Theoretical and Conceptual Frameworks in ICT Research

Agripah Kandiero
Insituto Superior Mutasa (ISMU), Mozambique & Mozambique Institute of Technology, Mozambique & Africa University, Zimbabwe

Stanislas Bigirimana
Africa University, Zimbabwe

Sabelo Chizwina
University of South Africa, South Africa

A volume in the Advances in Information Quality and Management (AIQM) Book Series

Published in the United States of America by
    IGI Global
    Information Science Reference (an imprint of IGI Global)
    701 E. Chocolate Avenue
    Hershey PA, USA 17033
    Tel: 717-533-8845
    Fax: 717-533-8661
    E-mail: cust@igi-global.com
    Web site: http://www.igi-global.com

Copyright © 2024 by IGI Global. All rights reserved. No part of this publication may be reproduced, stored or distributed in any form or by any means, electronic or mechanical, including photocopying, without written permission from the publisher.
Product or company names used in this set are for identification purposes only. Inclusion of the names of the products or companies does not indicate a claim of ownership by IGI Global of the trademark or registered trademark.

Library of Congress Cataloging-in-Publication Data

Names: Kandiero, Agripah, 1969- editor. | Bigirimana, Stanislas, editor. |
   Chizwina, Sabelo, 1979- editor.
Title: Theoretical and Conceptual Frameworks in ICT Research / Agripah
   Kandiero, Stanislas Bigirimana, and Sabelo Chizwina.
Description: Hershey PA : Engineering Science Reference, [2024] | Includes
   bibliographical references and index. | Summary: "This research book
   will initially address generic issues related to theorizing, theoretical
   and conceptual frameworks when conducting research followed by case
   studies from various countries to demonstrate the utilization of
   theoretical and conceptual frameworks in information systems research"--
   Provided by publisher.
Identifiers: LCCN 2022008814 (print) | LCCN 2022008815 (ebook) | ISBN
   9781799896876 (n/c) | ISBN 9781799896883 (s/c) | ISBN 9781799896890
   (ebook)
Subjects: LCSH: Information technology. | Industrial organization--Data
   processing. | Universities and colleges--Archives--Administration--Data
   processing. | Open educational resources. | Medical records--Data
   processing. | Electronic records--Management.
Classification: LCC T58.5 .T4965 2024 (print) | LCC T58.5 (ebook) | DDC
   004--dc23/eng/20220523
LC record available at https://lccn.loc.gov/2022008814
LC ebook record available at https://lccn.loc.gov/2022008815

This book is published in the IGI Global book series Advances in Information Quality and Management (AIQM) (ISSN: 2331-7701; eISSN: 2331-771X)

British Cataloguing in Publication Data
A Cataloguing in Publication record for this book is available from the British Library.

All work contributed to this book is new, previously-unpublished material.
The views expressed in this book are those of the authors, but not necessarily of the publisher.

For electronic access to this publication, please contact: eresources@igi-global.com.

Advances in Information Quality and Management (AIQM) Book Series

ISSN:2331-7701
EISSN:2331-771X

Editor-in-Chief: Siddhartha Bhattacharyya, RCC Institute of Information Technology, India

MISSION

Acquiring and managing quality information is essential to an organization's success and profitability. Innovation in information technology provides managers, researchers, and practitioners with the tools and techniques needed to create and adapt new policies, strategies, and solutions for information management.

The **Advances in Information Quality and Management (AIQM) Book Series** provides emerging research principals in knowledge society for the advancement of future technological development. This series aims to increase available research publications and emphasize the global response within the discipline and allow for audiences to benefit from the comprehensive collection of this knowledge.

COVERAGE

- Mobile Commerce
- IT Innovation and Diffusion
- Supply Chain Management
- Web Services and Technologies
- E-Collaboration
- Electronic Commerce Technologies
- Application of IT to Operation
- Emerging Technologies Management
- IT Management in Public Organizations
- Business Process Management and Modeling

IGI Global is currently accepting manuscripts for publication within this series. To submit a proposal for a volume in this series, please contact our Acquisition Editors at Acquisitions@igi-global.com or visit: http://www.igi-global.com/publish/.

The Advances in Information Quality and Management (AIQM) Book Series (ISSN 2331-7701) is published by IGI Global, 701 E. Chocolate Avenue, Hershey, PA 17033-1240, USA, www.igi-global.com. This series is composed of titles available for purchase individually; each title is edited to be contextually exclusive from any other title within the series. For pricing and ordering information please visit http://www.igi-global.com/book-series/advances-information-quality-management/73809. Postmaster: Send all address changes to above address. Copyright © 2024 IGI Global. All rights, including translation in other languages reserved by the publisher. No part of this series may be reproduced or used in any form or by any means – graphics, electronic, or mechanical, including photocopying, recording, taping, or information and retrieval systems – without written permission from the publisher, except for non commercial, educational use, including classroom teaching purposes. The views expressed in this series are those of the authors, but not necessarily of IGI Global.

Titles in this Series

For a list of additional titles in this series, please visit:
www.igi-global.com/book-series/advances-information-quality-management/73809

Digital Preservation and Documentation of Global Indigenous Knowledge Systems
Tlou Maggie Masenya (Durban University of Technology, South Africa)
Information Science Reference • copyright 2023 • 442pp • H/C (ISBN: 9781668470244)
• US $285.00 (our price)

Information Literacy Skills and the Role of Social Media in Disseminating Scholarly Information in the 21st Century
C. Baskaran (Alagappa University, India) and S. Dhanavandan (Central University of Tamil Nadu, India)
Information Science Reference • copyright 2023 • 236pp • H/C (ISBN: 9781668488058)
• US $215.00 (our price)

Library and Media Roles in Information Hygiene and Managing Information
Collence Takaingenhamo Chisita (Durban University of Technology, South Africa & University of South Africa, South Africa) Alexander Madanha Rusero (University of Johannesburg, South Africa) Ngoako Solomon Marutha (University of South Africa, South Africa) Josiline Phiri Chigwada (Chinhoyi University of Technology, Zimbabwe) and Oluwole Olumide Durodolu (Department of Information Science, University of South Africa, South Africa)
Information Science Reference • copyright 2022 • 268pp • H/C (ISBN: 9781799887133)
• US $215.00 (our price)

Using Information Technology Advancements to Adapt to Global Pandemics
Efosa C. Idemudia (Arkansas Tech University, USA) Tiko Iyamu (Cape Peninsula University of Technology, South Africa) Patrick Ndayizigamiye (University of Johannesburg, South Africa) and Irja Naambo Shaanika (Namibia University of Science and Technology, Namibia)
Engineering Science Reference • copyright 2022 • 276pp • H/C (ISBN: 9781799894186)
• US $270.00 (our price)

For an entire list of titles in this series, please visit:
www.igi-global.com/book-series/advances-information-quality-management/73809

701 East Chocolate Avenue, Hershey, PA 17033, USA
Tel: 717-533-8845 x100 • Fax: 717-533-8661
E-Mail: cust@igi-global.com • www.igi-global.com

Table of Contents

Preface xiii

Chapter 1
A Cross-Cultural Evaluation of Axiomatic Theories and Models of
Technology Acceptance: A Review of Literature 1
    Elisha Mupaikwa, National University of Science and Technology,
       Zimbabwe
    Kelvin Joseph Bwalya, University of Johannesburg, South Africa

Chapter 2
Application of Interpretivism Theoretical Framework on the Management of
University Records: Comparison of Selected Universities 29
    Nkholedzeni Sidney Netshakhuma, University of Mpumalanga, South
       Africa

Chapter 3
Conceptual Framework for the Application of the ANN Model in Accident
Prediction: A Study of Central Kolkata 50
    Amrita Sarkar, Birla Institute of Technology, Mesra, India
    Satyaki Sarkar, Birla Institute of Technology, Mesra, India

Chapter 4
Influences on the Decision to Implement Electronic Health Records in
Indonesia 77
    Ahmad Said, Bina Nusantara University, Indonesia
    Yulita Hanum P. Iskandar, Universiti Sains Malaysia, Malaysia

Chapter 5
Review and Analysis of Applications and Frameworks of Information
Systems in Supply Chain Management 94
    Manish Kumar, Indian Institute of Management, Indore, India

Chapter 6
The Viable System Model (VSM) in the Management of Institutions of
Higher Education in Zimbabwe 113
    Stansilas Bigirimana, Africa University, Zimbabwe
    Ganyanhewe Masanga, Chinhoyi University of Techology, Zimbabwe

Chapter 7
Theory and Theorizing in Information Systems 135
    Mampilo Phahlane, University of South Africa, South Africa

Chapter 8
Toward Comprehensive IS Project Alignment: The Case of Enterprise
Resource Planning Deployment Within a Logistics Service Provider...............155
    Eddy Bajolle, CERGAM, Aix-Marseille University, France
    Cécile Godé, CERGAM, Aix-Marseille University, France
    Nathalie Fabbe-Costes, CERGAM, Aix-Marseille University, France

Chapter 9
Cybernetics Principles in the Management of Intelligent Organizations 187
    Stanislas Bigirimana, College of Business, Peace, Leadership, and
      Governance, Africa University, Zimbabwe

Chapter 10
Customer Churn Prediction for Financial Institutions Using Deep Learning
Artificial Neural Networks in Zimbabwe..227
    Panashe Chiurunge, Chinhoyi University of Technology, Zimbabwe
    Agripah Kandiero, Instituto Superior Mutasa, Mozambique & Africa
      University, Zimbabwe
    Sabelo Chizwina, North-West University, South Africa

Compilation of References 266

About the Contributors 304

Index..310

Detailed Table of Contents

Preface..xiii

Chapter 1
A Cross-Cultural Evaluation of Axiomatic Theories and Models of
Technology Acceptance: A Review of Literature 1
    Elisha Mupaikwa, National University of Science and Technology,
        Zimbabwe
    Kelvin Joseph Bwalya, University of Johannesburg, South Africa

In analyzing the adoption and use of information systems, theories have been crucial.
The adoption of technology has been studied using several theories; however, very
few have taken into account cross-cultural influences on technology acceptance. This
chapter compares how technology acceptance theories have been used in various
cultures to identify cultural factors that might affect how technologies are embraced
by people from different cultural backgrounds. In this chapter, papers from referred
journals are reviewed. The reviews revealed that TAM and UTAUT were the two
most prevalent theories of technology adoption. The review also revealed that
different cultural factors, including power distance, individualism vs. collectivism,
aversion to uncertainty, long-term orientation, and masculinity vs. femininity, all
had an impact on people's acceptance of technology, but their significance depended
on the culture in question. The study suggested additional research to enhance the
parsimony of modern theories on technology acceptance and incorporate cultural
factors into these ideas.

Chapter 2
Application of Interpretivism Theoretical Framework on the Management of
University Records: Comparison of Selected Universities 29
    Nkholedzeni Sidney Netshakhuma, University of Mpumalanga, South
        Africa

This research assessed the adoption of interpretivism paradigm as a theoretical
framework. The interpretivism was adopted on a study comparing the University

of Venda and the University of Witwatersrand archives and records management programme. This research was undertaken as part of PhD thesis. The study found that adoption of interpretivism paradigm improves credibility, transferability, and authenticity of the research. The research recommend that research in information sciences are to incorporate other paradigm such as positivism.

Chapter 3
Conceptual Framework for the Application of the ANN Model in Accident Prediction: A Study of Central Kolkata 50
    Amrita Sarkar, Birla Institute of Technology, Mesra, India
    Satyaki Sarkar, Birla Institute of Technology, Mesra, India

Conceptual framework for accident prediction is an essential toolkit to curb accidents and fatalities globally. Different statistical methods and soft computing techniques are used to develop accident prediction models. Accident prediction models have been developed using two approaches, i.e., multiple linear regression (MLR) and artificial neural network (ANN). ANN has been applied to predict the frequency of traffic accidents. Adaptive neuro-fuzzy inference system (ANFIS) has been used as the feature selection method. Feature selection using ANFIS gets more accuracy with ANN was considered the most suitable based on prediction accuracy and measuring errors. It gives around 81.81% accuracy. The framework of hybrid model proposed in this chapter concludes that the prediction accuracy is high when ANN is applied for accident prediction, followed by the ANFIS as a feature selection method.

Chapter 4
Influences on the Decision to Implement Electronic Health Records in Indonesia 77
    Ahmad Said, Bina Nusantara University, Indonesia
    Yulita Hanum P. Iskandar, Universiti Sains Malaysia, Malaysia

Healthcare systems around the world are challenged by facing the COVID-19 outbreak. The expectation of high-quality care in hospitals, coupled with an aging population and more complex treatments, results in the system having increased productivity. The adoption of electronic health record systems (EHRs) is suitable for implementation as digital transformation in the healthcare industry. Despite the increase in demand and importance of EHR adoption, there is still a lack of comprehensive review and classification of the existing studies in this area. The authors are considering technology, organization, and environment (TOE) framework as the basis for EHR adoption. The objective of the study is to investigate the determinants of electronic healthcare record system adoption among hospitals in Indonesia. The findings are insightful and have important theoretical and practical implications for the hospital in Indonesia. This study may contribute to risk reduction throughout the adoption of EHRs, thereby fueling a technological revolution in Indonesia's healthcare industry.

Chapter 5
Review and Analysis of Applications and Frameworks of Information
Systems in Supply Chain Management..94
 Manish Kumar, Indian Institute of Management, Indore, India

In this era of information systems, humankind has benefitted enormously. The rapid growth in information system technology has made human life very easy and has significantly increased the efficiency, speed, and reliability of different processes. It is the need of the hour to study the interface between the information system and supply chain management. This chapter specifically tried to study the applications and frameworks of information systems in operation and supply chain management. For the study, the authors reviewed the articles published in top-quality journals. This chapter aimed to identify and discuss how different information systems frameworks solve problems related to operation and supply chain management. This study dealt with seven subsections involving supply chain, logistics, partnership, transparency, and decision-making. The study further identified that the use of information systems also contributes to competitive advantage. Finally, the understanding from the literature review has been concluded, and the existing gap has been highlighted for future research.

Chapter 6
The Viable System Model (VSM) in the Management of Institutions of
Higher Education in Zimbabwe 113
 Stansilas Bigirimana, Africa University, Zimbabwe
 Ganyanhewe Masanga, Chinhoyi University of Techology, Zimbabwe

This study aimed assessing the application of the viable system model (VSM) to institutions of higher learning in Zimbabwe. There is increased competition between the institutions themselves, and institutions of higher learning face decreasing budgets owing to the reduction in government financial support. These challenges threaten the viability of institutions of higher education in Zimbabwe and affect unprecedentedly their strategic orientation. The viable system model (VSM) has been recognised as a conceptual tool for understanding organizations, redesigning them (where appropriate) and supporting the management of change. From a sample of 150 respondents including vice chancellors, staff, parents and guardians, students, and other stakeholders, this study found principles of the viable system models are applied through existing organisational structures, although all institutions examined are suffering from various systems pathologies.

Chapter 7
Theory and Theorizing in Information Systems 135
    Mampilo Phahlane, University of South Africa, South Africa

Markus and Robey, in their seminal paper, assert that good theory guides research and when appropriately used it increases the likelihood that Information technology will be implemented with desirable results in any organization. This laments the importance of using theory in information systems research because of explanations it provides and paying attention to other areas that might otherwise be ignored. Researchers in the IS field such as Gregor, Grover, Corley and Gioia, Weber, and Whetten have discussed and classified theory and what constitutes a theoretical contribution. Despite the importance that many researchers ascribe to theory and theorising, the development of new theory and the refinement of existing theories there's a belief the information systems discipline has neglected theory and theorising. This, however, suggests that there's enough guidance on theory and theorising within the IS field and it is documented for different contexts and boundaries.

Chapter 8
Toward Comprehensive IS Project Alignment: The Case of Enterprise
Resource Planning Deployment Within a Logistics Service Provider...............155
    Eddy Bajolle, CERGAM, Aix-Marseille University, France
    Cécile Godé, CERGAM, Aix-Marseille University, France
    Nathalie Fabbe-Costes, CERGAM, Aix-Marseille University, France

Previous research offers limited and fragmented frameworks for information systems project alignment (ISPA). This study fills this gap by providing a comprehensive overview of the interplay between an IS project and its broader organizational context, and clarifying how contextual alignments relate to IS project success. ISPA is explored by observing a five-year implementation of an Enterprise Resource Planning (ERP) system within a logistics service provider based in Europe and North Africa. The study's findings and key contributions highlight the plural, complex, and multifaceted nature of ISPA resulting from the interaction of strategy, structure, process, people, and culture between the project, business, and IS organization. This chapter presents a comprehensive ISPA framework and is expected to increase project managers' awareness of the context in which IS projects are managed.

Chapter 9
Cybernetics Principles in the Management of Intelligent Organizations 187
    Stanislas Bigirimana, College of Business, Peace, Leadership, and
      Governance, Africa University, Zimbabwe

Against the background that mechanical principles were applied in management leading to bureaucracy, an application of cybernetics principles in management would imply (1) a behaviouralist approach to organisations, (2) teleology: reintroducing the notion of purpose, (3) managing complexity, (4) systems thinking, (5) managing as building intelligence, (6) managing as integrating knowledge domains. This overcomes the rigidity embedded in bureaucracy where organizations sought stability and equilibrium and operated in a relatively stable environment for a dynamic and integrative approach to organisations which are not closed stable entities but dynamic open systems. Organisations built on cybernetics principles are agile and continuously respond to their environment through information processing and feedback loops. In this context, there is a paradigm shift from top down management processes linked with hierarchy to cross-functional, flexible, adaptable, and open to learning management principles based on knowledge networks. Alternatives to bureaucracy can be suggested in terms of flat, inverted pyramids, matrix, networked and virtual organisational structures which may stipulate a change from Michael Porter's normative approach to strategic management to Mintzberg's descriptive approach. Organisational structures are not cast in stone but respond to changes in the environment, and there is a paradigm shift in corporate culture from organisations as closed stable entities to organisations as open dynamic systems, from competition to trust and collaboration including outsourcing, consortia, joint venture, and conglomerates become better ways of satisfying customer needs. From a corporate culture there is also a change from focusing on power and ownership in decision-making to focusing on knowledge and an increased use of information and communication technologies leading to virtualisation.

Chapter 10
Customer Churn Prediction for Financial Institutions Using Deep Learning Artificial Neural Networks in Zimbabwe 227
Panashe Chiurunge, Chinhoyi University of Technology, Zimbabwe
Agripah Kandiero, Instituto Superior Mutasa, Mozambique & Africa
    University, Zimbabwe
Sabelo Chizwina, North-West University, South Africa

The research was conducted to develop a customer churn predictive modelling using deep neural networks for financial institutions in Zimbabwe using a local leading financial institution. This was based on a need to perform a customer churn analysis and develop a very high accurate and reliable customer churn predictive model. In this era, every customer counts, hence once acquired a business should do everything in its power to keep that customer because the cost of acquiring a new customer is far greater than the cost of keeping an existing one. Therefore the need to ascertain customers who have churned and also be at a position to anticipate those who are churning or are about to churn then take corrective measures to keep such customers on board. The study followed one of the data science research methodologies called

CRoss industry standard process for data mining (CRISP-DM) which involves understanding the business, understanding the data, data preparation, modelling, validating the model then deployment of the model.

Compilation of References 266

About the Contributors 304

Index 310

Preface

Welcome to *Theoretical and Conceptual Frameworks in ICT Research*, a comprehensive compilation curated to address the critical role of theoretical and conceptual frameworks in advancing information systems research. As editors, we, Agripah Kandiero, Stanislas Bigirimana, and Sabelo Chizwina, are honored to present this collection of insightful contributions from esteemed scholars and practitioners in the field.

In an era dominated by technological advancements, the application of appropriate theoretical and conceptual frameworks has become paramount for researchers seeking to navigate the intricate landscape of information and communication technology (ICT). This book is a response to the evident need for guidance in employing these frameworks effectively, given their pivotal role in shaping credible research objectives and producing meaningful outcomes.

Despite the acknowledged significance of theoretical and conceptual frameworks, researchers often encounter challenges in their application. This book aims to bridge this gap by offering practical case applications that illuminate the process of integrating theories and concepts into information systems research. We believe that innovative and relevant knowledge emerges when researchers adeptly harness these frameworks, ultimately contributing to the broader discourse in the field.

The primary objectives of this publication are threefold:

1. Exposing readers to useful theories applicable in various contexts for solving business and day-to-day problems.
2. Testing and recommending the effectiveness and improvement of different theories and frameworks.
3. Identifying context-specific theoretical and conceptual frameworks that resonate with the unique challenges in information systems research.

This book is structured to serve as an essential reference source, enriching the existing literature in the field. We anticipate that it will provide a deeper understanding of the role played by theoretical and conceptual frameworks in conducting research in information systems, fostering a shared understanding among researchers regarding these tools as essential supports for empirical research.

Our intended audience includes policymakers, academicians, researchers, advanced-level students, and information systems professionals. We believe that this text will not only broaden their exposure to pertinent topics related to theoretical and conceptual frameworks but also aid in advancing their research endeavors in the ever-evolving field of information systems.

The chapters assembled in this volume cover a spectrum of themes related to theorizing and utilizing theoretical and conceptual frameworks in information systems research. The first part delves into generic issues associated with theorizing, while the second part presents compelling case studies from various countries, illustrating the application of these frameworks in diverse contexts.

Topics covered include the nature of a good theory, the relationship between theory and research, meta-theories, models, theoretical frameworks, conceptual frameworks, the distinction between theoretical and conceptual frameworks, the role of universal theories, theory borrowing, and case studies showcasing the practical application of these frameworks.

Chapter 1: In this opening chapter, the focus is on the critical role of theories in analyzing the adoption and use of information systems. The chapter delves into the various technology acceptance theories that have been employed, emphasizing the need to consider cross-cultural influences on technology acceptance. By reviewing papers from reputable journals, the authors highlight TAM and UTAUT as the predominant theories. The chapter reveals the impact of cultural factors, such as power distance and individualism, on technology acceptance, with a call for additional research to refine modern theories and incorporate cultural elements.

Chapter 2: This chapter undertakes an assessment of the adoption of the interpretivism paradigm as a theoretical framework in information sciences research. The research, embedded within a PhD thesis, compares archives and records management programs at the University of Venda and the University of Witwatersrand. The findings suggest that adopting the interpretivism paradigm enhances the credibility, transferability, and authenticity of research in information sciences. The chapter advocates for the inclusion of other paradigms, such as positivism, to enrich the research landscape in information sciences.

Chapter 3: The third chapter centers on the development of a conceptual framework for accident prediction, a crucial tool for global accident prevention. Employing statistical methods and soft computing techniques, the chapter explores accident prediction models using Multiple Linear Regression and Artificial Neural Network approaches. The study introduces a hybrid model, combining Adaptive Neuro-Fuzzy Inference System (ANFIS) as a feature selection method with ANN for accident prediction. The results showcase the efficacy of this hybrid approach,

Preface

providing valuable insights for enhancing prediction accuracy in accident-prone scenarios.

Chapter 4: Amid the challenges faced by healthcare systems globally, Chapter 4 explores the adoption of Electronic Health Record (EHR) systems using the Technology, Organization, and Environment (TOE) framework. Focusing on Indonesia, the study investigates the determinants of EHR adoption among hospitals. The findings contribute to the understanding of factors influencing EHR adoption, offering practical implications for the healthcare industry. The chapter emphasizes the potential of EHRs to drive digital transformation and improve productivity in the face of complex healthcare demands.

Chapter 5: Delving into the intersection of information systems and supply chain management, Chapter 5 reviews top-quality journal articles to identify and discuss applications and frameworks of information systems in operations and supply chain management. The study encompasses seven subsections, exploring various facets such as supply chain, logistics, partnership, transparency, decision-making, and the potential contribution of information systems to gaining a competitive advantage. The chapter concludes by highlighting areas for future research in this dynamic and critical field.

Chapter 6: Focused on the challenges faced by institutions of higher learning in Zimbabwe, Chapter 6 assesses the application of the Viable System Model (VSM). Through surveys involving stakeholders such as vice chancellors, staff, parents, and students, the study reveals the application of VSM principles within existing organizational structures. Despite systemic pathologies, the VSM proves to be a valuable conceptual tool for understanding and redesigning institutions, providing insights into strategic orientations and viability in the face of budget constraints.

Chapter 7: Chapter 7 addresses the pivotal role of theory in information systems research, echoing the assertions of Markus & Robey (1988). The chapter reviews the existing literature on theory and theorizing in information systems research, highlighting discussions by prominent researchers. While recognizing the importance of theory, the chapter also acknowledges a perceived neglect of theory development in the information systems discipline. This prompts a reflection on the guidance available within the field and encourages further exploration of theory and theorizing for different contexts.

Chapter 8: Chapter 8 fills a gap in existing research by providing a comprehensive overview of Information Systems Project Alignment (ISPA). Drawing on a five-year implementation of an ERP system in a logistics service provider, the study explores the complex interplay between the IS project and its broader organizational context. The findings underscore the multifaceted nature of ISPA, emphasizing the interactions between strategy, structure, process, people, and culture. The chapter introduces a comprehensive ISPA framework, enhancing project managers' awareness of contextual alignments for improved IS project success.

Chapter 9: This chapter explores the relationship between disruptive technological innovation and paradigm shifts in management, engineering, and science. Drawing on Kuhn's definition of paradigms and acknowledging the social impact of disruptive innovations, the chapter examines how technological innovations can lead to unprecedented societal changes. It contributes to the discourse on the transformative impact of disruptive innovations, shedding light on the dynamic interplay between technological advancements and societal shifts.

Chapter 10: The final chapter focuses on developing a customer churn predictive model using deep neural networks for financial institutions in Zimbabwe. Utilizing the CRoss Industry Standard Process for Data Mining (CRISP-DM), the study emphasizes the importance of customer retention in the financial sector. The chapter details the research methodology, from understanding the business to model validation, providing a comprehensive guide for implementing a high-accuracy customer churn predictive model.

In conclusion, we extend our gratitude to all contributors who have enriched this compilation with their valuable insights. It is our sincere hope that this book serves as a catalyst for advancing research in information systems and fosters a deeper appreciation for the pivotal role of theoretical and conceptual frameworks in shaping the future of ICT research.

Editors,

Agripah Kandiero
Insituto Superior Mutasa (ISMU), Mozambique & Mozambique Institute of Technology, Mozambique & Africa University, Zimbabwe

Stanislas Bigirimana
Africa University, Zimbabwe

Sabelo Chizwina
North-West University, South Africa

Chapter 1

A Cross–Cultural Evaluation of Axiomatic Theories and Models of Technology Acceptance:
A Review of Literature

Elisha Mupaikwa
iD https://orcid.org/0000-0002-0313-7139
National University of Science and Technology, Zimbabwe

Kelvin Joseph Bwalya
iD https://orcid.org/0000-0003-0509-5515
University of Johannesburg, South Africa

ABSTRACT

In analyzing the adoption and use of information systems, theories have been crucial. The adoption of technology has been studied using several theories; however, very few have taken into account cross-cultural influences on technology acceptance. This chapter compares how technology acceptance theories have been used in various cultures to identify cultural factors that might affect how technologies are embraced by people from different cultural backgrounds. In this chapter, papers from referred journals are reviewed. The reviews revealed that TAM and UTAUT were the two most prevalent theories of technology adoption. The review also revealed that different cultural factors, including power distance, individualism vs. collectivism, aversion to uncertainty, long-term orientation, and masculinity vs. femininity, all had an impact on people's acceptance of technology, but their significance depended on the culture in question. The study suggested additional research to enhance the parsimony of modern theories on technology acceptance and incorporate cultural factors into these ideas.

DOI: 10.4018/978-1-7998-9687-6.ch001

Copyright © 2024, IGI Global. Copying or distributing in print or electronic forms without written permission of IGI Global is prohibited.

INTRODUCTION

The production of new knowledge in information system research depends on the efficient application of theory to the field. Organizations that create information systems have recognized the potential presented by globalization. Globally, discussions about the appropriateness, application, and reliability of current theories and models of technology acceptance and adoption have come to characterize the field of information systems research (Straub, Keil and Brenner, 1997; Lin, 2014). The extensive use of information technologies across cultures makes it difficult to generalize research results across cultures and the connection between the cultural acceptability of technology has remained hazy. This necessitates an investigation into the effectiveness of modern theories in understanding the adoption and application of information systems in organizations. These calls have been made as a result of research that demonstrates how these theories have varied in their predictive validity across cultures in terms of explaining the adoption and use of information technologies. According to some researchers, among them Straub et al.,(1997) and Merchant (2007) the axiomatic links between the constructs vary according to the culture, indicating that diverse environmental and demographic factors have an impact on how people accept and use technology. Few scholars have made an effort to validate these ideas across cultures and situations, with particular attention to Hofstede's cultural aspects, despite the conspicuous lack of agreement on which theories best explain the acceptance or rejection of an information system.

Theory is a way to define relationships, constructions, declarations of relationships, and scope such that causal explanations, testable positions, and prescriptive statements can be made based on the theory's goals. These theoretical abstractions have significance for researchers' capacity to inform practice by illuminating axiomatic links that exist between variables of a theory, and they are not only academic. They foster a deeper comprehension of the phenomenon, assisting researchers in establishing their claims and placing their research in the proper context to justify investments in information systems investments. Globally investments in information systems development and adoption are justified by the corresponding usage among users. Park et al. (2009) claim that the underutilization of information systems in many developing nations is mostly due to the paucity of research on the user side of information system adoption. As a result, researchers have given the application of theory in information systems across broader settings greater consideration, which has led to the establishment of several IS research strands (Lim et al., 2014). According to Lim et al. (2014), theories from the fields of psychology, economics, sociology, and organizational science have been used in information system research. However, there are disagreements regarding whether information system research should continue to use theories from other fields, how these theories should be used,

Evaluation of Axiomatic Theories, Models of Technology Acceptance

and what contributions information system research should make to the fields from which these theories should come, according to Truex, Holmstrom, and Keil (2006). Other academics have advised against doing so, advising cautious selection of theories that might be applied to information system research. Even though Gregor (2006) agrees that there has been little theoretical discussion in IS forums, reliance on ideas from other disciplines has led to a need for IS researchers to create their own IS theories. Triuex, Holmstrom, and Keil (2006) advise researchers to take into account several aspects, such as what factors to take into consideration and the importance of theories in IS research, before borrowing a theory from another area. For the adoption and adaption of theories, they offer the following four recommendations:

i.   Take into account how well the chosen theory fits with the phenomenon of interest;
ii.   Take into account the theory's historical background;
iii. Take into account how the theory influences the choice of the research technique; and
iv.   Take into account the role of theory in the development of cumulative theory.

Gregor (2006) put up a taxonomy that divides information system theories into categories based on their objectives, which are analysis, explanation, prediction, and prescription. These objectives led to the emergence of four main categories of information systems theories: theories for analysis, theories for explanation, theories for prediction, and theories for design and action. Information systems and technology adoption have been the subject of single-country studies for several decades. Thoughtful of the many cultures and their effects on the reception of modern technologies, cross-country study on the adoption of new technologies has recently attracted more attention. In the past, the USA has been the primary location for research on how information and communication technologies are accepted across cultures, with a particular emphasis on corporate cultures. Only a small number of studies on the adoption of these technologies were based on ethnicity. The Diffusion of Innovation (DoI), Technology Acceptance Model (TAM), Theory of Reasoned Action (TRA), Theory of Planned Behaviour (TPB), Model of PC Usage (MPCU), Social Cognitive Theory (SCT), and the Theory of Planned Behavior (TPB) are among the dominant models that incorporate Hofstede's cultural research to explain how cultures adopt innovations. Some researchers have also integrated these models' cultural dimensions. These ideas and the corresponding variables are displayed in Table 1 below.

Although information systems have been spreading over the world, according to Dai and Palvia (2009), there haven't been many cross-cultural studies on how well-received technology is. Perez-Alvarez (2006) asserts that differences in the cross-

Evaluation of Axiomatic Theories, Models of Technology Acceptance

Table 1. Summary table of technology acceptance theories

Theory	Variables	
	Independent Variable	**Dependent variable**
TAM	PU	Attitude
	PEU	Attitude
	Attitude	BI
	BI	Usage
	External variables	PU & PEU
TRA	Attitude	BI
	Subjective norms	BI
	BI	Volitional behaviour
TPB	Attitude	Intention
	Subjective norm	Intention
	Perceived behavioural control	Intention
	BI	Behaviour
SCT	Behaviour	Environmental factors, Personal factors
	Environmental factors	Personal factors, Behaviour
	Personal factors	Behaviour, Environmental factors
DoI	Observability	Usage
	Relative advantage	Usage
	Compatibility	Usage
	Trialability	Usage
	Complexity	Usage
MPCU	Job fit	Attitude
	Complexity	Attitude
	Long-term consequences	Attitude
	Affect towards use	Attitude
	Social factors	Attitude
	Facilitating conditions	Attitude
UTAUT	PE	BI
	EE	BI
	SI	BI
	FC	Usage
	Moderators	
	Gender	SI, EE, PE
	Age	FC, SI, EE, PE
	Experience	FC, SI, EE
	Voluntariness of use	SI

4

Continued on following page

Table 1. Continued

Theory	Variables	
	Independent Variable	**Dependent variable**
UTAUT2	PE	BI
	EE	BI
	SI	BI
	FC	BI, Usage
	HM	BI
	PV	BI
	H	BI, Usage
	Moderators	
	Age	H, FC, HM, PV, BI
	Gender	H, FC, HM, PV, H
	Experience	FC, HM, H, PV, BI-Usage

*PU: Perceived usefulness; PEU: Perceived ease of use; BI: Behavioural intention; EE: Effort expectancy; FC: Facilitating conditions; SI: Social influence; HM: Hedonic motivation; PV: Price-value; H: Habit.

country adoption of technology like information systems are due to both economic and cultural variables. Cultural variations have had a considerable impact on how people perceive, believe, act, and behave when it comes to new technology, and people from diverse cultural backgrounds frequently exhibit distinct adoption and usage behavioural patterns. This chapter supports modern views of cross-cultural technology adoption. This chapter will therefore discuss how cultural differences influence the adoption and use of computer-based information systems across cultures, to broaden the scope of factors that influence the adoption of technologies across cultures and to provide insights into diverse reasons for technology adoption or rejection.

METHODOLOGY

Articles from peer-reviewed publications were downloaded for review from academic databases. 120 items were initially downloaded from Taylor and Francis, Elsevier, EmeraldInshight, JSTOR and PubMed. Following the creation of inclusion criteria; the author only chose publications published between 2000 and 2023 because this period witnessed increased publications on technology acceptance research across cultures. 'Cross-cultural adoption of technology' and 'validation of technology acceptance models across cultures' were key terms chosen to narrow down the

Table 2. Description of journal articles reviewed

Author	Theory	Description
Merhi, Hone and Tarhini (2009)	UTAUT extension with security, privacy and trust	A cross-cultural study on British and Lebanese use of mobile banking
Bandyopandyay and Fraccasto (2007)	UTAUT	Cross-cultural adoption of IT in the USA, Switzerland, Japan, Hong Kong, India, and Arabic countries
Teo, Luan and Sing (2008)	TAM	Cross-cultural use of technology in education in Malaysia and Singapore
Park (2009)	TRA	Testing theories across cultures
Metallo et al., (2022)	TAM	Testing Technology Acceptance in Hospitals in a cross-cultural Context
Oshylyansky, Cairns and Thimbleby (2007)	UTAUT	Validating UTAUT across cultures
Muk and Chung (2014)	TAM	Cross-cultural adoption of SMS advertising in the USA and Korea
Park et al.,(2009)	TAM	Cross-cultural acceptance of digital library technologies in Central and Latin America, Africa and Australia
Al-Gahtani et al., (2007)	UTAUT	ICT Acceptance in Saudi Arabia
Straub, Keil and Brenner(1997)	TAM	Technology adoption in Japan, Switzerland and the USA
Sharma et al., (2016)	TAM	Adoption of cloud computing in developing countries
Chopdar et al., (2018)	UTAUT2	Adoption of mobile shopping apps in India and the USA
Ahmad et al.,(2021)	UTAUT	Modelling behavioural intention to use travel reservation apps in the USA and China
Isaac et al., (2019)	UTAUT extension	Internet usage within organisations
Dhagarra, Goswami and Kumar (2020)	TAM, Trust and Privacy	Technology acceptance in Indian healthcare
Aboelmaged (2009)	TAM & TPB	E-procurement adoption in the developing world
Singh et al., (2004)	TAM	Website usage in Germany, Brazil and Taiwan for online shopping
Kwarteng et al.,(2023)	UTAUT with competitive pressures	Digitization adoption in Slovakia and the Czech Republic
Besbes et al., (2016)	Tourism Web Acceptance Model	Effects of culture on online booking acceptance in Tunisia and China
Göğüş,Nistor and Lerche(2012)	UTAUT	Educational technology acceptance across cultures in Turkey
Sineonova et al., (2014)	UTAUT	Use of VLE in Jordan, Russia and the UK

Continued on following page

Evaluation of Axiomatic Theories, Models of Technology Acceptance

Table 2. Continued

Author	Theory	Description
Khan et al., (2022)	UTAUT extension	Effects of culture on online banking adoption in Pakistan and Turkey
AlMuhanna, Hall and Millard(2023)	Technology acceptance and use under risks	Acceptance of Twitter across cultures
Hartzel et al., (2016)	TAM	Online social network adoption across cultures in the USA and China
Wu (2020)	TAM	Organisational acceptance of social media marketing across cultures in the USA and non-USA countries
Lowry (2004)	TAM	Validating TAM in the Arab world
Dinev et al.,(2009)	Hofstede's cultural dimension	User behaviour on Web Preventive Technologies in South Korea and the USA
Alsaleh and Elliot (2019)	TRA and TAM	Cultural differences in the adoption of social media
Huang, D'Ambra and Bhalla (2002)	TAM	Adoption of e-government among Australian citizens
Bandyopadhyay and Fraccastoro (2007)	TAM AND UTAUT	Adoption of prepayment metering systems
McCormick, Alavi and Hanham, (2015)	SCT	Cross-cultural adoption of technology
Minish-Majanja and Kiplang'at (2005)	DoI	Diffusion of ICT-based innovations
Botha and Atkins (2005)	DoI	Diffusion of ICT-based innovations
Gangwar, Date and Ramaswamy (2013)	MPCU variables	Adoption of cloud computing
Oliveira,Thomas and Espadanal (2014)	MPCU variables	Adoption of cloud computing
Albirini (2006)	MPCU variables	Adoption of information technologies

pool of papers for review. The primary findings of the study were based on the 36 articles based on the author's judgement on their suitability. The following Table 2 lists these articles along with the hypotheses that underpin specific studies:

HOFSTEDE'S CULTURAL DIMENSION AND TECHNOLOGY ADOPTION

Hofstede (2001) defined culture as the collective mental programming that distinguishes one group or category of people from another. This represents a set of norms, symbols, and values that apply to all members of a group of people, such as a nation. According to research by Dai and Palvia (2009), the five cultural aspects identified by Hofstede as having the ability to affect how a group of people adopts technology are power distance, uncertainty avoidance, individualism-collectivism, masculinity-feminism, and long-term temporal orientation. This concept is frequently used to discuss inequalities in societies and how nations aim to deal with such inequities. This variable frequently shows up in the economic disparity, social standing, and decision-making responsibilities that various people play in a community. Power-distance factors can have a direct impact on community access to resources and amenities. Because they rely so heavily on others who are more powerful, people from high power distance cultures don't need as much technology. For instance, in organizations, the general manager or another person in a position of responsibility would make decisions centrally. However, because they tend to be more independent, people from low power distance cultures are more likely to adopt technology because it gives them more power. The degree to which civilizations accept high levels of ambiguity and uncertainty in the environment is termed uncertainty avoidance. It outlines how people build circumstances and beliefs to avoid uncertainties because they feel frightened by ambiguous situations. According to Straub et al. (1997), uncertainty avoidance is a key factor in understanding why customers choose the technologies they do. According to the research, societies that are good at avoiding uncertainty favour tried-and-true innovations to take a chance on new ones. These cultures utilize rules and policies to reduce uncertainty because they are risk-averse (Veltri and Elgarah, 2009). Because of this, cultures with high degrees of uncertainty frequently perceive new technology as a danger and prefer to reject it in favour of tried-and-true norms and practices. Individualism-collectivism defines how one person interacts with other people. Strong relationships within groups enable the spread of ideas and collective adoption tendencies while weak ties between individuals in individualistic cultures are frequently characterized by individualistic and independent behaviors. People from low individualistic cultures prioritize face-to-face interaction while maintaining relationships on the personal and professional levels (Straub et al. 2001). However, those who come from very individualistic societies choose digital communication methods. They usually adopt Western ideas because they have more disposable income and utilize computers and the Internet more frequently than in low individualistic societies. The allocation of roles between the sexes to the extent that it is characterized by masculine or female features is referred to as masculinity or femininity. People from cultures with low levels of masculinity use technology to fulfil their needs on a personal and professional level. In these societies, women are more inclined to work, which hastens the development of technology. Most of these societies also had lower rates of poverty and illiteracy than societies with strong masculinity. Therefore, it is more likely that Internet banking will spread in nations or communities with low levels of masculinity. According to the long-term orientation theory, individuals place a high value on virtues like thrift, perseverance, and long-term relationships. The adoption and appreciation of new technologies as well as the formation of new attitudes about technology are outcomes of long-term orientation in the usage of technologies. According to Jan, Alshare, and Lane's (2022) application of Hofstede's cultural dimensions to technology adoption, these dimensions influence several variables generated from modern technology acceptance models and their associations are shown in Table 3.

According to Jan, Alshare, and Lane's (2022) findings, as shown in Figure 1 below, individualism-collectivism and power distance were the best predictors of behavioural intention, whereas uncertainty-avoidance and power distance were the best predictors of perceived ease of use (Effort expectancy). Although the

Table 3. Influence of cultural dimensions on technology acceptance (Jan et al., 2022)

Independent variable	Dependent variable	Relationship
Individual collectivism	BI	IDV-BI
	PEU	IDV-PEU
	PU	IDV-PU
Long-term orientation(LTO)	BI	LTO-BI
	PEU	LTO-PEU
	PU	LTO-PU
Masclunity-feminity (MAS)	BI	MAS-BI
	PEU	MAS-PEU
	PU	MAS-PU
Power-distance(PDI)	BI	PDI-BI
	PEU	PDI-PEU
	PU	PDI-PU
Uncertainty Avoidance(UA)	BI	UA-BI
	PEU	UA-PEU
	PU	UA-PU
	Use(U)	UA-U

Figure 1. Influence of cultural dimensions on technology adoption
(Jan et al., 2022)

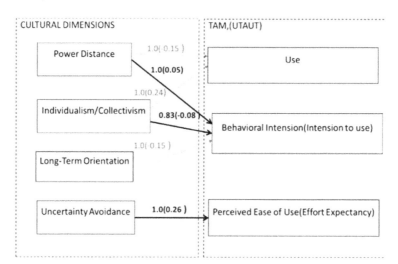

relationships were minor, individual-collective and long-term orientation were also related to usage and behavioural intention.

However, consumers from various cultures may engage in particular behaviours for personal and social reasons, claim Minton et al. (2018). For instance, Lee, Trimi, and Kim (2013) found that culture in the USA had a greater impact on technology adoption when compared to the Korean context, implying that in individualistic cultures, people tend to seek information on their own from direct formal sources while in collective cultures, people rely more on subjective evaluation of innovations conceptualized as a whole. Additionally, Minton et al.'s (2018) study on sustainable consumer behaviours among consumers in France, the USA, and Japan found similarities in technology use among consumers in these three countries, but these findings were different for Japanese consumers, whose behavioural scores were lower than those of the other two. The Arab cluster (Egypt, Iraq, Kuwait, Lebanon, Libya, United Arab Emirates, and Morocco as shown in Table 4 below), according to Veltri and Elgarah (2009), is characterized by high power distance and uncertainty avoidance, scoring 70 and 68, respectively, while the USA is characterized by higher scores for individualism and masculinity, scoring 91 and 62, respectively.

In comparison to nations like the USA, Arabic communities score lower on the masculinity scale, indicating that they are less assertive, more humble, and more competitive. Compared to the more individualistic cultures of the USA, Arabic communities are also communal. While acknowledging the greater number of research conducted in private organizations, Huang, D'Ambra, and Bhalla (2002)

Evaluation of Axiomatic Theories, Models of Technology Acceptance

Table 4. Comparison of cultural dimensions between Morocco and the USA

Dimension	Morocco*	USA	World Average
Power Distance	70	40	55
Individualism	46	91	43
Uncertainty Avoidance	68	46	64
Masculinity	53	62	50

bemoaned the dearth of studies on the use of information technology in organizational departments. Such arguments are based on the idea that Hofstede's cultural dimensions of power distance are connected to the cultural values that exist between private and public institutions.

DIFFUSION OF INNOVATION (DOI)

In the past, DOI research has concentrated on the factors that affect how quickly items get adopted. What influences the pace of adoption of an innovation is one of the key unanswered topics in the DoI study field. According to the literature, five categories of factors namely; perceived features of innovations, kind of innovation decision, communication channels, social system nature, and degree of change agents' promotion, determine the rate of adoption. DoI is characterized by individual uncertainty, which prompts people to ask people in their social network cycles for their subjective opinions on innovations, resulting in a shared understanding of innovations and adoption. Diffusion theories have drawn criticism from several scholars because they neglect the potential that even fully understanding people may reject a technology (Botha and Atkins, 2005). Few studies on technology acceptability across cultures have applied this idea, despite the prevalence of DoI-based studies. Takieddine and Sun (2015) are among the researchers who have used it to study how Internet banking was adopted across different cultures in Europe. They found that national culture is a key moderator since it affects how Internet banking spreads throughout distinct nations and groups. The results of their study, which show that Europe has a lower-than-average rate of Internet banking diffusion, support the need for further investigation into the root causes of the slow and late adoption of Internet banking in either the most or second most developed continent in the world. Europe has a higher average Internet access rate than the rest of the world (74.42%), which eliminates Internet connectivity as a barrier to the adoption of Internet banking. However, there are significant worries about Internet security and speed as basic barriers to the development of Internet banking in Europe.

MODEL OF PC UTILISATION (MPCU)

The MPCU was created by Thompson et al. (1991), and it put forth the concept that social variables, enabling circumstances, affect, and perceived consequences might all have a direct impact on how people use computers. The following constructs are included in this model, which was created to forecast individual acceptance of a variety of information technologies: job fit, complexity, long-term consequences, affect towards use, social factors, and facilitating conditions. The MPCU has not gained enough attention in cross-cultural studies of technology uptake and usage. The majority of investigations appear to have combined only a few of the variables with some of the DoI, TAM, and TOE framework theories of technological acceptance. DeGuinea and Webster (2015), who investigated the influence of culture on computer self-efficacy, were among the researchers who used variables from MPCU. The results showed that organizational culture affected computer self-efficacy indirectly through employees' preferences for individualism and task interdependence. The study also found that task interdependence and software personal innovativeness were favourably correlated with computer self-efficacy, whereas task ambiguity and software complexity were adversely correlated. In addition to this study, Gangwar, Date, and Ramaswamy (2013) examined the adoption of cloud computing and found that compatibility, relative advantage, organizational readiness, complexity, training, and management support all had a significant impact on adoption behaviour. Oliveira, Thomas, and Espadanal (2014) also identified relative advantage, complexity, technological maturity, competitive pressure, and management support as the primary drivers for cloud computing adoption in Portugal's manufacturing sectors. Computer attributes, cultural perceptions, computer competence, and personal characteristics were among the variables that influenced attitudes toward computers. Some of these variables also emerged as strong determinants in a study of the adoption of information technology by teachers in Syria by Albirini (2006).

SOCIAL COGNITIVE THEORY (SCT)

The social cognitive theory, which emphasizes that learning is a triadic and reciprocal process involving three constructs-personal factors, environmental variables, and behaviour-is an interpersonal theory. Information systems acceptability across various cultural situations is one of the research domains where the SCT has been applied. The SCT examines the reciprocal three-way dynamic causation among people, behaviours, and their environments and explores the psychological factors

Evaluation of Axiomatic Theories, Models of Technology Acceptance

that influence human thoughts, feelings, and behaviour. The SCT has received a lot of attention in both organizational and individual contexts and is one of the most comprehensive and cogent context-based theories that forecast human motivation and behaviour. Individual contexts influence behaviour, and each person's context is likely to be different (McCormick, Alavi and Hanham, 2015). Individual settings may contain elements like job satisfaction and leadership self-efficacy and are enmeshed in broader social contexts. Literature on SCT's uses in the field demonstrates how broadly it has been used in the utilization of new educational technologies in teaching and learning contexts. For example, Wei et al. (2011) demonstrated how the digital access disparity influences the digital divide among Singaporean pupils. The same study demonstrated a strong impact of the educational computing environment on students' computer self-efficacy. These elements did not, however, close the achievement disparity between pupils with and without access to personal computers. Similar research on academic self-efficacy among Turkish, former Soviet Union, and German students conducted in educational settings by Gebauer et al. (2021) revealed the difference in the importance of socialization contexts between Turkish and former Soviet Union students. For students without immigration backgrounds, mastery experience was the most important indicator of academic success in two cultural contexts, while verbal and social persuasion was the largest contributor in the other. Perkmen, Toy, and Caracuel (2023) claimed that previous technology acceptance models lacked parsimony and expanded the SCT to account for the adoption of technology by Turkish and Spanish pre-service teachers in their cross-cultural study of pre-service teachers' technology acceptance behaviours. According to the study's findings, openness, favourable conditions, self-efficacy, and outcome expectations are the main factors that explain instructors' technology adoption behaviours. Almogren and Aljammaz (2022) acknowledged the TAM's limitations in addressing the variables that influenced the adoption of mobile learning at King Saud University and combined it with the SCT. It was argued that the resulting model was reliable in explaining 52.5% of the variation in the adoption of mobile applications in higher education. The results of the study demonstrated that both social and technological factors have a positive impact on the adoption of new technologies. The degree of student collaboration was cited as a factor in the adoption of technologies. By accounting for 56% of the variance in health information professionals' behavioural intention to use web portals and identifying subjective usability and application-specific self-efficacy as significant antecedents to the model, Tao et al.'s (2019) integration of the SCT and usability provided additional support for these findings. The influence of subjective usability on perceived ease of use also mitigated the effect of self-efficacy in other ways.

TECHNOLOGY ACCEPTANCE MODEL (TAM) ACROSS CULTURES

One of the earliest models for examining the adoption of information systems is the Technology Acceptance Model (TAM), which Davis (1989) created. TAM is a sparse description of how perceptions and attitudes affect technology adoption and usage and has been empirically shown to predict 40% of system usage (Teo, Luan, and Sing 2008). It is based on two key constructs: perceived utility and perceived ease of use. Due to its clarity and simplicity, this model has been widely used to investigate the adoption and use of information systems. TAM aimed to get rid of the users' subjective norms because of the TRA's ambiguous theoretical and psychological position (Taherdoost, 2018). Since its creation, TAM has undergone many modifications, including the addition of external precursors like situational involvement, prior usage, or computer self-efficacy; the incorporation of factors suggested by other theories meant to improve TAM's predictive power, like subjective norm, expectation, task-technology fit, risk, and trust; the inclusion of contextual factors like gender, culture, and technology characteristics; and the inclusion of drawbacks. Among other modifications on TAM has been an investigation on information technology adoption and communication media in the United States, Switzerland, and Japan by Straub et al. (1997) who integrated TAM with Hofstede's cultural dimensions and found that there were significant differences among different cultures in terms of uncertainty avoidance, power distance, individualism, and assertiveness. There were also similarities in adoption tendencies reported by Park et al. (2009) in a study on the adoption of a digital library system in African, Asian, and Latin American institutions of higher learning as well as by Aboelmaged (2009) in a study on the adoption of e-procurement systems in the United Arab Emirates, indicating that TAM is a suitable theory to explain technology adoption. However, among the five African nations examined in Park et al.'s (2009) study on their use of information technology, Ghana, Malawi, Tanzania, and Kenya, the results on significant predictors were similar in Kenya and Nigeria but different in Ghana, Malawi, and Tanzania. Additional variations were also reported by Lin, Fofanah, and Liang (2011) and Tarhini et al. (2015) on the adoption of e-government services in Gambia and the adoption of e-learning, where all TA variables. The adoption of websites for online shopping by German, Brazilian, and Taiwanese consumers was the subject of a cross-cultural study by Singh et al. (2004). The results showed that TAM had a strong explanatory power for these technologies' adoption in Brazil, Germany, and Taiwan and that culture needed to be added to the theory when addressing cross-cultural issues. Compared to customers in other nations, Taiwanese consumers were more influenced by cultural adaption. Additionally, some researchers have combined TAM with other theories to increase its predictive

Evaluation of Axiomatic Theories, Models of Technology Acceptance

validity, while others have added new constructs that are related to cognitive beliefs and behavioural traits (Dhagarra, Goswami, and Kumar 2020; Wu and Wang, 2005); Blagoeva and Mijoska, 2017; Mohammed and Tejay, 2017; Bandyopadhyay and Fraccastro, 2007; Lim and Kim 2016). These researchers have considered privacy issues, trust, image, self-efficacy, trust and job opportunity, perceived danger, and cost as some of the constructs that explains technology adoptions in India, Tunisia and Taiwan (Besbes et al., 2016), China (Muk and Chung, 2015), the USA, Japan, Brazil, German, and Taiwan (Singh et al., (2004), in Macedonia (Blagoeva and Mijoska, 2017) and Japan, Switzerland and Hong Kong (Bandyopadhyay and Fraccastro, 2007) with results across these studies pointing to the influence of various cultural dimensions on technology adoption across various fields. Hofstede's cultural elements, particularly national cultures like individualism, have reportedly also been considered by certain researchers to impact the adoption of information systems, among them, Metallo et al., (2022), Faqih et al., (2015), Wu (2020) and Hartzel and Marley (2016) who all reported cultural differences in the use of social media among USA, Indian, and Chinese students. Their findings also revealed that there were significant differences between the relationships between behavioural intention and actual behaviour among students from these countries, and in each instance, students from the USA were less likely to have used online social network sites in search of the social cause. The study's findings also indicated that the ideas of cultural convergence and cultural divergence may either conflict with one another or work in concert with one another and that even in developed countries like the USA, the digital gap persisted and had an impact on the uptake of social media for marketing reasons. From these findings, one can conclude that while TAM is generally regarded as a reliable model to explain technology adoption, the impact of cultural variables plays a significant moderating role.

THEORY OF REASONED ACTION

The predictive validity of TRA has remained poor across cultures because various outside factors that can affect technology adoption were excluded from the theory. Attempts to include these external factors were made by Koo and Chung (2014), who found that both extrinsic and intrinsic factors affected the adoption of green IT. Similarly, in studying online political participation in Nigeria, Oni et al. (2017) identified external variables such as awareness, political efficacy, network recruitment networks, and citizens' attitudes toward adopting e-democracy systems to be significant determinants of technology adoption. Prior studies by Ramayah et al. (2009) had deconstructed TRA and produced new constructs namely, injunctive norms and descriptive norms, both of which were direct predictors of subjective norms, with associations between the new constructs and the original theory's constructs confirmed. Besides this, Park (2009), Arpaci and Baloglu (2016), and Arpaci and Baloglu (2016) sought to increase the predictive validity of TRA while studying attitudes toward knowledge-sharing information systems in Turkish educational institutions and reported that adoption was directly influenced by collectivism and subjective norms. Alsaleh et al.'s (2019) comparison of social media adoption trends in Kuwait and the USA included both TAM and TRA, and they discovered that the TAM variables of perceived enjoyment and trust were comparable with prior research across cultural boundaries. However, there were cultural differences between Kuwaiti and American students, with American students being more likely to have positive attitudes and trust in social media sites than Kuwaiti students. Dinev et al. (2009) made similar observations about information technology adoption behaviours in South Korea and the USA. This is because, whereas the association between behavioural intention and subjective norms was substantial in South Korea, it was not significant in the USA. The cultural factors of cumulative individualism, masculinity, power distance, and uncertainty avoidance identified by Hofstede are credited with producing these results. Their study, however, was unable to explain how cultural factors influenced the connection between perceived behavioural control and behavioural intention. Religious beliefs were cited by Lowry (2004) to document cultural factors that affected the adoption of technology in the United Arab Emirates. He suggested that these beliefs were strongly correlated with attitudes toward the perceived utility of technologies. These findings usually demonstrate that although the adoption of information technologies may be consistently explained by TRA's constructs, this is dependent on the setting as well as other cultural and religious values. From this then, one can conclude that social interactions within groups of people influence attitudes and intentions toward the adoption of technology and that these influences can occasionally be specific to an individual. This is because using technology is a "culturally embedded value-laden" activity that is frequently associated with individualism/collectivism and is reliant on the connections between people and society.

THEORY OF PLANNED BEHAVIOUR

TPB has not been extensively employed in cross-cultural studies to explain technology uptake and acceptability. The majority of research has only included studies of one country. The adoption of mobile commerce and the internet in India was examined by Fusilier and Durlabhji (2005) and Mishra (2014), who found correlations between the theory's constructs even though attitude and experience factors did not have any statistically significant associations. Despite Mathieson (1991) having said

Evaluation of Axiomatic Theories, Models of Technology Acceptance

that beliefs are particular to each context and cannot, therefore, be generalized, it appears that this research did not reflect on cultural differences that affected the adoption of technology. This raises questions concerning the predictive strength's perceived usefulness and usability as well as its perceived cultural adaptability. Then, Hassan, Shiu, and Parray (2016) made an effort to demonstrate the effectiveness of Hofstede's cultural dimensions in TPB-based studies, claiming that the associations between subjective norm and intention were strongly mediated by power distance in cultures with high power distance. In a previous study on the cross-cultural adoption of e-commerce in China and the USA, Pavlou and Chai (2002) showed that trust and consumer behavioural intention to engage in product purchases had an impact on the adoption of e-commerce. Uncertainties associated with conducting business online have an impact on trust as a variable. The study discovered that the cultural values of individualism/collectivism, power distance, and long-term orientation moderated the model's central interactions across variables across many cultures. Another study on the adoption of online shopping in Colombia and Spain by Pea-Garca et al. (2020) revealed that self-efficacy was a significant predictor of adoption in both cultures and that culture had a variety of moderating effects on the association between factors. According to their research, Colombians were more impacted by perceived usefulness on attitude than the Spanish population. Although there were considerable variations between these two groups, the research also revealed that perceived ease of use would influence purchasing intention, with a positive link in Columbia and a negative relationship in Spain.

UTAUT APPLICATIONS ACROSS CULTURES

In cross-cultural research on the adoption of information systems, UTAUT has been widely employed. For example, Oshlyansky, Cairns, and Thimbleby (2007) in researching the adoption of technologies in higher education institutions in the Czech Republic, Greece, India, Malaysia, New Zealand, Saudi Arabia, South Africa, United Kingdom, and the USA, reported that all variables had a strong influence on the intention to use adopt new technologies. UTAUT has also been extended to non-English speaking countries where anxiety towards using new technologies appeared to have a bigger effect on non-English speaking nations while having no discernible effect on English speakers. The study's findings revealed that although performance and effort constructs emerged as significant determinants in all nine countries and UTAUT provided some predictive explanation for the adoption of ICT, different constructs had varying degrees of influence in each country. For instance, social influence was a significant driver for website acceptance in all countries but the Czech Republic, whereas anxiety was a significant determinant in Saudi Arabia.

17

The acceptance of new technologies was influenced by the cultural variations between Istanbul and other Turkish regions, according to Göüş et al.'s (2012) validation of UTAUT in Turkey. Furthermore, the theory's predictive capabilities varied between STEM (science, technology, engineering, and math) and non-STEM disciplines. Simeonova et al.'s (2014) study into the factors influencing the adoption of virtual learning environments in Jordan, Russia, and the UK found that the study's findings could not be replicated in all three nations, indicating that cultural differences may have influenced the adoption of VLE in these nations.

To make UTAUT better, Kwarteng et al. (2023) combined UTAUT and Competitive Pressure (CP) to examine how SMEs in the Czech Republic and Slovakia are embracing digitalisation. The study found differences between the two nations' intentions to adopt new digitalization innovations, even though these differences were statistically insignificant, indicating that cultural differences between these two European nations had little impact on their adoption intentions. In general, however, the study found that intentions to adopt new digitalization innovations were influenced by performance expectations, enabling factors, and competitive pressure. Perceived value, perceived value outcomes, perceived risk, self-congruence, and novelty of the new product were other variables Karjaluoto (2019) offered as extensions to the original theory, and these were also shown to have a substantial impact on the uptake of mobile financial services. In research on Internet banking in England and Lebanon, Merhi, Hone, and Trahini (2019) added additional components such as trust, security, and privacy. The findings of their study demonstrated that among users in Lebanon and England, perceptions of security, habit, and trust affected users' intentions to embrace mobile banking services. The price value was significant in England but not Lebanon, but performance expectancy was a stronger factor in Lebanon. Both cultures' intentions to adopt mobile banking services were unaffected by social influence or hedonic motivation. Chopdar et al. (2018) explored the adoption of mobile banking applications using a cross-country study that encompassed the USA and India and reported the existence of cultural moderators on users' views toward privacy risk and security risk across the two nations investigated. In India compared to the USA, the impact of privacy and security risk on the adoption of mobile shopping applications was greater. According to Khan et al. (2022) and Jadil, Rana, and Dwivedi (2023), usage intention and behaviour among users in India, the USA, Turkey, and Pakistan were regulated by cultural factors such as facilitating conditions and effort expectations. According to the study's findings, performance expectations, hedonic motivation, habit, and perceived credibility were stronger predictors of behavioural intention to adopt online banking in Pakistan than they were in Turkey, where those factors were performance expectations, social influence, price value, habit, and perceived credibility. Collectivism and a long-term orientation were cultural factors that influenced customers' adoption of mobile banking in Pakistan, whereas uncertainty avoidance, power distance, and masculinity/femininity moderated the behavioural intention to embrace mobile banking among Turkish consumers. Ahmad et al. (2021) then incorporated cultural variables into the model in their study of mobile travel applications in China and the United States to provide reliable prediction strength in explaining behavioural intention to adopt travel reservation apps. A previous study conducted in Yemen by Isaac et al. (2019) similarly revealed differences in the theory's predictive validity across cultural boundaries. It is challenging for researchers to agree on the elements influencing technology utilization since these differences frequently lead to misunderstandings about how technologies are used. On the moderators of UTAUT, variations in prediction values have also been noted. Al-Gahtani, Hubona, and Wang, for instance, identified cultural differences between North American and Saudi Arabian users' use of IT in Saudi Arabia and further reported that there was no relationship between moderating variables, gender, or age on the relationship between performance expectancy and intention to use ICTs and that there was no relationship between effort expectancy and the moderating variables. Some studies, including Ahmad et al. (2021), have criticized the lack of predictive consistency across cultures since it ignores theoretically relevant correlations and omits potentially crucial factors. Additionally, because moderators are important in some settings, other academics have argued against keeping them in place.

DISCUSSIONS

From this review, the majority, the majority of research on cross-cultural studies have been carried out in English-speaking countries in the developed world, while a few studies have been carried out in the developing world for example, Takeiddine and Sun 2015). Across different cultures, however, it is evident that even among the widely used technology acceptance theories, no single theory can claim to be exhaustive in explaining technology acceptance and use. This is because the literature shows that cultural variables in addition to other external variables play a significant moderating role in the theories' constructs, while in some contexts, these variables, particularly those from Hifstede's cultural dimensions have a direct influence on users' intentions and usage behaviour of new technologies. These findings are supported by research by several authors and these research include the application of the SCT across cultures by McComick, Alavi and Hanham (2025) and Gebauer(2015), the application of TANM across cultures and the integration of the theory with Hoftedes's cultural dimensions by Straub et al., (2017), Aboelmaged (2009) and Dhagara, Gosswami and Kumar (2020). From the results of this review, therefore, contemporary theories have been proven to be inadequate in addressing the factors that influence technology adoption. The results show that power distance. Uncertainty avoidance, masculinity/

feminity, individualism/collectivism and long-term orientation all have a strong influence on users' intentions to use new technologies.

CONCLUSION

The chapter demonstrates the importance of theory in explaining technology adoption and usage. The use of theory has been generally accepted by researchers to provide valid reasons why some technologies are rejected in some cultures while they are adopted in other cultures. The review, therefore, recognizes the general validity of modern axiomatic ideas in understanding the acceptability and uptake of technology. However, different studies producing varying levels of predictive validity do not support the reliability of these hypotheses across cultures. This implies that there might be outside factors that control how variables from different axiomatic theories relate to one another. Hofstede's cultural dimensions classify these factors as power distance, uncertainty avoidance, individualism/collectivism, and masculinity/femininity, with their influence and strength varying across different user groups. These factors are embedded within the cultures of various communities of operation.

RECOMMENDATIONS

The study generally agrees that cultural variables that may affect the adoption and utilization of information systems across cultures are not addressed by current contemporary ideas on technology acceptance. And other researchers have created conceptual models for a variety of research activities to solve these limitations. This chapter suggests additional research to take into account the creation of fresh ideas to account for technology uptake and acceptability across cultural boundaries. Additionally, this chapter rejects the generalisation of theories across cultures and cautions against the universal application of theories of technology acceptance. The chapter therefore recommends user-centred research that takes into consideration the cultural variables of a community when studying the potential usage and usage of a new technology in an information system environment.

REFERENCES

Aboelmaged, M. G. (2010). Predicting e-procurement adoption in a developing country: An empirical integration of technology acceptance model and theory of planned. *Industrial Management & Data Systems*, *110*(3), 392–41. doi:10.1108/02635571011030042

Ahmad, W., Kim, W. G., Choi, H., & Haq, J. U. (2021). Modelling behavioural intention to use travel reservation apps: A cross-cultural examination between US and China. *Journal of Retailing and Consumer Services*, *63*, 102689. doi:10.1016/j. jretconser.2021.102689

Al-Gahtani, S. S., Hubona, G. S., & Wang, J. (2007). Information technology (IT) in Saudi-Arabia: Culture and the acceptance and use of IT. *Information & Management*, *44*(8), 681–691. doi:10.1016/j.im.2007.09.002

Albirini, A. (2006). Teachers' attitudes toward information and communication technologies: The case of Syrian EFL teachers. *Computers & Education*, *47*(4), 373–398. doi:10.1016/j.compedu.2004.10.013

Almogren, A. S., & Aljammaz, N. A. (2022). The integrated social cognitive theory with the TAM model: The impact of M-learning in King Saud University art education. *Educational Psychology*, *13*, 1050532. doi:10.3389/fpsyg.2022.1050532 PMID:36506961

Alsaleh, D. A., Elliott, M. T., Fu, F. Q., & Thakur, R. (2019). Cross-cultural differences in the adoption of social media. *Journal of Research in Interactive Marketing*, *13*(1), 119–140. doi:10.1108/JRIM-10-2017-0092

Arpaci, I., & Baloglu, M. (2016). The impact of cultural collectivism on knowledge sharing among information technology majoring undergraduates. *Computers in Human Behavior*, *56*, 65–71. doi:10.1016/j.chb.2015.11.031

Bandyopadhyay, K., & Fraccastoro, K. A. (2007). The Effect of Culture on User Acceptance of Information Technology. *Communications of the Association for Information Systems*, *19*(23). doi:10.17705/1CAIS.01923

Besbes, A., Legohérel, P., Kucukusta, D. M., & Law, R. (2016). A Cross-Cultural Validation of the Tourism Web Acceptance Model (T-WAM) in different cultural contexts. *Journal of International Consumer Marketing*, *28*(3), 211–226. doi:10.1 080/08961530.2016.1152524

Blagoeva, K. T., & Mijoska, M. (2017). Applying TAM to study online shopping adoption among youth in the Republic of Macedonia. *Management International Conference*, Venice, Italy.

Botha, N., & Atkins, K. (2005). *An assessment of five different theoretical frameworks to study the uptake of innovations.* Paper presented at the 2005 NZARES Conference, Tahuma Conference Centre, New Zealand.

Chopdar, P. K ., Korfiatis,N., Sivakumar, V.J. & Lytras, M. D. (2018). Mobile shopping app adoption and perceived risks: A cross-country perspective utilizing the Unified Theory of Acceptance and Use of Technology. *Computers in Human Behavior, 86(2018), 109e128.*

Dai, H., & Palvia, P. C. (2009). Mobile commerce adoption in China and the United States: A cross-cultural study. *The Data Base for Advances in Information Systems, 40*(4), 43–61. doi:10.1145/1644953.1644958

Davis, F. D. (1989). Perceived usefulness, perceived ease of use, and user acceptance of information technology. *Management Information Systems Quarterly, 13*(3), 319–340. doi:10.2307/249008

deGuinea, A. O., & Webster, J. (2015). The missing links: Cultural, software, task and personal influences on computer self-efficacy. *International Journal of Human Resource Management, 26*(7), 905–931. doi:10.1080/09585192.2012.655758

Dhagarra, D., Goswami, M., & Kumar, G. (2020). Impact of Trust and Privacy Concerns on Technology Acceptance in Healthcare: An Indian Perspective. *International Journal of Medical Informatics, 141*, 141. doi:10.1016/j.ijmedinf.2020.104164 PMID:32593847

Dinev, T., Goo, J., Hu, Q. & Nam, K. (2009). User behaviour towards protective information technologies: the role of national cultural differences. *Info Systems J, 19*(2009), 391-412. . doi:. doi:10.1111/j.1365-2575.2007.00289.x

Faqih, K. M. S., & Jarada, M. R. M. (2015). Assessing the moderating effect of gender differences and individualism-collectivism at individual-level on the adoption of mobile commerce technology: TAM3 perspective. *Journal of Retailing and Consumer Services, 22*, 37–52. doi:10.1016/j.jretconser.2014.09.006

Fusilier, M., & Durlabhji, S. (2005). An exploration of student internet use in India the technology acceptance model and the theory of planned behaviour. *Campus-Wide Information Systems, 22*(4), 233–246. doi:10.1108/10650740510617539

Gangwar, H., Date, H., & Ramaswamy, R. (2015). Understanding determinants of cloud computing adoption using an integrated TAM-TOE model. *Journal of Enterprise Information Management, 28*(1), 107–130. doi:10.1108/JEIM-08-2013-0065

Gebauer, M. M., McElvany, N., Köller, O., & Schöber, C. (2021). · Köller, O. & Schöber, C. (2021). Cross-cultural differences in academic self-efficacy and its sources across socialization contexts. *Social Psychology of Education, 24*(6), 1407–1432. doi:10.100711218-021-09658-3

Göğüş, A., Nistor, N., & Lerche, T. (2012). Educational technology acceptance across cultures: A validation of the Unified Theory of Acceptance And Use of Technology in the context of Turkish national culture. *The Turkish Online Journal of Educational Technology, 11*(4).

Gregor, S. (2006). The nature of theory in information systems. *Management Information Systems Quarterly, 30*(3), 611. doi:10.2307/25148742

Hartzel, K. S., Marley, K. A., & Spangler, W. E. (2016). Online Social Network Adoption: A Cross-Cultural Study. *Journal of Computer Information Systems, 56*(2), 87–96. doi:10.1080/08874417.2016.1117367

Hassan, L. M., Shiu, E., & Parry, S. (2016). Addressing the cross-country applicability of the theory of planned behaviour (TPB): A structured review of multi-country TPB studies. *Journal of Consumer Behaviour, 15*(1), 72–86. doi:10.1002/cb.1536

Hofstede, G. (2001). *Culture's Consequences: Comparing values, behaviors, institutions, and organizations across nations.* Sage.

Huang, W., D'Ambra, J., & Bhalla, V. (2002). An empirical investigation of the adoption of eGovernment in Australian citizens: Some unexpected research findings. *Journal of Computer Information Systems, 43*(1), 15–22.

Hussain, S. & Bashir-Dar, I. (2020). Comments on "The nature of theory in information systems". *Future Business Journal. 6*(1).

Isaac, O., Abdullah, Z., Aldholay, A. H. & Ameen, A. A. (2019). Antecedents and outcomes of Internet usage within organisations in Yemen: An extension of the Unified Theory of Acceptance and Use of Technology (UTAUT) model. *Asia Pacific Management Review, 24.*

Jadil, Y., Rana, N. P. & Dwivedi, Y. K. (2023). A meta-analysis of the UTAUT model in the mobile banking literature: The moderating role of sample size and culture. *Journal of Business Research, 132*, 354–372.

Jan, J., Alshare, K. A., & Lane, P. L. (2022). Hofstede's cultural dimensions in technology acceptance models: A meta-analysis. *Universal Access in the Information Society*. doi:10.100710209-022-00930-7

Karjaluoto, H., Shaikha, A. A., Saarijarvib, H., & Saraniemi, S. (2019). How perceived value drives the use of mobile *financial services apps. International Journal of Information Management, 47*, 252–261. doi:10.1016/j.ijinfomgt.2018.08.014

Koo, C., & Chung, N. (2014). Examining the eco-technological knowledge of Smart Green IT adoption behaviour: A self-determination perspective. *Technological Forecasting and Social Change, 88*, 140–155. doi:10.1016/j.techfore.2014.06.025

Kwarteng, M. A., Ntsiful, A., Diego, L. F. P., & Novak, P. (2022). Extending UTAUT with competitive pressure for SMEs digitalization adoption in two European nations: A multi-group analysis. *Aslib Journal of Information Management*. doi:10.1108/AJIM-11-2022-0482

Lee, S., Trimi, S., & Kim, K. (2013). The impact of cultural differences on technology adoption. *Journal of World Business, 48*(1), 20–29. doi:10.1016/j.jwb.2012.06.003

Lim, S., Saldanha, J. J. V., Mallachi, S., & Melville, N. P. (2014). Theories used in information system research: Insights from complex network analysis. [A publication of the Association for Information Systems.]. *Journal of Information Technology Theory and Application, 14*(2), 5–46.

Lin, C. A., & Kim, T. (2016). Predicting user response to sponsored advertising on social media via the technology acceptance model. *Computers in Human Behavior, 64*, 710–718. doi:10.1016/j.chb.2016.07.027

Lin, F., Fofanah, S. S & Liang, D. (2011). Assessing citizen adoption of e-government initiatives in the Gambia. *Validation of the tech,* 271-279.

Lin, H. (2014). An investigation of the effects of cultural differences on physicians' perceptions of information technology acceptance as they relate to knowledge management systems. *Computers in Human Behavior, 38*, 368–380. doi:10.1016/j.chb.2014.05.001

Lowry, G. (2004). Translation and Validation of the Technology Acceptance Model and instrument for use in the Arab World. *ACIS 2004 Proceedings. 105.* https://aisel.aisnet.org/acis2004/105

Mathieson, K. (1991). Predicting User Intentions: Comparing the Technology Acceptance Model with the Theory of Planned Behaviour. *Information Systems Research, 2*(3), 173–191. doi:10.1287/isre.2.3.173

McCormick, J., Alavi, S. B., & Hanham, J. (2015). *The importance of context when applying social cognitive theory in organisations. Faculty of Social Sciences, Papers (Archive)*. The University of Wollongong.

Merhi, M., Hone, K., & Tarhi, A. (2019). A cross-cultural study of the intention to use mobile banking between Lebanese and British consumers: Extending UTAUT2 with security, privacy and trust. *Technology in Society*, *59*, 101151. doi:10.1016/j.techsoc.2019.101151

Metallo, C., Agrifoglio, R., Lepore, L., & Landriani, L. (2022). Explaining users' technology acceptance through national cultural values in the hospital context. *BMC Health Services Research*, *2022*(22), 84. doi:10.118612913-022-07488-3 PMID:35039014

Minton, E. A., Spielmann, N., Kahle, L. R., & Kim, C. (2018). The subjective norms of sustainable consumption: A cross-cultural Exploration. *Journal of Business Research*, *82*, 400–408. doi:10.1016/j.jbusres.2016.12.031

Mishra, S. (2014). Adoption of M-commerce in India: Applying Theory of Planned Behaviour Model. *Journal of Internet Banking and Commerce*, *19*(1).

Mohammed, Z. A., & Tejay, G. P. (2017). Examining privacy concerns and e-commerce adoption in developing countries: The impact of culture in shaping individuals' perceptions toward technology. *Computers & Security*, *67*, 254–265. doi:10.1016/j.cose.2017.03.001

Muk, A., & Chung, C. (2015). Applying the technology acceptance model in a two-country study of SMS advertising. *Journal of Business Research*, *68*(1), 1–6. doi:10.1016/j.jbusres.2014.06.001

Muller, B., & Urbach, N. (2017). Understanding the Why, What and How of theories in IS research. *Communications of the Association for Information Systems*, *41*, 349–388. doi:10.17705/1CAIS.04117

Oliveira, T., Thomas, M., & Espadanal, M. (2014). Assessing the determinants of cloud computing adoption: An analysis of the manufacturing and services sectors. *Information & Management*, *51*(5), 497–510. doi:10.1016/j.im.2014.03.006

Oni, A. A., Oni, S., Mbarika, V., & Ayo, C. K. (2017). An empirical study of user acceptance of online political participation: Integrating Civic Voluntarism Model and Theory of Reasoned Action. *Government Information Quarterly*, *34*(2), 317–328. doi:10.1016/j.giq.2017.02.003

Oshlyyansky, L., Cairns, P., & Thimbleby, H. (2007). Validating the unified theory of acceptance and use of technology (UTAUT) tools cross-culturally. *Conference: Proceedings of the 21st British HCI Group Annual Conference on HCI 2007: HCI... but not as we know it - Volume 2, BCS HCI 2007*. University of Lancaster, United Kingdom.

Park, H. S. (2000). Relationships among attitudes and subjective norms: Testing the theory of reasoned action across cultures. *Communication Studies, 51*(2), 162–175. doi:10.1080/10510970009388516

Park, N., Roman, R., Lee, S., & Chung, J. E. (2009). User acceptance of a digital library system in developing countries: An application of the Technology acceptance model. *International Journal of Information Management, 29*(3), 196–209. doi:10.1016/j. ijinfomgt.2008.07.001

Peña-García, N., Gil-Saura, I., Rodríguez-Orejuela, A., & Siqueira-Juni, J. R. (2020). Purchase intention and purchase behaviour online: A cross-cultural approach. *Heliyon, 6*(6), e04284. doi:10.1016/j.heliyon.2020.e04284 PMID:32613132

Perez-Alvarez, C. (2006). Uncertainty avoidance, IT perceptions, use and adoption: Distributed teams in two cultures. *Journal of Academic and Business Ethics*.

Perkmen, S., Toy, S., & Caracuel, A. (2023). Extended Social Cognitive Model Explains Pre-Service Teachers' Technology Integration Intentions with Cross-Cultural Validity. *Computers in the Schools, 40*(2), 173–193. doi:10.1080/073805 69.2022.2157690

Ramayah, T., Rouibah, K., Gopi, M., & Rangel, G. J. (2009). A decomposed theory of reasoned action to explain the intention to use Internet stock trading among Malaysian investors. *Computers in Human Behavior, 25*(6), 1222–1230. doi:10.1016/j.chb.2009.06.007

Sharma, S. K., Al-Badi, A. H., Govindaluri, S. M., & Al-Kharusi, M. H. (2016). Predicting motivators of cloud computing adoption: A developing country perspective. *Computers in Human Behavior, 62*, 61–69. doi:10.1016/j.chb.2016.03.073

Simeonova, B., Bogolyubov, P., Blagov, E., & Kharabsheh, R. (2014). Cross-cultural validation of UTAUT: The case of University VLEs in Jordan, Russia and the UK. *Electronic Journal of Knowledge Management, 12*(1), 25–34.

Singh, N., Fassott, G., Chao, M. C. H., & Hoffmann, J. A. (2004). Understanding international website usage A cross-national study of German, Brazilian, and Taiwanese online consumers. *International Marketing Review, 23*(1), 83–97. doi:10.1108/02651330610646304

Straub, D., Karen, L., & Hill, C. E. (2001). Transfer of information technology to the Arab world: A test of cultural influence modelling. *Journal of Global Information Management, 9*(4), 6–28. doi:10.4018/jgim.2001100101

Straub, D., Keil, M., & Brenner, W. (1997). Testing the technology acceptance model across cultures: A three-country study. *Information & Management, 33*(1), 1–11. doi:10.1016/S0378-7206(97)00026-8

Taherdoost, H. (2018). A review of technology acceptance and adoption models and theories. *Procedia Manufacturing, 22,* 960–967. doi:10.1016/j.promfg.2018.03.137

Takieddine, S., & Sun, J. (2015). Internet banking diffusion: A country-level analysis. *Electronic Commerce Research and Applications, 14*(5), 361–371. doi:10.1016/j.elerap.2015.06.001

Tao, D., Shao, F., Wang, H., Yan, M., & Qu, X. (2019). Integrating usability and social cognitive theories with the technology acceptance model to understand young users' acceptance of a health information portal. *Health Informatics Journal, 26*(2), 1347–1362. doi:10.1177/1460458219879337 PMID:31603378

Tarhini, A., Hassouna, M., Abbasi, M. S., & Orozco, J. (2015). Towards the Acceptance of RSS to Support Learning: An empirical study to validate the Technology Acceptance Model in Lebanon. *Electronic Journal of e-Learning, 13*(1), 30–41.

Teo, T. M., Luan, W. S., & Sing, C. C. (2008). A cross-cultural examination of the intention to use technology between Singaporean and Malaysian pre-service teachers on application of the technology acceptance model (TAM). *Journal of Educational Technology & Society, 11*(4), 265–280.

Thompson, R. L., Higgins, C. A., & Howel, J. M. (1991). Personal Computing: Towards a Conceptual Model of Utilization. *Management Information Systems Quarterly, 15*(1), 125–143. doi:10.2307/249443

Truex, D., Holmstrom, J., & Keil, M. (2006). Theory in information systems research: A reflexive analysis of the adaptation of theory in information systems research. *Journal of the Association for Information Systems, 7*(12), 797–821. doi:10.17705/1jais.00109

Veltri, N. F., & Elgarah, W. (2009). The Role of national cultural differences in user adoption of social networking. *Proceedings of the Southern Association for Information Systems Conference*, Charleston, SC.

Wei, K., Teo, H., Chan, C., & Tan, C. (2011). Conceptualising and testing the social cognitive model of the digital divide. *Information Systems Research*, 22(1), 170–187. doi:10.1287/isre.1090.0273

Wu, J., & Wang, S. (2005). What drives mobile commerce? An empirical evaluation of the revised technology acceptance model. *Information & Management*, 42(5), 719–729. doi:10.1016/j.im.2004.07.001

Wu, M. (2020). Organizational Acceptance of Social Media Marketing: A Cross-Cultural Perspective. *Journal of Intercultural Communication Research*, 49(4), 313–329. doi:10.1080/17475759.2020.1771752

KEY TERMS AND DEFINITIONS

Cross-cultural Technology Acceptance: Acceptance of technology under the influence of cultural variables.

Hofstede cultural Dimensions: The variables that are used to identify differences in the cultural behaviours of communities.

Individualism: Refers to how one person interacts with other people.

Information Systems Theory: Theories that are used to study information systems.

Masculinity-Feminity: Behavioural differences and power dynamics in a community in based on gender.

Power-distance: Relates to a construct that refers to social relationships and power.

Technology Acceptance Model: A model developed by Davis(1989) to study technology acceptance in an information system environment.

Technology Across Cultures: The usage of technology across various cultures.

Chapter 2

Application of Interpretivism Theoretical Framework on the Management of University Records:
Comparison of Selected Universities

Nkholedzeni Sidney Netshakhuma

iD https://orcid.org/0000-0003-0673-7137
University of Mpumalanga, South Africa

ABSTRACT

This research assessed the adoption of interpretivism paradigm as a theoretical framework. The interpretivism was adopted on a study comparing the University of Venda and the University of Witwatersrand archives and records management programme. This research was undertaken as part of PhD thesis. The study found that adoption of interpretivism paradigm improves credibility, transferability, and authenticity of the research. The research recommend that research in information sciences are to incorporate other paradigm such as positivism.

INTRODUCTION

Interpretivism's theoretical framework is applied to a qualitative study. This is because the application of the interpretivism paradigm as fundamental affects the choice of the research approach. This case study was conducted to gain an understanding of a particular redesign process of university records management

DOI: 10.4018/978-1-7998-9687-6.ch002

Copyright © 2024, IGI Global. Copying or distributing in print or electronic forms without written permission of IGI Global is prohibited.

processes. Interpretivism theoretical framework was applied to research University archives and records. Studies conducted using interpretivism theoretical framework improved its credibility. Several researchers in archives and records management adopted the interpretivism paradigm to conduct their studies. For example, Mosweu (2016) applies the interpretivism paradigm to investigate success factors in electronic document and records management systems implementation at the Ministry of Trade and Industry in Botswana. Muhammad, Mat ISA and Miah (2021) also use the same paradigm on two Nigerian universities. Matlala (2019), Phiri (2016) applies the interpretivism approach to the management of universities archives and records management. This is an indication that the interpretivism paradigm is a major theory used by information scientists.

. The data collection and analyses determine the conduct of the study. Individuals build understandings, meanings, and identities through dialogue and discourse (Case 2012, p. 190).

There is a need to recognize the participants' viewpoints during the collection of data. The researcher unpacked the significance of the interpretive perspective on the management of university archives and records.

This chapter discusses the application of the interpretivism paradigm as fundamental that influences the choice of research methodology. The case study was conducted to assess the management of university archives and records. The study compared two selected universities in South Africa, archives and records management programs.

The data collected and interpreted determines the type of research. Individuals construct understandings, meanings, and identities through dialogue and discourse (Case 2012, p. 190). Interpretivism is mainstream within information science. It has been conventional to recognize that phenomena can be viewed from a multi-perspective (Clarke, Davison, and Jia 2020).

Paradigm shapes the researcher's viewpoints, interpretation, and understand (Babbie, 2017, p. 31). Paradigms are a set of expectations of what constitutes techniques to conduct a study. Research is based on a set of shared assumptions, concepts, values, and practices. Participants' viewpoints were recognized by the author. Paradigms are suitable ways of empathetic reality, building knowledge, and gathering information about the development of the university archive and records management program.

Interpretivism's viewpoint advance its position as a paradigm lies in the fact that is an ontological point of view of reality (Kankam, 2019, p. 850). This research depends on the participants' viewpoints during the data collection. The participants in this research include heads of divisions, units, and divisions selected to participate in this study

The interpretivism perspective viewed the world as interpreted and experienced by people during their interactions (Antwi and Hamza 2015, p. 219). People interact as a form of the social system. This interpretation is done to understand the process of management of university archives and records. interpretivism researchers must provide a rich, detailed contextual description (McChesney and Aldridge, 2019, p.234)

PURPOSE OF CHOOSING INTERPRETIVISM PARADIGM

The choice of interpretivism was determined by the research purpose and research questions. The research method was applied to answer research questions. This is because methodological thinking requires understanding the characteristics of questions that have the capability of leading high-quality research (Loseke, 2017, p. 38). Questions addressed in this research should be clear to address the objectives of the study. The researcher evaluated studies conducted by other scholars in information science. Any limitation on credibility methods that are considered acceptable severely limits the ability of a university to serve the needs of an organization.

Interpretivism is an epistemological lens incorporated as the researcher and the object of the research are inseparably linked. Interpretivism is a paradigm applied because the author aimed to explore the management of the university of records and archives management. The Interpretivism paradigm influence the researcher to develop an archives and records management framework. The purpose of investigating universities' archives and records management programs is to develop a framework to manage universities' archives and records.

The research applied inductively to generalize university archives and records management. Induction reasoning is the process to discuss the particular to the general phenomenon. Induction is a set of detailed observations to discover a pattern that represents a phenomenon. The research uses data to develop concepts and theories (Loseke 2017,p. 24). The research uses inductive logic because of various research on archives and records management conducted. Inductive reasoning determines reality and methodical inquiry takes place first, and the research tugs conclusions from the interpretations made. The Interpretivism paradigm represents a science to understand a phenomenon (Goldman, 2016, p. 7). The interpretivism paradigm is systematic but it distinguishes methical ideas differently from positivism because a set of views guides interpretation (Punch and Qancea, 2014 p.18). The author seeks to establish the meaning of a phenomenon from the participants' viewpoint (Creswell, 2014, p. 19).

The social world is accepted as a human construction with many attributes that cannot be observed and measured (Dana and Shaun, 2005, p.79). However, universities were the platform to conduct research. The interpretive multidimensional list deliberately sets out subjectively to understand these constructs.

The archives and records management programme is explained in detail through social science. This is an indication that interpretivism is concerned with individual meaning and contribution (Alharahsheh and Pius 2020, p. 42)

The author conducted this research with the purpose to improve the management of university archives and records. The participants' viewpoints on the management of archives and records management were analyzed. The researcher interpreted participants' sense of universities' archives and records management practices from record creation until the disposal stage. The Interpretivism paradigm requires an understanding of how participants define situations in which they are involved and the meanings they derive from their experiences (Kuada, 2012 p. 77).

Researchers' ontological stance and the nature of the research question shape the research ontological, epistemological, and methodological to guide the research. The author's viewpoint is that reality is subjective open for interpretation. Meaning does not emerge from the interplay of the subject and the outside world but is imposed on the subject by the subject. Subjects do not construct meaning but do so from within collective unconsciousness, from dreams and religious beliefs (Lyaruu, 2021, p. 74). This is so because the researcher understands the world by his views.

The researcher visited the selected universities with the view to assess the state of archives and records management.

Assess the level of compliance to statutory requirements of records management by the selected universities.

Set to evaluate the archives and records management maturity level of the selected universities;

Establish the Enterprise Information Management Business Process aligned to archives and records management process in the two selected universities.

Symbolic interactionism is interpreted as a social theory that has distinctive epistemological consequences and the hermeneutic-phenomenological tradition (Bryman and Bell 2015 p. 13). Participants assign meaning to the management of archives and records from creation until disposal. The subjective viewpoint is an instrument to analyze the management of records from creation until disposal. Interpretivism allows archives and records to be viewed differently by stakeholders due to varying beliefs, understanding, interests, experiences, and expectations (Hartz–Karp and Marinova, 2017, p. 11).

The author analyzed the participants' viewpoint on the management of university archives and records. The participants make sense of the management of records from creation until disposal. The integration of university Enterprise Information Management Business Processes to archives and records management processes has impacted a constructed understanding of the value of archives and records management programs (Grbich, 2013, p. 07). The researcher constructs and imposes an interpretation of archives and records management. The archives and records frames are derived from their own experiences, subjectivity, and inter-subjectivity.

LITERATURE REVIEW

The literature was reviewed to assess trends in the adoption of the interpretivism paradigm on information science. The literature review reflects current discussion debates of the research questions. This includes theories selected in this research (Largan and Morris, 2019, p. 74). The literature review was used to frame questions. The literature review should current discussion debates of the research questions. of the study. The literature exposure on paradigmatic issues demonstrated that consideration and discussion of pragmatism play a role in position philosophically and methodological. Interpretivism paradigm was the mainstream within information science, it has been conventional to recognize that phenomena can be viewed from a multi-perspective (Clarke, Davison, and Jia 2020).

QUALITATIVE AND QUANTITATIVE RESEARCH APPROACH

The research applies different research approaches such as quantitative, qualitative, and mixed. Based on the objectives and questions of this study, the researcher employed qualitative and quantitative methods. The selection of the interpretivism paradigm of this research was influenced by the nature of the research. The naturalistic perspective recognizes that understanding the reality of the phenomenon is essential for the reality as possible influences the qualitative research. University archives and records management principles may not be understood by applying research principles adopted from the natural science discipline.

Selecting a research approach requires the adoption of research philosophy. The researcher analyzed the management of university records through an interpretive perspective. This study applied interpretivism philosophy because it encompasses narrative research. The methodology related to interpretivism is associated with a qualitative approach (Ngulube 2016). The research used descriptive analysis to explain the data. The research emphasized the conceptions of participants and implies that the research understanding must be based on the experience of the staffs managing archives and records within an institution. (Bryman and Bell, 2015, p. 17). Interpretivism viewpoint encompasses participants engaged to make sense of archives, records. and interprets, creates, gives meaning, defines, justifies, and rationalizes activities.

The qualitative research approach is concerned with the interpretation of the meaning of the social phenomenon. Qualitative research creates narrative data. It is an approach selected to scientifically explain events, people, and matters associated with them. (Fox and Bayat, 2012 p. 07). Qualitative researchers tend to analyze data inductively. The qualitative researcher relies on judgment, experience, history, social contexts, and constructions of reality to enhance existing perceptions of university archives and records. The researcher used a variety of methods and perspectives, rather than approaching qualitative research from a single case study. The strength of qualitative research is its ability to interpret the records lifecycle throughout universities.

A qualitative approach was appropriate for this book chapter to generate rich and detailed data. The information generated by participants contributes to in-depth understanding management of university archives and records. Consideration was taken to combine constructivism and interpretivism paradigms to analyze data. Granting such combinations develops richer insights on the management of university records (De Vos, Strydom, Fouche and Delport 2017 p. 29). The researcher chooses interpretivism as the form of philosophical thinking because data analysis and interpretation were based on the researcher and participants' perspectives. In this study, positivism is the philosophical worldview underpinning the process of this study, since the study aims to capture the perceived experience of staff through numerical data and analysis. The recording of quantities or numbers is processed by using statistical techniques and reflects reality.

Constructivists' viewpoints are that people construct their understanding and knowledge of the world through experiencing things and developing the subjective meaning of their experiences while interpretivism informs methodologies about the nature of knowledge. The research is to develop a strategy to conduct the research. The author must acknowledge the contribution made by other researchers in the field of information science. The framework to be developed is informed by previous scholars on information science. The study seeks to develop an archives and records management framework to guide the implementation of records management programs in South African universities. The study is based on the narratives of the phenomenon.

The qualitative research methodology is grounded on the interpretivism paradigm. The methodology chosen for this research problem takes into account the nature of the data collected (Leedy and Ormrod, 2015 p. 97). The research was undertaken within a framework of a qualitative and quantitative approach because of philosophical assumptions of interpretivism and constructivism that seek to analyze data from participants' viewpoints. The qualitative and quantitative research approach was chosen in this research because the topic of the research and questions requires archives and records management phenomenon to be explored. Qualitative research was chosen because it gave a researcher a compelling description of the ARM in the university environment.

The types of qualitative and quantitative research designs were narrative statistical. This statement is alluded to by Patten and Newhart (2018 p. 165) who said that qualitative research assesses a case in detail. The researcher chooses a multiple case study because of its emphasis on the causes of a phenomenon and develops an in-depth analysis of records lifecycle.

RESEARCH METHODS AND DESIGN

Rather than conducting a single case study in all its complexity, the research opted for a multiplicity of cases (Flick, 2015 p. 98). To conduct the multiple case study was necessary to select organizations with similar functions. Universities' functions are teaching and learning research, engagement, and partnership. The education sector presents a rich area for investigation on archives and records management. According to Yin (2018, p.55), a case was selected to provide results or predict contrasting results to develop a records management framework to guide the implementation of records management programs. In this case, the historically disadvantaged university compared with the historically advantaged university. The selection of instruments for this study signifies a general view of the phenomenon under examination.

The cases were cross-analyzed on similarities and differences related to the management of archives and records. The author compared and contrast the findings deriving from each case. The selection of two cases provides a wider presentation of data than do a single case (Yin 2012 p. 131; and Struwig and Stead 2016 p. 6). The study was not meant to suggest prescriptive solutions to general archives and records management program problems but to develop an archives and records management framework to guide the implementation of records management programs in South African Universities.

The study contains an extensive study of several instrumental cases intended to understand, insight, or improved the ability to control records from creation until disposal (Berg 2009 p. 26).

Cases were understood in-depth, and their natural setting, recognizing its complexity and its context. This is alluded to by Merriam (2009, p. 51) who said that rich, thick description and analysis of a phenomenon is necessary to understand archives and records of universities. A case study provides a deep understanding of a phenomenon of organization. The purpose was to analyze the enterprise information management business Process alignment to archives and records management program.

Given the size of the population of the Selected universities in South Africa, a sample population of the study was the administrative staff. They are the custodians of divisions, departments, and units records. The author did not study an entire university population because of the limited time for this research. This statement is alluded to by Beins (2009 p. 108); and Aurini, Heath, and Howells (2016) who said that with a large sample size, the more time and effort takes to complete the research. Selecting a small size provided opportunities for an author to collect descriptive depth data (Aurini, Heath and Howells 2016; Fox and Bayt 2012 p. 67; and Merriam 2009 p. 94). There was a limit to this study thus why the researcher selected a limited forty sample for the study. From the population of the study, the sample was selected to actively participate in this study. Sampling is the process of selecting units of participants from a population of interest so that, by studying the sample, the researcher may transfer the results from the specific case to other cases from the finding of the research (Maxwell 2013, P. 78).

STUDY POPULATION AND SAMPLING STRATEGY

Purposive sampling is used to identify participants to understand the problem and the research question as described by Creswell (2009 p. 59). The researcher exercises a degree of judgment to select participants to provide the best perspectives on the phenomenon of interest and invites the participants into the study (Creswell, 2005, 203; Braun, Clarke, and Gray, 2017). The number of units at these universities was manageable. The total number of respondents targeted for the interview was forty (40). However, 35 agreed to complete the questionnaires. Purpose sampling was used to collect data from sources of information. The purpose sampling was used to select a sample that reflected the experience of management of university archives and records. The purposive sampling strategy was appropriate because it permitted the author to draw units from the sampling frame based on the participants' knowledge and experience on the management of university records and archives management (Padilla-Diaz 2015, p. 104). The researcher captured multiple perspectives on the management of university archives and records.

Small staff selected to participate in this research were representative of the university division, department, and unit. Heads of divisions, departments, and units with relevant skills and knowledge on archives and records management were selected t participate in this research. Studies conducted by Babbie (2016, p.187); Berg (2009, p. 50); and Hancock and Algozzine (2011 p.44) said that selection of participants of the study should be based on argued that appropriation of select a sample based on knowledge of a population enable the researcher to answers questions emanated from the research. Studies conducted by Babbie (2016, p.187);

and Hancock and Algozzine (2011 p.44) argued that selection of sample based on knowledge of a population to enable participants to answers questions emanated from the research questions.

The researcher secured was permitted to visit the selected institutions to conduct the research. The vast enable the researcher to Thirty-four (34) heads of business units from the University of Venda and the University of Witwatersrand agreed to participate in the research. The researcher's reason to include heads of business units in the study was because of their role in governance and management. These participants play a role to develop organizational strategy. The researcher's reason to include Heads of business units was due to their role in supervision and management. Over and above, they were chosen because of the strategic positions that enabled them to answer questions relating to universities archives and records management. Records managers and archivists were also selected based on their role and understanding of the university's records and archives management function.

DATA COLLECTION

A variety of data tools is used to collect data from sources points. The Interpretivism paradigm relies on data collection tools such as document analysis, interviews, and observation (Bryman, 2004). The researcher author emphasizes understanding the world through first-hand experience, truthful reporting, and quotations of actual observation.

Concepts are understood through analysis and interpretations of data. According to Wahyuni (2012) data collected through a qualitative approach was taken in the form of primary and secondary data. The form of data collection allowed a researcher to understand the management of archives and records. It also allowed a researcher to understand how they manage records. while documentary analysis includes records such as document

The researcher analyzes social activities how the staff universities archives and records from the research participants' point of view. This is so because in terms of university policy all staff is responsible for the management of records. It was essential to view an organization from its participants' views. Interpretivism views knowledge as socially constructed through language and interaction. Records are created when an organizations interact with stakeholders. For example, universities develop a memorandum of understanding with international organizations. Furthermore, it is the role of universities to interact with internal divisions such as legal services, Communication division, and registrar offices. Societal culture and ideological categories play an essential role in the participants' connection to the phenomenon under the study.

The researcher explored university staff's different experiences and understanding how differences result in the different construction and meanings people provide to the world (Blumberg, Boris Cooper, and Schindler, 2008, p.17). Social phenomena are characterized by complexity and are often unique. Most of the staff are not able to differentiate between documents and records. The fact that interpretivism research assesses the totality makes it most suitable when the researcher is dealing with research involving a smaller number of respondents and aiming at collecting qualitative data (Mabika, 2019, p. 61).

The purpose of triangulation is to gather data from multiple sources to allow the researcher to gain knowledge of the research under investigation (Braun, Clarke, and Gray, 2017, p. 37). The philosophy behind the use of multi-data sources was to understand the holistic picture. It was a strategy to strengthen the research design. According to Yin (2018, p. 130), a lack of multiple sources led to an invaluable advantage of the loss of a case study. Data were collected through a variety of instruments such as document review and, questionnaire (Yin, 2018 p.12). The selected instruments used for this study were as follows:

- both selected document review ;
- Questionnaire; and
- Observe how staff file university records.

Document Analysis

Documents reviewed include university records management policies, file Plans, strategic plans and the legislative documents kept by the universities archives were useful for this study. This statement is alluded to by Salkind (2018 p. 173); Braun, Clarke, and Gray,(2017, p. 502); and Pickard (2013, p. 253) who stated that researchers are to review organization strategic documents to understand institution history. According to Creswell (2005,p. 220) researchers are to develop processes and procedures to review documents collected by an organization. The reviewing of documents provided background information that assisted researchers to assist to understand the motives, objectives, and context on which universities manage records and archives. The documents were necessary to provide information about the history of universities.

Documents as sources of data are diverse, available in vast quantities, found in many forms, and numerous locations as sites of access (Largan and Morris, 2019: 122). The researcher reviewed university records management policies, annual reports, file plans, strategic plans, and legislative documents. These documents are secondary sources for analysis. Document sources were used to provide background information and an understanding of the university's functions and responsibilities.

Documents serve various purposes in an organization. The document provided supplementary data conducted through interviews and observation during the data collection. It is the view of the author that document analysis was the most effective means to collect data.

Interviews

Interviews were conducted with universities head of divisions, departments, and units. Interviews were conducted to understand the current situation concerning the management of university archives and records. The interviews conducted were unstructured. The researcher used an interview guide to proceed with the interviews. All the interviews conducted were recorded and were transcribed in appropriate form. The interviews provided additional information on the significance of records in universities.

The author applied one-on-one interviews with respondents to complete the questionnaire. One-on-one interviews are techniques a researcher visits respondents in a face-to-face setting. This is a data collection process to ask questions and records answers from only one participant in the study at a time (Gorman and Clayton, 2005, p. 126). There was a circumstance in selected universities wherein the researcher used a telephone interview. A telephone interview is a process to gather data over the telephone by an interviewer who asked questions and record responses (Fox and Bayat 2012 p.99). A telephone interview applied in the research participants may be geographically dispersed and unable to visit a central place to be interviewed (Creswell 2005:216; Braun, Clarke and Gray, 2017 p. 405; and DeFour-Howard, 2015 p. 134). The respondents completed the questionnaire in 2019.

Structured interviews through the completion of the questionnaire were used. The research conducted by Tracy (2013 p. 139) said that structured interviews are used to allow us to understand a phenomenon under study. Pickard (2013 p.199) postulates that…structured interviews are used to gain a holistic understanding of the business environment processes". The researcher conducted a structured interview to collect narrative data. Individual interviews contributed data from an individual's perspective but were time–consuming (Hancock and Algozzine 2011:44). This interview was concerned with closed-ended questions to allow the interviewee to explain the life-cycle of records.

The transcription was processed after the interview was conducted to document information. Recording of interviews offers data to achieve an l transcription of the interview (Braun, Clarke and Gray, 2014 p. 398; and Pickard, 2013 p. 202). Methods of recording interviews for documentation and analysis included audio recording and note-taking (Brinkmann and Kvale 2015 p. 205). The researcher recognized the emerging theme during the process of conducting research.

Observation

Observation is an instrument used to collect data by observing archives and records management divisions. Observation provides a thick description of data (Rule and John, 2011 p. 82). Data is provided in a detailed format. The observation was used as an instrument to collect data to supplement data collected through a questionnaire (Braun, Clarke and Gray, 2017; Creswell, 2015 p. 190). Observation yielded data to complement the questionnaire and document review. All observation involves the participation of the organization being studied (Denzin and Lincoln, 2013 p. 46).

The observation was carried out in the following manner:

It was conducted during the interviews and inspections of archives and records of universities. The author visited universities division, units, and sections to assess the management of university archives and records. During observation, the researcher ensures that notes on the positive and negative of records management systems were recorded. The researcher observed how participants said something during the interviews.

The author observed links between universities archives and records management functions Observation assisted the research to understand the relationships of universities' business processes (Flick 2015 p. 150). According to Creswell (2005 p. 212), observation can be conducted in the following manners:

- Select a case to be observed;
- Ease into the site slowly by looking around, getting a general sense of the site, and taking limited notes;
- Identify who or what to observe, when to observe, and how long to observe;
- Determine the role of an observer;
- Conduct multiple observations to understand business processes;
- Design means for recording notes during an observation; and
- After observing, slowly withdraw from the site.

The observation instrument provides opportunities for an author to understand the research setting (Rule and John 2011, p.84). Field notes based on observation were in a format that allows the researcher to find desired information easily.

A questionnaire is a list of themes covered in a case study interview to support the interview process with respondents (Hartz-Kap and Marinova 2017; Defour-Howard 2015 p. 131; and Bailey 2007, p. 96). A questionnaire was structured in in-depth qualitative interviews. A questionnaire was designed before conducting the interviews to ensure relevant themes of the research are covered while allowing unexpected themes to emerge.

The questionnaire assisted the author to formulate open-ended questions. It also assists the author to understand the fundamental questions on research. In a guided questionnaire, the researcher prepares a checklist to ensure that all relevant areas of the theme were covered (Pickard 2013 p. 200). This type of research allowed the researcher to explore, probe, and ask questions relevant to research purposes. The questionnaire was useful to be provided with information about the theme. A list of theme subheadings assists a researcher to gather information in an open and exploratory way. Structured interviews encompass standardization.

Data Analysis

The adoption of the interpretive paradigm enabled the researcher to assess the staff handling archives and records. The experience on how the staff handled records in their environment contributed to the management of records in universities. Data analysis is a process to interpret empirical data rationally. Data interpretation focuses on data integration to provide a coherent and meaningful understanding (Struwig and Stead 2016 p. 182). Rule and John (2011 p. 89) argued that data is analyzed through content and narrative. The researcher analyzed data in a narrative to allow the construction of thick descriptions, to identify themes, and to generate explanations. The research questions emanated from the research purpose of this study served as a guiding force during the analysis process. The aim of data analysis is the finding of patterns among the data, patterns that point to understanding records throughout (Babbie 2016 p. 388).

According to Braun, Clarke, and Gray (2017:604); De Vos, Strydom, Fouche, and Delport (2017 p. 400) the following must be considered during data analysis:

- Avoid misstatements, misinterpretations, or fraudulent analysis;
- Transcribe the data in detail;
- Review and amend the code;
- Reconsider the research questions;
- Similarities and differences of data should be considered to develop a coding scheme;
- Attended to all the evidence;
- Examine all plausible rival interpretations; and
- Get a sense of the data.

Data analyses identified themes that emerged during the research (Bailey 2007 p. 152). Themes from a study related to the research objectives (Kvale and BrinkMann 2015 p. 241). Thematic analyses were necessary when the researcher seeks themes that address research questions (Bailey 2007 p. 154). Themes were organized in a form of thematic organization that shows the objectives of the study. They were essential in developing a thematic structure (Kings, Horrocks, and Brooks 2017 p. 53). Patterning occurred because it was the way the researcher processed information. According to Miles, Huberman, and Saldana (2014 p. 86), "pattern-coding lays the basis for cross-cases analysis by developing themes aligned to research purposes and objectives. Data were summarised to identify patterns.

Data were cross-case analyzed. A cross-case is an analysis that assembles data from individual case studies (Miles, Huberman, and Saldana 2014 p. 101). Data obtained from one case was compared and contrasted with those of another case. According to Yin (2018 p.198), the significant requirement of conducting cross-case synthesis is that the cross-case patterns rely on argumentative interpretation. Analysis of data from the both University of Venda and the University of Witwatersrand found that information collected from both universities was not the same.

QUALITY CRITERIA FOR QUALITATIVE AND QUANTITATIVE RESEARCH

Qualitative and quantitative researchers use research principles to facilitate the quality of research. These research methods were used to answer the research questions. High-quality research is characterized by worthy topics, rich rigor, sincerity, credibility, trustworthiness, transferability, dependability, Confirmability, authenticity and transparency, resonance, significant contribution, ethics, meaningful coherence (Tracy 2013 p. 15). The author emphasizes issues of trustworthiness and credibility.

Confirmability is associated with the extent to which others can confirm the findings to ensure that the results reflect the understanding and experiences of participants (Wayhyuni, 2012, p. 77).

The author adopted the interpretivism paradigm with the purpose to improve research credibility. Credibility refers to reliability, trustworthiness, and articulating a reasonable reality. A case study has recorded the fullness and essence of the case reality to an extent. This is a demonstration that the evidence for the results reported is sound and that the argument made, based on the results, is strong. Trustworthiness promotes values such as transparent and professional ethics in the interest of qualitative research, thus gaining levels of trust within the research community (Rule and John, 2011, p. 107).

Credibility refers to the accuracy of data to reflect what is observed in the social phenomenon. This means the results reflect what is measured in the initial project (Wayhyuni 2012, p. 77). It is further referred to the accuracy of data, its sincerity, and the reliability of the producer of the document.

Interpretivism Theoretical Framework on the Management of University Records

Transferability implies that the application of research can be transferred to other settings or situations. This research can also be applied to another environment such as government agencies Qualitative research must be set in such a way that the findings are transferred to another environment.

Dependability implies that data is supposed to be replicable or repeatable. The research is explained in detail to provide detailed information of the research. Research step by step processes should be explained in detail to provide information about research in the organization.

Authenticity is the accuracy and completeness of data. This means that data is to be complete, correct, and accurate.

Transparent is essential for writing up research and the presentation and dissemination of findings; that is, the need to be explicit, clear, and open about the methods and procedures used. Transparent requires the researcher to be honest and open about the activities by which the research transpired (Tracy, 2013, p. 234).

Reliability is an assessment of the quality of the measurement procedure used to collect data Reliability is a matter of whether a particular technique applied to the same object, yields the same result each time (Babbie, 2016, p.146).

Pre-testing to conduct full research was conducted with the University of Mpumalanga records and archives management committee to determine whether further Interview guide revision was needed. After the feedback was received from the pilot group, the data collection instruments were revised.

The researcher ensured principles of honesty in communication; reliability; objectivity; impartiality and independence; openness and accessibility; and fairness in providing references and giving credit. The ethically appropriate research is informed consent," according to Curtis and Curtis (2011, p.15).

The researcher ensured that the following processes were followed during the collection of data (Yin, 2018, p. 88):

- Obtained informed consent from participants who may be part of the case study. The researcher ensured that participants were are of the following:
  - participating in research
  - Understand the purpose of the research
  - The procedures used to collect data during the research
  - Voluntary participation
  - Right to stop the research at any time
  - The procedures used to protect the confidentiality information
  - Their right to have all their questions answered at anytime
  - Other information relevant to their respondents
- Protect participants' privacy and confidentiality.

- Selecting participants equitably, so that no participants are unfairly included or excluded from the research".

During data analysis, the researcher avoided going naïve, disclosing only positive results, respect the privacy of the participants. The study conducted by Creswell (2014 p. 99) indicated that the researcher should avoid bias during the research. The researcher provided a full report of the outcome of the research without violating the rights of individuals.

Evaluation of Research Methodology

The application of the interpretivism paradigm was central to this research
This book chapter employed the viewpoint of the interpretivism paradigm method. The data instruments such as questionnaires, document review, and observation were used to collect data from universities. The selection of case study universities considered the nature of the research question, unit of analysis, and expected outcomes. Data obtained from the three instruments were coded and analyzed. The data were analyzed manually. The research methods were evaluated to determine their strengths and weaknesses and highlight what could have been done differently to yield better results.

Discussions

The researcher found that applications of interpretivism enable the researcher to understand the significance of organizations to keep records and archives management. The research was able to understand the management of Universities' archives and records through participants' viewpoints. The study conducted by Defour-Howard (2015 p. 80) said that qualitative and quantitative research requires the use and collection of a variety of empirical material. This research method is important to answer research questions.

FUTURE RESEARCH DIRECTIONS

Research should be conducted to assess the significance of adopting another paradigm such as positivism.

CONCLUSIONS

This research was framed by the interpretivism paradigm to enable the research to understand the management of university archives and records. This book attempted to emphasize a qualitative approach based on philosophical research paradigms of interpretivism. The researcher conducted research mainly using qualitative because of trying to maintain the quality of research. This chapter contributes to a wider discussion about the relationship between methods and paradigms. Interpretivism may be used for those who want to conduct a research case study on records and archives management.

REFERENCES

Alharahsheh, H. H., & Pius, A. (2020). A review of key paradigms: Positivism vs Interpretivism. *Global Academic Journal of Humanities and Social Science*, *2*(3), 39–43.

Antwi, K. S., & Hamza, K. (2015). Qualitative and Quantitative Research Paradigms in Business Research: A Philosophical Reflection. *European Journal of Business and Management*, *7*(3), 217–225.

Aurini, D. J., Health, M., & Howells, S. (2016). *The How to of Qualitative Research*. SAGE.

Babbie, C. (2017). *The basics of Social Research* (7th ed.). Cengage.

Bailey, C. A. (2007). *A guide to Qualitative Field Research* (2nd ed.). Pine Forge Press. doi:10.4135/9781412983204

Beins, B. C. (2009). *Research Methods. A tool for life* (2nd ed.). Pearson Education.

Berg, B. L. (2009). *Qualitative Research Methods for the Social Sciences* (7th ed.). Pearson.

Binkmann, S. C., & Kvle, S. (2005). Interviews learning the Craft of Qualitative Research Interviewing, 3rd edition. London. Thousand Oaks. CA.

Blumberg, F. Boris, Cooper, R.D & Schindler, P.S (2011). Business Research Methods (4th Edition). London: McGraw-Hill Higher Education.

Braun, V., Clarke, V., & Gray, D. (2017). *Collecting Qualitative Data. A practical Guide to Textual, Media and Virtual Techniques*. Cambridge University Press. doi:10.1017/9781107295094

Broadbent, J., & Unerman, J. (2011). Developing the relevance of the accounting academy. *Meditari Accountancy Research*, *19*(1/2), 7–21. doi:10.1108/10222521111178600

Bryman, A. (2004). *Social Research Methods* (3rd ed.). Oxford University Press.

Bryman, A., & Bell, E. (2014). *Research methodology, Business and Management Context*. Oxford University Press.

Case, O. D. (2012). Looking for information: A survey of Research on Information Seeking, Needs, and Behaviour. Third Edition. Library and Information Science. Emerald.

Clarke, R., Davison, M. R., & Jia, W. (2020). Researcher perspective in the IS discipline: An empirical study of articles in the basket of 8 journals. Researcher perspective in the IS discipline. *Information Technology & People*, *33*(6), 1515–1541. doi:10.1108/ITP-04-2019-0189

Creswell, J. W. (2005). *Educational Research. Planning, Conducting and Evaluating Quantitative and Qualitative Research* (2nd ed.). Pearson.

Creswell, J. W. (2014). Research Design: Qualitative, Quantitative, Mixed Methods approaches. International Students Edition 4th Edition. New Jersey: Pearson.

Curtis, B., & Curtis, C. (2011). Social Research: A practical introduction. London: SAGE: London. doi:10.4135/9781526435415

Dana, R., & Shaun, P. (2005). Some of the philosophical Issues underpinning research in information systems – from Positivism to Critical Realism. *SACTJT*, *35*, 50–79.

De Vos, A. S., Strydom, H., Fouche, C. B., & Delport, C. S. L. (2017). *Research at Grassroots. For the Social Sciences and Huan service professions eth edition*. Van Schaik.

Defour- Howard. S (2015). Research Methods. A handbook for Beginners. Denver: Outskirts Press.

Denzin, K. N., & Linoln, Y. S. (2013). *Collecting and Interpreting Qualitative Materials*. SAGE.

Flick, U. (2015). *Designing Qualitative Research*. SAGE.

Fox, W., & Bayat, M. S. (2012). *A guide to Managing Research*. Juta.

Goldman, G. A. (2016). Multiparadigmatic, Cooperative Opportunities for the Study of Business Management. *Management Dynamics*, *25*(3), 2–15.

Gorman, G. E., & Clayton, P. (2005). *Qualitative Research for the Information Professional: A Practical Handbook* (2nd ed.). Facet.

Grbich, C. (2013). *Qualitative Data Analysis: An introduction.* Sage. doi:10.4135/9781529799606

Hancock, D. R., & Algozzine, B. (2011). *Doing Case Study Research: A practical guide for beginning researchers* (2nd ed.). Teachers College Press.

Hartz-Karp, J., & Marinova, D. (2017). *Methods for Sustainability Research.* Edward Elgar. doi:10.4337/9781786432735

Kankam, K. P. (2019). The use of Paradigms in information research. *Library & Information Science Research, 41*(2), 85–92. doi:10.1016/j.lisr.2019.04.003

King, N., Horrocks, C., & Broks, J. (2017). *Interviews in Qualitative Research* (2nd ed.). SAGE.

Kuada, J. (2012). Research Methodology: A project Guide for University Students. Aalborg University, Denmark: Samfundslitteratur.

Largan, C., & Morris, T. (2019). *Qualitative Secondary Research. A step-by-step guide.* SAGE.

Leedy, D. P., & Ormrod, E. J. (2015). *Practical Research Planning and Design* (11th ed.). Pearson.

Leedy, P. D., & Ormrod, J. E. (2015). *Practical Research Planning and Design* (11th ed.). Pearson.

Loseke, R. D. (2017). Methodological Thinking Second Edition. Basic Principles of Social Research Design. London: SAGE

Lyaruu, T. (2021). *Integrating Records Management into the extractive industries transparency initiative in Tanzania.* [Thesis, University of South Africa]. Pretoria.

Mabika, B. (2019). *The Use of Mobile Phones in Disseminating Agricultural Information to Farmers in Mashonaland West Province of Zimbabwe.* [Thesis, University of South Africa]. Pretoria.

Matlala, E. (2019). Long-term preservation of digital records at the University of Kwazulu-Natal archives. *Journal of the South African Society of Archivists, 52,* 95–109.

Maxwell, J. A. (2013). *Qualitative Research Design. An Interactive Approach* (3rd ed.). SAGE.

McChesney, K., & Aldridge, J. (2019). Weaving an Interpretivist stance throughout mixed methods research. *International Journal of Research & Method in Education, 42*(3), 225–238. doi:10.1080/1743727X.2019.1590811

Miles, M. B., Huberman, A. M., & Saldana, J. (2014). Qualitative Data Analysis. Los Angels: SAGE.

Mosweu, O. (2016). Critical Success factors in electronic document and records management systems implementation at the Ministry of Trade and Industry in Botswana. *ESARBICA Journal, 35*(1), 1–13. doi:10.4314/esarjo.v38i1.1

Muhammad, S. J., Mat, I. S. A., & Miah, J. S. (2021). Constituent of an Information governance framework for a successful implementation in Nigerian Universities. *Education and Information Technologies, 26*(5), 6447–6460. doi:10.100710639-021-10528-w

Ngulube, P. (2016). *Postgraduate workshop on methodology at UNISA. (unpublished College of Graduate Studies.* UNISA: Pretoria Padilla-Diaz, M (2015). Phenomenology in Educational Qualitative Research: Philosophy as science or philosophical science? *International Journal of Educational Excellence, 1*(2), 101–110.

Pattern, L. M., & Newhat, M. (2018). *Understanding Research Methods. AN overview of the Essentials* (10th ed.). Routledge.

Phiri, M. J. (2016*). Managing university records and documents in the world of governance, audit and documents in the world of governance, audit and risk: case studies from South Africa and Malawi.* [Thesis, University of Glasgow, Glasgow].

Pickard, A. J. (2013). *Research Methods in information* (2nd ed.). Facet Publishing.

Punch, F. K., & Qancea, A. (2009). *Introduction to Research Methods in Education* (2nd ed.). SAGE.

Rule, P., & John, V. (2011). *Your Guide to Case Study Research*. Van Schaik.

Salkind, N. (2018). *Exploring Research* (9th ed.). Pearson.

Shanks, G. (2002). Guidelines for conducting positivist case study research in information systems. *AJIS. Australasian Journal of Information Systems, 10*(Special Issue), 76–85. doi:10.3127/ajis.v10i1.448

Struwig, F. W., & Stead, G. b (2016). Research: Planning, Designing Second Edition. Cape Town: Pearson Education South Africa (PTY).

Tracy, S. J. (2013). *Qualitative Research Methods. Collecting Evidence. Crafting analysis, Communicating impact.* Wiley Blackwell.

Wahyuni, D. (2012). The Research Design Maze: Understanding Paradigms, Cases. *Methods and Methodologies.*, *10*(2), 69–81.

Yin, R. K. (2018). *Case Study Research Design and Methods* (5th ed.). Sage.

KEY TERMS AND DEFINITIONS

Constructivism: The idea that participants create knowledge.

Epistemology: This theory of knowledge is about methods, validity, and scope.

Interpretivism: This is a philosophical system focused on human construction.

Positivism: This is a philosophy based on statistical data. Knowledge is generated through observation.

Qualitative methodology: It is concerned with interpreting the meaning of the social phenomenon.

Chapter 3
Conceptual Framework for the Application of the ANN Model in Accident Prediction:
A Study of Central Kolkata

Amrita Sarkar

 https://orcid.org/0000-0001-7415-2822
Birla Institute of Technology, Mesra, India

Satyaki Sarkar

 https://orcid.org/0000-0002-5161-2344
Birla Institute of Technology, Mesra, India

ABSTRACT

Conceptual framework for accident prediction is an essential toolkit to curb accidents and fatalities globally. Different statistical methods and soft computing techniques are used to develop accident prediction models. Accident prediction models have been developed using two approaches, i.e., multiple linear regression (MLR) and artificial neural network (ANN). ANN has been applied to predict the frequency of traffic accidents. Adaptive neuro-fuzzy inference system (ANFIS) has been used as the feature selection method. Feature selection using ANFIS gets more accuracy with ANN was considered the most suitable based on prediction accuracy and measuring errors. It gives around 81.81% accuracy. The framework of hybrid model proposed in this chapter concludes that the prediction accuracy is high when ANN is applied for accident prediction, followed by the ANFIS as a feature selection method.

DOI: 10.4018/978-1-7998-9687-6.ch003

Copyright © 2024, IGI Global. Copying or distributing in print or electronic forms without written permission of IGI Global is prohibited.

1. INTRODUCTION

Globally, 1.35 million deaths are recorded yearly due to road accidents. The number of injured due to road accidents counts 20–50 million and 27.5 deaths per 100,000 population (Yu, 2006). African countries record the highest number of deaths due to these accidents, while South-East Asia has the lowest (Yu, 2006). The number of death and injuries from road accidents may be reduced by 25% through the introduction of BRTS (Kapadia et al., 2022). Researchers in the field have also established a quadratic relationship between congestion and crash fatalities (Albalate & Xavier, 2021). It is accordingly of first concern to predict future traffic occurrences, to understand the severity related to speed to respond to it (Ebrahim & Hossain, ; Lee et al., 2019). Continuous inspection of significant determinants providing accidents admits researchers to act on computations concerning predicting the occurrence of severity (Mussone et al., 1999). Fact-finding on future accident spots has led to interlinking risk determinants like human traits, cab-related determinants, surroundings, and geometrical design-accompanying variables with accident severity (Chang, 2005). There are remnants of substantial significance for occurrence asperity models in forecasting city avenue accidents.

Models for predicting future road crashes are clear finishes for expressway security. Considering their skill to decide the accident occurrence helps label the determinants that transport tactics bear before identity (Abdulhafedh, 2017; Saccomanno et al., 1996). An able and trustworthy model of the asperity indicator is necessary for traffic accidents to effectively exercise an Intelligent Transport System (ITS) (Zheng et al., 2019). Researchers have established the frequency of crashes through a Poisson regression model. Few researchers have tried setting a relationship between risk factors with crash frequency (Abdulhafedh, 2016; Vogt & Barred,). One of the accepted techniques employed to evaluate predictions of severity due to injury resulting from crashes has used the logistic regression model. In this model, the categorical dependent variable was chosen over the numerical one (Pradhan & Sameen, 2020).

Similarly, a logistic regression model was applied in their analysis to derive the number of fatalities in accidents (Lui et al., 1988). It was improvised to establish that accident severity is determined by various indicators, including driver's fault, condition, visibility conditions on roads, road characteristics, and condition, time of occurrence, vehicle health, and use of safety parameters like seat belt use and the like. It was approached it using binary logit models (Sarkar & Sarkar, 2020). Though total accidents are more significant than the accident's character and number, the number of accidental injuries on roads exhibited better results in predicting severity due to accidents. Vogt and Barred 1998, identified the factors contributing to the severity of accidents on two-lane rural roads (Sarkar et al., 2016). Further, it was established through the log-linear model that the role of parameters like occurrence time, collision impact, driving condition, and driver's fault has an immense effect on the accident's severity (Chen & Jovanis, 2000). Different variables' contribution level to injury severity was established using logistic regression (Al-Ghamdi, 2002).

Dougherty, 1995, proposed that the prediction of driver behaviour, freight management, traffic health analysis, traffic health predictions, and traffic and their operation may be made using artificial neural networks (ANN) (Dougherty, 1995). Mussone et al. 1999, similarly applied the ANN method to understand road crashes occurring at intersections in Milan, Italy, and inferred that most accidents result in non-signalized junctions at night time (Oyedepo & Makinde, 2010). On the contrary, most literature studies suggest that merely human-centric behavioural indicators and surface and weather conditions still need to complete the cycle of research to predict the severity of accidents by applying artificial neural networks. Based on this conclusion, Abdelwahab and Abdel-Aty 2001, adopted the parameter of accident injuries to classify accident severity into three labels. The experiment for the accident was performed using a couple of vehicles at a signalized road intersection. They employed multilayer perceptron to classify data, which achieved an accuracy of classification up to 65.6% for training data and 60.4% for testing data (Abdelwahab & Abdel-Aty, 2001). Delen et al. 2006, further improvised the previous research by using data on injury severity intensity by applying neural models with eight binary inputs. Contributory factors governing accidents were established in developing the models discussed above(Delen et al., 2006). Chang 2005, while using ANN for frequency analysis of accidents, compared with negative binomial regression, inferred ANN as a suitable substitute for forecasting accidents on freeways (Chang, 2005). ANN analysis was also done to understand the nonlinear interrelationship between the severity of the injury and factors contributing to crashes (Delen et al., 2006). Multilayer perception (MLP) was applied with a back-propagation gradient-descent supervised learning algorithm and sigmoid activation functions (Delen et al., 2006). Yu 2006 further progressed this by developing an expert system using ANN for forecasting accidents (Zheng et al., 2019).

Further improvisation created a back-propagation artificial neural network model using data from intersections in urban areas facilitated by signals to predict vehicle crashes occurring at intersections. Reductions in car crashes were identified by improvising on this model (Sarkar et al., 2016; Shaik & Hossain, 2019). A multilayer perceptron neural network was further used to forecast road accident severity with data collected from hospitals in Thailand. Kunt et al. 2011, improvised on an existing model using various parameters related to the driver, vehicle weather, road, speed, time, and collision type (Mehmet et al., 2011). Chikaraishi et al. 2022 applied machine learning to congestion to predict the state of traffic and infer the results. They deduced that the XGBoost method best predicts accuracy, while neural network models best interpret results (Chikaraishi et al., 2022).

This paper discusses different models that may be developed to predict accidents on urban roads. The prediction models developed in this paper are primarily based on two approaches, i.e., Multiple Linear Regression (MLR) and ANN. Results of both the models employed for accident prediction have also been compared in this study. The coefficient of the determinant and R^2 made the comparison. In this proposed model, a newly recommended hybrid method, Sequential Adaptive Neuro-Fuzzy Inference System (ANFIS), and Artificial Neural Network (ANN), have been applied to infer accident prediction. The research employed two steps to execute the proposed accident prediction model. In the first step, the hybrid method was applied to reduce the features of the traffic accident dataset using Sequential ANFIS. After ignoring independent parts of less importance, ANN has been used to predict an accident in the next step.

Although its accident analysis is like traditional statistical analyses, ANN has unique features and capacities. The creation of accurate prediction models depends upon the selection of variables and aggregation and manipulation of the data of an accident employed in the model structure. The ANN model constructs a simple model by incorporating the accident data and calculating the weights of every variable. This research employs a dataset of accidents comprising thirty-one cases of crash data collected from 2016 to 2020 from Kolkata. These accident data were applied to train the Neural Network model, and another set of thirteen crashes has done for the model testing. Sensitivity analysis was done to describe the crash properties for each type (Sarkar et al., 2016). The methodology adopted in the research can provide a very accurate prediction (81.81%) of the crash types by using four features. Those features have been selected based on significance among sixteen crash properties using ANFIS. The results are optimistic and encourage further research by the expanded data sets to execute the accident prediction model.

2. METHODOLOGY

The accident dataset consists of twelve features used to predict accident occurrence on forty-four road segments during 2016 -2020 on Acharya Jagadish Chandra Bose Road, Kolkata. Primary and secondary source data collected from the Headquarters of Kolkata Police, and the Department of Transport, Government of West Bengal, forms the backbone for this study. An Expert Opinion Survey conducted on eminent stakeholders gave insight into possible secondary data sources. Some of the features are numerical, and others are categorical. Two groups of features have been taken for accident prediction, i.e., traffic-related features, geometry-related features, and other factors (Sarkar et al., 2012). The dataset includes the following features:

- Traffic-related variables
  - Annual Average Daily Traffic (AADT)
  - Traffic Volume (TV)
  - Peak Hour Factor (PHF)
  - Percentage of Left Turn Vehicles (PLTV)
  - Percentage of Right Turn Vehicles (PRTV)
  - Spot Speed of a major road (SS)
- Geometry related variables
  - Road Width (RW)
  - Width of Footpath (WF)
  - Length of Segments (LS)
- Other factors
  - Number of Left/Right Turn Signals (NS)
  - Number of Warning Signs (NWS)
  - Number of Congested Points (NCP)
  - Previous accident records that have been used in this analysis are shown below:
  - Number of Fatal Accidents (NFA)
  - Number of Non-Fatal Accidents (NNFA)

Two more parameters have been calculated from previous accident records for further analysis. Those are:

- Total no of the accident: The total number of accidents (TA) is the summation of accidents on a specific road segment for a particular year.
- Accident Index: The Accident Index (AI) is determined to recognize the most unsafe road segments. Forming this index requires an unambiguous relationship to compare the features of components (Mussone et al., 1999). It provides an analytical value and percentage of the degree of the unsafe situation at every segment relative to the most unsafe over a time of five years:

$$AI = N_i / N_{max} \qquad (1)$$

N_i is the number of accidents in the ith intersection, and N_{max} is the number of accidents in the most hazardous segment.

Framework for the Application of the ANN Model in Accident Prediction

2.1. Development of Accident Prediction Models

Several different modelling techniques are appropriate for accident prediction. The two most prominent modelling methodologies are continuous choice models (e.g., Linear Regression) and Machine Learning models (e.g., Neural Networks). Statistical methods have typically been applied in urban road safety to support accident analysis and construct an accident prediction model. It can be employed to select the significant features or find an association between accidents and characteristics. Continuous models have been chosen where the dependent variable is continuous or numerical outputs. The linear model method explains the association between numerical production and single or numerous independent variables. ANN was employed in the same dataset in the model mentioned above to evaluate the performance of another technique.

2.1.1 Multiple Linear Regression

The accident Index, the dependent variable in this research, is the continuous type variable for accident prediction. Each accident in the sampled data has been used to predict the number of casualties for a particular segment. Whether the independent variables could be numerical or categorical, linear regression determines the coefficients that make the observed outcome continuous. The following equation gives the linear regression model used for this case:

$$Y(\text{number of accidents}) = p(1)*x_1 + p(2)*x_2 + \ldots + p(n)x_n + c \ (2)$$

Where,
Y is the number of accidents at the considered site,
$x1$ to xn are the chosen predictor variables
$p(1)$ to $p(n)$ are required coefficients to be estimated from the model, and
c is defined as the intercept of the model.

At first, accident severity classification used twelve single variables. This process helped to understand each variable's effect on predicting road accidents. The overall impact of variables on accident prediction was comprehended from the cluster of variables. Table 1 shows the coefficients of individual independent variables calculated by linear regression.

Table 2 provides the respective linear regression models for individual variables. The p-values of 0.0442 for the Existence of a Warning sign and 0.0431 for the Peak Hour Factor prove the significance of these factors in determining accident severity. Hence the Linear regression models developed for individual variables in this study are:

Table 1. Contains coefficients of independent variables calculated by linear regression using individual variable

Features	P(1)	P(2)	Standard Error	pval
AADT	0.0000	0.1583	0.0000	0.2761
TV	0.0000	0.1453	0.0000	0.2802
PHD	-14.1463	13.9398	7.4107	0.0431
PLTV	0.0000	0.3718	0.0036	0.3957
PRTV	0.0035	0.3016	0.0030	0.1552
SCT	0.0147	-0.0872	0.0084	0.0889
GLT	0.0141	-0.0633	0.0159	0.1796
SS	0.1023	0.1942	0.1198	0.2977
RW	0.0818	0.2941	0.0643	0.1103
WF	0.0256	0.3372	0.0651	0.3959
ES	0.1217	0.3141	0.0742	0.1085
EWS	0.0011	0.2093	0.0005	0.0442

Table 2. Contains Linear regression model set for individual variables

Feature	Number of accident
AADT	$0.1583 + 0.0000*x$
TV	$0.1453 + 0.0000*x$
PHD	$13.9398 - 14.1463*x$
PTV	$0.3718 + 0.0000*x$
PTV	$0.3016 + 0.0035*x$
SCT	$-0.0872 + 0.0147*x$
GLT	$-0.0633 + 0.0141*x$
SS	$0.1942 + 0.1023*x$
RW	$0.2941 + 0.0818*x$
WF	$0.3370 + 0.0256*x$
ES	$0.3141 + 0.217*x$
NEWS	$0.2093 + 0.0011*x$

Framework for the Application of the ANN Model in Accident Prediction

Table 3. Contains coefficients of independent variables determined by linear regression using a group of variables

Regression Coefficients	Standard Error	pval
-13.4710	10.0473	0.1897
1.9550E-05	0.0000	0.6184
-1.2697E-05	0.0001	0.8293
-14.6632	10.0419	0.1543
-0.0102	0.0062	0.1101
0.0009	0.0049	0.8542
0.0144	0.0109	0.1951
0.0027	0.0195	0.8899
0.0987	0.1929	0.6123
0.2103	0.1427	0.1506
-0.0595	0.1098	0.5920
0.1650	0.0870	0.0672
-0.0002	0.0008	0.7753

The coefficients of independent variables determined by linear regression using a group of variables is shown in Table 3 (Kapadia et al., 2022). According to the previous analysis, the MLR model with the group of significant variables is as follows:

The final accident prediction model constructed by MLR is given below:

Number of Accidents = 13.4710+ 1.9550E-05* x1 (AADT) -1.2697E-05 *x2 (TV) -14.6632* x3 (PHF) -0.0102* x4 (PLTV) + 0.0009* x5 (PRTV) + 0.0144* x6 (SCT) + 0.0027 *x7 (GLT) + 0.0987* x8 (SS)+ 0.2103* x9 (RW) -0.0595* x10 (WF) +0.1650* x11 (ES) -0.0002* x12 (EWS)

Multiple linear regression employed to the sets of individual variables for accident prediction calculates the R^2, which varies from 0.20 to 0.6929. MSE computed by the regression method varies from 0.1023 to 0.1112, as shown in Table 4. When the outcome is near zero, the regression model calculates negative values in a few cases.

Table 5 explains that whenever group variables have been used, regression analysis gives an R^2 value of 0.5807, and MSE calculated on that regression model is 0.09.

The actual and predicted values for Accident Index for every road segment using MLR are shown in Figure 1.

The model represents AI as an output that states the level of accident-proneness for a specific road segment related to a particular dataset. The value of N_{max} is denoted as the number of accidents representing 8 in this study. This value of accidents has

Table 4. Contains measurement of performance determined by linear regression using individual variable

Features	Mean Squared Error (MSE)	Regression Coefficients
AADT	0.1104	0.4075
TV	0.1104	0.3073
PHD	0.1023	0.6798
PLTV	0.1112	0.2000
PTV	0.1078	0.5307
SCT	0.1037	0.4674
GLT	0.1092	0.3184
SS	0.1093	0.2171
RW	0.1071	0.2371
WF	0.1108	0.6037
ES	0.1045	0.2602
NEWS	0.1009	0.6929

Table 5. Contains measurement values of performance determined by linear regression using a group of variables

Feature	Mean Squared Error (MSE)	Coefficient of Determination (R-Square)	Adjusted R2 Statistic
Traffic and geometry-related variables and other factors	0.0999	0.5807	0.5373

Figure 1. Actual and predicted values for accident index for road segments using MLR

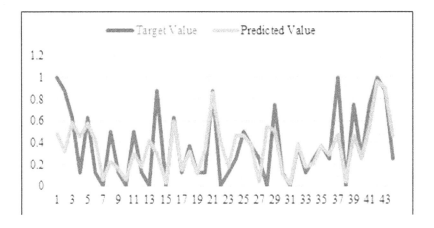

Framework for the Application of the ANN Model in Accident Prediction

Table 6. Contains predicted and the actual number of accidents for every link using MLR

Target	Predicted	Number of Accidents in a Most Dangerous Segment	Accident Number	Total No. of Accidents (Predicted)	Total No. of Accidents (Target)
1	0.4806	8	3.8449	4	8
0.875	0.3148	8	2.5186	3	7
0.625	0.5875	8	4.7002	5	5
0.125	0.4569	8	3.6554	4	1
0.625	0.5700	8	4.5602	5	5
0.125	0.4246	8	3.3967	3	1
0	0.0556	8	0.4449	0	0
0.5	0.2225	8	1.7804	2	4
0.125	0.1565	8	1.2524	1	1
0	0.0570	8	0.4563	0	0
0.5	0.2941	8	2.3530	2	4
0.125	0.1812	8	1.4496	1	1
0	0.4165	8	3.3324	3	0
0.875	0.2975	8	2.3804	2	7
0	0.0326	8	0.2605	0	0
0.625	0.5938	8	4.7504	5	5
0.125	0.1490	8	1.1918	1	1
0.375	0.3148	8	2.5186	3	3
0.125	0.1108	8	0.8866	1	1
0.125	0.3317	8	2.6532	3	1
0.875	0.8585	8	6.8681	7	7
0	0.4110	8	3.2881	3	0
0.125	0.1739	8	1.3908	1	1
0.25	0.4678	8	3.7421	4	2
0.5	0.4608	8	3.6862	4	4
0.375	0.3678	8	2.9420	3	3
0.25	0.0427	8	0.3418	0	2
0	0.5450	8	4.3597	4	0
0.75	0.5072	8	4.0576	4	6
0.125	0.1040	8	0.8317	1	1
0	0.0173	8	0.1383	0	0
0.375	0.3932	8	3.1457	3	3

Continued on following page

Framework for the Application of the ANN Model in Accident Prediction

Table 6. Continued

Target	Predicted	Number of Accidents in a Most Dangerous Segment	Accident Number	Total No. of Accidents (Predicted)	Total No. of Accidents (Target)
0.125	0.1819	8	1.4548	1	1
0.25	0.2056	8	1.6450	2	2
0.375	0.3682	8	2.9459	3	3
0.25	0.2904	8	2.3232	2	2
1	0.4722	8	3.7778	4	8
0	0.0427	8	0.3415	0	0
0.75	0.4640	8	3.7121	4	6
0.25	0.2519	8	2.0150	2	2
0.75	0.5368	8	4.2942	4	6
1	0.9647	8	7.7177	8	8
0.875	0.9080	8	7.2638	7	7
0.25	0.4674	8	3.7392	4	2

been obtained for the unsafe segments on the urban roads selected for this particular study. It may be inferred that if the AI for a definite set of input values is 0.5, the level of accident-proneness is represented as (8*0.5) or four accidents in five years. If the value of AI is 0.4, then the number of accidents can be calculated as (8*0.4) or 3.2 and represented as three accidents. The connection becomes more dangerous or accident-prone whenever AI for a particular link is high. Table 6 presents the predicted number of accidents determined by MLR for every link in the study area.

Table 7 presents the percentage of Accident Prediction (59.09%) determined by Linear regression. The prediction accuracy is inferior whenever MLR is used for accident prediction for a particular dataset.

Figure 2 represents the expected number of accidents and actual accidents in each road segment.

Table 7. Contains percentage of accident prediction determined by linear regression

Number of Segments	Number of Correct Prediction	Number of Incorrect Prediction	(%) of Accident Prediction
44	26	18	59.09

Figure 2. Number of accidents (predicted vs. happened)

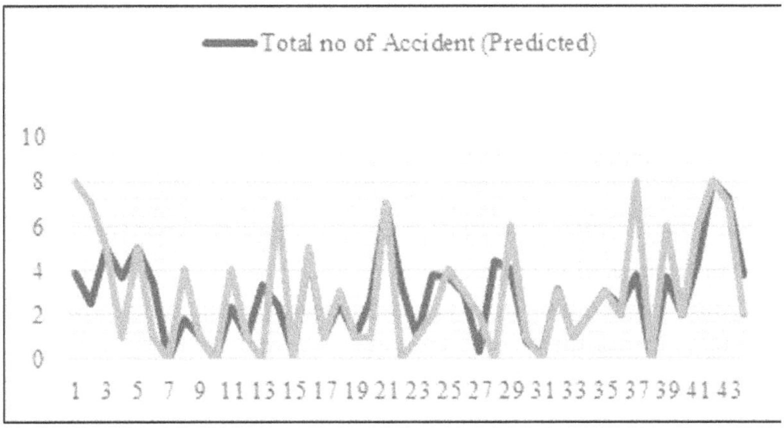

2.2 Artificial Neural Network (ANN) Model

This method consists of three stages. The data subset is randomly divided into two sets in the first stage. Two sets are required as separate datasets for training, and testing is necessary for the learning process of the ANN model. The second and third stage comprises two methods, i.e., validation and testing, which are repeated till the optimum network is decided. Optimum defines the minimization of ANN model error and maximization of coefficient of determination. There is no theoretical limitation to selecting the number of inputs and outputs. This method, therefore, enhances the computation time for establishing an optimum network.

Several types of ANN models have been developed to predict AI using different combinations of datasets engaged in accidents. The primary focus has been to select the best model which models the dataset in the best way using other ANN models. In this study, Multilayer Perceptron, a feed-forward neural network, has been applied with a back-propagation learning method to develop the accident prediction model. The activation function propagates from the input to the output layer forward. The error propagates backward from the output to the input layer. The model computes the outcome and is compared with the actual output. The difference between tangible and predicted outcomes influences the weights on the links of the back-propagation method. This process helps reduce the error difference until the tolerance is achieved.

The model constructed by the ANN is shown in Figure 3. The previous research illustrates that the input layer comprises sixteen nodes representing sixteen variables. The hidden layer formed several combinations of nodes, and the output consisted of one node. Two transfer functions are employed for the input, hidden, and output layers, i.e., hyperbolic tangent and identity functions. In this study, the number of hidden layers, the number of nodes in the hidden layer, and the activation function have been altered to obtain the best model of ANN using the accident dataset. Here, the main focus of this model is to minimize the MSE (Mean Square Error) and maximize the R^2 value for getting the most significant Accident Prediction Model using ANN. The outer output layer includes a node representing the Accident Index (AI) joined by the nodes of hidden layers. The features of the input layer incorporate either a numerical or a categorical value. AI, considered the outcome of the ANN model, corresponds to the intensity of risk for a particular segment related to a specific set of features of the input layer.

The learning method has been executed repeatedly using the different datasets to describe the relationship between the input and output of specific segments. The number of instances employed is forty-four, out of which thirty-one cases have been applied for training, and the rest thirteen have been used for testing. The best solution minimizes the MSE and the determination of coefficients computed by the testing dataset considering learning of 500 cycles. Table 8 presents the performance of ANN models using the values of correlation coefficients.

Table 8. Contains performance of ANN models

ANN model	Number of hidden layers	Number of neurons in hidden layers	Activation function	MSE	SSE	R	R^2
ANN 1	1	3	tansig	0.0407	1.7921	0.8048	0.6273
ANN 2	1	6	tansig	0.0362	1.5907	0.8147	0.6622
ANN 3	1	9	tansig	0.0347	1.5286	0.8455	0.7066
ANN 4	2	3,2	tansig-tansig-tansig	0.0482	2.1209	0.7402	0.5476
ANN 5	2	6,2	tansig-tansig-tansig	0.0312	1.3927	0.8572	0.7127
ANN 6	2	9,2	tansig- tansig-tansig	0.0317	1.3741	0.8434	0.7082
ANN 7	2	6,2	tansig-tansig-purelin	0.0596	2.6234	0.6698	0.4440
ANN 7	2	6,2	tansig-tansig-purelin	0.0537	2.3620	0.7379	0.4950
ANN 8	2	6,2	tansig-purelin-purelin	0.0386	1.6967	0.8054	0.6443
ANN 9	2	6,2	tansig-purelin-tansig	0.0468	2.0587	0.7698	0.5894

Framework for the Application of the ANN Model in Accident Prediction

Figure 3. Accident Index for road segments using ANN (actual vs. predicted)

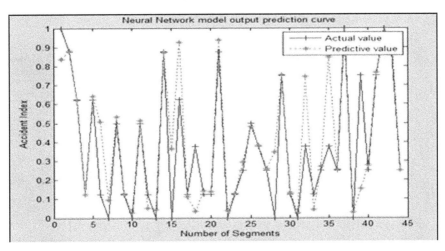

Figure 4. Graphical representation of the determination of coefficients (a) by applying training data, (b) by using validation data, (c) by using testing data, and (d) by using all three types of data together

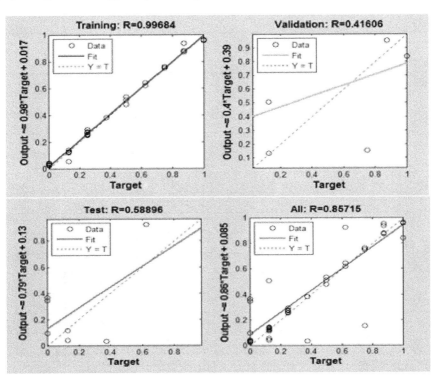

Framework for the Application of the ANN Model in Accident Prediction

Table 9. Contains predicted and the actual number of accidents for every segment using the ANN model

Target	Predicted	Number of Accidents in the Most Dangerous Segment	Accident Number	Total No. of Accidents (Predicted)	Total No. of Accidents (Target)
1	0.8383	8	6.706462	7	8
0.875	0.8808	8	7.046645	7	7
0.625	0.6202	8	4.961261	5	5
0.125	0.1230	8	0.984257	1	1
0.625	0.6430	8	5.143967	5	5
0.125	0.5078	8	4.062111	4	1
0	0.0951	8	0.760827	1	0
0.5	0.5350	8	4.279604	4	4
0.125	0.1264	8	1.010991	1	1
0	0.0265	8	0.212292	0	0
0.5	0.5136	8	4.108575	4	4
0.125	0.0523	8	0.418646	0	1
0	0.0410	8	0.328256	0	0
0.875	0.8733	8	6.986734	7	7
0	0.3653	8	2.922043	3	0
0.625	0.9264	8	7.411048	7	5
0.125	0.1139	8	0.911391	1	1
0.375	0.0322	8	0.257614	0	3
0.125	0.1410	8	1.127627	1	1
0.125	0.1393	8	1.114407	1	1
0.875	0.9363	8	7.490352	7	7
0	0.0379	8	0.303335	0	0
0.125	0.1272	8	1.017804	1	1
0.25	0.2924	8	2.339336	2	2
0.5	0.4799	8	3.839261	4	4
0.375	0.3812	8	3.049444	3	3
0.25	0.2584	8	2.066883	2	2
0	0.3452	8	2.76163	3	0
0.75	0.7524	8	6.019363	6	6
0.125	0.1335	8	1.067706	1	1
0	0.0248	8	0.198428	0	0
0.375	0.7427	8	5.941675	6	3

Continued on following page

Framework for the Application of the ANN Model in Accident Prediction

Table 6. Continued

Target	Predicted	Number of Accidents in the Most Dangerous Segment	Accident Number	Total No. of Accidents (Predicted)	Total No. of Accidents (Target)
0.125	0.0423	8	0.338674	0	1
0.25	0.2710	8	2.168203	2	2
0.375	0.8457	8	6.765231	7	3
0.25	0.2529	8	2.023281	2	2
1	0.9580	8	7.664202	8	8
0	0.0271	8	0.216639	0	0
0.75	0.1526	8	1.220845	1	6
0.25	0.2755	8	2.204064	2	2
0.75	0.7637	8	6.109973	6	6
1	0.9656	8	7.725105	8	8
0.875	0.9553	8	7.642131	8	7
0.25	0.2512	8	2.009373	2	2

The increment of the number of nodes in the hidden layer minimizes the MSE from 0.0407 to 0.0347 while considering one hidden layer. Then ANN structure was selected with two hidden layers to minimize the MSE and maximize the determination of coefficients. The ANN5 model provided the best results for both MSE (0.0312) and coefficient of determination (0.7127) simultaneously amongst all ANN models. So ANN5 model is considered a best-fit Accident Prediction model in this study. This model includes two hidden layers, where the first hidden layer considers a hyperbolic tangent faction as an activation function. The second hidden layer and output layer also consider the same activation function. The actual and predicted values for Accident Index for every road segment using ANN5 are shown in Figure 3. Figure 4 is the graphical representation of the determination of coefficients by applying training, validation, and testing data individually and all three types of data together.

The model represented with AI as an output state the level of accident-proneness for a specific road segment related to a particular dataset. The connection becomes highly accident-prone whenever the accident index for a specific link increases. Table 9 shows below the predicted and actual number of accidents for every link in the study area.

Table 10. Contains percentage of accident prediction using ANN model

Number of Segments	Number of Correct Prediction	Number of Incorrect Prediction	(%) of Accident Prediction
44	32	12	72.72

Figure 5. Predicted (using ANN) and the actual number of accidents that happened for each road segment

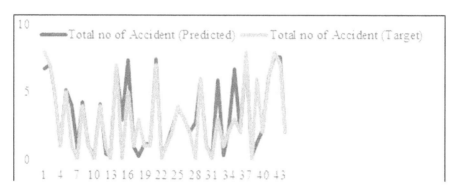

Table 10 shows that ANN5, with the highest percentage of correct accident prediction (72.72%), may be considered the best model. The prediction accuracy is likely good when ANN is applied for accident prediction with a particular dataset. Feature selection is the most suitable method to get more precision with the application of ANN using the same dataset.

Figure 5 represents the predicted accidents and the accidents in each road segment using ANN5.

2.3 Results of Feature Selection

In this section, features have been selected based on the minimum MSE value. Table 11 shows the stages and features chosen in this method. Finally, five significant features were selected for accident prediction and black spot identification. These features are SS, NS, PHF, RW, and LS.

Framework for the Application of the ANN Model in Accident Prediction

Table 11(a). Contains results of feature selection method using sequential ANFIS

Feature	MSE	Features	MSE	Features	MSE
AADT	0.2714	SS+AADT	3.1860	SS+NS+AADT	4413.4538
TV	0.1576	SS+TV	0.2185	SS+NS+TV	133.1339
PHD	0.0711	SS+PHF	0.5241	**SS+NS+PHF**	**0.0080**
PTV	0.0922	SS+PLTV	1.5775	SS+NS+PLTV	115.4242
PTV	0.0730	SS+PRTV	2.5670	SS+NS+PRTV	16041.0128
SS	**0.0412**				
RW	0.1336	SS+RW	3.2820	SS+NS+RW	119.2353
WF	0.0645	SS+WF	0.0791	SS+NS+WF	0.1144
NS	0.0659	**SS+NS**	**0.0084**		
NWS	0.0566	SS+NWS	0.0589	SS+NS+NWS	0.1066
NCP	0.1519	SS+NCP	0.4495	SS+NS+NCP	0.2422
LS	0.0494	SS+LS	0.3949	SS+NS+LS	27.8408

Table 11(b). Contains results of feature selection method using sequential ANFIS

Features	MSE	Features	MSE
SS+NS+PHF+AADT	1.3490	SS+NS+PHF+RW+AADT	0.162687
SS+NS+PHF+TV	4.6473	SS+NS+PHF+RW+TV	0.076625
SS+NS+PHF+PLTV	0.2494	SS+NS+PHF+RW+PLTV	0.254332
SS+NS+PHF+PRTV	0.0168	SS+NS+PHF+RW+PRTV	0.13421
SS+NS+PHF+RW	**0.0067**		
SS+NS+PHF+WF	0.1285	SS+NS+PHF+RW+WF	0.148175
SS+NS+PHF+NWS	0.1691	SS+NS+PHF+RW+NWS	0.079894
SS+NS+PHF+NCP	0.1954	SS+NS+PHF+RW+NCP	0.21013
SS+NS+PHF+LS	0.7539	**SS+NS+PHF+RW+LS**	**0.036009**

3. RESULTS OF ACCIDENT PREDICTION AFTER FEATURE SELECTION

The learning method has been executed repeatedly using the different datasets to describe the relationship between the input and output of specific segments. The

Table 12. Contains data obtained from measurement of performance determined by ANN

ANN model	Number of hidden layers	Number of neurons in hidden layers	Activation function	MSE	SSE	R	R^2
ANN 1	1	2	tansig	0.0454	1.9956	0.7737	0.5982
ANN 2	1	3	tansig	0.0447	1.9650	0.7623	0.5794
ANN 3	2	4	tansig	0.0412	1.8113	0.7941	0.6280
ANN 4	2	4,2	tansig-tansig-tansig	0.0369	1.6220	0.8142	0.6576
ANN 5	2	4,3	tansig-tansig-tansig	0.0385	1.6950	0.8008	0.6408
ANN 6	2	4,4	tansig-tansig-tansig	0.0246	1.0807	0.8849	0.7735
ANN 7	2	4,4	tansig-purelin -tansig	0.0667	2.9352	0.6174	0.3812
ANN 8	2	4,4	tansig-tansig-purelin	0.0448	1.9697	0.7665	0.5804
ANN 9	2	4,4	purelin-tansig-tansig	0.0569	2.5049	0.7026	0.4640

number of instances employed is forty-four, out of which thirty-one cases have been applied for the training and the rest thirteen for testing. The best solution that minimizes the MSE and maximizes the determination of coefficients computed by the testing dataset considering learning of 500 cycles has been selected. Table 12 presents the performance measurement using the decision of the correlation coefficient using the ANN method.

The increment of the number of nodes in the hidden layer minimized the MSE from 0.0454 to 0.412 for considering one hidden layer. Then ANN structure was selected with two hidden layers to minimize the MSE and maximize the determination of coefficients. The ANN6 model provided the best results for both MSE (0.0246) and coefficient of determination (0.7735) simultaneously amongst all ANN models. So ANN6 model may be considered this study's best-fitting Accident Prediction model. This model includes two hidden layers where the first, second, and the hidden output layers think of hyperbolic tangent faction as an activation function. The actual and predicted values for Accident Index for every road segment using ANN are shown in Figure 6. Figure 7 demonstrates the graphical representation of the determination of coefficients by applying training, validation, and testing data individually and all three data types together.

The model represented AI as an output, stating the level of accident-proneness for a specific road segment related to a particular dataset. Table 13 shows the predicted and actual number of accidents for each link in the study area, and Table 14 offers the prediction accuracy of the accident prediction model that uses ANN. Figure 8 represents the predicted number of accidents and the number of accidents for

Framework for the Application of the ANN Model in Accident Prediction

Figure 6. Actual and predicted values for accident Index for every road segment using ANN

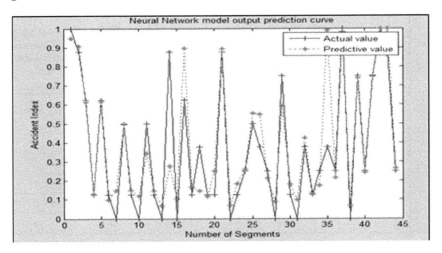

Figure 7. Graphical representation of the determination of coefficients (a) by applying training data, (b) by using validation data, (c) by using testing data, and (d) by using all three types of data together

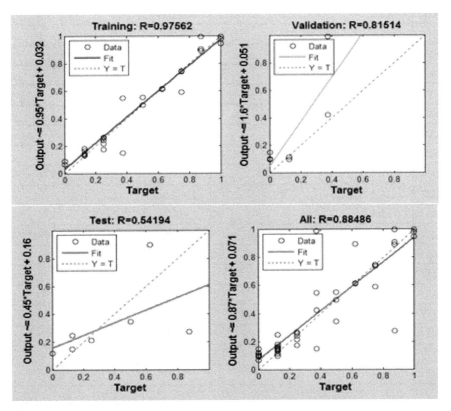

Framework for the Application of the ANN Model in Accident Prediction

Table 13. Contains predicted and the actual number of accidents for every segment using ANN

Target	Predicted	Number of Accidents in the Most Dangerous Segment	Accident Number	Total No. of Accidents (Target)	Total No. of Accidents (Predicted)
1	0.9483	8	6.706462	8	8
0.875	0.9075	8	7.046645	7	7
0.625	0.6117	8	4.961261	5	5
0.125	0.1290	8	0.984257	1	1
0.625	0.6156	8	5.143967	5	5
0.125	0.0977	8	4.062111	1	1
0	0.0482	8	0.760827	0	0
0.5	0.4959	8	4.279604	4	4
0.125	0.1490	8	1.010991	1	1
0	0.0184	8	0.212292	0	0
0.5	0.3447	8	4.108575	4	3
0.125	0.1441	8	0.418646	1	1
0	0.0560	8	0.328256	0	0
0.875	0.8249	8	6.986734	7	7
0	0.0528	8	2.922043	0	0
0.625	0.8968	8	7.411048	5	7
0.125	0.1654	8	0.911391	1	1
0.375	0.1456	8	0.257614	3	1
0.125	0.1145	8	1.127627	1	1
0.125	0.2494	8	1.114407	1	2
0.875	0.8934	8	7.490352	7	7
0	0.0573	8	0.303335	0	0
0.125	0.1814	8	1.017804	1	1
0.25	0.2588	8	2.339336	2	2
0.5	0.5529	8	3.839261	4	4
0.375	0.5471	8	3.049444	3	4
0.25	0.2132	8	2.066883	2	2
0	0.0594	8	2.76163	0	0
0.75	0.5914	8	6.019363	6	5
0.125	0.1805	8	1.067706	1	1
0	0.0612	8	0.198428	0	0
0.375	0.4218	8	5.941675	3	3

Continued on following page

Framework for the Application of the ANN Model in Accident Prediction

Table 6. Continued

Target	Predicted	Number of Accidents in the Most Dangerous Segment	Accident Number	Total No. of Accidents (Target)	Total No. of Accidents (Predicted)
0.125	0.1328	8	0.338674	1	1
0.25	0.1936	8	2.168203	2	2
0.375	0.9901	8	6.765231	3	8
0.25	0.2138	8	2.023281	2	2
1	0.9798	8	7.664202	8	8
0	0.0569	8	0.216639	0	0
0.75	0.7396	8	1.220845	6	6
0.25	0.2417	8	2.204064	2	2
0.75	0.7466	8	6.109973	6	6
1	0.9996	8	7.725105	8	8
0.875	0.9993	8	7.642131	7	8
0.25	0.2640	8	2.009373	2	2

each road segment. From Table 14, the percentage of correct Accident Prediction of ANN6 is 81.81%. This result concludes that the prediction accuracy is high whenever ANN is applied for accident prediction, followed by the ANFIS as a feature selection method.

Figure 8. Predicted (using ANN) and the actual number of accidents that happened for each road segment

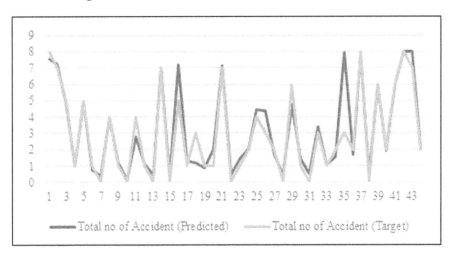

Table 14. Contains percentage of an accident prediction model using ANFIS and ANN

Number of Segments	Number of Correct Prediction	Number of Incorrect Predictions	Percentage of Correct Accident Predictions
44	36	8	81.81

4. DISCUSSION

In this research, ANFIS as a feature selection method and ANN have been applied to predict the frequency of traffic accidents. This method has been selected as the most suitable based on prediction accuracy and measuring errors. The results recommend that the model is ideal for predicting accident frequency. The study focuses only on the probability of accidents in the mid-block of a road and not at intersections. Statistical methods have typically been applied in urban road safety for accident analysis and the development of accident prediction models. The same is employed to select the significant features or find an association between accidents and characteristics. Another technique, ANN, has also been used in the same dataset to evaluate the performance. The model represents AI as an output that states the level of accident-proneness for a specific road segment related to a particular dataset.

The percentage of correct accident prediction is 20.45% by linear regression, which could be better when MLR is applied for accident prediction using traffic and geometry-related dataset. It has been found that the percentage of correct accident prediction is 72.72%, referred to as good when ANN5 is applied for accident prediction using traffic and geometry-related dataset. Feature selection was made using ANFIS to get more accuracy with ANN using the same dataset. Since each feature is represented by a numerical value specified by the linguistic hedges, utilization of the Adaptive Neuro-Fuzzy Inference System (ANFIS) is better in selecting linguistic hedges' features. Finally, five contributory features were selected for predicting accident and the black spot identification method using ANFIS. These are Spot Speed (SS), Number of Left/Right Turn Signals (NS), Peak Hour Factor (PHF), Road Width (RW), and Length of Segments (LS). Among all accident prediction models, the best-fitted model is ANN6, as the percentage of correct accident prediction of the ANN6 model is 81.81%. The prediction accuracy is likely high when ANN is applied for accident prediction, followed by the ANFIS as a feature selection method.

5. CONCLUSION

To conclude, it may be stated that the ANN model results are more accurate with minimal errors as compared with the MLR models at the time of accident prediction. Adaptive Neuro-Fuzzy Inference System (ANFIS) got better results in selecting the features comprising linguistic hedges. Five significant features proposed for accident prediction and black spot identification method Using ANFIS are Spot Speed (SS), Number of Left/Right Turn Signals (NS), Peak Hour Factor (PHF), Road Width (RW), and Length of Segments (LS). The percentage of correct Accident Prediction becomes better when the ANN method is applied along with ANFIS feature selection. It is considered high accuracy compared with the prediction accuracy whenever ANN is employed as a single method.

ACKNOWLEDGMENT

The authors are thankful for the support provided by Birla Institute of Technology Mesra in carrying out the work and accident spot data provided by Kolkata Police.

REFERENCES

Abdelwahab, H. T., & Abdel-Aty, M. A. (2001). Development of Artificial Neural Network Models to Predict Driver Injury Severity in Traffic Accidents at Signalized Intersections *Transportation Research Record: Journal of the Transportation Research Board*, *1746*(1), 6–13. doi:10.3141/1746-02

Abdulhafedh, A. (2016). Crash frequency analysis *Journal of Transportation Technologies*, *6*(4), 169–180. doi:10.4236/jtts.2016.64017

Abdulhafedh, A. (2017). Road crash prediction models: Different statistical modeling approaches. *Journal of Transportation Technologies*, *7*(2), 190–205. doi:10.4236/jtts.2017.72014

Al-Ghamdi, A. (2002). Using Logistic Regression to Estimate the Influence of Accident Factors on Accident Severity. *Accident; Analysis and Prevention*, *34*(6), 729–741. doi:10.1016/S0001-4575(01)00073-2 PMID:12371778

Albalate, D., & Xavier, F. (2021). On the relationship between congestion and road safety in cities. *Transport Policy*, *105*, 145–152. doi:10.1016/j.tranpol.2021.03.011

Chang, L. (2005). Analysis of Freeway Accident Frequencies: Negative Binomial Regression Versus Artificial Neural Network. *Safety Science*, *43*(8), 541–557. doi:10.1016/j.ssci.2005.04.004

Chen, W. H., & Jovanis, P. P. (2000). Method for Identifying Factors Contributing to Driver-Injury Severity in Traffic Crashes. *Transportation Research Record: Journal of the Transportation Research Board*, *1717*(1), 1–9. doi:10.3141/1717-01

Chikaraishi, M., Garg, P., Varghese, V., Yoshizoe, K., Urata, J., Shiomi, Y., & Watanabe, R. (2022). On the possibility of short-term traffic prediction during disaster with machine learning approaches: An exploratory analysis. *Transport Policy*, *98*, 91–104. doi:10.1016/j.tranpol.2020.05.023

Delen, D. R., Sharda, R., & Bessonov, M. (2006). Sharda., Bessonov, M.: Identifying significant predictors of injury severity in traffic accidents using a series of artificial neural networks. *Accident; Analysis and Prevention*, *38*(3), 434–444. doi:10.1016/j.aap.2005.06.024 PMID:16337137

Dougherty, M. (1995). A review of Neural Network applied to Transport. *Transportation Research Part C, Emerging Technologies*, *3*(4), 247–260. doi:10.1016/0968-090X(95)00009-8

Ebrahim, S., & Hossain, Q. S. (2018). An Artificial Neural Network Model for Road Accident Prediction: A Case Study of Khulna Metropolitan City. *Proceedings of the 4th International Conference on Civil Engineering for Sustainable Development (ICCESD 2018)*.

Kapadia, M., Sarkar, S., Roy, B. C., & Sinha, R. C. (2022). Critical Appraisal of Parameters for Successful Implementation of BRTS in India. *Periodica Polytechnica Transportation Engineering*, *50*(2), 165–183. doi:10.3311/PPtr.16508

Lee, J., Yoon, T., Kwon, S., & Lee, J. (2019). Model evaluation for forecasting traffic accident severity in rainy seasons using machine learning algorithms: Seoul city study. *Applied Sciences (Basel, Switzerland)*, *10*(1), 129. doi:10.3390/app10010129

Lui, K. J., McGee, D., Rhodes, P., & Pollock, D. (1988). An Application of a Conditional Logistic Regression to a Study the Effects of Safety Belts, Principal Impact Points, and Car Weights on Drivers' Fatalities. *Journal of Safety Research*, *19*(4), 197–203. doi:10.1016/0022-4375(88)90024-2

Mehmet, K. M., Aghayan, I., & Noii, N. (2011). Prediction for traffic accident severity: Comparing the artificial neural network, genetic algorithm, combined genetic algorithm and pattern search methods. *Transport*, *26*(4), 353–366.

Mussone, L., Ferrari, A., & Oneta, M. (1999). An analysis of urban collisions using an artificial intelligence model. *Accident; Analysis and Prevention, 31*(6), 705–718. doi:10.1016/S0001-4575(99)00031-7 PMID:10487346

Oyedepo, O. J., & Makinde, O. (2010). Accident Prediction Models for Akure – Ondo Carriageway, Ondo State Southwest Nigeria; Using Multiple Linear Regressions. *African Research Review, 4*(2), 30–49. doi:10.4314/afrrev.v4i2.58286

Pradhan, B., & Sameen, M. I. (2020). Review of traffic accident predictions with neural networks. In *Advances in Science, Technology, and Innovation book series (ASTI)* (pp. 97–109). Springer. doi:10.1007/978-3-030-10374-3_8

Saccomanno, F. F., Nassar, S. A., & Shortreed, J. H. (1996). Reliability of Statistical Road Accident Injury Severity Models. *Transportation Research Record: Journal of the Transportation Research Board, 1542*(1), 14–23. doi:10.1177/0361198196154200103

Sarkar, A., Sahoo, G., & Sahoo, U. C. (2016). Feature Selection in Accident Data: An Analysis of its Application in Classification Algorithms. *International Journal of Data Analysis Techniques and Strategies, 8*(2), 108–121. doi:10.1504/IJDATS.2016.077484

Sarkar, A., Sahoo, U. C., & Sahoo, G. (2012). Accident prediction models for urban roads. *International Journal of Vehicle Safety, 6*(2), 149–161. doi:10.1504/IJVS.2012.049020

Sarkar, A., & Sarkar, S. (2020). Comparative Assessment Between Statistical and Soft Computing Methods for Accident Severity Classification. *Journal of Institution of Engineers India Series A, 101*(1), 27–40. doi:10.100740030-019-00422-7

Shaik, M. E., & Hossain, Q. S. (2019). Accident prediction by using Poisson regression for unsignalised junction in Khulna Metropolitan City, Bangladesh. In *Proceedings of International Conference on Planning, Architecture and Civil Engineering*. Rajshahi University of Engineering & Technology.

Vogt, A. & Barred, J. G. (n.d.). *Accident Models for Two-Lane Rural Road: Segment and Intersection*. Federal Highway Administration, McLean, Virginia. FHWA-RD-98-133.

World Health Organization. (2018). *Global status report on road safety*. WHO.

Yu, C. C. (2006). An artificial neural network-based expert system for the appraisal of two-car crash accidents. *Accident; Analysis and Prevention, 38*(4), 777–785. doi:10.1016/j.aap.2006.02.006 PMID:16556433

Zheng, Z., Yang, Y., Liu, J., Dai, H. N., & Zhang, Y. (2019). Deep and embedded learning approach for traffic flow prediction in urban informatics. *IEEE Transactions on Intelligent Transportation Systems, 20*(10), 3927–3939. doi:10.1109/TITS.2019.2909904

Chapter 4

Influences on the Decision to Implement Electronic Health Records in Indonesia

Ahmad Said
Bina Nusantara University, Indonesia

Yulita Hanum P. Iskandar
iD https://orcid.org/0000-0002-8037-5800
Universiti Sains Malaysia, Malaysia

ABSTRACT

Healthcare systems around the world are challenged by facing the COVID-19 outbreak. The expectation of high-quality care in hospitals, coupled with an aging population and more complex treatments, results in the system having increased productivity. The adoption of electronic health record systems (EHRs) is suitable for implementation as digital transformation in the healthcare industry. Despite the increase in demand and importance of EHR adoption, there is still a lack of comprehensive review and classification of the existing studies in this area. The authors are considering technology, organization, and environment (TOE) framework as the basis for EHR adoption. The objective of the study is to investigate the determinants of electronic healthcare record system adoption among hospitals in Indonesia. The findings are insightful and have important theoretical and practical implications for the hospital in Indonesia. This study may contribute to risk reduction throughout the adoption of EHRs, thereby fueling a technological revolution in Indonesia's healthcare industry.

DOI: 10.4018/978-1-7998-9687-6.ch004

Copyright © 2024, IGI Global. Copying or distributing in print or electronic forms without written permission of IGI Global is prohibited.

Figure 1. Healthcare ecosystem of the future
Source: McKinsey Report, 2020

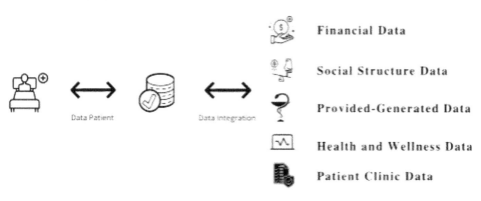

INTRODUCTION

The Coronavirus, which was found in 2019, has transformed the habits that individuals and organizations have practiced on a regular basis, resulting in the emergence of a "New Normal" as a new activity in which all activities previously carried out on site are now carried out online. Pandemics wreak havoc on economies all around the world, and public health is one of the industries that must be prepared (Alrahbi, Khan, Gupta, Modgil, & Chiappetta Jabbour, 2020). Due to the significant growth in the impact of the present pandemic, the health- care business is being pressed to innovate swiftly by employing adoption technology for time efficiency in handling patients. Artificial intelligence, blockchain, and IoT (internet of things) are examples of health technologies that have developed and are being employed by various service facilities to support operating systems in hospitals in the industrial era 4.0. (Clipper, 2020; Palas & Bunduchi, 2021; Sivathanu, 2018). Patients and their families benefit from the increased use of health technology because it makes it easier to obtain information and comprehend diseases, treatment alternatives, and readily access and choose hospitals or health facilities that meet their needs (Stablein, Loud, DiCapua, & Anthony, 2018).

Patients and their families benefit from the increased use of health technology because it makes it easier to obtain information and comprehend diseases, treatment alternatives, and readily access and choose hospitals or health facilities that meet their needs (Stablein, Loud, DiCapua, & Anthony, 2018).

Companies in the health industry, particularly hospitals, have taken the initiative to include digital transformation into their management systems to create better quality health services, according to Singhal, Kayyali, Levin, and Greenberg (2020). However, not all Indonesian health facilities are prepared to meet the disruption 4.0

age, which is characterized by digitization. Human resources, financial sources, business procedures, government rules, and legislation, as well as the lack of a data integration system, are all common roadblocks to achieving this goal (Badan Pengkajian dan Penerapan Teknologi, 2020; Hospital Insights Asia, 2019). Currently, hospitals and clinics use tangible documents to keep track of their patients' medical information, making patient monitoring difficult. The Electronic Health Record System (EHRs) is a collection of data technology, medical information science, such as Electronic Health IT, and telemedicine that could provide a solution for hospital and clinic identification systems to reduce data concerns. (Jianxun, Arkorful, & Shuliang, 2021; Rasmi et al., 2020; Simons, Cillessen, & Hazelzet, 2016); Rasmi et al., 2020; Simons, Cillessen, & Hazelzet, 2016).

Data relating to the patient's health history, laboratory reports, vaccines, and pharmaceuticals used by patients will be available on the EHR system, allowing for correct data to lead to the right decision making (Mathai, McGill, & Toohey, 2020; zer, zkan, & Budak, 2020). Furthermore, technological advancements and the availability of EHR will have a positive impact on increasing hospital service quality (Atasoy, Greenwood, & McCullough, 2019; Coffey et al., 2008; Cook et al., 2020). Mathai et al. are a good place to start (2020), Because electronic health records are regularly exchanged among healthcare professionals, they are considered important, highly sensitive, and confidential information. When any person or organization producing, receiving, administering, or paying for this service is in doubt, concerns about the security and privacy of health information in electronic health records arise.

THEORETICAL/CONCEPTUAL FRAMEWORK

Several emerging and developed countries are implementing EHRs in order to stimulate digitalization in the healthcare industry and thereby promote the health revolution (Jianxun et al., 2021). The current issue in Indonesia is that adoption of electronic health records is relatively low owing to a number of factors that must be provided by the hospital or by supporting factors (Rahmadiliyani, Putri, & Gunarti, 2019). Hospitals, physicians, and nurses today require the creation of EHRs in order to examine information and track patient health records in order for timely choices to be made regarding patient care and for the government to set COVID-19 rules (Alsalman et al., 2021). The speed with which patients are handled will have a significant impact on the activity, resulting in higher service quality (Cook et al., 2021).

Technology development or innovation in Indonesia must be examined, particularly in the health sector. According to an analysis by Oliver Wyman, an estimated $303 billion in healthcare potential cost is lost each year. The total economic output lost due to diseases and outbound medical tourism has a significant economic impact. However, $130 billion of this opportunity cost might be recovered if unmet healthcare needs are addressed.

Due to a lack of market competition at the time, technological developments caused the healthcare business to expand; normally, market competition breeds, so the function of technology as a basic asset to prepare accurate information to generate acceptable service quality. (Hossain, Quaresma, & Rahman, 2019; Richards, Prybutok, & Ryan, 2012; Richards, Prybutok, & Ryan, 2012) The healthcare ecosystem, according to Anand & Fosso Wamba (2013), is in desperate need of a transformative transition to recoup from this tremendous economic loss.

Furthermore, the installation of EHRs must take into account not only the availability of technology to be used, but also the availability of human resources with adequate IT skills. Currently, Indonesia's health-care industry is employing heavily in the IT field to support everyday operations and provide better service to patients (Hospital Insights Asia, 2019). According to Wang & Hajli (2017a), in order for technological advancements to result in changes in hospital operations, hospitals must have IT people who are qualified to support the hospital's operations. From operating as a core business or as a supporter, an organization that does not strengthen its human resource competences will have issues in competitiveness and changing market dynamics (Baloc, Sha, & Panhwar, 2014).

Environment support, whether from government regulation or IS infrastructure, makes EHR deployment even more difficult. The availability of high-tech facilities is a challenge for Indonesia to support the Indonesia Hospital-centric market, according to Bain & Company's "Asia-Pacific Front Line of Healthcare Report 2020." The lack of infrastructure, on the other hand, is a barrier to establishing Electronic Health Records because infrastructure allows for data transmission and even data storage for EHRs (Frisina, Munene, Finnie, Oakley, & Ganesan, 2020; Wang & Hajli, 2017b). Aside from infrastructural issues, the goal of EHR adoption is to provide a centralized interchange of information so that data management can enable the transmission of data among healthcare providers in Indonesia (Badan Pengkajian dan Penerapan Teknologi, 2020). However, when using enormous and diverse data from numerous sources, the impact of data streams on data quality is unknown, and there is a lack of knowledge of the importance of data quality, which makes governance more difficult (Janssen, Brous, Estevez, Barbosa, & Janowski, 2020). In order to cope with uncertainty, rapid environmental changes, globalization, and rising complexity in the execution of every function, organizations must improve (Suprapto, 2018; Tepic, 2013).

Influences on the Decision to Implement EHR in Indonesia

There is a present situation in Indonesia with the COVID-19 epidemic and the development of digital transformation, and support for the digital revolution in hospitals is required. This study adds to the original Technology-Organization-Environment Framework (Tornatzky & Fleischer, 1990) by including supporting variables, and it also builds on previous research by Shahzad et al., (2020), which identifies another factor that influences innovation adoption in the Indonesian context.

To begin, digital transformation must assist the operational hospital in providing excellent care to all patients (Wang & Hajli, 2017a). EHRs have a favorable impact on the hospital's everyday operations (Ayaad et al., 2019; Shahzad et al., 2020). When there is data sharing across healthcare in Indonesia, EHRs examine the availability of data quality and security (Mathai et al., 2020). As a result, the goal of this study is to look at characteristics that can lead to higher electronic health record usage in Indonesian hospitals. As a result, the purpose of this research is to fill in the gaps by looking into data governance for electronic health record adoption.

Second, the context of the organization is critical for decision-makers to make a go/no- go judgment on technology adoption. According to previous study, size and top management support have a positive impact on technology adoption (Ahmadi, Nilashi, Shahmoradi, & Ibrahim, 2017). Unfortunately, this rapid and vast technological growth has resulted in a slew of other issues relating to the usage of digital data, as all data is now available in digital form and can be easily accessed by anyone with reliable technological capabilities (Smallwood, 2020). As a result, the purpose of this research is to fill in the gaps by looking into data governance for electronic health record adoption.

Third, the Technology-Organization-Environment model has been tested in other countries, including Taiwan (Lin, 2014), Malaysia (Ahmadi et al., 2017)(Ahmadi, Nilashi, & Ibrahim, 2015), North America (Herath, Herath, & D'Arcy, 2020), Vietnam (Hue, 2019), Nigeria (Awa, Ukoha, & Igwe, 2017), Pakistan (Shahzad (Cruz-Jesus, Pinheiro, & Oliveira, 2019). However, in the context of electronic health record adoption in Indonesia, the Technology-Organization-Environment architecture and data governance have not been widely implemented.

A.   Technology Context

The technical context, according to (Tornatzky & Fleischer, 1990), contains both internal and external technologies that are relevant to a corporation. Relative advantage refers to the process of analyzing whether to employ HIS technology to lower hospital operating expenses and obtain relative operational benefits for a specific institution (Ahmadi et al., 2015), and today's technology allows for the building of increasingly complex systems. Attractive software tools and hardware at reasonable prices, stable networking, and industry standards increase the likelihood of this feeling becoming a reality (Tachinardi, Gutierrez, Moura, & Melo, 1993). Compatibility in the ISS context is described in terms of perceived compatibility with current telecommunications infrastructure, business operations, and the relative ease with which these technologies and regulations can be applied, according to Herath, Herath, & D'Arcy (2020). Digital transformation and the complexity of the environment have changed the work system that exists in a business to help generate efficient operations and increase service quality in the last decade. Due to the impact of pandemics and technological revolutions on the healthcare business, the use of electronic health records (EHRs) has expanded in developing nations in order to improve service quality (Adetoyi & Raji, 2020). Electronic health records are regarded for data quality and data security because they are constantly transmitted among healthcare providers, according to Mathai et al. (2020). Data governance, on the other hand, entails systems and controls to ensure that, at the most basic level, the raw data that the organization collects and inputs is truthful, accurate, and unique (not redundant) 2020 (Smallwood)

The availability and characteristics of technology must be coupled with present operating processes, according to Gillani, Chatha, Sadiq Jajja, and Farooq (2020). As a result, one of the most essential aspects of technology is that it will be utilized to handle archive data (Hawash, Mokhtar, Yusof, & Mukred, 2020). Data governance, on the other hand, is used to examine the outcomes of a technology implementation in a business case as well as the technology's influence. EHRs technology has a substantial effect on services and the quality of health services, according to previous research by Ayaad et al. (2019), therefore the system is required in hospital operations. The favorable influence of technology environment on technology adoption is explained by the same findings previously examined by Shahzad et al. (2020). Technology Aspect has a good link with electronic health record adoption and data governance, according to the preceding arguments. As a result, consider the following hypothesis:

H1: Technology and electronic health record adoption have a positive association.

B.   Organization Context

The organization dimension refers to the organization's features and assets, such as connecting configurations amongst users; it also includes communication methods, the size of the organization, and the amount of assets (Hawash, Mokhtar, Yusof, & Mukred, 2020). Organizational size is one of the most important distinguishing factors between IS adopters and non-adopters in organizations of various sizes (Ahmadi et al., 2017). According to H.-F. Lin (2014), large firms are better at technology innovation than small organizations. Large facility size was substantially associated with electronic health use, according to a prior study by Bhuyan, Zhu, Chandak, Kim, and Stimpson (2014). Nonetheless, H.-F. Lin (2014) discovered that the size of the organization had no bearing on the adoption of technology.

Managers who collaborate closely with other stakeholders (such as end-users, IT personnel, and other department heads) can better grasp the issues and mandate, negotiate, persuade, motivate, and support the resources needed to implement ISS (Herath et al., 2020). In other words, the organization's senior management must provide a clear communication route for the dissemination of information to all stakeholders. According to prior research, top management of an organization has sufficient expertise and understanding about the benefits and drawbacks of hospital information systems, and their attitude will favorably influence the adoption of hospital information systems, according to Shahzad et al. (2020).

Readiness resource and forecasting contribute to the adoption of other factors in order to increase healthcare resilience, whereas operational failure detection either has no links with other variables or is solely caused by them, in particular, collaborative variables (Rubbio, Bruccoleri, Pietrosi, & Ragonese, 2019). Lack of human resources for technology advancements to be regarded for preparing appropriate competence to support the hospital's operations, according to Wang & Hajli (2017a). In this example, technology is used to tackle difficult issues (operational failures) by collaborating with an external entity to gain a better knowledge of the event.

In today's business environment, data management is required in organizations where data will become an asset for internal decision-making or can be interpreted as "data driven," implying that the organization recognizes the value of data and requires data management from the input process to operations (Ladley, 2020). Good data governance can help to ensure that faulty data doesn't have a detrimental influence later on, and that future reports, analyses, and conclusions are based on reliable and trustworthy data (Smallwood, 2020). Because effective data governance necessitates cross-functional collaboration among multiple stakeholders, the support of the data provider organization's top management will facilitate the establishment of effective data governance through ongoing participation and commitment based on defined responsibilities (Haneem, Kama, Taskin, Pauleen, & Abu Bakar, 2019). According to previous research (Elliott et al., 2013), top management support will ensure the effectiveness of data governance through their participation and accountability in the governance committee, whereas low top management support and a lack of budget allocation will result in poor coordination between employees, IT, and the business, posing a significant barrier to quality data management. The following hypothesis can be posited as a result of these findings:

H2: The organization and electronic health record adoption have a good association.

C.   Environment Context

According to (Tornatzky & Fleischer, 1990), a significant determinant for environmental context includes industrial characteristics (competitive pressure), information technology infrastructure, and a secondary primary element for regulatory assistance. Firms' innovation decisions are influenced by competition pressure, which has long been acknowledged as a significant driver (Hue, 2019). Healthcare businesses must keep an eye on the outside world to keep up with developments in the legal, political, economic, and competitive arenas (Vaishnavi, Suresh, & Dutta, 2019). When emerging countries (competitors) use HIS in their hospitals and reap the benefits, such as greater facilities for patients, competition pressure may rise (Shahzad et al., 2020). Several studies have shown that competition pressure has an impact on technology adoption (Awa et al., 2017; Cruz-Jesus et al., 2019; Shahzad et al., 2020).

The system's integrity must match user expectations and enhance their faith in the network, but infrastructure is also a key component in determining whether or not technology is adopted, as well as supporting and meeting current infrastructure requirements (Hughes et al., 2019). According to Mathai et al. (2020), electronic health records are vital and highly sensitive for real-time exchange among healthcare providers. To improve the efficiency and precision of the working process, the company uses computer-aided planning, design, and production systems. To enable flawless and error-free execution, communication technology fosters real-time communications with customers and other functional divisions (Gillani et al., 2020). As a result, the government must fund infrastructure development and design a strategy to facilitate networking access.

Furthermore, the government should recognize the benefits of meaningful use and work on nationwide implementation of the EHR system, which can include training programs, conferences, technical help, policies, and use certification to encourage primary care physicians to embrace EHR (Iqbal et al., 2013). The impact of government policies and business norms on the adoption of essential technologies' institutional effects (Ahmadi et al., 2017). Data governance, according to Janssen et al. (2020), should assist minimize the cost of data administration and produce value from data. Data is frequently split across multiple organizations with varying data regulations. When it comes to managing access to public papers and interagency data interchange, a corporation that prioritizes safety may need to focus on standards and processes, while a government entity may need to focus on preserving individual privacy (Ladley, 2020). The environment has a beneficial link with electronic health record adoption and data governance, according to the aforementioned reasons and supporting claims. As a result, consider the following hypothesis:

H3: There is a link between the environment and the adoption of electronic health records.

AIM AND OBJECTIVES

This study proposes that the Technology-Organization-Environment framework (Tornatzky & Fleischer, 1990) and Resource Base Theory be combined to create a framework that emphasizes data governance as a mediator and has an impact on hospital EHR adoption in Indonesia. The key of technological context, organization context, and environment context is used as an independent variable in this study. The adoption of EHRs is the study's dependent variable. For this investigation, data governance is a mediator variable. Data governance and EHR adoption are moderated by complexity.

Figure 2. Technology-Organization-Environment framework

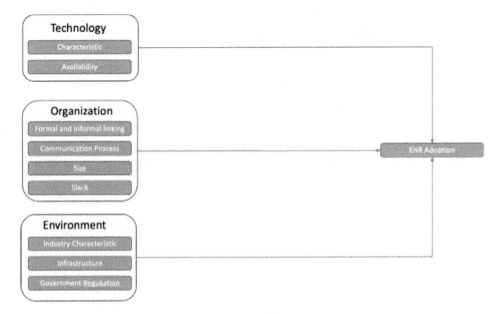

Figure 3. Explanatory sequential mixed methods flow

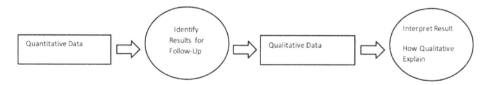

RESEARCH METHODS AND DESIGN

The explanatory sequential mixed techniques will be explained by the recommended resign design of this investigation. It is a two-part data collecting project in which the researcher gathers quantitative data in the first phase, analyzes the findings, and then plans (or builds on) the second qualitative phase using the findings.

The research design is to provide effects to empirical evidence elements for linking technology, organization, environment, and data governance with complexity as a moderating factor in electronic health record adoption.

SIGNIFICANCE AND CONCLUSION

In summary, this study intends to examine the technological elements, organizational aspects, and environmental aspects that were used to suit electronic health record adoption across hospitals in the Indonesia setting, which is one of the Indonesian government's programs. In order to adopt electronic health records in Indonesia, it is expected that the integration of technology, organization, and environment will increase. Understanding the factors that influence technology adoption decision-making can help to reduce risk during the installation of EHRs, resulting in a technological revolution in Indonesia's healthcare industry. The goal of this project is to teach insiders about the importance of data governance in building an integrated system during the post-pandemic recovery stage. We are confident that this will help in the decision-making process in both research and business.

REFERENCES

Adetoyi, O. E., & Raji, O. A. (2020). Electronic health record design for inclusion in sub- Saharan Africa medical record informatics. *Scientific African, 7*, e00304. doi:10.1016/j.sciaf.2020.e00304

Ahmadi, H., Nilashi, M., & Ibrahim, O. (2015). Organizational decision to adopt hospital information system: An empirical investigation in the case of Malaysian public hospitals. *International Journal of Medical Informatics*, *84*(3), 166–188. doi:10.1016/j.ijmedinf.2014.12.004 PMID:25612792

Ahmadi, H., Nilashi, M., Shahmoradi, L., & Ibrahim, O. (2017). Hospital Information System adoption: Expert perspectives on an adoption framework for Malaysian public hospitals. *Computers in Human Behavior*, *67*, 161–189. doi:10.1016/j.chb.2016.10.023

Ali, O., Shrestha, A., Osmanaj, V., & Muhammed, S. (2020). Cloud computing technology adoption: An evaluation of key factors in local governments. *Information Technology & People*, *34*(2), 666–703. doi:10.1108/ITP-03-2019-0119

Alrahbi, D. A., Khan, M., Gupta, S., Modgil, S., & Chiappetta Jabbour, C. J. (2020). Challenges for developing healthcare knowledge in the digital age. *Journal of Knowledge Management*.

Alsalman, D., Alumran, A., Alrayes, S., Althumairi, A., Almubarak, S., Agrawal, S., & Alanzi, T. (2021). Implementation status of health information systems in hospitals in the eastern province of Saudi Arabia. *Informatics in Medicine Unlocked, 22*, 100499.

Ames, G. M., Duke, M. R., Moore, R. S., & Cunradi, C. B. (2009). The impact of occupational culture on the drinking behavior of young adults in the US navy. *Journal of Mixed Methods Research, 3*(2), 129–150. doi:10.1177/1558689808328534

Anand, A., & Fosso Wamba, S. (2013). The business value of RFID-enabled healthcare transformation projects. *Business Process Management Journal*, *19*(1), 111–145. doi:10.1108/14637151311294895

Atasoy, H., Greenwood, B. N., & McCullough, J. S. (2019). The Digitization of Patient Care: A Review of the Effects of Electronic Health Records on Health Care Quality and Utilization. *Annual Review of Public Health*, *40*(1), 487–500. doi:10.1146/annurev-publhealth-040218-044206 PMID:30566385

Awa, H. O., Ukoha, O., & Igwe, S. R. (2017). Revisiting technology-organization-environment (T-O-E) theory for enriched applicability. *The Bottom Line (New York, N.Y.)*, *30*(01), 2–22. doi:10.1108/BL-12-2016-0044

Ayaad, O., Alloubani, A., ALhajaa, E. A., Farhan, M., Abuseif, S., Al Hroub, A., & Akhu-Zaheya, L. (2019). The role of electronic medical records in improving the quality of health care services: Comparative study. *International Journal of Medical Informatics, 127*(April), 63–67. doi:10.1016/j.ijmedinf.2019.04.014 PMID:31128833

Badan Pengkajian dan Penerapan Teknologi. (2020). *Strategi Nasional Kecerdasan Artifisial Indonesia.*

Bain & Company. (2020). *Asia-Pacific Front Line of Healthcare Report 2020.* Bain & Company.

Baloc, R. A., Sha, N., & Panhwar, K. N. (2014). The relationship of slack resources with subjective wellbeing at work: Empirical study of sugar mills from Pakistan. *International Strategic Management Review, 2*(2), 89–97. doi:10.1016/j. ism.2014.10.002

Bhuyan, S. S., Zhu, H., Chandak, A., Kim, J., & Stimpson, J. P. (2014). Do service innovations influence the adoption of electronic health records in long-term care organizations? Results from the US National Survey of residential care facilities. *International Journal of Medical Informatics, 83*(12), 975–982. doi:10.1016/j. ijmedinf.2014.09.007 PMID:25453201

Boneva, B., Kraut, R., & Frohlich, D. (2001). Using e-mail for personal relationships: The difference gender makes. *The American Behavioral Scientist, 45*(3), 530–549. doi:10.1177/00027640121957204

Clipper, B. (2020). The Influence of the COVID-19 Pandemic on Technology: Adoption in Health Care. *Nurse Leader, 18*(5), 500–503. doi:10.1016/j. mnl.2020.06.008 PMID:32837346

Coffey, R. M., Buck, J. A., Kassed, C. A., Dilonardo, J., Forhan, C., Marder, W. D., & Vandivort-Warren, R. (2008). Transforming mental health and substance abuse data systems in the United States. *Psychiatric Services (Washington, D.C.), 59*(11), 1257–1263. doi:10.1176/ps.2008.59.11.1257 PMID:18971401

Cook, K., Cochran, G., Gali, H., Hatch, T., Awdishu, L., & Lander, L. (2021). Pharmacy students' readiness to use the electronic health record: A tale of two institutions. *Currents in Pharmacy Teaching & Learning, 13*(4), 327–332. doi:10.1016/j. cptl.2020.11.005 PMID:33715792

Creswell, J. W., & Creswell, J. D. (2018). Research Design: Qualitative, Quantitative, and Mixed Methods Approaches. SAGE Publishing (Five Edit). California: SAGE Publisher.

Cruz-Jesus, F., Pinheiro, A., & Oliveira, T. (2019). Understanding CRM adoption stages: Empirical analysis building on the TOE framework. *Computers in Industry, 109*, 1–13. doi:10.1016/j.compind.2019.03.007

Elliott, T. E., Holmes, J. H., Davidson, A. J., La Chance, P.-A., Nelson, A. F., & Steiner, J. F. (2013). Data Warehouse Governance Programs in Healthcare Settings: A Literature Review and a Call to Action. *EGMs (Generating Evidence & Methods to Improve Patient Outcomes), 1*(1), 15.

Frisina, P. G., Munene, E. N., Finnie, J., Oakley, J. E., & Ganesan, G. (2020). Analysis of end- user satisfaction with electronic health records in college/university healthcare. *Journal of American College Health, 0*(0), 1–7. PMID:32529959

Gillani, F., Chatha, K. A., Sadiq Jajja, M. S., & Farooq, S. (2020). Implementation of digital manufacturing technologies: Antecedents and consequences. *International Journal of Production Economics, 229*, 107748. doi:10.1016/j.ijpe.2020.107748

Haneem, F., Kama, N., Taskin, N., Pauleen, D., & Abu Bakar, N. A. (2019). Determinants of master data management adoption by local government organizations: An empirical study. *International Journal of Information Management, 45*(October 2018), 25–43.

Hawash, B., Mokhtar, U. A., Yusof, Z. M., & Mukred, M. (2020). The adoption of electronic records management system (ERMS) in the Yemeni oil and gas sector: Influencing factors. *Records Management Journal, 30*(1), 1–22. doi:10.1108/RMJ-03-2019-0010

Herath, T. C., Herath, H. S. B., & D'Arcy, J. (2020). Organizational Adoption of Information Security Solutions. *The Data Base for Advances in Information Systems, 51*(2), 12–35. doi:10.1145/3400043.3400046

Hospital Insights Asia. (2019). *How this hospital is overcoming the IT skills shortage.*

Hossain, A., Quaresma, R., & Rahman, H. (2019). Investigating factors influencing the physicians' adoption of electronic health record (EHR) in healthcare system of Bangladesh: An empirical study. *International Journal of Information Management, 44*(September 2018), 76–87.

Hue, T. T. (2019). The determinants of innovation in Vietnamese manufacturing firms: An empirical analysis using a technology–organization–environment framework. *Eurasian Business Review, 9*(3), 247–267. doi:10.100740821-019-00125-w

Hughes, L., Dwivedi, Y. K., Misra, S. K., Rana, N. P., Raghavan, V., & Akella, V. (2019). Blockchain research, practice and policy: Applications, benefits, limitations, emerging research themes and research agenda. *International Journal of Information Management, 49*(February), 114–129. doi:10.1016/j.ijinfomgt.2019.02.005

Iqbal, U., Ho, C.-H., Li, Y.-C., Nguyen, P.-A., Jian, W.-S., & Wen, H.-C. (2013). The relationship between usage intention and adoption of electronic health records at primary care clinics. *Computer Methods and Programs in Biomedicine, 112*(3), 731–737. doi:10.1016/j.cmpb.2013.09.001 PMID:24091088

Janssen, M., Brous, P., Estevez, E., Barbosa, L. S., & Janowski, T. (2020). Data governance: Organizing data for trustworthy Artificial Intelligence. *Government Information Quarterly, 37*(3), 101493. doi:10.1016/j.giq.2020.101493

Janz, N. K., Zimmerman, M. A., Wren, P. A., Israel, B. A., Freudenberg, N., & Carter, R. J. (1996). Evaluation of 37 AIDS prevention projects: Successful approaches and barriers to program effectiveness. *Health Education & Behavior, 23*(1), 80–97. PMID:8822403

Jianxun, C., Arkorful, V. E., & Shuliang, Z. (2021). Electronic health records adoption: Do institutional pressures and organizational culture matter? *Technology in Society, 65*(96), 101531. doi:10.1016/j.techsoc.2021.101531

Johnson, R. D., & Diman, K. (2017). An Investigation of the Factors Driving the Adoption of Cloud-Based Human Resource Information Systems by Small- and Medium-Sized Businesses. In *Electronic HRM in the Smart Era* (pp. 1–31). Emerald Publishing Limited. doi:10.1108/978-1-78714-315-920161001

Ladley, J. (2020). *Data Governance*. Elsevier.

Lim, J., Sharma, S., Colyer, T., & Lee, S. (2018). *The Future of the Indonesian Healthcare Ecosystem, 21*.

Lin, H.-F. (2014). Understanding the determinants of electronic supply chain management system adoption: Using the technology–organization–environment framework. *Technological Forecasting and Social Change, 86*, 80–92. doi:10.1016/j.techfore.2013.09.001

Mathai, N., McGill, T., & Toohey, D. (2020). Factors Influencing Consumer Adoption of Electronic Health Records. *Journal of Computer Information Systems, 00*(00), 1–11.

Mikalef, P., Boura, M., Lekakos, G., & Krogstie, J. (2019). Big data analytics and firm performance: Findings from a mixed-method approach. *Journal of Business Research, 98*(July 2018), 261–276.

Neaverth, M. P. (2015). Project management and governance in the Project Management Office (PMO): Analysis of the variables associated with project success. *ProQuest Dissertations and Theses*, (March), 153.

O'Halloran, K. L., Tan, S., Pham, D. S., Bateman, J., & Vande Moere, A. (2018). A digital mixed methods research design: Integrating multimodal analysis with data mining and information visualization for big data analytics. *Journal of Mixed Methods Research, 12*(1), 11–30. doi:10.1177/1558689816651015

Özer, Ö., Özkan, O., & Budak, F. (2020). The Relationship between the Nurses' Perception of Electronic Health Records and Patient Privacy. *Hospital Topics, 98*(4), 155–162. doi:10.1080/00185868.2020.1799729 PMID:32757888

Palas, M. J. U., & Bunduchi, R. (2021). Exploring interpretations of blockchain's value in healthcare: A multi-stakeholder approach. *Information Technology & People, 34*(2), 453–495. doi:10.1108/ITP-01-2019-0008

Rahmadiliyani, N. R., Putri, P., & Gunarti, R. (2019). Implementasi Electronic Health Record (EHR) Pada Poli Rawat Jalan Di Rumah Sakit Umum Daerah Ratu Zalecha Martapura. *Jurnal Kesehatan Indonesia, 9*(3), 135. doi:10.33657/jurkessia.v9i3.186

Rasmi, M., Alazzam, M. B., Alsmadi, M. K., Almarashdeh, I. A., Alkhasawneh, R. A., & Alsmadi, S. (2020). Healthcare professionals' acceptance Electronic Health Records system: Critical literature review (Jordan case study). *International Journal of Healthcare Management, 13*(sup1, S1), 48–60. doi:10.1080/20479700.2017.14 20609

Richards, R. J., Prybutok, V. R., & Ryan, S. D. (2012). Electronic medical records: Tools for competitive advantage. *International Journal of Quality and Service Sciences, 4*(2), 120–136. doi:10.1108/17566691211232873

Rubbio, I., Bruccoleri, M., Pietrosi, A., & Ragonese, B. (2019). Digital health technology enhances resilient behaviour: Evidence from the ward. *International Journal of Operations & Production Management, 40*(1), 34–67. doi:10.1108/ IJOPM-02-2018-0057

Shahzad, K., Jianqiu, Z., Zubedi, A., Xin, W., Wang, L., & Hashim, M. (2020). DANP-based method for determining the adoption of hospital information system. *International Journal of Computer Applications in Technology, 62*(1), 57. doi:10.1504/ IJCAT.2020.103900

Simons, S. M. J., Cillessen, F. H. J. M., & Hazelzet, J. A. (2016). Determinants of a successful problem list to support the implementation of the problem-oriented medical record according to recent literature. *BMC Medical Informatics and Decision Making, 16*(1), 1–9. doi:10.118612911-016-0341-0 PMID:27485127

Singhal, S., Kayyali, B., Levin, R., & Greenberg, Z. (2020). *The next wave of healthcare innovation: The evolution of ecosystems How healthcare stakeholders can win within evolving healthcare ecosystems.*

Sivathanu, B. (2018). Adoption of internet of things (IoT) based wearables for healthcare of older adults – a behavioural reasoning theory (BRT) approach. *Journal of Enabling Technologies, 12*(4), 169–185. doi:10.1108/JET-12-2017-0048

Smallwood, R. F. (2020). *Information Governance.* John Wiley & Sons.,Inc.

Stablein, T., Loud, K. J., DiCapua, C., & Anthony, D. L. (2018). The Catch to Confidentiality: The Use of Electronic Health Records in Adolescent Health Care. *The Journal of Adolescent Health, 62*(5), 577–582. doi:10.1016/j.jadohealth.2017.11.296 PMID:29422435

Suprapto, Y. L., Wibowo, A., & Harsono, H. (2018). Intra-firm causal ambiguity on cross- functional project team's performance: Does openness and an integrative capability matter? *International Journal of Managing Projects in Business, 11*(4), 901–912. doi:10.1108/IJMPB-09-2017-0109

Tachinardi, U., Gutierrez, M. A., Moura, L., & Melo, C. P. (1993). Integrating Hospital Information Systems. The challenges and advantages of (re-)starting now. *Proceedings / the ... Annual Symposium on Computer Application [Sic] in Medical Care. Symposium on Computer Applications in Medical Care,* (pp. 84–87). NIH.

Tan, M. L., Prasanna, R., Stock, K., Doyle, E. E. H., Leonard, G., & Johnston, D. (2020). Usability factors influencing the continuance intention of disaster apps: A mixed-methods study. *International Journal of Disaster Risk Reduction, 50*(April), 101874. doi:10.1016/j.ijdrr.2020.101874

Tepic, M., Kemp, R., Omta, O., & Fortuin, F. (2013). Complexities in innovation management in companies from the European industry: A path model of innovation project performance determinants. *European Journal of Innovation Management, 16*(4), 517–550. doi:10.1108/EJIM-05-2012-0053

Tornatzky, L. G., & Fleischer, M. (1990). *Processes of Technological Innovation.* Lexington Books.

Vaishnavi, V., Suresh, M., & Dutta, P. (2019). Modelling the readiness factors for agility in healthcare organization: An TISM approach. *Benchmarking, 26*(7), 2372–2400. doi:10.1108/BIJ-06-2018-0172

Wang, Y., & Hajli, N. (2017a). Exploring the path to big data analytics success in healthcare. *Journal of Business Research*, *70*, 287–299. doi:10.1016/j.jbusres.2016.08.002

Wang, Y., & Hajli, N. (2017b). Exploring the path to big data analytics success in healthcare. *Journal of Business Research*, *70*, 287–299. doi:10.1016/j.jbusres.2016.08.002

Weitzman, P. F., & Levkoff, S. E. (2000). Combining Qualitative and Quantitative Methods in Health Research with Minority Elders: Lessons from a Study of Dementia Caregiving. *Field Methods*, *12*(3), 195–208. doi:10.1177/1525822X0001200302

Chapter 5

Review and Analysis of Applications and Frameworks of Information Systems in Supply Chain Management

Manish Kumar
Indian Institute of Management, Indore, India

ABSTRACT

In this era of information systems, humankind has benefitted enormously. The rapid growth in information system technology has made human life very easy and has significantly increased the efficiency, speed, and reliability of different processes. It is the need of the hour to study the interface between the information system and supply chain management. This chapter specifically tried to study the applications and frameworks of information systems in operation and supply chain management. For the study, the authors reviewed the articles published in top-quality journals. This chapter aimed to identify and discuss how different information systems frameworks solve problems related to operation and supply chain management. This study dealt with seven subsections involving supply chain, logistics, partnership, transparency, and decision-making. The study further identified that the use of information systems also contributes to competitive advantage. Finally, the understanding from the literature review has been concluded, and the existing gap has been highlighted for future research.

DOI: 10.4018/978-1-7998-9687-6.ch005

Copyright © 2024, IGI Global. Copying or distributing in print or electronic forms without written permission of IGI Global is prohibited.

1. INTRODUCTION

The rapid growth in information system technology is having a huge impact on all aspects of human life. Information systems are also significantly contributing to supply chain management by improving its efficiency, speed and reliability. There has been a significant number of research happening in the interface of information systems and supply chain management. The future is also very bright for this area. The world is continuously witnessing the growth of information systems and their applicability in operation and supply chain management (Narasimhan et al., 2000; Gunasekaran et al., 2004; White et al., 2005; Lu et al., 2013). So, it is very important for researchers as well as practitioners to have updated knowledge of the application and frameworks of information systems in operation and supply chain management. To the best of the author's knowledge, there are no research articles that specifically deal with the application and frameworks of information systems in operation and supply chain management. So, this book chapter is an attempt to address this gap.

Information system solves many deep rotted problems related to operation and supply chain management, and information systems-enabled operation and supply chain network is the need of the hour (Gunasekaran et al., 2004). For a fast, optimised and reliable operation and supply chain, information systems research and frameworks are very necessary. The chapter aims to cater to this need of researchers wherein they can find all the frameworks, their application, and their result in the operation and supply chain context. This chapter will help the target audience to further their exposure to theoretical and conceptual frameworks in the context of information system-enabled operation and supply chain management. This paper tries to analyse how the different aspects of operation and supply chain management have evolved due to advances in information system technology. The chapter mainly focuses on the application of information system technologies in operation management, supply chain management, logistics management, supply chain transparency and decision-making. The study also identifies certain frameworks for the integration of information systems in operation and supply chain networks. Finally, the study also shows whether information systems can be effectively used for the purpose of fast, optimised and reliable decision-making. With these objectives, the study is presented in the following sections:

- section-1 dealt with the introduction of the study
- section-2 presents the research methodology
- in section-3 and its subsections, the application and frameworks of information systems in operation and supply chain management are presented
- in the last section, the conclusion and future research directions are discussed

2. RESEARCH METHODOLOGY

For fulfilling the objective of this paper, the literature survey is used as the methodology. Articles mostly from top-quality journals have been chosen for the study. According to the ABDC (Australian Business Deans Council) journal ranking, the papers selected are mostly from A and A* category journals, with few being from B or lower category journals. The keyword used for identifying the articles on google scholar revolved around the application and frameworks of information systems in supply chain management. Only top-quality articles were chosen after manual filtering to maintain the rigour of the study. The chosen articles were further classified into seven categories, and those categories are as:

- Dynamics of operation management and information systems
- Information system in supply chain management
- Inter-organisational information system in supply chain management
- Supply chain partnership and information systems
- Information technology in logistics
- Information system and transparency in the supply chain
- Decision-making based on information systems

So, this review paper will deal with the application and frameworks of information systems in the above-defined seven dimensions. For studying this, thirty-five articles from top-quality journals or publishers are selected. The name of journals or publishers from which the articles are selected is summarised in Table 1, along with the number of articles from each source. Articles for this study are chosen in such a way that all the dimensions of the information system-enabled operation and supply chain management can be studied in detail. So, the articles for this study have been chosen for all the seven defined dimensions. The detailed breakup of the chosen articles for different dimensions has been summarised in Table 2. The articles are interlinked, and the article mentioned in one dimension is also used to understand the other dimension, but articles mentioned for the study of one specific dimension mainly focus on that dimension. The different dimension is also defined as classification criteria for studying the information system-enabled operation and supply chain management.

So, the objective of this paper is to analyse the application and frameworks of information systems in operation and supply chain management and find out the implications of this with the help of existing literature. For this, the study has been classified into seven dimensions, and each dimension has been studied separately in order. So, the next section deals with the study of each dimension of information system-enabled operation and supply chain management as defined above with the

Frameworks of Information Systems in Supply Chain Management

Table 1. Article Resources

Title of the journal or publisher	Number of articles
Annals of Operations Research	1
Boston: Kluwer Academic Publishers	1
Computers in Industry	1
Computers & Industrial Engineering	3
European Journal of Operational Research	2
European Journal of Purchasing & Supply Management	1
Expert Systems with Applications (Elsevier)	1
IEEE Transactions on Engineering Management	1
Industrial Management & Data Systems	1
Information Systems Research	1
International Journal of Computer Integrated Manufacturing	1
International journal of information management	1
International Journal of Physical Distribution & Logistics Management	3
International Journal of Production Economics	1
International Journal of Production Research	3
International Journal of Technology Management	1
Journal of Business Logistics	1
Journal of Cleaner Production	2
Journal of Industrial Information Integration	1
Journal of Management Information System	1
Journal of Operations Management	1
Journal of the Academy of Marketing Science	1
Management Information Systems Quarterly	1
Technological Forecasting and Social Change	1
Technovation (Elsevier)	2
The Journal of Strategic Information Systems	1

help of existing literature. Finally, the concluding statement has been made stating the existing gap in the literature and the implications of the information system-enabled operation and supply chain management.

Table 2. Classification of reviewed articles

Classification Criteria	References
Dynamics of operation management and information systems	Shtub et al. (1999), Jayaram et al. (2000), White et al. (2005), Dolgui et al. (2022), Grover et al. (2022)
Information system in supply chain management	Narasimhan et al. (2001), Kim et al. (2002), Subramani et al. (2004), Kim et al. (2006), Gunasekaran et al. (2004), Lu Panetto et al. (2013)
Inter-organisational information system in supply chain management	Holland et al. (1995), Humphreys et al. (2001), Shah et al. (2002), Qu et al. (2022)
Supply chain partnership and information systems	Lau et al. (2000), Yu Z et al. (2001), Zhou et al. (2007)
Information technology in logistics	Closs et al. (1997), Helo et al. (2005), Chounard et al. (2005)
Information system and transparency in the supply chain	Sunny et al. (2020), Agarwal et al. (2021), Bai et al. (2022), Hader et al. (2022), Latino et al. (2022), Chou et al. (2023)
Decision-making based on information systems	Gupta et al. (2003), Themistocleous et al. (2004), Yazdani et al. (2017), Belhadi et al. (2022)

3. INFORMATION SYSTEM ENABLED OPERATION AND SUPPLY CHAIN MANAGEMENT

With advances in information systems over the years, information systems have expanded to almost every activity of humankind. The main reason behind this extent of expansion is the inherent property of the information system, which makes the activity fast, efficient and reliable. So, for improving the overall performance of the operation and supply chain management, mainly in terms of speed, reliability and efficiency, the use of information systems has seen significant growth over the years. This study mainly focuses on studying the growth and implications of the interface of information systems with operation and supply chain management over the years. So, to study this interface, the literature has been classified into seven dimensions, and this section will deal with all those dimensions one by one.

3.1 Dynamics of Operation Management and Information System

Operation management is all about converting materials and labour into goods and services in an efficient way. The term efficient is very important for the introduction of information systems in operation management. Information system basically contributes to the speed, efficiency and reliability of any process. So, the introduction of an information system in operation management increases the efficiency, speed and reliability of the operation, which further contributes to maximising the profit, which is the ultimate goal of any firm.

Information systems can be introduced in operation management in many ways, but for that understanding, the process and its requirements become very important. Merely introducing information systems everywhere will incur an unnecessary cost that is not desired. Shtub et al. (1999), in the article "ERP: The dynamics of operation management", have tried to explain all the dimensions of operation management. According to the article, the information system can be introduced in operation management in the integration of processes, the integration of organisational units, and the integration of data and models, which helps in decision-making. The article further explains that enterprise resource planning is an information system tool that helps in communicating between different departments in a firm which further helps in being efficient, serving the customer better and taking smart decisions. The article also talks about the core processes of a firm where there is scope for the introduction of information systems which involves the development process of a new product or facility, existing process or facility, analysing market for sale or any other purpose, and the delivery and service process. The article has also emphasised the importance of data and its use in decision-making.

White et al. (2006) talk about information systems contributing to the agility and flexibility of operation management. The paper discusses that there is always scope for uncertainty in a firm or any operation, and the information system must possess the ability to overcome that uncertainty. The paper also has involved case studies in finding the effect of information systems in operation management. Two companies, IBM and E2Open, have been studied in the paper, and the results show that the integration of information systems provides increased flexibility and agility. The effect of information system infrastructure in operation management has also been studied by Jayaram et al. (2000) with the help of case studies in which 57 suppliers of the automotive industry are studied. The paper emphasised that information systems and process improvement in operation management have a positive and complementary effect. The paper finally concludes that the joint deployment of information systems and process improvement in operation management significantly improves performance.

The article by Grover et al. (2022) talks about the use of artificial intelligence (AI) in different operation management elements, such as supply chain, product development, and manufacturing. The results of the article suggest that there are six factors which include facilitating conditions, job fit, long-term consequences, social factors, complexity, and affect toward use as the criteria for the use of AI in different elements of operation management. The article uses literature and Twitter data to derive the results. Similarly, the paper by Grover et al. (2022) talks about the use of 5G technology in operation management to ensure end-to-end connectivity, flexibility and real-time visibility. The paper focuses on the digital supply chain, and its results suggest that the use of 5G can improve connectivity, transparency, intelligence, networking and visibility of the supply chain. Information system technologies have progressed over time, and their use in operation management has also evolved with the main aim of making the supply chain more transparent and visible for improving efficiency and ensuring trust among all stakeholders.

3.2 Information System in Supply Chain Management

Operation management basically deals with producing goods and services from raw materials and labour, and it is internally focused on the company. In comparison, the supply chain is externally focused and deals with the flow of goods and services. Operation management is basically about managing the processes of producing goods and services, whereas supply chain management is about managing the flow of finished goods, work-in-process inventory and raw materials to the point of consumption from the point of origin. This section deals with a broader picture of the interface of information systems in supply chain management.

The use of information systems in supply chain management and integration has been discussed in detail by Gunasekaran et al. (2004), who tried to figure out the framework for the development and implementation of information technology in supply chain management. The paper extensively reviewed the existing literature and came up with the framework. The framework developed in the paper involves strategic planning, virtual enterprise, e-commerce, infrastructure, knowledge and implementation. The findings of the paper also show that the use of information systems in supply chain management provides flexibility and responsiveness, which in turn contributes to competitive advantage. Suppliers are the most important component in the supply chain network. Gunasekaran et al. (2004) concluded that information system integration in the supply chain gives a competitive advantage, but this integration from the supplier's perspective is discussed by Subramani et al. (2004). They talked about two patterns of supply chain management systems by suppliers; exploitation and exploration. The paper used a survey-based approach and collected data from 131 suppliers. The result of the article concludes that the use of information systems in supply chain management leads to close buyer-seller relationships. The result of the study also suggests that the information system-enabled supply chain also helps the supplier in creating value and helps the supplier in making the entire process efficient.

Gunasekaran et al. (2004) and Subramani et al. (2004) discussed the use of information systems from the organisation and suppliers' perspective, but the supply chain communication system and its effect on channel relationship and firm performance are discussed by Kim et al. (2006). The authors argued that a supply

Frameworks of Information Systems in Supply Chain Management

chain communication system is a resource for the firm, and innovation in that leads to capability building which further contributes to the firm's performance. The results of the study also tell that the inter-_rm system integration mediates the relationship between innovations in the supply chain communication system and its capabilities. The method used in this paper was an empirical study in which a survey was done with US supply chain managers, which validates the results.

All the review done above tells that information system is very advantageous and should be implemented in supply chain practices as it enhances capabilities and gives a competitive advantage, but the strategies for information system utilisation in supply chain management is given by Narasimhani et al. (2001) and Kim et al. (2002). They have used empirical data from manufacturing firms to find the recommended system for the integration of information systems in supply chain management. The results show that value creation management and logistic operations should be focused more than the infrastructural support, which can further lead to competitive advantage.

Another thing that can contribute to the competitive advantage in the supply chain context is the infrastructure of a supply chain information system. Lau et al. (2000) have tried to discuss and propose an infrastructure for the system. They have also discussed all the components of the infrastructure and described the creation of all the modules. The proposed system allows effective data exchange, which further leverages the responsiveness of the supply chain network. The result of this study talks about the formulation of a customer-driven supply chain network that allows cross-platform data exchange. The study concludes that this cross-platform data exchange infrastructure of the supply chain information system contributes to a competitive advantage on local as well as global levels.

3.3 Inter-Organisational Information System in Supply Chain Management

This section studies the implications of inter-organisational information systems in supply chain management. The general understanding of inter-organisational information systems is shared information among a group of companies. Electronic data interchange is the most common form of inter-organisational information system in which information from computer to computer is transferred instantaneously (Premkumar et al., 1994). The importance of aligning the inter-organisational information system has been discussed by Shah et al. (2002) in detail. The authors first find that the alignment of inter-organisational information systems with supply chain management gives a competitive advantage to the firm. They have further tried to introduce a framework in the form of a matrix known as the "supply chain management-inter-organisational information system" framework. The alignment of inter-organisational information system capabilities with the needs of the supply chain network is understood by the given matrix. Industry's week census data of manufacturers has been used by the authors to validate the framework.

Humphreys et al. (2001) also discussed a framework for inter-organisational information systems from an information system provider's perspective. Inter-organisational relationship within a supply chain concept is also studied in the paper. The proposed framework has been studied in Hong Kong to China supply chain network. Holland et al. (1995) have also discussed the impact of inter-organisational information systems in the supply chain network in the textile industry. The analysis by them is done in terms of a managerial perspective. The study also shows that the market structure is integrating organisational boundaries using information systems. A case-based longitudinal study of different retail organisations and manufacturers is done in detail to derive the results.

The role of supply chain integration, when aligned with green information systems, significantly contributes to the green innovations of the organisation. This important result is derived from a study by Qu et al. (2022), in which the authors collected data from 231 organisations and used confirmatory factor analysis to derive the results. The study basically analyses how green innovation is being impacted by customer orientation and supplier integration and how the green information system is moderating or mediating this relationship. This study uses information processing theory and does empirical analysis to prove the hypothesis. The results of the study provide important guidelines to the organisational decision-makers regarding investment in the green information system.

3.4 Supply Chain Partnership and Information Systems

Information systems play a very important role in supply chain partnerships. The previous section mainly dealt with the inter-organisational information system framework for supply chain management. This section will deal with the use and implication of information systems in supply chain partnerships. Lee et al. (2000) argue that supply chain-wide performance can be optimised with tight coordination among supply chain partners. The paper further discusses that information sharing among supply chain partners is the most important thing for achieving tight coordination. The paper further emphasises the fact that information sharing can be made efficient, fast and reliable with the help of an information system. The paper also discusses the type of information that can be shared among supply chain partners and industry has been taken to find how and why particular information sharing is needed. The paper also proposes three models of information sharing and discusses the associated with each model. The paper concludes that information sharing among supply chain partners is very important, and the full value of information sharing should be utilised by overcoming challenges associated with the model used by the firm, and this will contribute to the competitive advantage.

Frameworks of Information Systems in Supply Chain Management

Zhou et al. (2000) also emphasise the fact that information sharing and effective supply chain practice among partners contribute to enhanced supply chain management. The study tried to investigate the same by collecting data from a survey targeting 125 North American manufacturing companies. The paper proposes the hypothesis for realising the objective of the paper, and structural equation modelling is also done. The findings of the paper show that effective information sharing among supply chain partners enhances effective supply chain practices. The results also show that with a higher level of information, effective supply chain practices become more important to optimise the output and gain a competitive advantage. The paper concludes that effective supply chain practices in coordination with effective information sharing among partners contribute to better supply chain performance.

The literature studied above shows that information sharing among supply chain partners is very important, which enhances the overall supply chain performance and contributes to the competitive advantage but measuring the effectiveness of this supply chain coupling is discussed by Barut et al. (2002). The authors firstly emphasise the fact that integration among supply chain partners in terms of information has become vital nowadays, and information systems help in achieving integration very effectively and reliably. The paper further talks about the need to measure the magnitude of such integration. The paper then tries to develop a generic measure to gauge the degree of such integration. The measure developed, also known as the degree of supply chain coupling, accounts for the extent and intensity of the information owed among supply chain partners. The paper also talks about the practical or managerial implications of the measure at the micro as well as macro level.

3.5 Information Systems in Logistics

The previous section discussed the use of information systems in operation management and supply chain management. As discussed above, operation management is internal to the firm and mainly focuses on processes to convert material and labour into goods and services, whereas the supply chain is external to the company and mainly talks about the flow of goods, work-in-process inventory and raw material from the point of origin to the point of consumption. The supply chain involves coordination and collaboration among all the supply chain partners ranging from suppliers, customers, intermediaries, and third-party service providers. Logistics is a subpart of the supply chain which only focuses on the flow of goods, services and related information to the point of consumption from the point of origin. Logistics only involves one organisation, whereas supply chain involves multiple organisations. This section exclusively discusses the use of information systems in logistic management.

Helo et al. (2005) tried to review the efforts to integrate information systems in logistics management. The paper basically investigates the development of information systems in logistics and their functionality and benefits. The paper reviewed the existing academic and non-academic literature and used practical views to identify this integration. However, the paper could not involve interviews or surveys of managers or consultants or any person from the company to test the objective, which is a limitation of this study. The paper also highlighted the problem of choosing and implementing a new information system. The paper further highlighted that integrating a new information system requires a positive attitude from the employee, the expertise of the firm, and significant money and time. The paper finally concluded that the integration of information systems in logistics improves visibility as well as contributes significantly to performance, but choosing a suitable information system for a particular purpose is very important. Bad analysis may lead to wrong information system selection, which may further lead to the wastage of organisational resources instead of giving a competitive advantage.

The paragraph discussed above talks about the integration of information systems in logistics management, but it fails to involve the industry perspective by including surveys or interviews with industry people. The paper by Closs et al. (1997) discusses the integration of information systems in logistics and also involves an industry perspective by using data taken from 111 firms. The paper firstly emphasises that the use of information systems enhances logistic competitiveness. The paper also talks about evidence of world-class performances resulting from logistics information capabilities. The paper also highlighted the fact that there may be a scenario in which the integration of information systems may lead to the wastage of the firm's resources. The paper is also trying to find logistic information capabilities which lead most to logistic competence. Firstly, the paper uses the literature review method to understand the relation between logistic competence and logistic information capabilities and then uses multiple regression analysis and t-tests on the data taken from 111 firms to derive the relationship. The paper has finally concluded with managerial implications, and the final results show a weak relationship between logistic competence and logistic information capabilities.

The above-discussed paragraph mainly focuses on the integration of information systems in logistic management. However, the implication of the use of information systems in reverse logistics is studied in detail by Chouinard et al. (2004). According to the paper, the recovery and processing of unused products and redistribution of reusable products come under the banner of reverse logistics. The paper firstly emphasises the fact that the use of information systems in reverse logistics is very much required, and this can increase the speed, reliability and efficiency of reverse logistics. The paper then tries to propose new approaches and information support systems to control and manage reverse logistics better. The paper has taken the problem of a rehabilitation centre and proposed an information system for operational processes and organisational resources. The paper further extends the conclusion that the proposed information system can be applied to other centres also, along with application in a network context.

3.6 Information Systems and Transparency in Supply Chain

With increasing awareness among consumers and various types of adulteration, counterfeiting and unsustainable practices, transparency in the supply chain is the need of the hour. The paper by Latino et al. (2022) highlights the importance and then drawbacks of Industry 4.0 technologies in making the supply chain transparent. The paper highlights the problem of supply chain players and consumers regarding data visualisation and the standard adopted for data collection as the main drawbacks of the current system, including the unfulfillment of Industry 4.0 standards. The paper further provides a framework which overcomes the drawbacks of simply using Industry 4.0 technologies. The proposed framework is based on digital technologies and uses mapping of processes, identification of data generating processes and use of appropriate technologies for collecting and processing the data as the three pillars. The article then uses a case of the organic oil (olive oil) firm to test the developed framework, and the results from the case study suggest the proposed framework is a very effective mechanism for ensuring supply chain transparency by eliminating the drawbacks of the existing practices.

In contrast to Latino et al. (2022), Hader et al. (2022) discuss how the Industry 4.0 technologies, such as Big Data, can help in effective supply chain traceability and effective supply chain information sharing. Hader et al. (2022) take the example of the textile industry and highlights that problems such as delay in product delivery, tempering with the delivered product, very poor traceability and very poor information sharing lead to very poor performance of the supply chain. The paper further highlights that emerging technologies such as blockchain and big data can be pathbreaking solutions for such problems by having certain very important features, which include transparency, decentralisation and immutability. The paper then proposes a unique framework and applies this framework to the supply chain of the textile industry. The proposed framework is based on blockchain technology because of its unique properties, which help in immutable transparency among all the supply chain members. The use of the proposed framework results in the building of better synchronisation and trust among all the stakeholders of the supply chain. The use of the proposed framework further results in a reduction in counterfeit products, a reduction in recall of the product, and an increase in the efficiency of the overall supply chain. The paper also highlights the problem in the wide implication of the framework and emphasises that blockchain being a new technology, scalability can be an issue with very big data. Therefore, the paper further proposes a new framework integrating blockchain technology and big data technology. This integration of the technologies helps in the elimination of the drawback by having a decentralised system with all the benefits of blockchain technology with the option of scalability, even in the presence of very big data. The paper finally concludes that both frameworks are good, but the final framework involving blockchain technology as well as big data technology can be very useful in today's supply chain networks which are very complex and need transparency for various reasons, including the awareness among end consumers.

The paper by Agarwal et al. (2021) also talks about the use of the framework based on blockchain technology in the textile industry supply chain traceability. The paper also highlights that present-day consumers need quality assurance and transparency, and that's why traceability has become the main need of the supply chain. The paper highlights that the textile supply chain lacks visibility, and information asymmetry is very prevalent in this sector. So this leads to the creation of doubts among consumers regarding the product authenticity and use of ethical as well as sustainable practices for the manufacturing of the product. The paper also highlights the problems from the supply chain player's side, which involves problems such as the risk of data tempering in an insecure environment and the risk of losing the advantage of having information. Therefore, the study proposes a framework based on blockchain technology in the context of a complex textile supply chain having multiple tiers. The proposed framework captures the network of the supply chain, the interaction of the supply chain players and the new contracting and validating techniques (smart contracts). The paper demonstrates this framework in the organic cotton industry, and the results suggest that the proposed framework, along with the smart contract, is very effective for traceability as well as building trust among all the supply chain players.

Another paper by Sunny et al. (2020) also supports the results from Agarwal et al. (2021) that a blockchain-based framework for traceability of the supply chain can be very effective if used along with smart contracts. The paper also highlights one very important fact that blockchain technologies can not totally replace the existing technologies but support the existing technology and mechanism for better traceability and information sharing. Another important contribution of this paper is demonstrating the implication of using blockchain-based solutions in the cold supply chain developed in the Microsoft Azure environment. The paper also highlights that the use of blockchain technology in supply chain transparency is not the best solution and has some drawbacks. So, the paper finally highlights that the technologies such as smart contracts and the Internet of Things improves the efficiency and applicability of blockchain technology for the traceability of the supply chain.

The use of blockchain technology in ensuring transparency in the sustainable supply chain is discussed by Bai et al. (2022). The authors first highlight that the lack of transparency in the agriculture supply chain leads to very poor farming as

Frameworks of Information Systems in Supply Chain Management

well as minimum social responsibility, which further leads to environmental damage. The use of blockchain technology for ensuring transparency in such a complex agriculture supply chain is very problematic. So, the paper develops a framework using TOE (Technology Organization Environment) theoretical framework for ensuring transparency in the sustainable supply chain in the context of the cocoa industry. The developed framework is a hierarchical enablers framework, and therefore, for calculating the weights of the main as well as the sub-enablers, the popular BWM (Best Worst Method) is used in the context of the African cocoa supply chain. The results of the case study identify technical characteristics as the main enablers and blockchain security, smart contracts, and tracking of product components as the sub-enablers. The results of this study support the results of other studies, such as Sunny et al. (2020) and Agarwal et al. (2021). The results of this study can be used by the decision-makers to effectively use blockchain technology to improve the transparency and efficiency of the sustainable supply chain.

The paper by Chou et al. (2023) also highlights the fact that the use of blockchain technology increases supply chain transparency as well as trust among supply chain stakeholders. The paper also highlights that the use of blockchain technology while collaborating with competitors and other partners in a dynamic environment can be risky as well because transparency can risk confidentiality, privacy, and the information advantage. The paper is an attempt to solve this issue by building a permissioned blockchain in a Hyperledger environment using a proposed multichain framework which takes care of multiple assets, multiple processes, confidentiality and privacy. The results of the study show that the channels in the proposed framework help the organisation maintain information confidentiality and privacy with other collaborators, including partners and competitors, and also make the supply chain more transparent and efficient. The analysis of the results further suggests that the proposed framework in permissioned blockchain is the way ahead and far better than public blockchain for such cases where privacy and confidentiality are an issue. So, the use of information system technology, mainly emerging technology such as blockchain, big data, and smart contracts, can play a pivotal role in ensuring supply chain transparency.

3.7 Information Systems in Decision Making

All the above sections discussed talk about the use or integration of information systems in operation management, supply chain management and logistics, but this section will exclusively deal with the use of information systems in decision-making, which is very important for a firm. Gupta et al. (2003) discussed the use of information systems in decision-making. The paper firstly highlights the fact that strategic decision-making was earlier done with the help of cost accounting, and the use of information system-based activity-based costing/management (ABC/M) enhances the usefulness and helps in decision-making in a better way. The paper then tries to show that operations decision-making processes can also be benefited by the ABC/M. The paper further tries to propose a conceptual framework for the use of the ABC/M information system for various decisions related to operation management. The paper shows that the ABC/M information system can help in taking operation-related decisions ranging from planning, inventory, quality, capacity and workforce management. The paper finally concludes that the ABC/M information systems can help managers in more effective decision-making.

Themistocleous et al. (2003) also did a case study to evaluate the integration of information systems with the supply chain. The paper talks about enterprise application integration (EAI) as an emerging information system technology to facilitate the integration of all supply chain partners, which helps in effective decision making, but choosing the supply chain provider, like the logistic provider, is also a very important decision which is discussed in detail by Yazdani et al. (2017). The paper by Yazdani et al. (2017) proposed a decision support system based on quality function deployment for selecting a logistic provider. The research in the paper has been carried out in the context of the agriculture supply chain in France. The result of the study shows that the group decision-making system, as proposed in the study, helps in selecting the third-party logistic provider in an efficient and reliable way. So, the overall conclusion of the study is that the use of information systems makes decision-making very easy and also increases the speed, quality, efficiency and reliability of the decision-making process.

Similarly, the paper by Belhadi et al. (2022) also uses Artificial Intelligence (AI) techniques for building a decision-making framework for supply chain resilience. The paper talks about how AI techniques like Wavelet Neural Networks (WNN), Evaluation based on Distance from Average Solution (EDAS), and Fuzzy systems can power multi-criteria decision-making (MCDM) for supply chain resilience. The article uses data from 479 companies and suggests that machine learning big data and fuzzy logic programming are best suited for supply chain resilience. The finding from the study provides an integrated framework to the decision makers for building supply chain resilience using artificial intelligence.

4. CONCLUSION AND FUTURE WORK

This study tries to investigate the implication of integrating information systems in operation and supply chain management. The review of the existing literature is done in the operation and supply chain management context by classifying the literature into seven parts to simplify the study. Each part of the literature reviews the implication of information systems in different segments of operation and supply chain management ranging from the operation, supply chain, inter-organisational supply chain, supply chain partnership, logistics, supply chain transparency, and decision making.

The results of the review study show that the use of information systems contributes to higher speed, efficiency and reliability. The study further identifies that the use of information systems also contributes to competitive advantage. The findings of the study also show that choosing information systems is very purpose-specific, and utmost care should be given while choosing an information system for a particular operation. Otherwise, the use may backfire by contributing to the wastage of the organisation's resources. The study shows that the use of the right information system makes the operation very fast, efficient and reliable. The study also finds that the use of information systems improves inter-organisational information sharing, improves supply chain partnership and thus, enhances the organisational capabilities and gives a competitive advantage. The study also identifies certain frameworks for the integration of information systems in operation and supply chain networks. Finally, the study also shows that information systems can be effectively used for the purpose of fast, optimised and reliable decision-making.

Future studies can be done towards building a reliable framework for suitable information system selection for a particular purpose, which can be further tested by practical implementation of the framework. Further study can also be done towards measuring the effect of information systems on the existing network so that those information systems which are wasting organisational resources and not contributing to the organisational capabilities and competitiveness as desired can be identified, and corrective measures can be taken.

REFERENCES

Agrawal, T. K., Kumar, V., Pal, R., Wang, L., & Chen, Y. (2021). Blockchain-based framework for supply chain traceability: A case example of textile and clothing industry. *Computers & Industrial Engineering, 154*, 107130. doi:10.1016/j.cie.2021.107130

Bai, C., Quayson, M., & Sarkis, J. (2022). Analysis of Blockchain's enablers for improving sustainable supply chain transparency in Africa cocoa industry. *Journal of Cleaner Production, 358*, 131896. doi:10.1016/j.jclepro.2022.131896

Barut, M., Faisst, W., & Kanet, J. J. (2002). Measuring supply chain coupling: An information system perspective. *European Journal of Purchasing & Supply Management, 8*(3), 161–171. doi:10.1016/S0969-7012(02)00006-0

Belhadi, A., Kamble, S., Fosso Wamba, S., & Queiroz, M. M. (2022). Building supply-chain resilience: An artificial intelligence-based technique and decision-making framework. *International Journal of Production Research*, *60*(14), 4487–4507. doi:10.1080/00207 543.2021.1950935

Bharadwaj, S., Bharadwaj, A., & Bendoly, E. (2007). The performance effects of complementarities between information systems, marketing, manufacturing, and supply chain processes. *Information Systems Research*, *18*(4), 437–453. doi:10.1287/ isre.1070.0148

Chou, C. C., Hwang, N. C. R., Li, C. W., Wang, T., & Wang, Y. Y. (2023). Implementing a multichain framework using hyperledger for supply chain transparency in a dynamic partnership: A feasibility study. *Computers & Industrial Engineering*, *175*, 108906. doi:10.1016/j.cie.2022.108906

Chouinard, M., D'Amours, S., & Ait-Kadi, D. (2005). Integration of reverse logistics activities within a supply chain information system. *Computers in Industry*, *56*(1), 105–124. doi:10.1016/j.compind.2004.07.005

Closs, D. J., Goldsby, T. J., & Clinton, S. R. (1997). Information technology influences on world class logistics capability. *International Journal of Physical Distribution & Logistics Management*, *27*(1), 4–17. doi:10.1108/09600039710162259

Dolgui, A., & Ivanov, D. (2022). 5G in digital supply chain and operations management: Fostering flexibility, end-to-end connectivity and real-time visibility through internet-of-everything. *International Journal of Production Research*, *60*(2), 442–451. doi:10.1 080/00207543.2021.2002969

Grover, P., Kar, A. K., & Dwivedi, Y. K. (2022). Understanding artificial intelligence adoption in operations management: Insights from the review of academic literature and social media discussions. *Annals of Operations Research*, *308*(1-2), 177–213. doi:10.100710479-020-03683-9

Gunasekaran, A., & Ngai, E. W. (2004). Information systems in supply chain integration and management. *European Journal of Operational Research*, *159*(2), 269–295. doi:10.1016/j.ejor.2003.08.016

Gupta, M., & Galloway, K. (2003). Activity-based costing/management and its implications for operations management. *Technovation*, *23*(2), 131–138. doi:10.1016/ S0166-4972(01)00093-1

Hader, M., Tchoffa, D., El Mhamedi, A., Ghodous, P., Dolgui, A., & Abouabdellah, A. (2022). Applying integrated Blockchain and Big Data technologies to improve supply chain traceability and information sharing in the textile sector. *Journal of Industrial Information Integration*, *28*, 100345. doi:10.1016/j.jii.2022.100345

Frameworks of Information Systems in Supply Chain Management

Helo, P., & Szekely, B. (2005). Logistics information systems: An analysis of software solutions for supply chain coordination. *Industrial Management & Data Systems*, *105*(1), 5–18. doi:10.1108/02635570510575153

Holland, C. P. (1995). Cooperative supply chain management: The impact of interorganizational information systems. *The Journal of Strategic Information Systems*, *4*(2), 117–133. doi:10.1016/0963-8687(95)80020-Q

Humphreys, P. K., Lai, M. K., & Sculli, D. (2001). An inter-organisational information system for supply chain management. *International Journal of Production Economics*, *70*(3), 245–255. doi:10.1016/S0925-5273(00)00070-0

Jayaram, J., Vickery, S. K., & Droge, C. (2000). The effects of information system infrastructure and process improvements on supply-chain time performance. *International Journal of Physical Distribution & Logistics Management*, *30*(3/4), 314–330. doi:10.1108/09600030010326082

Kim, D., Cavusgil, S. T., & Calantone, R. J. (2006). Information system innovations and supply chain management: Channel relationships and _rm performance. *Journal of the Academy of Marketing Science*, *34*(1), 40–54. doi:10.1177/0092070305281619

Kim, S. W., & Narasimhan, R. (2002). Information system utilisation in supply chain integration efforts. *International Journal of Production Research*, *40*(18), 4585–4609. doi:10.1080/0020754021000022203

Latino, M. E., Menegoli, M., Lazoi, M., & Corallo, A. (2022). Voluntary traceability in food supply chain: A framework leading its implementation in Agriculture 4.0. *Technological Forecasting and Social Change*, *178*, 121564. doi:10.1016/j.techfore.2022.121564

Lau, H. C., & Lee, W. B. (2000). On a responsive supply chain information system. *International Journal of Physical Distribution & Logistics Management*, *30*(7/8), 598–610. doi:10.1108/09600030010346242

Lu, Y., Panetto, H., Ni, Y., & Gu, X. (2013). Ontology alignment for networked enterprise information system interoperability in supply chain environment. *International Journal of Computer Integrated Manufacturing*, *26*(1-2), 140–151. doi:10.1080/09511 92X.2012.681917

Narasimhan, R., & Kim, S. W. (2001). Information system utilisation strategy for supply chain integration. *Journal of Business Logistics*, *22*(2), 51–75. doi:10.1002/j.2158-1592.2001. tb00003.x

Premkumar, G., Ramamurthy, K., & Nilakanta, S. (1994). Implementation of electronic data interchange: An innovation diffusion perspective. *Journal of Management Information Systems*, *11*(2), 157–186. doi:10.1080/07421222.1994.11518044

Qu, K., & Liu, Z. (2022). Green innovations, supply chain integration and green information system: A model of moderation. *Journal of Cleaner Production*, *339*, 130557. doi:10.1016/j.jclepro.2022.130557

Shah, R., Goldstein, S. M., & Ward, P. T. (2002). Aligning supply chain management characteristics and interorganizational information system types: An exploratory study. *IEEE Transactions on Engineering Management*, *49*(3), 282–292. doi:10.1109/TEM.2002.803382

Shtub, A., & Karni, R. (1999). *Enterprise resource planning (ERP): the dynamics of operations management*. Kluwer Academic Publishers.

Subramani, M. (2004). How do suppliers benefit from information technology use in supply chain relationships? *Management Information Systems Quarterly*, *28*(1), 45–73. doi:10.2307/25148624

Sunny, J., Undralla, N., & Pillai, V. M. (2020). Supply chain transparency through blockchain-based traceability: An overview with demonstration. *Computers & Industrial Engineering*, *150*, 106895. doi:10.1016/j.cie.2020.106895

Themistocleous, M., Irani, Z., & Love, P. E. (2004). Evaluating the integration of supply chain information systems: A case study. *European Journal of Operational Research*, *159*(2), 393–405. doi:10.1016/j.ejor.2003.08.023

Whang, S. (2000). Information sharing in a supply chain. *International Journal of Technology Management*, *20*(3/4), 373–387. doi:10.1504/IJTM.2000.002867

White, A. E. D. M., Daniel, E. M., & Mohdzain, M. (2005). The role of emergent information technologies and systems in enabling supply chain agility. *International Journal of Information Management*, *25*(5), 396–410. doi:10.1016/j.ijinfomgt.2005.06.009

Yazdani, M., Zarate, P., Coulibaly, A., & Zavadskas, E. K. (2017). A group decision making support system in logistics and supply chain management. *Expert Systems with Applications*, *88*, 376–392. doi:10.1016/j.eswa.2017.07.014

Yu, Z., Yan, H., & Edwin Cheng, T. C. (2001). Benefits of information sharing with supply chain partnerships. *Industrial Management & Data Systems*, *101*(3), 114–121. doi:10.1108/02635570110386625

Zhou, H., & Benton, W. C. Jr. (2007). Supply chain practice and information sharing. *Journal of Operations Management*, *25*(6), 1348–1365. doi:10.1016/j.jom.2007.01.009

Chapter 6

The Viable System Model (VSM) in the Management of Institutions of Higher Education in Zimbabwe

Stansilas Bigirimana
iD https://orcid.org/0000-0002-3735-6102
Africa University, Zimbabwe

Ganyanhewe Masanga
Chinhoyi University of Techology, Zimbabwe

ABSTRACT

This study aimed assessing the application of the viable system model (VSM) to institutions of higher learning in Zimbabwe. There is increased competition between the institutions themselves, and institutions of higher learning face decreasing budgets owing to the reduction in government financial support. These challenges threaten the viability of institutions of higher education in Zimbabwe and affect unprecedentedly their strategic orientation. The viable system model (VSM) has been recognised as a conceptual tool for understanding organizations, redesigning them (where appropriate) and supporting the management of change. From a sample of 150 respondents including vice chancellors, staff, parents and guardians, students, and other stakeholders, this study found principles of the viable system models are applied through existing organisational structures, although all institutions examined are suffering from various systems pathologies.

DOI: 10.4018/978-1-7998-9687-6.ch006

Copyright © 2024, IGI Global. Copying or distributing in print or electronic forms without written permission of IGI Global is prohibited.

1. INTRODUCTION

Higher education refers to postsecondary institutions such as universities, polytechnics, teachers colleges, and other units in government ministries, government parastatal organisations and the private sector as well as other non-governmental organisations (Shizha & Kariwo 2011). In Zimbabwe at independence in 1980, there were five teachers' colleges, two polytechnic colleges, and one university (Mumbengegwi 2001). By 1990, teachers' colleges had increased to 14, technical colleges to eight, and two new vocational training centres (VTCs) were established –but there remained only one university (Mumbengegwi 2001). Zimbabwe educational reforms since 1990 were more focused on the relevance and quality of education. They included new approaches to curriculum content, new technologies and teaching methodologies, skills provision, decentralization of colleges, and the establishing of college advisory boards (Kapungu 2008). The 1999 Presidential Commission on Education and Training, known also as the Nziramasanga Commission, recommended a wide range of educational reforms with a primary focus on teacher education, the sciences, technology, and skills (Kapungu 2008). Many of the country's tertiary institutions have successfully computerized their operations through Educational Management Information Systems (EMIS).

However, institutions of higher learning in Zimbabwe are facing unprecedented competition owing to rapid internationalization of institutions in other countries (Altbach and Knight 2007) and a virtually unstoppable global migration movement for educational purposes (Varghese 2008). Majoni (2014) has identified challenges ranging from instruction and teaching, research and publication, quality assurance, staffing (loss of qualified and experienced staff) and decrease in the student population. These challenges occured in a context where institutions of higher learning face decreasing budgets owing to the reduction in government financial support (Mhukahuru 2015, Mawonde 2015, Dzimbo (2015). Moreover, potential students in Zimbabwe have access to universities in other countries because of increased internationalization and globalization (Magwa 2015, Altbach and Knight 2007, Varghese 2008). Internal competition is also on the increase given the unprecedented expansion of the higher education sector in Zimbabwe (Zindi 2015) leading to increased competition for resources, students and qualified staff. Moreover, potential students in Zimbabwe have alternative modes of delivery such as open and distance learning (Kurasha 2015) and online learning (Rourke & Coleman 2011).

These challenges threaten the viability of institutions of higher education in Zimbabwe and affect unprecedentedly their strategic orientation. The Viable System Model (VSM) has been recognised by Espejo and Gill (1997) as a conceptual tool for understanding organizations, redesigning them (where appropriate) and supporting the management of change. Viability refers to the capacity of an organism to maintain a separate existence, that is, to survive regardless of the changes in its environment (Rios 2010). In these changing circumstances, institutions of higher education may need to revisit business models they have applied so far such as operating within the context of state bureaucracy and devise ways of generating revenue in order to cover their expenses or even to make a profit. This study aims at assessing how the Viable System Model (VSM) as a conceptual tool for understanding organizations, redesigning them (where appropriate) and supporting the management of change is being applied in institutions of higher education in Zimbabwe.

2. LITERATURE REVIEW

According to Puche, Ponte, Costas, Pino, de la Fuente (2016) the VSM offers the possibility to scientifically design an organization as a system with regulatory learning and adaptive capabilities necessary to ensure its survival (viability) when facing changes that may occur in its environment over time, even though they were not foreseen in its design. As Hilder (1995) has pointed out, the VSM is a tool for diagnosis and an instrument for improvement. The VSM originated from cybernetics, and cybernetics was defined by Wiener (1948) as the science of control and communication in the animal and the machine. Although the concept originated from engineering it was successfully introduced in management by Stafford Beer (1989) creating the discipline of "management cybernetics". Management cybernetics is applied by means of good regulations, supervision and communication, in a business context. This can help managers intervene in complex situations (Van Vliet 2011). Unlike the bureaucratic model which is based on the principle of the division of labour and which strived on fragmenting tasks to make them simple, Management Cybernetics acknowledges that organisations are inherently complex. According to Beer (1984) in order to persist in a complex environment an organization must be viable i.e. "capable of independent existence". Viable Systems have necessary and sufficient conditions for their independent existence (Beer 1979). Moreover, there is a "set of rules" (management principles) that applies to all viable systems, be it a human or an organization that comprises humans (Beer 1984).

Consequently, according to Beer (1989) for a cybernetic model of any viable system, there are five necessary and sufficient subsystems interactively involved in any organism or organization that is capable of maintaining its identity independently of other such organisms within a shared environment. A viable system is composed of five interacting subsystems which may be mapped onto aspects of organizational structure (Beer, 1972). In broad terms Systems 1–3 (Beer 1972) are concerned with the 'here and now' of the organization's operations, System 4 is concerned with the 'there and then' – strategical responses to the effects of external, environmental

Figure 1. Representation of the viable system model
Source: Espejo and Gill (1997)

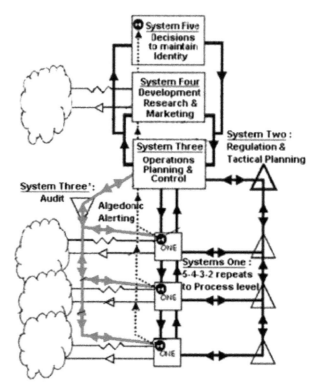

and future demands on the organization (Beer 1972). System 5 is concerned with balancing the 'here and now' and the 'there and then' to give policy directives which maintain the organization as a viable entity (Beer 1972). According to Espejo and Gill (1997) the VSM has can be represented as follows:

System 1 in a viable system contains several primary activities. Each System 1 primary activity is itself a viable system due to the recursive nature of systems as described above. These are concerned with performing a function that implements at least part of the key transformation of the organization.

System 2 represents the information channels and bodies that allow the primary activities in System 1 to communicate between each other and which allow System 3 to monitor and co-ordinate the activities within System 1. Represents the scheduling function of shared resources to be used by System 1.

System 3 represents the structures and controls that are put into place to establish the rules, resources, rights and responsibilities of System 1 and to provide an interface with Systems 4/5. Represents the big picture view of the processes inside of System 1.

System 4 – The bodies that make up System 4 are responsible for looking outwards to the environment to monitor how the organization needs to adapt to remain viable.

System 5 is responsible for policy decisions within the organization as a whole to balance demands from different parts of the organization and steer the organization as a whole.

Espejo and Gill (1997) have reconceptualised the VSM in by renaming the five systems as (1) implementation, (2) coordination, (3) monitoring (and 3* auditing), (4) intelligence and (5) policy. Steinhaeusser, Elezi, Tommelein, Lindemann (2015) has called system 1 "operational control", system 2 "coordinating function", system 3 "managing the inside and now", system 3* 'auditing and monitoring, system 4, "managing the outside and future" and system 5, the Three-Four Balancer.

The VSM is founded on Ashby (1956)'s law of requisite variety. Variety is defined by Ashby (1956) total number of distinct states of a <u>system</u>. Beer (1981) has rephrased this definition by pointing out that variety is the total number of *possible* states of a system, or of an element of a system." Variety implies the degree of complexity of an entity and it is an indicator of its ability to match the pressures faced by it from other entities (Gautam & Batra 2011). The management of an operation unit increases its variety and decreases the variety of the operational unit using variety amplifiers and variety attenuators respectively (Gautam & Batra 2011). These amplifiers and attenuators are specific organisational interactions and information filtering mechanisms (Gautam & Batra 2011). The notion of variety was introduced in management cybernetics by Beer (1979) in his book the *Heart of the Firm*. According to the law of requisite variety if a system is to be stable, the number of states of its control mechanism must be greater than or equal to the number of states in the system being controlled (Ashby 1956). In other words, "variety can destroy variety" (Ashby 1956) or in Beer (1979)'s terms "variety absorbs variety".

The notion of variety led to Beer (1979) four principles of organisation. These principles are as follows:

(1)   The first principle of organization: Managerial, operational and environmental varieties, diffusing through an institutional system, tend to equate; they should be designed to do so with minimum damage to people and to cost.

(2)   The second principle of organization: The four directional channels carrying information between the management unit, the operation, and the environment must each have a higher capacity to transmit a given amount of information relevant to variety selection in a given time than the originating subsystem has to generate it in that time. (Beer 1979)

(3)   The third principle of organization: Wherever the information carried on a channel capable of distinguishing a given variety crosses a boundary, it undergoes

transduction; the variety of the transducer must be at least equivalent to the variety of the channel (Beer 1979:)

(4)   The fourth principle of organization: The operation of the first three principles must be cyclically maintained through time without hiatus or lags (Beer 1979:)

The notion of variety implies i.e. taking into account of the sum total of possible states of a system. This implies that, as Hilder (1995) has pointed out, Beer believes that effective organizations should maximize the freedom of their participants, within the practical constraints of the requirement for those organizations to fulfill their purpose.

Therefore, the VSM is of strategic importance because of the need to give requisite variety to strategic and implementation processes (Espejo 1997) and information systems (Espejo 1993) that is, capable of independent existence. One of the main challenges for organisations is how do they maintain their identify in a complex and constantly changing enviroments. Hence, the main task of the VSM is managing complexity and creating intelligent organisations (Espejo & Reyes 2011, Schwaninger 2000).

Another important aspect of the Viable System Model (VSM) is the principle of recursion. According to Warnecke (1995) the viability, cohesion, and self-organization of an enterprise depend upon the specified functions being recursively operating at all levels of organization. Recursion is a key characteristic of viable systems. In other words, viable systems contain viable systems that can be modeled using an identical cybernetic description as the higher (and lower) level systems in the containment hierarchy (Beer 1972). Beer calls this characteristic cybernetic isomorphism (Beer 1972). Malik (2016) defines the principle of recursion by pointing out that in a constellation of systems, which in general systems terminology can be referred as systems, subsystems, supersystems, each system no matter what level it is on is structured in a similar way.

Therefore, the basic structure of a system hierarchy structured according to the recursion principle does not follow a pyramid-like structure i.e. a top-down bureaucratic system based on the principle of "command and control". Rather it consists of systems that are nested with each other, almost like Chinese boxes or Polish dolls (Malik 2016). In other words, every sub-entity of a viable system – which in a business context would be a division – has to be a viable system in itself (Malik 2016). This implies that each division has to have the overall structure of a viable system i.e. at the divisional level there will also be system 1 through system 5.

Management cybernetics is oriented towards the effect of processes within an organization and looks at the cohesive part of these processes (Van Vliet 2011). That is why, one of the most crucial inherent principle of management of cybernetics is the principle of syntegrity (Malik 2010). The word syntegrity is derived from the words "synergistic" and "tensegrity" (Malik 2010). Its etymology signifies the ideal balance of tension and compression that makes structures stronger and more stable as they grow (Malik 2010). Management cybernetics is based on the fact that today's organizations are highly complex hybrids of man and technology, the results of human thought and action (Malik 2007). Malik (2007) has further noted that today's organisastions like natural biological systems are characterised by complexity, right practice, orientation (or direction). They have inbuilt early warning systems that monitor their continuous interaction with their environment; these systems survive through self-organisation, efficient coordination, integration, communication and adaptation (Malik 2007). They are the opposite of bureaucratic systems which are characterised by fragmentation both vertically and horizontally.

The Viable System Model (VSM) and corollary concepts from cybernetics and management cybernetics have been applied in various areas of business. Bozeman and Kacmar (1997) have suggested a cybernetic model of impression management. Schwaninger (2006) tested the power of the viable system model (VSM) in five corporations of various sizes and orientations and found that the five cases examined corroborated the viable system model (VSM) claim to provide necessary and sufficient conditions for the viability of an organization. Although literature on cybernetics and its application to management is abundant, very few studies have examined how cybernetics and its derivative concepts such as management cybernetics, systems thinking and the viable system model (VSM) apply to the management of institutions of higher education.

Nevertheless, Liber (1998) has noted that the adoption of learning technologies has not fulfilled expectation in any sector of education. Arguably, it is the structure of educational institutions which is the main obstacle (Liber 1998). In a study conducted at the Isfahan Medical Sciences University, in Isfahan (Iran) Falsafinejad and Hashembeik (2013) findings showed that faculty members of Isfahan Medical Sciences University use cybernetic patterns in organizing their activities. However, Falsafinejad and Hashembeik (2013) limited their study to three aspects, namely, decision making, leadership, and equilibrium. There is, therefore, a need to study other aspects of university management such as financing, recruitment and student and staff welfare.

3. METHODOLOGY

This study used a qualitative design. Qualitative research is a method of inquiry employed in many different academic disciplines, including in the social sciences and natural sciences, but also in non-academic contexts including market research, business, and service demonstrations by non-profit organisations (Denzin & Lincoln,

Figure 2. Universities in the sample and their characteristics

Ownership	Public		Private	
	Chinhoyi University of Technology (CUT); Great Zimbabwe University (GZU) Zimbabwe Open University (ZOU)		Africa University (AU) The Catholic University in Zimbabwe (CUZ)	
Mode of Delivery	**Contact Tuition**	**Open and Distance Learning**	**Blended**	
	Chinhoyi University of Technology (CUT); Great Zimbabwe University (GZU)	Zimbabwe Open University	Africa University (AU) The Catholic University in Zimbabwe (CUZ)	
Location	**One Campus**		**Multiple Locations**	
	Chinhoyi University of Technology (CUT)		Africa University (AU) The Catholic University in Zimbabwe (CUZ) Zimbabwe Open University (ZOU) Great Zimbabwe University (GZU)	

2005). The population was constituted of stakeholders in all institutions of higher education in Zimbabwe. The researchers used purposive sampling. Purposive sampling, one of the most common sampling strategies, groups participants according to preselected criteria relevant to a particular research question (Mack et al., 2005). Stakeholders in institutions of higher education are a diverse group. This study focused on those involved in the daily management of universities, students, parents and guardians. Universities were selected following three criteria, namely, (1) the ownership structure (public vs private), location (single or multiple campus) and (3) the mode of delivery (contact tuition vs Open and Distance Learning or ODL) and were classified as follows:

Other stakeholders included conveniently selected students, parents and guardians. When convenience sampling is used, members of the population are chosen based on their relative ease of access (Lucas 2014).

The research instruments used in the study consisted of questionnaires, in-depth interviews and participant observations. Questionnaires consist of a series of questions and other prompts for the purpose of gathering information from respondents (Gault, 1907), while in-depth interviewing is a qualitative research technique that involves conducting intensive individual interviews with a small number of respondents to explore their perspectives on a particular idea, program, or situation (Boyce & Neale, 2006). A total of 150 questionnaires was administered and 46 were returned while participant observation is the process of learning through exposure to or involvement in the day-to-day or routine activities of participants in the researcher setting (Schensul, Schensul and Le Compte, 1999:91).

4. DATA ANALYSIS

The viability of each institution was analysed using five parameters, namely, the degree of complexity escalation of the institution being assessed, secondly whether the institutions have the 5 sub-systems that Stafford Beer (1989) considers as part of nay viable system, thirdly whether the organization abides to Beer (1989)'s management principles and also whether the organization has proper intelligence channels. The last parameter was whether the organization is not suffering from "organisational pathologies".

4. 1 Complexity Escalation

Complexity escalation or "complexity unfolding" is a measure of which sub-environments are of interest, and which organizations (sub-systems) will handle these environments (Rios, 2010). Measuring complexity escalation implies a process of "vertical unfolding" (Rios, 2010) which can be carried out following different "criteria", depending upon the purpose of the study or intervention (i.e. geographical, commercial, political, etc.) (Rios, 2010). In this research, The 5 universities assessed displayed different levels of complexity escalation. While two (2) state owned universities stated clearly that they have a national mandate given by the government who is both their founder and owner, one private universities was described as Pan-African while the other described itself as global given the fact that it has "replicates" in other countries the world over. Another state owned university described itself as "global" given the fact that it has students in other countries in Africa but also in America, Europe and Asia as well.

Table 1. Complexity escalation

		Frequency	Percent	Valid Percent	Cumulative Percent
Valid	National	14	30.4	30.4	30.4
	Regional	19	41.3	41.3	71.7
	Pan-African	5	10.9	10.9	82.6
	Global	7	15.2	15.2	97.8
	Other	1	2.2	2.2	100.0
	Total	46	100.0	100.0	

Table 2. Existence of Beer (1989)'s five sub-systems

		Frequency	Percent	Valid Percent	Cumulative Percent
Valid	Implementation	29	63.0	63.0	63.0
	Coordination	14	30.4	30.4	93.5
	Control	1	2.2	2.2	95.7
	Intelligence	1	2.2	2.2	97.8
	Planning and Policy	1	2.2	2.2	100.0
	Total	46	100.0	100.0	

4.2 Existence of Sub-Systems

Beer (1989) indicated that for an organization to be viable, it must have 5 subsystems, which Beer (1989) numbered from 1 to 5. Espejo and Gill (1997) have reconceptualised the VSM by renaming the five systems as follows: (1) implementation, (2) coordination, (3) monitoring (and 3* auditing), (4) intelligence and (5) policy. Steinhaeusser et al. (2015) has called system 1 "operational control", system 2 "coordinating function", system 3 "managing the inside and now", system 3* 'auditing and monitoring, system 4, "managing the outside and future" and system 5, the Three-Four Balancer.

The 5 universities assessed acknowledged that they have no dedicated teams or units to handle the implementation, coordination, audit, control, and planning units. One university has an internal audit unit while another has a planning and corporate services unit and a quality assurance department. However, respondents noted that these functions are carried out within the framework of existing structures and reporting relationships within faculties/schools or units. Although only one university has a full-time planning and corporate services unit, respondents from two universities pointed out that activities pertaining to the planning function are carried ex-officio by the office of the Pro-Vice Chancellor (PVC) - Institutional Development and Resources Mobilisation.

In other two universities respondents pointed out that the planning function is carried through ad-hoc committees where all the units and faculties/schools are represented by ex-officio members (e.g. deans or directors) and coopted members. In these two (2) universities the planning function sometimes implies carrying strategic planning workshops facilitated by external consultants. No university claimed to have an intelligence unit or a "spying agency" and all the institutions based their decisions either on information which is available in the public domain or on directives from the government or respective university boards.

Table 3. Generic strategies

		Frequency	Percent	Valid Percent	Cumulative Percent
Valid	Cost Leadership/Reduction	16	34.8	35.6	35.6
	Product Differentiation	11	23.9	24.4	60.0
	Focus	13	28.3	28.9	88.9
	Other	5	10.9	11.1	100.0
	Total	45	97.8	100.0	
Missing	System	1	2.2		
Total		46	100.0		

4.3 Strategic Orientation

According to Porter (1980) there are three (3) generic strategies i.e. cost leadership, differentiation, and, focus. In this study it was noted that various levels of complexity escalation point to differences in goals, scope and influence. Among the five universities assessed, no university uses only one strategic orientation in isolation. Two state owned universities indicated that they use mostly focus and cost reduction. One state owned university added that it uses product differentiation by adding block-release programmes to traditional campus-based instruction. The private universities assessed pointed that in addition to cost reduction they use product differentiation by offering evening and weekend-based programmes and one of them offers short courses (6 months certificate level) in the areas of Project Management, Monitoring and Evaluation, Business Administration, NGO Management, Computer Packages and Applications, Peace Building Studies, Chaplaincy and Church Administration. One university pointed out that it has a strategy of regional expansion while respondents from another university indicated that their university uses "results-based management." Regional expansion and "result-based management" were not initially suggested by the researcher in the questionnaire and appeared under the category "Others". Another respondent from a state-owned university underscored the complementarity of the strategies by indicating that "we have adopted a mixed strategy i.e. cost reduction (freeze recruitment), product differentiation (offering "unique" degrees) while in the same university another respondent indicated that the strategy adopted may dependent on the unit involved.

4.4 Compliance With Stafford Beer's Principles of Management

Stafford Beer (1984:9) noted that there is a "set of rules" (management principles) that applies to all viable systems, be it a human or an organization that comprises humans. These principles imply that (1) managerial, operational and environmental varieties, diffusing through an institutional system, tend to equate; they should be designed to do so with minimum damage to people and to cost (Beer 1979: 97). Hence the need of a clear delineation between operational, tactical and strategic functions. Otherwise, a lack of delineation between operational and tactical functions leads to the collapse of system 3 (monitoring) and system 3* (audit) into system 1 (implementation) bypassing system 2 (coordination). This leads to a culture of policing rather than supervision. The other possibility is when system 5 (policy and planning) collapses into system 3 (monitoring) and 3* (audit) bypassing system 4 (intelligence). This creates a situation where an organization is excessively centralized and inward looking and reacts to problem ad-hoc as they occur instead of charting ways for the future.

In this study, all universities assessed were compliant with Stafford Beer's principles of management but to various extents. There was (1) a clear delineation between operational, tactical and strategic roles, (2) inbuilt systems to ensure financial viability to a great extent. However, all universities scored low on (3)

Figure 3. Compliance to Beer (1989)'s management principles

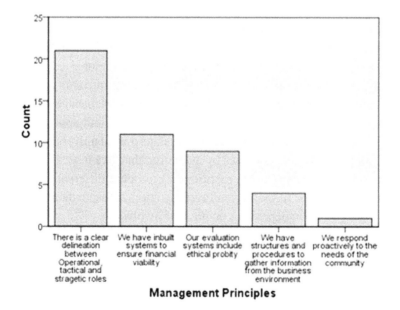

the existence of the existence of evaluation systems which include ethical probity, (4) the existence of structures and procedures to gather information from business environment, and (5) responding proactively to the needs of the community. Morover, these compliance to these principles decreases from principle one to principle 5. Figure 3 attests to that decrease.

4.5 Intelligence

4.5.1 External Communication

The second principle of organization implies that the four directional channels carrying information between the management unit, the operation, and the environment must each have a higher capacity to transmit a given amount of information relevant to variety selection in a given time than the originating subsystem has to generate it in that time (Beer 1979: 99). However, as Figure 3 indicates, the universities assessed scored low on the existence of structure and procedures to gather information from the environment and proactive response to the needs of the community. This shows a weakness of the intelligence function. The weakness of the intelligence function is also attested by the preferred modes of external communication.

Table 4 shows that despite the unprecedented development of information and communication technologies (ICTs) most universities assessed handle their external communication through face-to-face communication at offices, letters, and newspaper advertisement and statements.

Table 4. Preferred means of external communication

		Frequency	Percent	Valid Percent	Cumulative Percent
Valid	Face-to-face at our offices	15	32.6	33.3	33.3
	Letters	13	28.3	28.9	62.2
	Telephone	4	8.7	8.9	71.1
	E-mail	4	8.7	8.9	80.0
	Newspaper Advertisement and Statement	9	19.6	20.0	100.0
	Total	45	97.8	100.0	
Missing	System	1	2.2		
Total		46	100.0		

Table 5. Preferred means of internal communication

		Frequency	Percent	Valid Percent	Cumulative Percent
Valid	Face-to-face at our offices	20	43.5	44.4	44.4
	Letters	14	30.4	31.1	75.6
	Telephone	3	6.5	6.7	82.2
	E-mail	8	17.4	17.8	100.0
	Total	45	97.8	100.0	
Missing	System	1	2.2		
Total		46	100.0		

4.5.2 Internal Communication

A similar pattern is observed in internal communication (See Table 5) and this violates Beer (1979)'s the third principle of organization which stipulates that wherever the information carried on a channel capable of distinguishing a given variety crosses a boundary, it undergoes transduction; the variety of the transducer must be at least equivalent to the variety of the channel (Beer 1979:101). In other words, internal communications take a similar pattern to external communication with face-to-face communication at offices still leading, and letters coming in the second position. In internal communication, the use of the telephone is lower than the use of the e-mail although both are below average. No internal communication takes place in newspapers. The weaknesses of internal communication point to a failure to abide to Beer (1979)'s fourth principle of organization i.e. that the operation of the first three principles must be cyclically maintained through time without hiatus or lags (Beer 1979:258).

4.6. Organisational Pathologies

4.3.1 Alvarado's Pathologies

All organisations assessed suffered from Alavarado's pathologies to various extents. Bureaucratitis was leading accounting for 50% of the pathologies. As part of "bureaucratitis." "bad planning" or "no planning at all" was mentioned especially "repeated last minutes of changes of timetable in module based programmes when students have taken leave from their workplaces or cancelled international trips". Projectitis came second in the order of importance. Projectitis was also manifested, according to some respondents, in the way some members who are involved into projects that bring additional remuneration tend to neglect their normal duties but also staff who are not involved in the project tended to set aside work that is project related. Respondents reported lack of transparency and a veil of secrecy in externally funded projects. Respondents pointed out that in some externally funded projects both internal and outsourced employees were allocated "juicy" consultancy contracts without advertising or following proper tender procedures, while in another institution, respondents pointed to what they called "double dipping" this is a situation where a member of staff would be assigned on a project and get additional remuneration even when the member of staff used time and resources provided for his or her normal duties.

The third pathology in importance is technologytisis. Alvarado (1998) called it computerosis or informatosis i.e. plaguing organizations with specialized personnel, with marvelous machines and producing millions of characters printed on paper or displayed on video screens (Alvarado, 1998). In one organization, a respondent lamented that despite the presence of a computer on each desk, the use of interoffice memos is still very high. Meetingtisis was noted in one organization where meetings take precedence to teaching and research activities. Conflictitisis manifested itself in faculties and department fighting for recognition and resources. A respondent lamented that sometimes lecturers in the STEM (Science Technology Engineering and Mathematics) department "mocked" their colleagues in the humanities and social sciences for offering "useless" degrees. In another institutions, conflict erupted over the use of facilities. Other forms of conflicts were over resources especially faculties that hand funded projects or income generating programmes claiming that they should

Figure 4. Levels of Alvarado (1998)'s pathologies

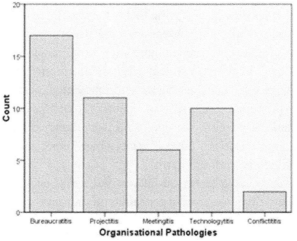

get more remuneration than those "who do not bring money." Sometimes personal conflicts spilled into the official business of an institution such as in one university a respondent claimed that one senior official (a woman) refused to approve the leave of a junior employee whose spouse was sick because "he spread rumours about her adulterous life," while in another institution, one respondent claimed that he was not shortlisted for an internal advertisement because he once chaired a disciplinary hearing where a senior member in the personel office that was being accused of sexually harassing students.

4.3.2 Beer's Pathologies

Stafford Beer (1989) pathologies were also noted in all universities. One was a collapse of system 3 i.e. "monitoring" into system 1 "implementation" bypassing system 2 i.e. "coordination". This situation was found in situation were senior administrators were given teaching duties, especially in part-time programmes although they never applied for teaching positions or shown passion for academic work. In another situations, an administrator prohibited her secretary from reading her "official" mail while in another university a respondent noted that the form of supervision they were receiving which included classroom visits by deans, PVCs and sometimes the VC "reminded him of his teaching time, several years ago".

The second of Beer's pathology was described by the respondents as most organisations being inward looking and hence either lacking system 4 "intelligence" or using the information available sparingly. As noted in 4.4 the intelligence function in all organization assessed is weak. One respondent noted that "we get to know about what other universities are doing only by hearsay or reading it in the newspapers." Another respondent noted that most of the institutions in Zimbabwe are now led by former students and staff of the university of Zimbabwe, hence they tendency to copy the practices that took place during their time at college although the context has totally changed. Another respondent point that currently institutions of higher learning in Zimbabwe are preoccupied more with complying to the directives of the regulating body, the Zimbabwe Council for Higher Education (ZIMCHE) rather than following market trends. This is an obstacle to innovation, according to the same respondent, since programmes take several months or sometimes years to be approved for years. The same respondent also indicated that whenever a university applies for a new programme, ZIMCHE "always wants a benchmark, as if in Zimbabwe we cannot bring anything new on this earth".

Many respondents noted that most universities suffer excessive centralization with some of them failing to separate academic programmes and political agenda.

One respondent noted for instance that from the time the government introduced The Zimbabwe Agenda for Sustainable Socio-Economic Transformation (ZIMASSET) and the need to build capacity in STEM (Science, Technology, Engineering and Mathematics) related disciplines, ZIMASSET and STEM are in all academic forums. The respondent noted that there is "a faint voice in favor of psychomotor disciplines, but it seems this is a personal initiative of the President". Another respondent pointed out that universities are normally managed within the context state bureaucracy hence even private universities do not have the agility it takes to follow market trends. They are subject to long administrative and regulatory procedures like their state owned counterparts.

The least suffered pathology is identity crisis. Many respondents noted that most universities can still recognize themselves although changes have taken place. However, one professor rejected this view noting that "the problem with universities in Zimbabwe is that they are all similar. Normally universities are put in a community in order to serve. However in Zimbabwe, even the so called technical universities are obliged to offer programmes in business, humanities and social sciences in order to increase the number of students and break-even." The ideas that commercial imperative are taking precedence over quality and academic excellence was also mentioned by a respondent who castigated, "the proliferation of parallel, block-release programmes which takes people below the cut point". However, another professor noted that "there is a need to demystify higher education in Zimbabwe." He added that we should not confuse a problem of poverty and a problem of ability. When higher education was introduced in Zimbabwe we had only one university hence the need to keep the cut point higher in order to avoid the overcrowding of that highly covered but small space. Now with more than 15 universities, we need to come to our sensesand acknowledge that education is a right and no longer a privilege. We cannot continue to structure universities as "inaccessible ivory towers".

Paradoxically, although the intelligence function is weak in all the university assessed and that around 25% of the respondents described universities as "inward looking", less than 10% of the responds described the universities assessed as "lacking external feedback". External feedback comes in diverse forms such as reports of visits by the regularity body ZIMCHE, complaints from students, parents, guardians and the public in general. Although around 40% of the respondents noted that their institutions do not have a "suggestion box", a respondent noted that universities receive feedback most of the time informally and in unexpected ways. "Universities are sometimes in the newspapers unfortunately for the wrong reasons such as when students or members staff have misbehaved or when an exam paper has leaked", he added. "However, in all those circumstances, university authorities take note and act." He concluded.

Figure 5. Levels of Beer (1989)'s pathologies

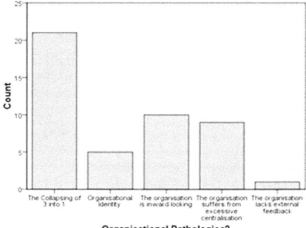

5. CONCLUSION

This study aimed at assessing the application of the Viable System Model (VSM) to Institutions of higher education in Zimbabwe. Principles of the VSM such as keeping adequate levels of "complexity escalation", designing organisations in ways that equip them with Beer (1989)'s five sub-systems for any viable system, complying with Beer (1989)'s four principles of management, having functioning intelligence channels and the absence of "organisational pathologies." The institutions assessed have no dedicated units for implementation, coordination, monitoring (and audit), intelligence and planning but these activities are carried through establish operation and reporting structures. One of them has an internal audit unit while another has a planning and corporate services and a quality insurance unit. Some of these activities are carried through ad-hoc committees and sometimes the assistance of external consultants is sought. All institutions assessed abide to Beer (1989) management principles to various degrees but they suffer from both Alvarado (1998)'s pathologies such as various forms of bureaucratitis, projectititis, meetingtitis, technologytitis and conflictitis. Beer (1989)'s pathologies are also prevalent including the collapose of system 3 into 1 i.e. collapsing of monitoring into operation (suppressing coordination) and this leads to policing rather than supervising. All the organisations assessed managed to maintain their identity in a changing environment but most of them are inward looking, extremely centralized and lack external feedback owing the weakness of the intelligence function.

6. RECOMMENDATIONS

This study recommends that in order to ensure the viability of institutions of higher education in Zimbabwe, the government should give universities a certain autonomy in terms of income generation and expenditure. Moreover, the government should ensure that the regulatory framework allows universities to generate income in order to cover their expenses and even make a profit. The government also should allow private institutions to create their own institutions in order to complement the government's effort in terms of education services provision, skills development, research and innovation. The institutions of higher education themselves should be aware that they are operating in a different environment hence the nee do increase their "requisite variety". The researchers recommend that the current level of "complexity escalation" of institutions of higher education in Zimbabwe should be maintained as it is unless there is change of mandate by the government or by the founding institutions. For a system to remain viable as a whole, all the sub-systems have to be viable. Institutions of higher education in Zimbabwe should explore ways of transforming or simply discarding faculties and units which are not viable. The intelligence function should be considered as part and parcel of good business, hence universities need to put in place mechanisms of getting information from the environment. In order to quicken their external and internal communications, universities needs to adopt information and communication technologies (ICTs) as their preferred modes of communication unlike the current situation where communication is done mainly through letters or face-to-face in the office although there is increased use of e-mails in internal communications. All organisations assessed need to initiate restructuring and change processes in order to end or at least minimize organizational pathologies. Institutions of higher education need to ensure their viability by enrolling more students, adopting value chain and integrated approach to service provision, recruiting and retaining competent and experienced academic and non-academic staff and ensuring transparency at all levels. Entrepreneurs should explore higher education as a possible investment area while communities should initiate synergies with institutions of higher for research-informed policy and science based solutions to societal and technical problems. More empirical studies are needed in order to create the awareness of the Viable System Model (VSM) as a tool for diagnosis, design and improvement and success stories should be made available to the public as case studies.

REFERENCES

Altbach, P. A., & Knight, J. (2007). The Internationalisation of Higher Education: Motivations and Realities. *Journal of Studies in International Education*, *11*(3-4), 290–305. doi:10.1177/1028315307303542

Alvarado, G. S. M. (1988). *Organizational pathology. 26th International Conference of the Institute of Management Sciences*, Copenhagen, Denmark.

Aminbeidokhti, A. A., Talebi, A., & Nemati, M. A. (2014). Studying the Effect of Cybernetic Pattern on Quality Assurance by Reviewing The Role of Learning Organisation Mediator Variable in General Universities of Tehran. *Kuwait Chapter of Arabian Journal of Business and Management Review*, *3*(10), 12–22. doi:10.12816/0018387

Ashby, W. R. (1956). *An Introduction to Cybernetics*. Chapman & Hall. doi:10.5962/bhl.title.5851

Beer, S. (1959). *Cybernetics and Management*. English University Press.

Beer, S. (1989). *The Viable System Model: Its Provenance, Development, Methodology and Pathology*. Cwarel Isaf Institute.

Bozeman, D. P., Kacmar, K. M. (1997) A Cybernetic Model of Impression Management Processes in Organizations, *Organisational Behaviour and Human Decision-Processes, 69*(1), 9-30.

Burgess, N., & Wake, N. (2012). The applicability of the Viable Systems Model as a diagnostic for small to medium sized enterprises. *International Journal of Productivity and Performance Management*, *62*(1), 29–46. doi:10.1108/17410401311285282

Clarke, F., Dean, G., & Edwards, J. R. (2013) *An historical perspective from the work of Chambers from: The Routledge Companion to Accounting Communication*. Routledge. https://www.routledgehandbooks.com/doi/10.4324/9780203593493.ch3

Espejo, R. (1993) Giving Requisite Variety to Strategy and Information Systems in Stowell et al. (1993). Systems Science, New York, Plenum Press.

Falsafinejad, M., & Hashembeik, N. (2013, September). A Cybernetic Modelling Framework in Higher Education Administration (Case study: Isfahan Medical Sciences UniversityIsfahan Medical Sciences University). *International Journal of Scientific and Research Publications*, *3*(9), 1–4.

Gault, R. H. (1907). A history of the questionnaire method of research in psychology. *Research in Psychology.*, *14*(3), 366–383. doi:10.1080/08919402.1907.10532551

Heylighen, F. (1992). Principles of Systems and Cybernetics: an evolutionary perspective. In Trappl, R. (1992) (ed.) Cybernetics and Systems. Singapore: World Science.

Hilder, T. (1995). *The Viable System Model Cavendish Software Ltd.*

Kapungu, R. S. (2008). *The Pursuit of Higher Education in Zimbabwe:A Futile Effort?* Center for International Private Enterprise Economic Reform Feature Service.

Kay, R., Alder, J., Brown, D., & Houghton, P. (2013). Management Cybernetics: A New Institutional Framework for Coastal Management. *Coastal Management, 31*(3), 213–227. doi:10.1080/08920750390198513

Kurasha, P. (2015, July). The Future of Higher Education in Zimbabwe: A Constantly Moving Target. *Zimbabwe Journal of Educational Research, 27*(2), 204–220.

Lucas, S. R. (2014). Beyond the Existence Proof: Ontological Conditions, Epistemological Implications, and In-Depth Interview Research. *Quality & Quantity, 48*(1), 387–408. doi:10.100711135-012-9775-3

Mack, N., Woodsong, C., MacQueen, K. M., Guest, G., & Namey, E. (2005). *Qualitative research methods: A data collector's field guide.* Family Health International.

Magwa, W. (2015, July). Enhancing Africa's Renewal through Internationalisation of Higher Education: A Review of Management Strategies and Issues. *Zimbabwe Journal of Educational Research, 27*(2), 255–272.

Malik, F. (2016). *Strategies for Managing Complex Systems: A Contribution to Management Cybernetics for Complex Systems, Frankfurt-am-Main.* Campus Verlag.

Matua, G. A. (2015). Choosing phenomenology as a guiding philosophy for nursing research. *Nurse Researcher, 22*(4), 30–34. doi:10.7748/nr.22.4.30.e1325 PMID:25783150

Mawonde, A. (2015). Government to Wean Off Universities. *The Herald.*

Mhukahuru, C. (2015) Universities brace for 50% government cuts to salaries. *University World News,* 367. https://www.universityworldnews.com/article. php?story=20150513172957289

Preece, G., Shaw, D., & Hayashi, H. (2015). Application of the Viable System Model to analyse communications structures: A case study of disaster response in Japan. *European Journal of Operational Research, 243*(1), 312–322. doi:10.1016/j. ejor.2014.11.026

Puche, J., Ponte, B., Costas, J., Pino,R., de la Fuente, D. (2016) Systemic approach to supply chain management through the viable system model and the theory of constraints. *Production Planning & Control, 27*(5), 421-430.

Rios, J. P. (2012). *Design and Diagnosis for Sustainable Organisations: The Viable System Model*. Springer-Verlag. doi:10.1007/978-3-642-22318-1

Rourke, A. J., & Coleman, K. S. (2011). Pedagogy Leading Technology in higher education: New Technologies, New Pedagogies. Champaign, Il: Common Ground Publishing.

Saunders, M., Lewis, P., & Thornhill, A. (2009). *Research methods for business students* (4th ed.). Person Education Limited.

Schwaninger, M. (2006). Design for Viable Organisations: The Diagnostic Power of the Viable System Model, Kybernetes. *The International Journal of Systems and Cybernetics, 35*(7/8), 955–971. doi:10.1108/03684920610675012

Shizha, E., & Kariwo, M. (2011). *"The Development of Higher Education in Zimbabwe" in Shizha, E. &Kariwo, M. (2011) Education and Development in Zimbabwe: A Social, Political and Economic Analysis*. Springer.

Steinhaeusser, T., Elezi, F., Tommelein, I. D., & Lindemann, U. (2015). Management Cybernetics as a Theoretical Basis for Lean Construction Thinking. *Lean Construction Journal*, 01-14

Umpleby, S. (2006). *Fundamentals and history of cybernetics: Development of the theory of complex adaptive systems*. SCIIIS. http://info-sciiis.org/IIIS_Videos/website/IIISV06.asp

Van Vliet, V. (2011). *Management cybernetics*. ToolsHero. https://www.toolshero.com/change-management/management-cybernetics

Varghese, N. V. (2008) Globalisation of higher education and cross border student mobility. *UNESCO IIEP Research Paper.* Springer.

Wiener, N. (1948) Cybernetics: Or Control and Communication in the Animal and the Machine. Mass. MIT Press.

Chapter 7

Theory and Theorizing in Information Systems

Mampilo Phahlane
University of South Africa, South Africa

ABSTRACT

Markus and Robey, in their seminal paper, assert that good theory guides research and when appropriately used it increases the likelihood that Information technology will be implemented with desirable results in any organization. This laments the importance of using theory in information systems research because of explanations it provides and paying attention to other areas that might otherwise be ignored. Researchers in the IS field such as Gregor, Grover, Corley and Gioia, Weber, and Whetten have discussed and classified theory and what constitutes a theoretical contribution. Despite the importance that many researchers ascribe to theory and theorising, the development of new theory and the refinement of existing theories there's a belief the information systems discipline has neglected theory and theorising. This, however, suggests that there's enough guidance on theory and theorising within the IS field and it is documented for different contexts and boundaries.

INTRODUCTION

Markus & Robey (1988) in their seminal paper assert that good theory guides research and when appropriately used it increases the likelihood that Information technology will be implemented with desirable results in any organization, for its users and those affected by it. This laments the importance of using theory in information systems research because of explanations it provides and paying attention to other areas that might otherwise be ignored. Researchers in the IS field such as Gregor (2006),

DOI: 10.4018/978-1-7998-9687-6.ch007

Copyright © 2024, IGI Global. Copying or distributing in print or electronic forms without written permission of IGI Global is prohibited.

Grover et al. (2008), Corley and Gioia (2011), Weber (2012) and Whetten (1989) have discussed and classified theory and what constitutes a theoretical contribution. The works of Hassan et al. (2019), Guillemette & Paré (2012), Grover & Lyytinen (2023) and many others have contributed to theorizing in the IS discipline.

Despite these progresses made in the field, there's still a belief that the information systems discipline has neglected theory and theorising. By their very nature, theories are incomplete, for no one theory can explain and include all phenomena, and thus, they can only be approximations (Hassan et al., 2019). This chapter, however, suggests that there's enough guidance on theory and theorising within the IS field and that it is done in different ways and needs to be formulated and assessed according to the different contexts. Further, if researchers wish to continue to expand theory and theorising within the IS field, they should continue to do so with some of the guidelines mentioned in this paper. The aim of this paper is to highlight some of the ways in which researchers in the information systems field have developed and how theorizing has happened. The rest of the chapter is structured as follows: what is theory is discussed next, what theory is not follows this discussion and the field of IS theory and theorising follow and conclusion discussed last.

WHAT IS THEORY

Theory largely depends on assumptions related to philosophy and discipline (Gregor, 2006). Within the natural sciences, theory is viewed as providing explanations, and predictions and as being testable positivist stance (Popper, 2005). Within the interpretive tradition however, theory is constructed from "lived experiences", "understanding meaning", "multiple knowledges existing". Weber (2012) describes theory as a specific kind of model that is intended to describe for some subset of events in the real world. Theory describes reality because of collaborative consensus, and it is an artifact built by humans to achieve a specifics purpose. Theory by nature represents a platform for research to be transdisciplinary, multidisciplinary, and interdisciplinary as most fields develop, apply, and evaluate theories, this makes theories interconnected ideas with predictive and explanatory properties (Kerlinger et al., 2000).

(Joseph, 2021) asserts that theory offers to ability to predict, validate or disproof hypotheses for quantitative research-based methodology to develop theory within this paradigm. It also offers explanatory power and value on the process of conceptualising and demystifying social phenomena.

There are other words or names used in synonym as theory, these concepts are used interchangeably with the term theory. The concepts include words such as paradigm, model, view/worldview, principle, approach, framework, perspective,

Theory and Theorizing in Information Systems

and thesis, (Stoeffler & Joseph, 2020; Zastrow & Kirst-Ashman, 2016). Grant theories, such as systems theory (ST), activity theory (AT), actor-network theory (ANT), contingency theory (CT), diffusion of innovation (DOI) theory, structuration theory (ST), and the technology acceptance model (TAM) are endorsed by more than one discipline and are the most used theories in the IS field (Iyamu, 2021). Hence, theories are inherently transdisciplinary.

Types of Theories

Marcus & Robey (1988) differentiate between variance and process theories. They explain variance theory as entities that explain the behaviour of another entity. Variance theories are concerned with predicting levels of outcome from levels of contemporaneous predictor variables; variance theories are concerned with explaining how outcomes develop over time. Process theories is about how entities change and develop and outcomes are not conceived as variables that can take on a range of values, but rather as discrete or discontinuous phenomena. Their three dimensions of causal structure as causal agency, logical structure, and level of analysis.

Table 1. variance and process theory comparison, logical structure (Marcus & Robey, 1988)

Variance theory Process theory		
Role of time	Static	Longitudinal
Definition	Entities that explain the behaviour of other entities, they are mostly concerned with the "what" of theory	A system of ideas that explain how an entity changes over time. Chance and random events play a role
Assumptions	An outcome will occur when necessary and sufficient conditions are met	Outcomes may not be met even when conditions are present
Elements	Variables	Discrete outcomes
Logical form	If x then y, then if more x then more y	If not x then not y, cannot be extended to more x or more y

Logical structure in theory refers to the nature of the relationship between elements identified as antecedents and those identified as outcomes. In variance theories, ante cedents are conceived as necessary and sufficient conditions for the outcomes to occur.

Theory According to Gregor (2006)

Gregor (2006) in her seminal work *Nature of Theory in Information Systems* classified theory as theory for analysis, explanation, prediction, explanation and prediction and design and action, the table below describes the theory types.

Table 2. Theory types in Information systems (2006)

Theory type	Distinguishing attributes
Analysis (Type I)	Focused on "what is" The theory describes and analyses and doesn't go beyond that. No causal relationships among phenomena are inferred and no predictions made
Explanation	Describes "what is, how, why, when and where Explanation theory is focused on explanations but does not aim to predict with any precision, there are no testable propositions
Prediction	Describes "what is and what will be" The theory provides predictions and testable propositions but does not have well-developed justifiable causal explanations
Explanation and prediction	Describes "what is, how, when, where and what will be" Provides descriptions and has testable propositions and explanations
Design and action	Describes a "way of doing something" Design and action theory provides a detailed prescription in the form of methods, techniques for creating an artefact

Theory for analysis describes what is and doesn't explain causality and no predictions are made and are descriptive and is most valuable when little is known about phenomena. Theory for explanation describes how and why certain things happen, and it is used to understand. Theory of prediction say what will be but not why it will be like that; this type of theory is able to predict outcomes from a set of explanatory factors without explaining underlying causal connections between dependent and independent variables in any detail. Theory of explanation and prediction This type of theory is focused on how, what is, why, what will be and when, and it implies an understanding of underlying causes and prediction, as well as description of theoretical constructs and relationships among them. Theory of design and action discusses how to do something, and it is about form, function, methods used for IS development, research associated with design sciences.

Theory and Theorizing in Information Systems

Critique of Gregor's Typology Theories

Weber (2012) counter argues Gregor's typology of theories in the following ways: Weber says theory for analysis is not a theory but a typology; and that typologies underpin the exact definition of the construct in a theory but lack certain characteristics that are important to theory. Theory for explaining and theory for predicting may or may not constitute theory, Weber further argues that both types of theories sometimes lack clarity and precision with constructs, their relationships, states, and events they cover, and since theory for explaining is associated with interpretivist paradigm; they often lack rigor, they can be regarded as models because of lack of qualities needed to constitute a theory. Theory for design and action can be categorized with theory for explaining and theory for predicting.

Weber (2012) asserts that his view of theory is associated with Gregor (2006)'s theory for explaining and predicting as there's precision with constructs, their relationships, and often have clear descriptions of states and events as they occur, and a rigorous research methodology is defined.

Theory According to Weber (2012)

Theories provide a representation of someone's perceptions of how a subset of real-world phenomena should be described. In this view, theory can be conceived as specialized ontologies. Therefore, careful analysis of the notion of and components of a theory must be rooted in a rigorously formulated nature of that reality The elements of a specific theory can then be evaluated in terms of how well they map to or instantiate this generalized reality.

Weber conceptualised formalised generalised ontology as a basis of their analysis, and it is based on the work of Bunge (1977 and 1979) to include the following constructs.

These constructs and their explanations are linked to what constitutes theory, and terms theory as an artifact built by humans to achieve some purpose and it is deemed as *conceptual* rather than a concrete thing. Weber further proposed a framework to evaluate the quality of theory that is unfolding, and it includes the following to be considered based on Grifith et al.'s (2003) work.

This criteria for evaluating the quality of theory can used to define an existing theory or to build a new theory.

139

Table 3. Ontological constructs (Weber, 2012)

Construct	Explanation
Thing	Things that exist in the world such as substantial (concrete) or conceptual
Composite thing	Things made up of other things which can be referred to as components
Property	Concrete things possess properties, and describe different features of the world
Class	Things that share common property make up a class of things
Attribute	Properties are because of our perceptions of them, and these perceptions may or may not be true. Various attributes exist: *Attributes in general* belong to a class of things. *Attributes in particular* are attributes that belong to *specific* things in a class of things. *Intrinsic attributes* represent properties of individual things. *Mutual attributes* represent properties of two or more things. *Emergent attributes* (or in general) are attributes of composite things that do not belong to their components. *Complex attributes* (or in general) are attributes that are made up of the conjunction of simple attributes. A vector of *attributes represents* a state of a thing (its attributes in general along with their associated values). States can also be conceived as a complex attribute. The complex attribute *in general* might be called "perceived utilities and for the particular user it has the value.
Lawful state	Some states of a thing are deemed *lawful* (they obey natural or human-made laws); others are deemed unlawful
Event	An event that a thing undergoes is represented by a change from one of its states to another of its states (at least one of its attributes changes values).
Lawful event	Some events that a thing undergoes are deemed *lawful* (they obey natural or human-made laws); others are deemed unlawful. If an event has an unlawful beginning or end state, it will be unlawful.
History of a thing	The history of a thing is a *sequence* (ordered set) of its states (e.g., the states that a thing traverses over time are ordered by time).
Interaction between things	Two things interact when the history of one thing is not independent of the history of the other thing.

Grover & Lyytinen's (2023) Pursuit of Innovative Theory Description

Grover & Lyytinen's (2023) paper discussed the pursuit of innovative theory in the digital age and scrutinize further the idea of blue-ocean theorizing and review the characteristics, impediments, and merits of developing innovative theory. They further suggest six assumptions that guide dominant, legitimate forms of the field's theorizing. They identify and review institutional barriers that limit the development of innovative theory. These barriers form a part of shared institutionalized known assumptions guiding research and justifying beliefs concerning research legitimacy and value. and they are categorised according to *theory building*, *use of reference theories* and *theoretical imagination*.

Theory and Theorizing in Information Systems

Table 4. Weber's (2012) criteria for evaluating theory based on Grifith et al.'s (2003)

Criteria	Evaluation
Parts	
Constructs	The extend to which individuals rely on knowledge and made available to those who seek to access it
Associations	Associations are related to interactions between the constructs
States	States are boundaries defined to fall within the theory and those outside the theory
Events	An occasion defined as either inside or outside of the boundary of the theory
Whole	
Importance	The meaning of the theory/paper for practice and other researchers
Novelty	Refers to phenomena or constructs that have not received attention prior
Parsimony	Choosing a simple explanation to define constructs
Level	The level which the theory can reference (mid-range, grand theory etc)
Falsifiability	If the hypotheses or constructs can be proven wrong

Constraints Related to Theory Building

Barrier 1: Building innovative theory requires that all elements of theorizing: observations, constructs, and logic, this could be done by embedding constructs related to the IS field.

Barrier 2: Good theory needs solid descriptive foundations and rigorous descriptive inquiries and field work.

Barrier 3: Is related to the belief that empirical data complicates the need for innovative theory. Inductive approaches whether qualitative and quantitative needs to be above the study so that generalizability could apply.

Constraints Related Use of Reference

Barrier 4: Reference theories are treated as absolute truths. The focus should be on falsifying rather than corroborating reference theories with tendencies such as publishing only significant results, deploying reference theory with high plausibility to digital phenomena and building operational models and not theoretical models.

Barriers Relates to Theoretical Imagination

Barrier 6: Literature and empirical evidence need to be integrated in research articles by breaking up the research paper genre and loosen the tight link between theory and evidence by grounding it in literature or testing through data.

Barrier 7: Misplaced parameter values to evaluate innovative theory have the potential to change the direction and organization of the discourse in the topic.

What Theory Is Not

Theory building is rather a daunting task and unfortunately, the literature on theory building can leave a reader more confused about how to write a paper that contains strong theory (Freese, 1984). Sutton & Staw (1995) described what theory is not, this includes the following: *references are not theory*- this includes listing references to existing theories and mentioning the names of those and calling that a theory. *Data is not theory*- and both play different roles in during the research process, data describe which empirical patterns were observed and theory explains why empirical patterns were observed or are expected to be observed. *Lists of variables of constructs are not theory*- lists of constructs or variables do not make a strong theoretical argument but rather why certain variables are expected to be strong predictors. Diagrams are not theory- good theory is representational and with logical explanations. Hypotheses or predictions are not theory- hypotheses are crucial as they serve as a bridge between theory and data. An analysis on Sutton and Staw's *What theory is not* done by DiMaggio (1995) and they suggested two modifications as an enhancement to Sutton and Staw's paper, that good theory is challenging to create routinely, because goodness is multidimensional, and that theory combines approaches theorizing and this requires compromise between competing and mutually incompatible values. The second one is that theory construction is a cooperative venture between author and readers which is theory acceptance in a field of study rides on much more than scientific potential to exercise judgment and pluck, the second suggests the importance of environment and luck.

POPULAR IS THEORIES IN LITERATURE

Ramírez-Correa (2016) documented the most popular theories in information systems, and they were identified as *dynamic capabilities* which is about restructuring organizations' internal and external competencies according to competitive market conditions and situations based on the organization's rare resources (Eisenhardt & Martin, 2000).

Transaction cost economics considers the transaction as the most basic unit of measure and focuses on how much effort, resources, or cost is necessary for two parties to complete an exchange (Williamson, 1998). A*bsorptive capacity theory* is an organization's ability to recognize the value of new information, assimilate it, and apply it when necessary to gain competitive advantage in the field (Cohen & Levinthal, 1990). *Competitive strategy* identifies how an organization contends in a specific industry and gets an edge on a competitive advantage over other competitors by using different strategies to do so (Porter, 1990).

Resource based view of the firm alleges that organizations can achieve strategic success through acquiring, developing, and deploying scarce resources and skills over time and gain competitive advantage over other organizations (Barney et al., 2001). *Knowledge based theory* of the firm explains how organizations establish soft power in the market to gain competitive advantage over others using knowledge and information resources to do so (Grant, 1996). *General theory of entrepreneurship* seeks to understand and describe the societal phenomenon observable in the creation of new economic activity and its processes (Shane, 2003).

Institutional theory is based on the belief that the internal and external environment which the organization operates in exerts certain pressures and that influences how the organization react to certain events and processes (Meyer& Rowan, 1977). *Stakeholder theory* acknowledges the interconnected relationships between a business and its customers, suppliers, employees, investors, communities, and others who have an interest in the organization and the value created by the organization must be shared with the stakeholders and not just shareholders (Freeman, 2001). Another category of theories used in information systems are related to the acceptance of technologies and include theories such as *sense making theory which* is about employees in an organization make sense of unexpected events through a process of action, selection, and interpretation (Weick, 1995).

Administrative behaviour theory which is about how decisions in organizations are made through administrative processes such as training, information dissemination, and other standard operating procedures (Simon, 1950). *Organizational learning theory* is about the process which organizations acquire new skills, knowledge and capabilities that enable them to adapt to the changing environment and improve performance (Levitt & March, 1988). *Prospect theory* is a behavioural theory that demonstrates how people decide between alternatives that involve risk and uncertainty (Kahneman & Tversky, 2013). *Contingency* theory is related to leadership and well a leader in an organization adjusts their leadership style matches a specific situation (Miller, 1981).

Resource dependency theory asserts that organizations develop strategies and engage in some activities is decreasing dependency on resources, so gaining bargaining power against the providers of those resources and getting a competitive advantage (Pfeffer, 2005). *Cultural dimensions theory* is about how societal culture influences the values of organizational members, and how these values relate to individual behaviour (Hofstede, 2011). *Theory of planned behaviour* asserts that behaviours are influenced by intentions, which are determined by three factors, which are attitudes, subjective norms, and perceived behavioural control (Ajzen, 1991).

IS success model is about system quality, information quality, service quality, (intention to) use, user satisfaction, and net benefits of the system (DeLone & McLean, 2003). *Task technology fit* (Goodhue and Thompson, 1995) is based on adopted information system to have a positive impact on user performance, it must be used and must match the task it was designed for. *Theory of reasoned action* is about beliefs, attitudes, intentions, and behaviour forming a causal chain, so that beliefs lead to attitudes, and attitudes in turn lead to intentions and behaviour (Fishbein, 1979).

Diffusion of innovations explain how, why, and at what rate new ideas and technology is adopted in society or a group of individuals (Rogers et al., 2014). Most of these theories are organization level theories and are used to underpin phenomena at a societal, group or organizational level. There are theories focused on an individual level of analysis and they're usually borrowed from disciplines such as psychology and these include *self-determination theory* which is about understanding social conditions and how they influence motivation and what makes individuals feel more motivated to act when they think that what they do will influence the outcome (Deci & Ryan, 2012). *Social cognitive theory* is an interpersonal level theory that is focused on the interaction between individuals, the environment, and their behaviour (Bandura, 1999). *Technology acceptance model* (TAM) explains how to encourage users on how to use technology (Davis, 1987). TAM has many variations such as the unified theory of acceptance and use of technology (UTAUT) (Venkatesh et al., 2003) and other variations of it that followed.

The Field of IS Theory and Theorising

Hassan &Lowry (2015) describe two central constituents of theory that have not received much attention from the IS field: concepts and propositions. Using these descriptions, they distinguish between grand theories, meta-theories, empirical observation, and conceptual formation, and propose the IS community consider and engage theories of the middle range.

Sandberg & Alvesson (2021) categorised theory in management and organizational studies as a typology consisting of five main theory types: explaining, comprehending, ordering, enacting and provoking theories.

Theory and Theorizing in Information Systems

Zhang & Gable (2017) suggest theorizing IS studies or building theory in IS from a multilevel perspective and as this approach offers an alternative means to examine phenomena by simultaneously accounting for multiple levels of analysis.

Hassan et al (2022) focused on the products of theorizing rather than on what theories are, and assemble and analyse products, question, paradigm, law, framework, myth, analogy, metaphor, model, concept, construct, statement, and hypothesis—that are rarely discussed together in any depth in the IS field and combine them into a coherent theorizing framework.

Markus & Rowe (2018) suggested that three dimensions of a framework concerning the theorist's views about the reality and meaning of causation (Causal Ontology), about that which is changed in causation (Causal Trajectory), and about the role of humans and/or technology in bringing about the change (Causal Autonomy).

Burton-Jones et al. (2015) define a perspective as a researcher's choice of the types of concepts and relationships used to construct a theory, and examine three perspectives: process, variance, and systems.

Rivard (2021)'s article proposes that theory building resembles a craft more than an art or a science and proposed an iterative model which consists of activities and outcomes.

Mueller & Urbach (2017) transposed Whetten's (1989) seminal thoughts on the why, what, and how in theories and structured the discussion according to the why, what, and how of theory and theorizing in IS research. They conclude the paper by suggesting that we engage in theory and theorizing not merely for the sake of theory. What is more important is a genuine intention to make sense of the world around us; to advance our collective ability to describe, explain, and predict the phenomena we study; and to inform managerial practice.

Niederman & March (2019a) discuss the "theoretical lens" concept and assert that despite its growing prevalence in the literature, the term theoretical lens is not a major element of the prevalent conceptualization of the philosophy of science, nor is it part of the standard approach to the scientific method. And they conclude that the term lens implies three elements: the lens or transforming device itself, the observation target, and the observer.

Niederman & March (2019b) present an alternative view of theory that emphasizes a variety of ways in which theory can be conceptualized, i.e., a variety of meta-theories. Specifically, examine three alternative metatheories: network, process, and co-evolution. The study compared underlying conceptualizations, entities, relationships, and methodologies with each other and with variance meta-theory.

Hirscheim (2019) however says that instead of focusing on what contributions one's research makes to theory, we should focus on the contributions one's research makes to understanding—What new insights does the research generate, as they relate to changing or helping practice? Do the insights resonate with practitioners? How would these insights change the way practitioners see problems, particular solutions?

Post et al (2020) suggested that advancing theory with review articles requires an integrative and generative approach. They propose a non-exhaustive set of avenues for developing theory with a review article: exposing emerging perspectives, analysing assumptions, clarifying constructs, establishing boundary conditions, testing new theory, theorizing with systems theory, and theorizing with mechanisms.

Gorver et al. (2008) propose ways to improve the rigor and originality of forward-looking theory in the IS field. This is accomplished by proposing a set of guidelines outlining how prospective authors should prepare their manuscripts or approach their research problems to enhance theory.

Hassan et al., (2019) suggested that a focus on the theorizing process within the context of discovery holds the key to building exciting IS theories. They suggest that focusing on the foundational and generative broad practices of theorizing within the context of discovery, holds the key to building exciting IS theories.

IS THEORISING AS A DISCURSIVE PRACTICE

Foundational practice are discursive theorizing practices that involve high level concepts such as discourse formulation, leveraging the paradigm or disciplinary questions shared by the community and bridging no discursive practices that assist the field in recognising opportunities for creating theories and applying them. *Generative theorizing* practices support or modify the development of the discourse and include analogising, metaphorizing, mythologising, and modelling and constructing frameworks. Theory components include frameworks, concepts, models, claims and boundaries. Guillimet and Paré (2012) wrote about theory of the contributions of the IT function in organizations, this included a typology of ideal IT management profiles and proposes a contingency explanation of the contribution made by IT functions in organizations, and lastly it explores the circumstances under which ideal profiles are adopted in organizations. Whetten (1989) discussed what constitutes a publishable theory paper by asking these seven questions.

Whetten's guide for evaluating theoretical contribution focuses on questions that are common with reviewers and editors of academic papers.

Corley & Gioia (2011) What Constitutes a Theoretical Contribution

The researchers start by asking "what is a theoretical contribution" as in what implies a significant theoretical advancement in understanding phenomena. A synthesis that

146

Theory and Theorizing in Information Systems

Table 5. Whetten (1989) Theoretical contribution evaluation questions

Question	Explanation
What's new?	Does the paper make a significant, value-added contribution to current thinking, how different is it from current thinking. Proposed changes can be calibrated in terms of scope and degree
So what?	Are linkages to research evident (either explicitly laid out or easily reliably deduced) Are solutions proposed for remedying alleged deficiencies in current theories. Simply tweaking a conceptual model is not enough as the aim is to alter research practice.
Why so?	Are the underlying logic and supporting evidence compelling? Are the authors view and assumptions explicit and believable? Theory development papers should be built on a foundation of convincing arguments and grounded in reasonable, explicit views of human nature and practice.
Well done?	Does the paper reflect seasoned thinking, conveying completeness and thoroughness? Are these theoretical elements (What, How, why, When, Where Who) covered, giving the paper a conceptually well rounded, rather than a superficial quality
Done well?	Is there a logical flow of ideas? Is it enjoyable to read? Is the paper long enough to cover the subject but short enough to be interesting?
Why now?	Is the topic of current interest to scholars in this area? Will it likely advance current discussions, stimulate new discussions, or revitalize old discussions?
Who cares?	This is related to the academic community interest and broader audience, to make a more significant contribution to current thinking and research practice

they have conducted reveal that *originality* and *utility* dominate considerations for theoretical contribution. Originality represents either an incremental or a more about advancing an understanding of phenomena, these could be described as incremental insight, revelatory or transformative thinking as factors affecting the creation of a theoretical framework. The insights mentioned must also be useful as well, it must have potential to either improve current research or managerial practice. Specific utility refers to the rigor or the potential to be operationalised and tested and practical utility when theory can be directly applied to the problems practicing managers and other organizational practitioners face.

CONCLUSION

The IS field and theory is one that keeps evolving, this evolution however has yielded many branches on what theory is and how to theorise in the field. For example, there is still little agreement on the universal definition on what theory is and why is it so difficult to develop strong theory (Sutton & Staw, 1995). Despite this, Mueller &

Urbach (2017) assert that the IS discipline has a strong need for conceptual plurality and the promotion of a vast array of different philosophical approaches that each produce different notions of what theory and theorizing mean.

Interpretive researchers could gain from the guidance of Walsham (1995), that there's several ways of using theory in interpretive research in IS; as an initial guide to design and data collection (midrange inductive, deductive approach); as an iterative process of data collection and analysis (grounded theory approach) and as a final product of the research. These approaches are all important and assist in the development of theory (Grover & Lyytinen, 2023). Further, theories should be understood as sets of credible, persuasive, penetrating ideas about IT and its interaction with human being shared by a community that is constantly reshaping, redefining, and repositioning itself due to the emergence of new ideas, new phenomena, and new data. Authors and reviewers in the IS field need to understand that innovative theorizing comes in different forms and needs to be formulated and assessed differently in different contexts. Although some have deemed the endeavour of theorising difficult, seeking to better understand the characteristics of the choices that lead to developing of high impact and high-quality theories focused on phenomena that clearly defines its constructs, associations and inside boundary states and events. These events are curial choices as they affect the quality of the whole; a theory's importance, its novelty, its parsimony (Weber 2012). Despite all these efforts by researchers in the field, (Nierderman & March, 2019a) assert that there's still a long-unresolved debate about the nature of the discipline: whether one can better define it in a narrow way as a discipline that studies primarily how IS operates in organizations or as a broader area which considers any application of computing technology how it is used by humans and, in turn, what effects on humans individually and collectively it creates.

Despite the numerous ways of theory and theorising in IS, Rindova (2008) provides general guidelines for publishing theory when you're a developing researcher, a start of some sort as a guideline intended for those starting in the field, but I do think they could be applicable for all researchers who want to build and develop theory in the IS field. These guidelines include *avoid isolation*- Discussing and presenting ideas is the process through which one can understand how one's audience, rather than one's mind, views the potential contribution. *Put your best foot forward*- published papers tend to look different from the papers originally submitted. The published versions have acquired additional elegance and polish from the additional crafting that has taken place during the review process. *Rejoice but revise*- carefully crafted and original submission often will generate a revise-and resubmit, which is the proverbial foot in the door. *Revise not resent*-Everyone knows how difficult it is to deal with criticism and rejection, especially early in one's career, when so

Theory and Theorizing in Information Systems

much hinges on the success of a single paper. Its best to realise how these negative emotional reactions to a hinder our own progress.

Another important consideration is boundary conditions and context as important in IS theorising. given the field's fast changing phenomena. Therefore, we need to search for new concepts that contribute to explaining why, and how, and/or explaining and predicting IS phenomena. Given the pervasiveness and speed of digitalization, accelerated by the pandemic, and its poorly understood impact—it is critical to foster flexibility in our theorizing. We believe that this will facilitate our ownership of the intellectual regime where digital technologies and human enterprise interact; other fields will have ample reasons to look to us for deeper insights at this critical junction (Grover & Lyytinen, 2023).

Implications of the Paper

The paper constitutes a series of ways on how to theorise in the IS field and how researchers can use phenomena to develop theory and theorise, therefore influencing the practice and researchers in the field. In other words, that it reflects the social sciences as diverse and essential in theory building exercises. It is worth emphasizing that because theories drive vital policies and shape public interest, the research community should be more involved in evaluating their worth. This chapter suggests the various ways of using theory and how to theorise in the IS discipline.

What Can Future Researchers on The Topic Build On

For researchers seeking to articulate a new theory, their first concern should be the choice of the focal phenomena. They must select focal phenomena that the field and colleagues will deem to be important, either because the focal phenomena's importance is readily apparent, or the rhetoric the researchers provide to support the importance of the focal phenomena is compelling. Sometimes a key issue is to reframe well-known phenomena in new, interesting ways or to point out important phenomena that previously had gone unseen (Weber, 2003). The focal phenomena must also be conceived at a level that allows a meso-level theory to be formulated. Once the focal phenomena are defined clearly, researchers can then build the parts of the theory – constructs, associations, inside-boundary states, and inside-boundary events. They can seek to ensure the theory is falsifiable through clear, precise definitions or specification of the theory's parts. Through selective choice of constructs, associations, and inside-boundary states and events, they can also seek to ensure the theory is parsimonious. They must then realistically evaluate their theory's "utility" and "originality" (Corley & Gioia, 2011). If they deem it to be useful and novel, they must carefully craft their rhetoric with the objective of convincing their colleagues that their theory has these characteristics (Locke & Golden-Biddle, 1997).

What Are Future Gaps That Can Be Investigated

This review has hopefully shed some light and potential applications for innovations such as technology for future researchers to conceptualize, distinguish and comprehend the underlying models and theories that may affect the previous, current and future application of technology adoption and use especially in organizations. Theorising and theory building has always happened in well-known and defined fields such as organizational studies, education, healthcare, finance etc. Emerging technology fields such as ethics in computing adaptive artificial intelligence, datafication, sustainable technology, super apps, wireless value realization, metaverse, industrial cloud, digital immune system, quantum computing, robotics, and internet of things could be used as phenomena to develop theory and theorising in the IS field.

REFERENCES

Ajzen, I. (1991). The theory of planned behavior. *Organizational Behavior and Human Decision Processes*, *50*(2), 179–211. doi:10.1016/0749-5978(91)90020-T

Bandura, A. (1999). Social cognitive theory of personality. Handbook of personality, 2, 154-96.

Barney, J., Wright, M., & Ketchen, D. J. Jr. (2001). The resource-based view of the firm: Ten years after 1991. *Journal of Management*, *27*(6), 625–641. doi:10.1177/014920630102700601

Bunge, M. (1977). Treatise on basic philosophy: Vol. 3. *Ontology I: The furniture of the world*. D. Reidel Publishing Company.

Bunge, M. (1979). Treatise on basic philosophy: Vol. 4. *Ontology II: A world of systems*. D. Reidel Publishing Company.

Burton-Jones, A., McLean, E. R., & Monod, E. (2015). Theoretical perspectives in IS research: From variance and process to conceptual latitude and conceptual fit. *European Journal of Information Systems*, *24*(6), 664–679. doi:10.1057/ejis.2014.31

Cohen, W. M., & Levinthal, D. A. (1990). Absorptive capacity: A new perspective on learning and innovation. *Administrative Science Quarterly*, *35*(1), 128–152. doi:10.2307/2393553

Theory and Theorizing in Information Systems

Corley, K. G., & Gioia, D. A. (2011). Building theory about theory building: What constitutes a theoretical contribution? *Academy of Management Review*, *36*(1), 12–32. doi:10.5465/amr.2009.0486

Davis, F. D. (1987). *User acceptance of information systems: the technology acceptance model*. TAM.

Deci, E. L., & Ryan, R. M. (2012). Self-determination theory. Handbook of theories of social psychology, 1(20), 416-436.

DeLone, W. H., & McLean, E. R. (2003). The DeLone and McLean model of information systems success: A ten-year update. *Journal of Management Information Systems*, *19*(4), 9–30. doi:10.1080/07421222.2003.11045748

DiMaggio, P. J. (1995). Comments on" What theory is not. *Administrative Science Quarterly*, *40*(3), 391–397. doi:10.2307/2393790

Eisenhardt, K. M., & Martin, J. A. (2000). Dynamic capabilities: What are they? *Strategic Management Journal*, *21*(10-11), 1105–1121. doi:10.1002/1097-0266(200010/11)21:10/11<1105::AID-SMJ133>3.0.CO;2-E

Fishbein, M. (1979). *A theory of reasoned action: some applications and implications*.

Freeman, R. E. (2001). A stakeholder theory of the modern corporation. *Perspectives in Business Ethics Sie*, *3*(144), 38–48.

Freese, L. (1984). Cumulative problem solving in family sociology. *Journal of Family Issues*, *5*(4), 447–469. doi:10.1177/019251384005004002

Goodhue, D. L., & Thompson, R. L. (1995). Task-technology fit and individual performance. *Management Information Systems Quarterly*, *19*(2), 213–236. doi:10.2307/249689

Gregor, S. (2006). The nature of theory in information systems. *Management Information Systems Quarterly*, *30*(3), 611–642. doi:10.2307/25148742

Griffith, T. L., Sawyer, J. E., & Neale, M. A. (2003). Virtualness and knowledge in teams: Managing the love triangle of organizations, individuals, and information technology. *Management Information Systems Quarterly*, *27*(2), 265–287. doi:10.2307/30036531

Grover, V., & Lyytinen, K. (2023). The pursuit of innovative theory in the digital age. *Journal of Information Technology*, *38*(1), 45–59. doi:10.1177/02683962221077112

Grover, V., Lyytinen, K., Srinivasan, A., & Tan, B. C. (2008). Contributing to rigorous and forward-thinking explanatory theory. *Journal of the Association for Information Systems*, *9*(2), 40–47. doi:10.17705/1jais.00151

Guillemette, M. G., & Paré, G. (2012). Toward a new theory of the contribution of the IT function in organizations. *Management Information Systems Quarterly*, *36*(2), 529–551. doi:10.2307/41703466

Hassan, N. R., & Lowry, P. B. (2015, December). Seeking middle-range theories in information systems research. In *International Conference on Information Systems (ICIS 2015), Fort Worth, TX, December.*

Hassan, N. R., Lowry, P. B., & Mathiassen, L. (2022). Useful products in information systems theorizing: A discursive formation perspective. [JAIS]. *Journal of the Association for Information Systems*, *23*(2), 418–446. doi:10.17705/1jais.00730

Hassan, N. R., Mathiassen, L., & Lowry, P. B. (2019). The process of information systems theorizing as a discursive practice. *Journal of Information Technology*, *34*(3), 198–220. doi:10.1177/0268396219832004

Hirschheim, R. (2019). Against theory: With apologies to Feyerabend. *Journal of the Association for Information Systems*, *20*(9), 8.

Hofstede, G. (2011). Dimensionalizing cultures: The Hofstede model in context. *Online Readings in Psychology and Culture*, *2*(1), 8. doi:10.9707/2307-0919.1014

Iyamu, T. (2021). *Applying theories for information systems research*. Routledge. doi:10.4324/9781003184119

Joseph, R. (2021). Determining the singularity and transdisciplinarity properties of the theory evaluation scale: A literature review. *Journal of Evidence-Based Social Work*, *18*(6), 650–662.

Kahneman, D., & Tversky, A. (2013). Prospect theory: An analysis of decision under risk. In Handbook of the fundamentals of financial decision making: Part I (pp. 99-127).

Kerlinger, F. N., Lee, H. B., & Bhanthumnavin, D. (2000). Foundations of behavioral research: The most sustainable popular textbook by Kerlinger & Lee (2000). *Journal of Social Development*, *13*, 131–144.

Levitt, B., & March, J. G. (1988). Organizational learning. *Annual Review of Sociology*, *14*(1), 319–338. doi:10.1146/annurev.so.14.080188.001535

Markus, M. L., & Robey, D. (1988). Information technology and organizational change: Causal structure in theory and research. *Management Science*, *34*(5), 583–598. doi:10.1287/mnsc.34.5.583

Markus, M. L., & Rowe, F. (2018). Is IT changing the world? Conceptions of causality for information systems theorizing. *Management Information Systems Quarterly*, *42*(4), 1255–1280.

Meyer, J. W., & Rowan, B. (1977). Institutionalized organizations: Formal structure as myth and ceremony. *American Journal of Sociology*, *83*(2), 340–363. doi:10.1086/226550

Miller, D. (1981). Toward a new contingency approach: The search for organizational gestalts. *Journal of Management Studies*, *18*(1), 1–26. doi:10.1111/j.1467-6486.1981.tb00088.x

Mueller, B., & Urbach, N. (2017). Understanding the Why, What, and How of Theories in IS Research. *Communications of the Association for Information Systems*, *41*(17), 349–388. doi:10.17705/1CAIS.04117

Niederman, F., & March, S. (2019a). The "theoretical lens" concept: We all know what it means, but do we all know the same thing? *Communications of the Association for Information Systems*, *44*(1), 1–33. doi:10.17705/1CAIS.04401

Niederman, F., & March, S. T. (2019b). Broadening the conceptualization of theory in the information systems discipline: A meta-theory approach. *The Data Base for Advances in Information Systems*, *50*(2), 18–44. doi:10.1145/3330472.3330476

Pfeffer, J. (2005). Developing resource dependence theory: how theory is affected by its environment. In K. G. Smith & M. A. Hitt (Eds.), *Great Minds in Management: The Process of Theory Development*. Oxford University Press. doi:10.1093/oso/9780199276813.003.0021

Popper, K. (2005). *The logic of scientific discovery*. Routledge. doi:10.4324/9780203994627

Porter, M. E. (1997). Competitive strategy. *Measuring Business Excellence*, *1*(2), 12–17. doi:10.1108/eb025476

Post, C., Sarala, R., Gatrell, C., & Prescott, J. E. (2020). Advancing theory with review articles. *Journal of Management Studies*, *57*(2), 351–376. doi:10.1111/joms.12549

Ramírez-Correa, P. (2016, May). Most popular theories in information systems research. In *Anais Do XII Simpósio Brasileiro de Sistemas de Informação* (pp. 582–584). SBC. doi:10.5753bsi.2016.6017

Rivard, S. (2021). Theory building is neither an art nor a science. It is a craft. *Journal of Information Technology*, *36*(3), 316–328. doi:10.1177/0268396220911938

Rogers, E. M., Singhal, A., & Quinlan, M. M. (2014). Diffusion of innovations. In *An integrated approach to communication theory and research* (pp. 432–448). Routledge.

Sandberg, J., & Alvesson, M. (2021). Meanings of theory: Clarifying theory through typification. *Journal of Management Studies*, *58*(2), 487–516. doi:10.1111/joms.12587

Shane, S. A. (2003). *A general theory of entrepreneurship: The individual-opportunity nexus*. Edward Elgar Publishing. doi:10.4337/9781781007990

Simon, H. A. (1950). Administrative behaviour.

Sutton, R. I., & Staw, B. M. (1995). What theory is not. *Administrative Science Quarterly*, *40*(3), 371–384. doi:10.2307/2393788

Venkatesh, V., Morris, M. G., Davis, G. B., & Davis, F. D. (2003). User acceptance of information technology: Toward a unified view. *Management Information Systems Quarterly*, *27*(3), 425–478. doi:10.2307/30036540

Weber, R. (2012). Evaluating and developing theories in the information systems discipline. *Journal of the Association for Information Systems*, *13*(1), 2. doi:10.17705/1jais.00284

Weick, K. E. (1995). *Sensemaking in organizations* (Vol. 3). Sage.

Whetten, D. A. (1989). What constitutes a theoretical contribution? *Academy of Management Review*, *14*(4), 490–495. doi:10.2307/258554

Williamson, O. E. (1998). Transaction cost economics: How it works; where it is headed. *De Economist*, *146*(1), 23–58. doi:10.1023/A:1003263908567

Zhang, M., & Gable, G. G. (2017). A systematic framework for multilevel theorizing in information systems research. *Information Systems Research*, *28*(2), 203–224. doi:10.1287/isre.2017.0690

Chapter 8
Toward Comprehensive
IS Project Alignment:
The Case of Enterprise Resource Planning Deployment Within a Logistics Service Provider

Eddy Bajolle
iD https://orcid.org/0000-0002-3943-6667
CERGAM, Aix-Marseille University, France

Cécile Godé
iD https://orcid.org/0000-0002-9148-2820
CERGAM, Aix-Marseille University, France

Nathalie Fabbe-Costes
iD 0000-0001-5857-7994
iD https://orcid.org/
CERGAM, Aix-Marseille University, France

ABSTRACT

Previous research offers limited and fragmented frameworks for information systems project alignment (ISPA). This study fills this gap by providing a comprehensive overview of the interplay between an IS project and its broader organizational context, and clarifying how contextual alignments relate to IS project success. ISPA is explored by observing a five-year implementation of an Enterprise Resource Planning (ERP) system within a logistics service provider based in Europe and North Africa. The study's findings and key contributions highlight the plural, complex, and multifaceted nature of ISPA resulting from the interaction of strategy, structure, process, people, and culture between the project, business, and IS organization. This chapter presents a comprehensive ISPA framework and is expected to increase project managers' awareness of the context in which IS projects are managed.
DOI: 10.4018/978-1-7998-9687-6.ch008

Copyright © 2024, IGI Global. Copying or distributing in print or electronic forms without written permission of IGI Global is prohibited.

INTRODUCTION

Each year, thousands of information system (IS) projects are launched "using hardware, software, and/or networks to create a product, service, or result" (Schwalbe, 2019, p.3). Worldwide, IS spending was expected to reach 4.5 trillion dollars in 2022, representing an increase of 5.5% from 2021 (Gartner, 2021). Moreover, the COVID-19 pandemic compelled companies to accelerate digital transformation to remain competitive and adapt to clients' move toward online channels (Seiler, 2020). Hence, IS projects have become essential for companies' survival after the pandemic and continued development in an uncertain era. The 2020 Standish Group CHAOS Report indicates that almost half (47%) of all IS projects are late, over budget, or do not meet original specifications, and about one-fifth (19%) are canceled before completion (Johnson, 2020). These alarming considerations indicate significant difficulties for IS projects' delivery of expected outcomes on schedule and budget.

Project misalignment has been determined as the origin of disappointing business results and project failure (Box & Platts, 2005; Srivannaboon & Milosevic, 2006; Patanakul & Shenhar, 2012; Alsudiri et al., 2013). Specifically, IS project alignment (ISPA) is defined as "the degree to which information system (IS) project deliverables are consistent with the project's objectives, which are shaped by the organization's IS strategy" (Jenkin & Chan, 2010, p.35). According to Jenkin and Chan (2010), ISPA influences project and firm performance. Project alignment, specifically ISPA research, has primarily focused on aligning project management (PM) with business strategy and ensuring alignment among project stakeholders. The broader organizational context in which IS projects are executed mainly revolves around strategic and social factors. Scarce are the studies that adopt a more open system approach to ISPA. Yet, the interplay between projects and their surrounding permanent organizations has long been the subject of research (Blomquist & Packendorff, 1998; Grabher, 2002; Engwall, 2003; Manning, 2008; Klimkeit, 2013) and still are in recent literature (Ren et al., 2019; Sydow & Windeler, 2020; Nilsson Vestola et al., 2021). These studies fall under the organizational perspective of project (Winter et al., 2006), considering projects as complex temporary systems (Packendorff, 1995) strongly influenced by the organizational context in which they are embedded. Organizational context can be understood at the project level as permanent organizational characteristics that facilitate or constrain successful project implementation. These characteristics have been addressed by previous research (Shenhar, 1999; Engwall, 2003; Manning, 2008; Klimkeit, 2013; Ren et al., 2019; Pinto, 2019), which advocates consideration of the interplay of critical elements (i.e., strategy, structure, system or process, people, politics and culture) between projects and their parent organization. Contextual alignment issues (i.e., alignment between projects and their organizational context) are even more salient within the framework of IS projects as management of information system (MIS) literature repeatedly documents misfits between information technology (IT) artifacts (such as ERP system) and their implementing organization (Soh et al., 2000; Krumbholz & Maiden, 2000; Yusuf et al., 2004; Leidner & Kayworth, 2006; Sia & Soh, 2007; Strong & Volkoff, 2010; Hustad et al., 2016; Morquin et al., 2023) that significantly influences IS project success (Holland & Light, 1999; Nah et al. 2001; Hong & Kim 2002; Ram & Corkindale, 2014). Based on previous research, we suggest that gaining a deeper insight into the success or failure of IS projects requires a comprehensive perspective on project alignment. This perspective should consider IS projects as open systems that influence and are influenced by the context of their immediate surroundings. However, limited attention has been paid to the linkages between IS projects and their parent system and few studies have attempted to explain how contextual alignments influence IS project success. For five years, we were immersed in the international implementation of an ERP project within a logistics service provider, allowing us to enhance the ISPA construct and explore the influence of contextual alignments on IS project success. Through a longitudinal case study, we address the following research questions:

RQ1. *What are contextual alignments between IS projects and their parent organization?*

RQ2. *How do contextual alignments between IS projects and their parent organization influence project success?*

By addressing these questions, we contribute to the literature by providing scholars and practitioners with a comprehensive framework of ISPA, including 15 contextual alignments related to strategy, structure, process, people, and culture between the project organization, the business organization, and the IS organization as well as their influence on IS project success. This framework is expected to help project managers improve their understanding of the surrounding context in which IS projects are managed so that they can identify contextual strengths and weaknesses early and act accordingly to increase the likelihood of success.

The remainder of this paper is structured as follows: we first present the project alignment and ISPA literatures and their limitations that led us to explore project organizational context and its influence on IS project success. Second, we detail our methodology and expose our findings, paving the way for our subsequent discussion. In the conclusion, implications for theory and practice, limitations, and suggestions for future research are outlined.

LITERATURE REVIEW

The benefits of project alignment are known across the Information Systems (Jenkin & Chan, 2010), Construction (Griffith & Gibson, 2001), and PM (Srivannaboon & Milosevic, 2006) literatures. To provide an overview of existing literature on project alignment, we first investigate studies related to project alignment independently of their research field. Then, we focus on research on IS projects with particular attention dedicated to ISPA.

Project Alignment

Research addressing alignment at the project level remains scarce. Scholars have offered various definitions of project alignment, emphasizing the need for a common understanding of the project's mission, goals, objectives, tactics and plans (Skulmoski & Hartman, 1999), uniformly defined and understood set of project objectives (Griffith & Gibson, 2011) and shared vision of success (Villachica et al., 2004). Overall, studies on project alignment focused on the strategic and social aspects of alignment. The former emphasizes the connection between PM and business strategy (Srivannaboon & Milosevic, 2006; Jenkin & Chan, 2010; Alsuridi et al., 2013); the latter addresses alignment of different project stakeholders' worldviews and interests (Griffith & Gibson, 2001; Van der Horn & Whitty, 2017; Gilchrist et al., 2018).

The strategic view of project alignment has been studied by Srivannaboon and Milosevic (2006), who investigate the relationship between business strategy and project alignment. They highlight that competitive attributes such as time-to-market, quality, and cost influence the configuration of PM and, conversely, that PM configuration can influence the business strategy. In addition, Alsudiri et al. (2013) examine both internal (effective communication, executive support, project manager involvement in the business strategy development, project manager leadership competence) and external factors (government agencies, vendors and contractors, telecommunications market, site acquisition) that affect the process of aligning PM to the business strategy. They conclude that companies with a stronger alignment between their business strategy and PM show more successful project outcomes. For IS projects, Jenkin and Chan (2010) conceptualize ISPA as consisting of three dimensions (strategy-to-project-objectives congruence, project-objectives-to-deliverables congruence, and project social congruence) and provide a process view of aligning final project deliverables with IS project objectives and strategy. Their findings underscore the significance of the evolutionary process, learning, and adaptation to change for achieving project alignment.

Griffith and Gibson (2001) discuss the social view of project alignment and identify critical alignment issues (concerning execution processes, culture, information, and

Toward Comprehensive IS Project Alignment

tools) influencing team alignment and, ultimately, project success. Similarly, Van der Hoorn and Whitty (2017) find that project managers can employ diverse praxis, to build rapport, trust, and empathy between project teams to achieve alignment. For IS projects, Gilchrist et al. (2018) explore the process of social alignment and misalignment in a complex IS project and investigate how social alignment develops or dissolves over time. Their qualitative study leads to constructing a dynamic model involving eight stages, including four for social misalignment (separation, disrespect, lack of cross-discipline participation, and social misalignment) and four for social alignment (learning, respect, cross-discipline participation, and social alignment). Similarly, O'Leary and Williams (2012) investigate an IS-enabled business change project and develop a project model based on social trajectories in which progress depends on a complex "alignment-seeking" process between parties with different worldviews and interests. Highlighting the dynamic and inter-organizational settings in which projects are evolving, Nilsson (2015) asserts that ISPA concerns the "management task dealing with the relationship between the IS project and the surrounding environment" (p.30). To reach this objective, the author provides a model of ISPA that strongly emphasizes the social dimension of ISPA, highlighting the significance of the human aspects of alignment and the need to consider various individuals' perceptions of the world.

As the larger organizational context in which IS projects are embedded has been superficially considered by previous studies, we could not find studies providing a comprehensive overview of project alignment. Although Jenkin and Chan's (2010) ISPA construct is helpful, the authors narrowed the achievement of project alignment to a reciprocal relationship between project deliverables and project objectives on the one hand and between project objectives and IS strategy on the other. This restrictive view of ISPA raised several limitations. First, the current ISPA construct implicitly considers that a strategic alignment exists a priori of project execution; that is, business and IS strategies are aligned (Henderson & Venkatraman, 1993). Following this premise, as soon as project objectives are aligned with IS strategy, they are mechanically aligned with business strategy so that the project alignment process enables strategy execution (Jenkin & Chan, 2010). However, it is not clear that a strategic alignment is systematically existing within the implementing organization (El-Telbany & Elragal, 2014). In case of a lack of such alignment (i.e., between IS and business strategies), regardless of whether projects are executed under IS strategy, the firm's expected benefits may not be fully realized as IS projects might fail to execute business strategy. Thus, IS strategy is not the sole organizational element with which project objectives should be consistent to produce successful outcomes. In other words, IS projects must align with a set of critical elements of the parent organization (including business and IS strategies) to deliver expected benefits. To the best of our knowledge, only one research dedicated to ISPA by Nilsson (2015) attempted to consider the IS project's external environment. Although Nilsson (2015) attempt to consider relationships between IS projects and their surrounding context is helpful, the latter has been limited to the social aspect of alignment, whereas past studies described the project surrounding context as having a much larger scope (Shenhar, 1999; Manning, 2008; Morris & Geraldi, 2011; Klimkeit, 2013; Svejvig & Andersen, 2015; Pinto, 2019; Ren et al., 2019; Schwalbe, 2019; Sydow & Windeler, 2020). Considering the limitations described above and aiming to increase our understanding of project alignment, we adopt a more comprehensive approach to ISPA, including the broader organizational context in which IS projects are implemented.

Project Organizational Context

From the traditional and rationalistic PM theory perspective, projects are viewed as closed and autonomous systems isolated from their embedded context (Blomquist & Packendorff, 1998; Engwall, 2003). Influenced by organizational theories, the organizational perspective of projects deals with integrating the temporary project organization into the permanent one (Winter et al., 2006). Within this perspective, projects are considered complex temporary systems (Packendorff, 1995) interacting with their surrounding permanent contexts (Blomquist & Packendorff, 1998; Engwall, 2003; Manning, 2008; Klimkeit, 2013; Pinto, 2019; Sydow & Windeler, 2020; Nilsson Vestola et al., 2021). Without this holistic view, "it is unlikely that those projects will ever truly serve the needs of the organization" (Schwalbe, 2019, p.49). However, contextual issues concerning the implemented IT artifact have not been considered by current ISPA research. The latter is considered a black box aligned with the implementing organization. Nevertheless, the alignment between the IT artifact and the implementing organization is far from obvious (Soh et al., 2000; Hong & Kim, 2002; Yusuf et al., 2004; Leidner & Kayworth, 2006; Sia & Soh, 2007; Strong & Volkoff, 2010; Hustad et al., 2016; Morquin et al., 2023). Therefore, the current ISPA study would benefit from considering the organizational context in which IS projects are implemented. At the project level, the surrounding permanent organization (i.e., organizational context) can be understood as permanent organizational characteristics that facilitate or constrain successful project implementation (Table 1). These characteristics have been revealed through various studies described below.

Investigating the effect of organizational context on collaboration in international projects, Klimkeit (2013) considers governance and structure, policies and procedures, systems, people, and organizational culture to embody the permanent organizational context. In addition, Ren et al. (2019) analyze the impact of organizational context on inter-project knowledge transfer, determining that the meeting and reward system

Table 1. Project organizational context characteristics

Article	Project organizational context characteristics
Shenhar (1999)	Strategy, organization (structure and people), process, culture, tools
Engwall (2003)	Institutionalized norms, values, and routines
Manning (2008)	Strategy, structure, culture
Marchewka (2012)	Strategy, structure, culture, politics
Klimkeit (2013)	Governance and structure, policies and procedures, system, people, culture
Ren et al. (2019)	Meeting and reward systems and culture
Schwalbe (2019)	Structure, people, culture, politics
Pinto (2019)	Strategy, structure, culture

and shared culture constitute factors of organizational context that influence social relations between project teams. According to Manning (2008) and Pinto (2019), projects' organizational context is represented by parent organizations' organizational strategies, structures, and cultures "together they create the environment in which a project will flourish or founder" (Pinto, 2019, p.40). As a complement, Marchewka (2012) and Schwalbe (2019) added politics as part of the project's organizational context. Exploring how a project is influenced by its surrounding environment, Engwall (2003) argues that projects must be conceptualized as "contextually-embedded open systems" (p.790) and analyzed in consideration of more permanent historical and organizational contexts. In his study, project organizational context is represented by institutionalized norms, values, and routines of the parent system. To help organizations and project managers successfully turn projects into strategic competitive advantages, Shenhar (1999) proposes a comprehensive framework connecting projects to their broader organizational context. The latter is relevant to organizational (or corporate) and project levels and includes five factors: strategy, culture, organization (i.e., structure and people), processes, and tools.

The PM literature suggests that the organizational context in which projects are embedded comprises the following parent organization's essential elements: strategy, structure, culture, people, politics, system (or process) and tools. To further develop these insights, we reviewed the influence of organizational context on project success and, more specifically, how alignment between projects and their organizational context, i.e., contextual alignment, increases the likelihood of project success.

Contextual Alignments and Project Success

Few scholars have highlighted the influence of organizational context on project success. In their study, the larger environment in which projects operate is considered a strength or a weakness that supports or hinders their execution and success. For example, Pinto (2019) asserts that organizational context (i.e., strategy, structure, and culture of the parent organization) in which projects are managed is "a key determinant of the likelihood of their success or failure" (Pinto, 2019, p.68). Specifically, the parent organization's ability to provide clear strategic goals (i.e., organizational strategy), allocate sufficient skilled resources to the project team (i.e., organizational structure), and create a supportive atmosphere for the development of projects (i.e., organizational culture) strongly influence the likelihood of project success. In the same vein, Marchewka (2012) states that understanding the organizational context can help the project team "identify potential risks and issues that could impede the project" (p.15). Within the framework of IS projects, alignment between IT and the implementing organization has been considered a critical success factor that significantly influences project success (Holland & Light, 1999; Nah et al., 2001; Hong & Kim 2002; Ram & Corkindale, 2014). Therefore, organizational context can be supportive or non-supportive of projects. A supportive organizational context promoting projects and increasing the likelihood of success will be aligned (i.e., contextual alignment), whereas a non-supportive organizational context hindering projects and decreasing the likelihood of success will be considered misaligned (i.e., contextual misalignment).

Various approaches have been adopted to evaluate project success, from the traditional and straightforward 'iron triangle' to a more complex and holistic framework, including impact on the customer, benefits to the organization, and preparing for the future (Jugdev & Müller, 2005). A distinction has been made between project management success and product success (de Wit, 1988; Shenhar et al., 1997; Baccarini, 1999; Cooke-Davies, 2002). The former considers the successful project execution in terms of time, cost, and quality objectives, representing the short-term project management success efficiency, and the latter focuses on achieving strategic organizational goals and satisfaction of users and stakeholders' needs, representing the long-term project result or effectiveness. Therefore, the assessment of project success has been made through hard and soft criteria (Müller & Jugdev, 2012; Baccarini, 1999). Hard criteria (i.e., cost, time, and quality) are objective, tangible, and measurable, whereas soft criteria (i.e., user and stakeholder satisfaction) are subjective, subtle, and more difficult to evaluate (Baccarini, 1999). Regarding IS projects, success criteria generally encompass project management, technical (or system), and business aspects (Thomas & Vernàndez, 2008). In this vein, Iriarte and Bayona (2020) consolidate project success into project management success criteria (time, budget, specifications and scope, process efficiency, quality of PM, goals achievement, project stakeholder satisfaction, and team satisfaction) and product success criteria (system quality, information quality, user satisfaction, intention to use/use, business impact and impact on users). Furthermore, Shenhar et al. (1997)

Toward Comprehensive IS Project Alignment

state that project efficiency can be assessed during execution and immediately after completion. In contrast, stakeholder satisfaction can be measured after a short time when the project has been delivered to the customer (or users) and the customer is using its product.

Summary of Key Elements From the Literature

A limitation in the literature on ISPA is that few papers consider the organizational context in which IS projects are embedded. Most papers focus on strategic and/ or social aspects of alignment, while extant literature highlights the importance of adopting a holistic approach to PM that considers the organizational context in which projects are executed. To anticipate and understand project success or failure, we posit that current ISPA frameworks could benefit from a comprehensive view that considers projects as open systems influencing and influenced by the context of their immediate surroundings. However, no integrated framework connects IS projects with their organizational context. By conducting a longitudinal case study allowing us to explore ISPA over a considerable period, our research goals were to provide a comprehensive framework of contextual alignments that should be considered between IS projects and the parent organization on the one hand and investigate the role of these contextual alignments on project success on the other hand. In this regard, this chapter contributes to establishing that connection and overcoming the limitations mentioned earlier.

METHODS

Our study presents a single, multi-year case study to explore ISPA examining an international transportation and logistics company's deployment of an ERP system across all its subsidiaries in Europe (France, Italy) and North Africa (Morocco and Tunisia) involving a wide range of operational activities (i.e., import, export, transport, customs, and warehousing) with 300 final users. The selected case study presents a rich and varied organizational context characterized by various interdependent structures, processes, people, and cultures suitable for exploring contextual alignments between the temporary (IS project) and permanent organization (the implementing organization). Given the exploratory nature of this research and our commitment to investigating the ISPA phenomenon in a natural setting, an in-depth case study approach was used (Benbasat et al., 1987), choosing a rich and complex setting that provided fertile ground for exploring ISPA dynamics and revealing multiple facets (Siggelkow, 2007).

The Case: The Large Deployment of an ERP System in Europe and North Africa

We investigated ISPA, focusing on an international logistics service provider and leader of roll on–roll off transport in North Africa. For anonymity, we refer to the organization as ROROL. Operating in a highly competitive market, ROROL's survival depends on its ability to optimize transport flows in and between Europe and North Africa and to offer superior services to its clients. The organization identifies cost control, process standardization and optimization, and collaboration as critical success factors for outperforming competition and increasing market share. To support business development, in 2018, the company decided to replace its dated in-house transport management system (TMS), implementing ERP software. A dedicated project team, including three project managers based in the French headquarters, was appointed to manage the IS project. In addition, business experts were chosen at subsidiary levels to facilitate dialog between the central project team and local key users. In September 2019, ROROL selected a web-enabled transport ERP system designed by an Andorran software vendor (referred to as vendor A in this study) for implementation across European and North African subsidiaries. The ROROL internal IS team and the external software vendor A team shared software development and configuration processes. Our immersion in the IS project lasted five years, from 2019 to 2023, and included three main phases. The first phase, extending from January 2019 to June 2021, suffered a significant turnover of project managers and key users, tensions leading to a temporary interruption with vendor A, poor internal communication, repeated postponement of the go-live date, and budget overrun. A fourth-month interruption arose between ROROL and vendor A in this period. A second phase, from July 2021 to January 2023, is characterized by recruitment, heightened autonomy, decision power granted to the project team, and more trust placed in vendor A. During this second period, the organization learned from its past mistakes and implemented corrective actions. Overall, project stakeholders significantly improved the project's progress, relationships with vendor A, and cost control during this second project period. The third and last phase, from February 2023 to September 2023, corresponded to the implementation phase and was marked by intensive user training and testing and, finally, ERP system deployment across all subsidiaries. To limit risks associated with a brutal ERP system deployment, the project team decided to run the new ERP system in parallel with the old one for several months before disconnecting the old in-house system. During the implementation phase, users had to use both systems, which allows more control and flexibility to solve user errors or system bugs. The pre-implementation phase

Toward Comprehensive IS Project Alignment

(composed of phases 1 and 2) served as a basis for assessing project management success The third and last phase allowed us to assess the final product (i.e., product success) issued by the project.

Data Collection

When collecting data, we gathered multiple sources of evidence (direct and participant observations, interviews, and documentation) (Eisenhardt, 1989). First, researchers were involved in the ERP project early on and could attend most project events. Consequently, direct participant observations were practiced extensively throughout the project. Overall, 700 hours of observation were tracked through four significant activities (1) user requirement collection, (2) workshops with software vendors, (3) internal project team meetings, and (4) user training. In addition, a daily research diary was used to keep track of project events, ideas, and reflections representing the researchers' experience. During these activities, it was possible to observe stakeholders in action in their working environment. Second, we conducted semi-structured interviews with line managers, key users, business executives, IS managers, consultants, and project managers. Follow-up interviews were organized with key informants whose roles, actions, and involvement were particularly determinant for the project's progression.

In summary, 24 interviews were conducted with 18 participants, and theoretical saturation was reached after 17 interviews. At the beginning of each interview, the period (phase 1, 2, or 3) to which questions were related was specified to respondents. Overall, we conducted 11 interviews concerning the first phase, six interviews concerning the second, and seven interviews concerning the third and last phase. We used a guide for interviews that included a brief introduction followed by semi-structured questions, most of which were open-ended to allow respondents to express themselves and elicit detailed and contextualized answers freely. In addition, probing follow-up questions were frequently used to encourage interviewees to expand their descriptions and explanations. Interviews lasted from 45 to 90 minutes. They were all recorded and transcribed. Each interview transcription was presented to and discussed with respondents to ensure mutual understanding and clarify specific points addressed during the interview. Third, we collected and reviewed various documents, including the project charter, functional and technical specifications, internal reports, meeting minutes, contracts, emails, and mock-ups. Table 2 details the interviewees' characteristics and the complementary qualitative research processes applied in this study.

Table 2. Overview of collected data (Sources of Evidence)

	Interviews					
Resp.	Role in the IS project	Position	Company	Phase 1	Phase 2	Phase 3
R1	Project Director	Project Director	ROROL	[R1–P1]		
				[R1–P1]		
R2	Project Manager	Project Manager	ROROL	[R2–P1]	[R2–P2]	
R3	IS Expert	IS Project Manager	ROROL	[R3–P1]	[R3–P2]	
R4	ERP Consultant	President	Vendor A	[R4–P1]	[R4–P2]	
R5	Key User / Final user	Operating Officer	ROROL	[R5–P1]		
R6	Sponsor	President	ROROL	[R6–P1]		[R6–P3]
R7	Financial Expert	Chief Financial Officer	ROROL	[R7-P1]		
R8	ERP Consultant	Software Vendor Consultant	Vendor A	[R8–P1]		
R9	Key User / Final user	Operation Director	ROROL	[R9–P1]		[R9–P3]
R10	Key User / Final user	Operating Officer	ROROL	[R10–P1]		
R11	IS Expert	IS Project Manager	ROROL		[R11–P2]	
R12	Key User / Final user	Commercial Agent	ROROL		[R12–P2]	
R13	Key User / Final user	Commercial Agent	ROROL		[R13–P2]	
R14	Key User / Final user	Operating Officer	ROROL			[R14–P3]
R15	Key User / Final user	Operating Officer	ROROL			[R15–P3]
R16	Key User / Final user	Operating Officer	ROROL			[R16–P3]
R17	Key User / Final user	Invoicing Officer	ROROL			[R17–P3]
R18	Key User / Final user	Commercial Agent	ROROL			[R18–P3]
N = 24				$P_1 = 11$	$P_2 = 6$	$P_3 = 7$
Participant Observation						
Seven hundred hours of participant observation were tracked and divided into four major activities (1) user requirement collection, (2) workshops with software vendors, (3) internal project team meetings, and (4) user training.						
Field Notes						
A daily diary was used to track project events (meetings, participants' arrivals and departures, routine and unusual occurrences, and other relevant notations) and record researchers' overall reflections.						
Documentation						
Project charter, functional and technical specifications, internal reports and communication, meeting minutes, contracts, emails, mock-ups, and related materials.						

Toward Comprehensive IS Project Alignment

Data Analysis

Our data analysis referenced the method of Miles et al. (2020) for qualitative analysis, including three steps (1) data condensation, (2) data display, and (3) conclusion drawing and verification. We selected a mid-range accounting scheme to construct our codes, "partway between the a priori and inductive approaches" (Miles & Huberman, 1994, p. 61). Our data were coded using Nvivo 12 software. We began with open coding of the transcribed interviews and field notes to identify emergent recurring patterns and establish categories. This first coding cycle allowed us to identify three distinct categories, including "Organization," "Information system," and "Project." We then included codes from the preexisting theoretical framework (i.e., strategy, structure, system/process, people, tools, politics, and culture), which led to the development of various subcategories from the initial three categories (e.g., organizational strategy, IS strategy, project strategy, organizational structure, IS structure, and project culture). A total of 15 subcategories were created, some of which referenced existing concepts, leading us to return to the literature to verify our application as to their meaning and content. We then reanalyzed the data (second cycle coding) using deductive coding. We applied a network format to present our data and identify the relationships between subcategories, between subcategories and categories, and between categories (Miles et al., 2020). These relationships represent circumstances of alignment and/or misalignment and were labeled Phase 1, Phase 2, or Phase 3, depending on the period the respondents were referencing. With the help of existing conceptualization described by literature (Iriarte & Bayona, 2020), the ERP project success was divided into two categories, namely "Project management success" and "Product success." In the first category (project management success), we include codes concerning the success criteria "On-time," "On-budget," "Within specification," "Process efficiency," "Quality of PM," "Goals achievement," "Project stakeholder satisfaction," and "Team satisfaction." In the second category (product success), we include codes concerning the success criteria "Information quality," "System quality," "User satisfaction," "Intention to use/Use," "Business impact," and "Impact on users."

Several techniques were used to reinforce our data quality and validity. First, during our interviews, we intentionally refrained from using the terms "alignment" or "misalignment" to prevent any potential influence on respondents' answers. Moreover, the interviewees reviewed all transcripts to allow them to specify or correct elements if needed. To avoid elite bias, we conducted semi-structured interviews with various participants in the company at different hierarchical levels (strategic, tactical, and operational) (Miles & Huberman, 1994). Finally, using multiple sources of evidence allowed us to triangulate the data to strengthen the validity of our findings (Eisenhardt, 1989).

FINDINGS

Our findings reveal three contextual dimensions of ISPA, including (1) Alignment between the business organization and the project organization, (2) Alignment between the IS organization and the project organization, and (3) Alignment between the IS organization and the business organization. From the original key organizational elements in the literature, strategy, structure, process, people, and culture were the most salient within our data. The above dimensions identified a series of contextual alignments between the project, business, and IS organizations. A total of 15 contextual alignments were revealed in our data analysis, each salient in the data at certain times in the first, second, or third project period. Our results also highlighted the influence of each contextual alignment on IS project success, specifically project management and product success. Our findings led to building a comprehensive ISPA framework emphasizing the multifaceted nature of ISPA, intertwining strategic, structural, processual, social, and cultural aspects (Figure 1). A summary of respondents' verbatim reply content is centralized in Appendix A, showing the applicable alignment, the associated period, and the status (fit or misfit) for each quote. References to Appendix A are added in square brackets to facilitate reader understanding.

Alignment Between Business Organization and Project Organization

Although the global implementation of new software was planned to support ROROL's organizational goals [1][2] (i.e., alignment between organizational strategy and project strategy), the first project period was marked by an evident lack of skilled resources and authority provided by the parent organization to the project structure (i.e., alignment between organizational structure and project structure). Indeed, ROROL's weak matrix structure conferred extremely minimal authority to project managers who had more of a coordinating role between functional experts as the latter remained under the authority of their departmental directors. In this organizational context, project managers encountered challenges in obtaining skilled and available resources from the parent organization's functional silos [3][4]. This critical situation significantly delayed the collecting requirements process and negatively impacted functional specification quality. To address this shortcoming, a competent functional resource has been transferred from the permanent organization to the project organization full-time, significantly aiding the project team in executing daily tasks within the due deadline in the second project phase [5].

To collect organizational requirements and produce relevant functional specifications in connection with target organizational processes (i.e., alignment

Toward Comprehensive IS Project Alignment

between organizational process and project process), project managers collaborated intensely with key users from all subsidiaries through various meetings and workshops [6][7]. Notwithstanding the largely successful regular exchanges between local key users and project managers [9], the first period revealed significant gaps, wherein effective communication between parties was sometimes very poor [10][11] (i.e., alignment between organizational and project people). Although the project team was reinforced, the short deadlines enforced by project planning did not always allow project managers to suitably collect user needs [8]. Consequently, functional specifications did not always accurately reflect organizational requirements, which led to various change requests from project managers to vendor A, involving additional development costs and time waste.

Moreover, some tensions arose between project managers and top management for at least two reasons. First, the project culture was based on close collaboration and consensus with functional experts, whereas the organizational culture was shaped by authority and centralized decision-making power held by the company's top management. Systematic consultation with various functional members was incompatible with top management's centralized decision-making method [12]. Second, the flexible and dynamic project team culture made project managers uncomfortable with the slow decision-making process, which was considered too centralized [13]. The cultural differences between the two (permanent and temporary) organizations (i.e., alignment between organizational culture and project culture) led to various debates and tensions between project managers and top management. To cope with this situation, top management increased the delegation power granted to project managers who were subsequently empowered to decide and engage in initiatives independently [14]. This change enabled a more expedient decision-making process, which was far more consistent with the project culture [15].

Alignment Between IS Organization and Project Organization

Project objectives were determined according to IS strategic focus [16][17][18] and regularly referred to with the project team to encourage project managers' focus when designing each ERP module (i.e., alignment between IS strategy and project strategy). However, the launch of various IS projects in a short period primarily mobilized the IS department that could no longer support the project team and ensure software development [19][20] (i.e., alignment between IS structure and project structure). Consequently, the lack of IS resources prompted top management to postpone the implementation phase. Software developers were recruited in the second project phase to join the ROROL IS team to address the lack of IS resources and support the IT development effort previously initiated on the project [21].

Each functional specification was reviewed to ensure mutual understanding between project and IS experts before being translated into the technical specifications intended for software development [22]. This process should ensure that software development was initiated under organizational requirements (i.e., alignment between IS and project process). Although one of the ERP consultants had a good understanding of the transport domain [25], the ROROL functional project managers' business backgrounds did not always facilitate their understanding of the technical considerations inherent to the IS project [26] (i.e., alignment between IS people and project people) which was regularly at the origin of misunderstanding and conflicts between parties. However, a better understanding of the software functionality and scope allowed project functional project managers to improve their technical knowledge [27]. Despite this review process, functional project managers often noted significant gaps between the requirements communicated and the software releases delivered by the vendor team [23][24] (i.e., alignment between the IS process and the project process). These gaps involved multiple change requests and software-level corrections to accurately match the functional specifications, negatively impacting the project's progress.

Having participated in the conception, implementation, and maintenance of the current TMS, the project team developed master software functionalities and, more broadly, managed the system with autonomy. However, replacing the custom in-house software with a standard ERP package owned by an external company drastically altered the associated methods and activities of the project team [28] (i.e., alignment between IS culture and project culture). Even if vendor A allowed some changes in its ERP software, such changes were restricted and costly, which involved extension discussion, negotiation, and conflicts between the project and vendor teams. Therefore, the project team had much less freedom and power on system functionality and customization decisions and often had to adapt to the ERP software [29].

Alignment Between Organization Business and IS Organization

As current information systems could no longer adequately support organizational strategy [30][31] (i.e., alignment between organizational strategy and IS strategy) and requirements [33][34][35][36] (i.e., alignment between IS structure/process and organizational structure/process), ROROL decided to replace its outdated in-house IS with an ERP software. Given that an external supplier owned the ERP software identified, the project required a close and long-term collaboration between ROROL and software vendor A. However, the relationships between vendor A and organizational professionals quickly suffered from a lack of mutual trust (i.e., alignment between IS people and organizational people). Indeed, ROROL's top management reproached the supplier for being disorganized, and the latter was also suspected of deliberately inflating workloads and associated invoicing. Similarly, the supplier team also perceived a lack of confidence from ROROL's top management [42][43]. This mutual distrust led to a progressive deterioration of business relationships between ROROL and vendor A, interrupting the collaboration. Despite multiple tensions and a four-month break in their business relationship, ROROL's top management and vendor A established a common ground concerning development costs, project planning, and scope. This significant change made communication smoother and drastically reduced conflicts between the parties [44].

After several years of planning, collecting requirements, configuring, developing, and testing the ERP system, the latter was deployed across all subsidiaries during the third phase. Even if the project was delivered late and the budget was exceeded, the final product was recognized by top management and users as successful. On the one hand, the ROROL president considered that ERP systems and, more broadly, information systems better supported organizational strategy and goals [32]. On the other hand, most final users were satisfied with ERP functionalities, system and information quality, and support to accomplish their daily activities [37][38][39][40][41]. However, as ROROL was divided into various departments, different functions include subunits with unique cultures (or subcultures) coexisting within the larger organization as part of the larger organizational culture. Among them, the commercial function plays a crucial role in managing the relationship between ROROL and its clients. In their daily work, commercial agents are highly committed to client contracts and price confidentiality. From their perspective, access to information related to commercial offers should be restricted only to commercial

Figure 1. IS project alignment framework

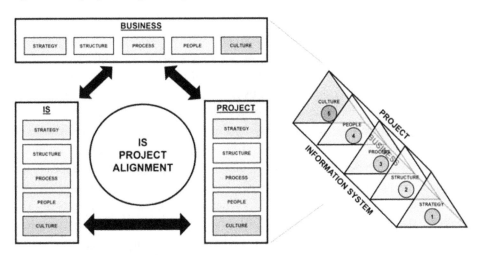

agents and top management; however, one of the objectives of the ERP software was to improve cross-functional communication by offering greater information transparency to raise each department's awareness of the importance of optimization and profitability. As a consequence, the transparency promoted by the software conflicted with commercial agents' perceptions of privacy inherent to commercial activity [45][46][47].

DISCUSSION

Although previous studies represent notable contributions to the field, there is a lack of framework adopting a comprehensive view of ISPA that considers the interplay between IS projects and the larger organizational context in which they are embedded. Most studies focus on the strategic and/or social dimensions of alignment (Jenkin & Chan, 2010; Gilchrist et al., 2018; Nilsson, 2015; O'Leary & Williams, 2013), underestimating the influence of other organizational characteristics such as structure, process, and culture. By including these missing elements in our analysis, our research fills the gap in the literature by providing a comprehensive framework of ISPA emphasizing contextual alignments between a temporary and a permanent organization. In this section, we discuss our framework and, more specifically, (1) the multifaceted nature of ISPA, and (2) contextual alignments as success factors.

The Multifaceted Nature of ISPA

Our results lead to the construction of a comprehensive framework highlighting the plural, complex, and multifaceted nature of ISPA resulting from the interaction of strategy, structure, process, people, and culture between the project, business, and IS organizations (Figure 1). Specifically, we identified three main dimensions of ISPA: (1) Alignment between the business organization and the project organization, (2) Alignment between the IS organization and the project organization, and (3) Alignment between the IS organization and the project organization, as well as 15 contextual alignments (Table 3). We investigated the extant literature for each of them to verify if they had been described and discussed a priori. Among the various alignments revealed by our data analysis, four are exemplified in previous ISPA literature, two are addressed in PM literature, eight are discussed in MIS literature, and one is unique to our findings. Our results highlight trust as an essential aspect of social alignment. Consequently, they partly support the conclusions of other scholars regarding the different factors to consider when studying the social aspects of ISPA (Jenkin & Chan, 2010; Gilchrist et al., 2018; Nilsson, 2015). Specifically, our study shows that social alignment influences ISPA by establishing shared information,

Toward Comprehensive IS Project Alignment

understanding, and mutual trust between project, organizational, and IS professionals (or people). Our results differ materially from other ISPA studies, such as Gilchrist et al. (2018), who stated that "we believe social alignment can occur without trust" (p. 850). Instead, trust between ROROL and software vendor teams proved crucial to maintaining long-term relationships. Distrust and suspicion between parties were salient during the first project period, which caused frequent conflicts followed by a temporary interruption of business relationships. In other words, parties involved in the project could not collaborate effectively without trusting each other. Among all alignments listed in Table 3, alignment between organizational culture and project culture (i.e., the subculture of the project team) was scarce in the literature. In our study, alignment between organizational culture and project culture refers to the ability of organizational culture to support the presence and development of a project culture. Temporary organizations that oversee projects develop unique cultures, constituting a subculture within the base organization that is best represented as a task culture (Handy, 2020). In a task culture, members' expertise and knowledge are more important than hierarchical positions. The task culture of the project team, characterized by flexibility, creativity, and cross-functional collaboration (Handy, 2020), clashed with that of the parent organization culture, which was based on power and influence. In contrast, transferring power to the project team during Phase 2 enabled improved relationships with top management.

Contextual Alignments as Success Factors

Our findings highlight that not all contextual alignments have the same influence on project success. Specifically, some alignments directly affected project management success, while others influenced product success. Furthermore, some contextual alignments were complementarity; they were both required to produce the expected outcome. For example, (1) alignment between organizational structure and project structure and (2) alignment between IS structure and project structure were complementary as the project structure required both organizational and IS skilled resources to complete project tasks within time, budget, and quality and positively influence project management success. In the same vein, (1) alignment between organizational people and project people, (2) alignment between IS people and project people, and (3) alignment between IS people and organizational people were complementary as sufficient communication, coordination, and shared understanding between all involved parties were necessary to avoid conflicts and misunderstanding, allow a smooth project progression and positively affect project management success.

Moreover, some contextual alignments influenced others. For example, (1) alignment between organizational process and project process and (2) alignment between IS process and project process were complementary, and they affected

(3) alignment between IS process and organizational process; to produce software supporting tasks (Goodhue & Thompson, 1995) and more broadly organizational processes, functional project managers had to first produce specifications in relation to target organizational requirements, and IT developers then had to produce technical specifications and configure the ERP system depending on these functional specifications. Alignment between the IS and organizational process affects system quality, information quality, intention to use/use, user satisfaction, and product success. Similarly, (1) alignment between organizational strategy and project strategy and (2) alignment between IS strategy and project strategy were complementary, and they impacted (3) alignment between IS strategy and business strategy; to strengthen strategic alignment (Henderson & Venkatraman, 1993), project strategy had to both support IS strategy and organizational strategies. Alignment between IS strategy and organizational strategy will contribute to achieving long-term organizational goals and, consequently, product success. Cultural issues were salient throughout the IS project and originated resistance, tensions, and disputes between project participants. In that sense, (1) alignment between organizational culture and project culture and (2) alignment between IS culture and project culture impacted project advancement and, by extension, project management success. Finally, alignment between organizational culture and IS culture was not uniform because of different subcultures. This alignment was mitigated as the user satisfaction related to the ERP system was not the same according to the functional silos in which users were affected. Similar to the alignment between organizational processes and IS processes, alignment between organizational culture and IS culture affects user satisfaction and intention to use the ERP system and, consequently, product success. Considering our findings, contextual alignments can be considered success factors or "elements of a project which, when influenced, increase the likelihood of success" (Müller & Jugdev, 2012, p. 758). The implementation phase allowed us to assess product success. For the parent organization, this phase represents the beginning of a transition phase (Lundin & Söderholm, 1995), where the initial level of alignment between (1) organizational strategy and business strategy, (2) organizational structure/ process and IS structure/process and (3) organizational culture and IS culture will be gradually updated either positively or negatively in the near future depending on the satisfaction of final users and top management regarding the ability of the IS to support organizational strategy, processes and culture.

Toward Comprehensive IS Project Alignment

Table 3. IS project alignment framework

Dimension	Contextual alignment	(1)	(2)	(3)	(4)	Description	Project success	
							PMS	PD
Alignment between the **business organization** and the **project organization**	Organizational strategy < > Project strategy		X			...depends on the degree to which the project establishes competitive advantage (or value) for customers (or users) and contributes to the organization's business and long-term strategic goals (Patanakul & Shenhar, 2012).		X
	Organizational structure < > Project structure		X			...depends on the degree to which the surrounding organization provides (either by recruiting new resources or transferring existing resources) the project structure with sufficiently skilled resources and authority to accomplish its missions (Lidow, 1999).	X	
	Organizational process < > Project process			X		...depends on the degree to which project managers create functional specifications connected with target organizational requirements (Wiegers & Beatty, 2013).	X	
	Organizational culture < > Project culture				X	...depends on the degree to which organizational culture supports the presence and development of a project culture characterized by flexibility, creativity, and cross-functional collaboration.	X	
	Organizational people < > Project people	X				...depends on the social interactions throughout the project, which affect communication, coordination, and shared understanding between organization people and project people (Jenkin & Chan, 2010).	X	
Alignment between the **IS organization** and the **project organization**	IS strategy < > Project strategy	X				...depends on the degree to which the project objectives reflect the current IS strategy, which may change throughout the project (Jenkin & Chan, 2010).		X
	IS structure < > Project structure			X		...depends on the degree to which the internal and/or outsourced IS structure provides the project structure with sufficient IS-skilled resources to ensure IS application development, configuration, and maintenance (Nah & Delgado, 2006).	X	
	IS process < > Project process			X		...depends on the degree to which IS experts develop, configure, and deliver an IS application that supports the organizational requirements described by functional specifications (Aversano et al., 2016)	X	
	IS people < > Project people	X				...depends on the social interactions that occur throughout the project that affect communication, coordination and shared understanding between IS people and project people (Jenkin & Chan, 2010).	X	
	IS culture < > Project culture			X		...depends on the degree to which the values embedded in the technology match project team values (representing a subunit of the organization) or the group's IT values (Leidner & Kayworth, 2006).	X	

continued on following page

Table 3. Continued

Dimension	Contextual alignment	(1)	(2)	(3)	(4)	Description	Project success	
							PMS	PD
Alignment between the **IS organization** and the **business organization**	IS strategy < > Organizational strategy			X		...depends on the degree to which IS shapes and supports organizational strategy (Henderson & Venkatraman, 1993).		X
	IS structure < > Organizational structure			X		...depends on the delivery capability of the IS function to support organizational requirements and expectations[11] (Henderson & Venkatraman, 1993).		X
	IS process < > Organizational process			X				X
	IS culture < > Organizational culture			X		...depends on the degree to which the values embedded in technology match with organizational values or the group's IT values (Leidner & Kayworth, 2006).		X
	IS people < > Organization people	X				...depends on the social interactions throughout the project, which affect communication, coordination, and shared understanding between IS people and organizational people (Jenkin & Chan, 2010).	X	

(1) Alignments addressed by ISPA literature (four alignments)
(2) Alignments addressed by PM literature (two alignments)
(3) Alignments addressed by MIS literature (eight alignments)
(4) Alignments revealed by our findings (one alignment)

CONCLUSION

To explore ISPA, we performed a five-year longitudinal case study of the international implementation of an ERP project within a logistics service provider. The organizational context characterized by various and interdependent structures, processes, people, and culture allowed us to uncover contextual alignments between the temporary organization represented by the IS project and its parent system represented by the implementing organization. Our research constructed a comprehensive framework of ISPA consisting of three main dimensions and 15 contextual alignments. Specifically, our study investigated the plural, complex, and multifaceted nature of ISPA resulting from the interaction of strategy, structure, process, people, and culture between the project, business, and IS organizations.

Contributions to Theory and Practice

By constructing a comprehensive framework of ISPA that includes the organizational context in which projects evolve, this research expands and refines our understanding of ISPA. In that sense, our study contributes to the ISPA literature and, more broadly,

Toward Comprehensive IS Project Alignment

the PM literature. Specifically, our findings emphasize the multifaceted nature of ISPA, intertwining strategic, structural, processual, social, and cultural aspects that must be brought into alignment for successful IS project implementation. Our main contribution is linking the advancements of different streams of literature (PM, MIS, and ISPA) together into a unique and comprehensive framework of ISPA composed of 15 contextual alignments between the project organization, the business organization, and the IS organization. Thus, within the scope of IS projects, a third organization (or sub-organization) can also be part of the project's larger organizational context (in addition to the business organization), which the IS organization represents. The latter also has a unique strategy, structure, processes, people, and culture; various elements can raise inherent fit and misfit challenges for the project and the business organizations. By introducing technological alignment issues to ISPA, we contribute to the MIS literature. Overall, to understand ISPA dynamics, separate investigations of the project, business, and IS organizations led to a partial and fragmented view of alignment. Instead, we demonstrated that interactions between these organizations (permanent and temporary) involved multiple alignment and misalignment scenarios that influence ISPA and, ultimately, project success.

This research also has implications for practitioners. Given that the organizational context in which projects evolve influences their success or failure (Pinto, 2019), project managers must consider the surrounding environment in which IS projects operate and identify contextual strengths and weaknesses early in the project life cycle. Our comprehensive ISPA framework enables project managers to deepen their understanding of how contextual alignments influence project success, encompassing project management and product success. Our framework enables project managers to assess the supportiveness of the organizational context in which their projects are managed so that they can concentrate on contextual alignments with lower levels, pinpointing areas for improvement and determining where changes should be implemented.

Limitations

Our research contains some limitations. First, the main limitation of our study is that it is restricted to a case study in a single organization. Consequently, the findings are closely tied to the specific context in which we gathered our data. While a longitudinal case study enabled a thorough exploration of ISPA dimensions, further research is warranted to validate or contest our findings in diverse contexts. The second limitation of our study is related to product success assessment. Although the ERP system had already been implemented and benefited from user feedback, it ran concurrently with the old in-house system. Such a situation did not allow us to fully assess product success and the organizational benefits.

Research Agenda

Although this study has enhanced our comprehension of ISPA and developed a rich understanding of ISPA, the proposed framework could be validated and/or improved by additional replications across other IS projects in different organizational contexts. Additionally, further research could investigate if some contextual alignments are more critical than others for project success, requiring particular attention from the project team. Future research related to ISPA could delve into the processes associated with some of the identified alignments (among the fifteen) and emphasize the steps and events leading to alignment. For example, future research could investigate how to reach cultural alignment between IT and the adopting organization. Last, additional intriguing avenues for extending this research involve investigating external factors beyond the parent organization's scope that influence ISPA.

REFERENCES

Alsudiri, T., Al-Karaghouli, W., & Eldabi, T. (2013). Alignment of large project management process to business strategy: A review and conceptual framework. *Journal of Enterprise Information Management*, *26*(5), 596–615. doi:10.1108/JEIM-07-2013-0050

Aversano, L., Grasso, C., & Tortorella, M. (2016). Managing the alignment between business processes and software systems. *Information and Software Technology*, *72*, 171–188. doi:10.1016/j.infsof.2015.12.009

Baccarini, D. (1999). The logical framework method for defining project success. *Project Management Journal*, *30*(4), 25–32. doi:10.1177/875697289903000405

Benbasat, I., Goldstein, D. K., & Mead, M. (1987). The case research strategy in studies of information systems. *Management Information Systems Quarterly*, *11*(3), 369–386. doi:10.2307/248684

Blomquist, T., & Packendorff, J. (1998). Learning from renewal projects: Content, context and embeddedness. In R. A. Lundin & C. Midler (Eds.), *Projects as arenas for renewal and learning processes* (pp. 37–46). Springer. doi:10.1007/978-1-4615-5691-6_4

Box, S., & Platts, K. (2005). Business process management: Establishing and maintaining project alignment. *Business Process Management Journal*, *11*(4), 370–387. doi:10.1108/14637150510609408

Cooke-Davies, T. (2002). The "real" success factors on projects. *International Journal of Project Management*, *20*(3), 185–190. doi:10.1016/S0263-7863(01)00067-9

De Wit, A. (1988). Measurement of project success. *International Journal of Project Management*, *6*(3), 164–170. doi:10.1016/0263-7863(88)90043-9

Eisenhardt, K. M. (1989). Building theories from case study research. *Academy of Management Review*, *14*(4), 532–550. doi:10.2307/258557

El-Telbany, O., & Elragal, A. (2014). Business-information systems strategies: A focus on misalignment. *Procedia Technology*, *16*, 250–262. doi:10.1016/j.protcy.2014.10.090

Engwall, M. (2003). No project is an island: Linking projects to history and context. *Research Policy*, *32*(5), 789–808. doi:10.1016/S0048-7333(02)00088-4

Gartner. (2021). *Gartner forecasts worldwide IT spending to exceed $4 trillion in 2022*. Gartner Consulting. https://www.gartner.com/en/newsroom/press-releases/2021-10-2 0-gartner-forecasts-worldwide-it-spending-to-exceed-4-trilli on-in-2022

Gilchrist, A., Burton-Jones, A., & Green, P. (2018). The process of social alignment and misalignment within a complex IT project. *International Journal of Project Management*, *36*(6), 845–860. doi:10.1016/j.ijproman.2018.04.004

Goodhue, D. L., & Thompson, R. L. (1995). Task-technology fit and individual performance. *Management Information Systems Quarterly*, *19*(2), 213–236. doi:10.2307/249689

Grabher, G. (2002). Cool projects, boring institutions: Temporary collaboration in social context. *Regional Studies*, *36*(3), 205–214. doi:10.1080/00343400220122025

Griffith, A. F., & Gibson, G. E. Jr. (2001). Alignment during preproject planning. *Journal of Management Engineering*, *17*(2), 69–76. doi:10.1061/(ASCE)0742-597X(2001)17:2(69)

Handy, C. B. (2020). *Gods of management: The four cultures of leadership*. Profile Books.

Henderson, C., & Venkatraman, N. (1993). Strategic alignment: Leveraging information technology for transforming organizations. *IBM Systems Journal*, *32*(1), 4–16. doi:10.1147j.382.0472

Holland, C. R., & Light, B. (1999). A critical success factors model for ERP implementation. *IEEE Software*, *16*(3), 30–36. doi:10.1109/52.765784

Hong, K.-K., & Kim, Y.-G. (2002). The critical success factors for ERP implementation: An organizational fit perspective. *Information & Management, 40*(1), 25–40. doi:10.1016/S0378-7206(01)00134-3

Hustad, E., Haddara, M., & Kalvenes, B. (2016). ERP and organizational misfits: An ERP customization journey. *Procedia Computer Science, 100*, 429–439. doi:10.1016/j.procs.2016.09.179

Iriarte, C., & Bayona, S. (2020). IT projects success factors: A literature review. *International Journal of Information Systems and Project Management, 8*(2), 49–78. doi:10.12821/ijispm080203

Jenkin, T. A., & Chan, Y. E. (2010). IS project alignment – A process perspective. *Journal of Information Technology, 25*(1), 35–55. doi:10.1057/jit.2009.10

Johnson, J. (2020). *CHAOS 2020: Beyond infinity*. The Standish Group. https://www. standishgroup.com/news/49

Jugdev, K., & Müller, R. (2005). A retrospective look at our evolving understanding of project success. *Project Management Journal, 36*(4), 19–31. doi:10.1177/875697280503600403

Klimkeit, D. (2013). Organizational context and collaboration on international projects: The case of a professional service firm. *International Journal of Project Management, 31*(3), 366–377. doi:10.1016/j.ijproman.2012.08.001

Krumbholz, M., & Maiden, N. A. M. (2000). How culture might impact on the implementation of enterprise resource planning packages. In B. Wangler & L. Bergman (Eds.), *Advanced Information Systems Engineering* (pp. 279–293). Springer. doi:10.1007/3-540-45140-4_19

Leidner, D. E., & Kayworth, T. (2006). Review: A review of culture in information systems research: Toward a theory of information technology culture conflict. *Management Information Systems Quarterly, 30*(2), 357–399. doi:10.2307/25148735

Lidow, D. (1999). Duck alignment theory: Going beyond classic project management to maximize project success. *Project Management Journal, 30*(4), 8–14. doi:10.1177/875697289903000403

Lundin, R. A., & Söderholm, A. (1995). A theory of the temporary organization. *Scandinavian Journal of Management, 11*(4), 437–455. doi:10.1016/0956-5221(95)00036-U

Manning, S. (2008). Embedding projects in multiple contexts – A structuration perspective. *International Journal of Project Management, 26*(1), 30–37. doi:10.1016/j.ijproman.2007.08.012

Marchewka, J. T. (2012). *Information technology project management: Providing measurable organizational value* (4th ed.). Wiley.

Miles, M. B., & Huberman, A. M. (1994). Qualitative data analysis: An expanded sourcebook. *Sage (Atlanta, Ga.).*

Miles, M. B., Huberman, A. M., & Saldaña, J. (2020). Qualitative data analysis: A methods sourcebook. *Sage (Atlanta, Ga.).*

Morquin, D., Ologeanu-Taddei, R., Paré, G., & Wagner, G. (2023). A method for resolving organisation-enterprise system misfits: An action research study in a pluralistic organisation. *Information Systems Journal, 33*(5), 995–1028. doi:10.1111/isj.12433

Morris, P. W., & Geraldi, J. (2011). Managing the institutional context for projects. *Project Management Journal, 42*(6), 20–32. doi:10.1002/pmj.20271

Müller, R., & Jugdev, K. (2012). Critical success factors in projects: Pinto, Slevin, and Prescott–the elucidation of project success. *International Journal of Managing Projects in Business, 5*(4), 757–775. doi:10.1108/17538371211269040

Nah, F. F. H., Lau, J. L. S., & Delgado, S. (2006). Critical success factors for enterprise resource planning implementation and upgrade. *Journal of Computer Information Systems, 46*(5), 99–113. doi:10.1080/08874417.2006.11645928

Nah, F. F. H., Lau, J. L. S., & Kuang, J. (2001). Critical factors for successful implementation of enterprise systems. *Business Process Management Journal, 7*(3), 285–296. doi:10.1108/14637150110392782

Nilsson, A. (2015). IT project alignment in practice. In S. Gao & L. Rusu (Eds.), *Modern techniques for successful IT project management* (pp. 21–47). Business Science Reference. doi:10.4018/978-1-4666-7473-8.ch002

Nilsson Vestola, E., Eriksson, P. E., Larsson, J., & Karrbom Gustavsson, T. (2021). Temporary and permanent aspects of project organizing–operation and maintenance of road infrastructure. *International Journal of Managing Projects in Business, 14*(7), 1444–1462. doi:10.1108/IJMPB-09-2020-0279

O'Leary, T., & Williams, T. (2012). Managing the social trajectory: A practice perspective on project management. *IEEE Transactions on Engineering Management, 60*(3), 566–580. doi:10.1109/TEM.2012.2228206

Packendorff, J. (1995). Inquiring into the temporary organization: New directions for project management research. *Scandinavian Journal of Management, 11*(4), 319–333. doi:10.1016/0956-5221(95)00018-Q

Patanakul, P., & Shenhar, A. J. (2012). What project strategy really is: The fundamental building block in strategic project management. *Project Management Journal, 43*(1), 4–20. doi:10.1002/pmj.20282

Pinto, J. K. (2019). *Project management: Achieving competitive advantage* (5th ed.). Pearson.

Ram, J., & Corkindale, D. (2014). How "critical" are the critical success factors (CSFs)? Examining the role of CSFs for ERP. *Business Process Management Journal, 20*(1), 151–174. doi:10.1108/BPMJ-11-2012-0127

Ren, X., Yan, Z., Wang, Z., & He, J. (2019). Inter-project knowledge transfer in project-based organizations: An organizational context perspective. *Management Decision, 58*(5), 844–863. doi:10.1108/MD-11-2018-1211

Schwalbe, K. (2019). *Information technology project management* (9th ed.). Cengage.

Seiler, D. (2020). *How COVID-19 has pushed companies over the technology tipping point—and transformed business forever.* Strategy & Corporate Finance. https://www.mckinsey.com/business-functions/strategy-and-cor porate-finance/our-insights/how-covid-19-has-pushed-companie s-over-the-technology-tipping-point-and-transformed-business -forever

Shenhar, A. J. (1999). Strategic project management: The new framework. *PICMET '99: Portland International Conference on Management of Engineering and Technology (Vol-1).* 10.1109/PICMET.1999.808262

Shenhar, A. J., Levy, O., & Dvir, D. (1997). Mapping the dimensions of project success. *Project Management Journal, 28*(2), 5–13.

Sia, S. K., & Soh, C. (2007). An assessment of package–organisation misalignment: Institutional and ontological structures. *European Journal of Information Systems, 16*(5), 568–583. doi:10.1057/palgrave.ejis.3000700

Siggelkow, N. (2007). Persuasion with case studies. *Academy of Management Journal, 50*(1), 20–24. doi:10.5465/amj.2007.24160882

Skulmoski, G. J., & Hartman, F. T. (1999). Project alignment: The key to successful cost engineering. *AACE International Transactions*, PM41.

Soh, C., Kien, S. S., & Tay-Yap, J. (2000). Enterprise resource planning: Cultural fits and misfits: Is ERP a universal solution? *Communications of the ACM, 43*(4), 47–51. doi:10.1145/332051.332070

Srivannaboon, S., & Milosevic, D. Z. (2006). A two-way influence between business strategy and project management. *International Journal of Project Management, 24*(6), 493–505. doi:10.1016/j.ijproman.2006.03.006

Strong, D. M., & Volkoff, O. (2010). Understanding organization—Enterprise system fit: A path to theorizing the information technology artifact. *Management Information Systems Quarterly, 34*(4), 731–756. doi:10.2307/25750703

Svejvig, P., & Andersen, P. (2015). Rethinking project management: A structured literature review with a critical look at the brave new world. *International Journal of Project Management, 33*(2), 278–290. doi:10.1016/j.ijproman.2014.06.004

Sydow, J., & Windeler, A. (2020). Temporary organizing and permanent contexts. *Current Sociology, 68*(4), 510–531. doi:10.1177/0011392120907629

Thomas, G., & Fernández, W. (2008). Success in IT projects: A matter of definition? *International Journal of Project Management, 26*(7), 733–742. doi:10.1016/j.ijproman.2008.06.003

van der Hoorn, B., & Whitty, S. J. (2017). The praxis of 'alignment seeking' in project work. *International Journal of Project Management, 35*(6), 978–993. doi:10.1016/j.ijproman.2017.04.011

Villachica, S. W., Stone, D. L., & Endicott, J. (2004). Project alignment ensuring successful development and implementation from day one. *Performance Improvement, 43*(10), 9–15. doi:10.1002/pfi.4140431005

Wiegers, K., & Beatty, J. (2013). *Software requirements* (3rd ed.). Pearson.

Winter, M., Smith, C., Morris, P., & Cicmil, S. (2006). Directions for future research in project management: The main findings of a UK government-funded research network. *International Journal of Project Management, 24*(8), 638–649. doi:10.1016/j.ijproman.2006.08.009

Yusuf, Y., Gunasekaran, A., & Abthorpe, M. S. (2004). Enterprise information systems project implementation: A case study of ERP in Rolls-Royce. *International Journal of Production Economics, 87*(3), 251–266. doi:10.1016/j.ijpe.2003.10.004

KEY TERMS AND DEFINITIONS

IS Project Alignment: Alignment between an IS project and its larger organizational context comprising the business organization and the IS organization.

IS project organizational context: The permanent organizational characteristics (i.e., strategy, structure, process, people, and culture of the business and the IS organizations) that can facilitate or constrain successful IS project implementation.

IS Project Contextual Alignments: The set of alignments between an IS project and its larger organizational context that influence project success, encompassing project management and product success.

Alignment Between the Business Organization and the Project Organization: The extent to which organizational strategy, structure, process, people, and culture support and are supported by project strategy, structure, process, people, and culture.

Alignment Between the IS Organization and Project Organization: The extent to which IS strategy, structure, process, people, and culture support and are supported by project strategy, structure, process, people, and culture.

Alignment Between the IS Organization and the Business Organization: The extent to which IS strategy, structure, process, people, and culture support and are supported by organizational strategy, structure, process, people, and culture.

IS Project Supportive Organizational Context: A supportive organizational context promotes IS projects and increases the likelihood of success.

IS Project Non-Supportive Organizational Context: A non-supportive organizational context hinders IS projects and decreases the likelihood of success.

ENDNOTES

[1]   In their seminal article "*Strategic alignment: Leveraging information technology for transforming organizations*", Henderson and Venkatraman (1993) defined alignment between I/S infrastructure and processes and organizational infrastructure and processes (or operational integration) as "ensuring internal coherence between the organizational requirements and expectations and the delivery capacity within the I/S function" (p.476). Drawing on Henderson and Venkatraman (1993) definition, we selected one definition for two alignments in our above framework.

Toward Comprehensive IS Project Alignment

APPENDIX

Appendix A. Summary of respondents' verbatim reply content

Alignment Between Business Organization and Project Organization	
Alignment between **organizational strategy** and **project strategy**	[1] "Thanks to the data [provided by the single ERP database], we will have decision-making tools that will provide us with reliable indicators and will allow us to optimize our operations at the group level." [R1 – P1] [Fit] [2] "The new ERP software will bring new services and more value to our clients." [R6 – P1] [Fit]
Alignment between **organizational structure** and **project structure**	[3] "They [speaking about key users and the project team] are juniors without business expertise and without technical expertise of the software itself." [R2 - P1] [Misfit] [4] "I was unable to complete the tasks assigned to me within the framework of the project. Why all that? Because I have other missions in the company and afterward, I lose the train and I can't catch up..." [R5 - P1] [Misfit] [5] "I think it's very positive since there was a change of profile; now we have someone [speaking about the new project team recruit] who has good business knowledge, so that helps us a lot!" [R2 - P2] [Fit]
Alignment between **organizational process** and **project process**	[6] "I am very happy about the organizational requirements we [speaking about the project team] wrote because nothing existed before and now we have a clear picture of functional needs for each domain!" [R2 – P1] [Fit] [7] "I greatly appreciated all the work we [speaking about the project team] have done to formalize the different aspects of our business; in return, it took a very long time!" [R9 – P1] [Fit] [8] "In the first phase, before transmitting a functional need to [vendor A], we had meetings with our key users to present and validate organizational requirements; however, in the second phase, we never called our referents as we did before." [R3 – P2] [Misfit]
Alignment between **organizational people** and **project people**	[9] "I think the right choice you made was to share the project with the different teams and listen to them, but at the same time, to make decisions because you can't ask everyone what they think." [R10 – P1] [Fit] [10] "We were not sufficiently involved in the project. In fact, we had no information about what you [speaking about the project team] do!" [R5 – P1] [Misfit] [11] "The typical example is the period from January [2021] to today; for nine months, the key users heard nothing from the project team, so that reduces the motivation of people!" [R9 – P1] [Misfit]
Alignment between **organizational culture** and **project culture**	[12] "We [speaking about the project team] started to listen to everyone but not everyone knew the purpose of it all; that's what caused the mess!" [R6 – P1] [Misfit] [13] "The decision-making process is too centralized, it was [ROROL President] who made the decisions and it took too long!" [R8 – P1] [Misfit] [14] "We gave you [speaking about the project team] the power and accountability for the project, before you had none..." [R7 – P1] [Fit] [15] "Today, it is the three of us who decide [speaking of the two functional project managers and himself]. We must preserve this autonomy." [R3 – P2] [Fit]
Alignment Between IS Organization and Project Organization	
Alignment between **IS strategy** and **project strategy**	[16] "One of our guidelines for the project was to allow smoother communication with our clients. The ERP allows us to automatically send notifications and documentation depending on certain events in the system." [R3 – P1] [Fit] [17] "Project objectives were clearly defined from the beginning. We had to replace the current old software with an ERP at group level. The new system was chosen to harmonize IS applications by implementing a single system with various modules." [R2 – P1] [Fit] [18] "By centralizing all business data in a unique and monitored system, our goal was to avoid re-keying of the same data by various people in different Excel files which leads to a lot of entry errors today. In addition, we implemented a drop-down list to limit free user entry and avoid inaccuracies." [R1 – P1] [Fit]
Alignment between **IS structure** and **project structure**	[19] "We had a lot of stuff to do and not enough resources. There were really two of us; me, who worked on the project and [a developer], who did imports in the system as well as a few developments..." [R3 – P1] [Misfit] [20] "We have not acted fast enough to expand our IT team, we need to have a strong IT team composed of analysts and developers." [R6 – P1] [Misfit] [21] "Frankly, the recruitment in the IS team helped us because today we have people who can really work on the project. We no longer depend on me. That was a big problem before. If I was not here, we couldn't do anything in the system..." [R3 – P2] [Fit]
Alignment between **IS process** and **project process**	[22] "We had several meetings in which functional project managers expressed their needs. [...] We got them involved by explaining what we were going to do in the software." [R11 – P2] [Fit] [23] "[Talking about the different versions of the software that were delivered by the software vendor A] As we are making functional tests, we realize that a lot of things are missing. Each time we are obliged to repeat the same things and stay alert because it is not correct!" [R2 – P2] [Misfit] [24] "[Comparing functional specifications and software releases] There were some developments missing and a lot of bugs during this period. It was two weeks before the new year." [R3 – P2] [Misfit]

Toward Comprehensive IS Project Alignment

Alignment between **IS people** and **project people**	**[25]** "[Speaking about one of software vendor A's consultants] He has good knowledge and understanding of the transport domain!" [R3 – P2] [Fit] **[26]** "You need people [speaking about one of the ROROL project managers] who have a little understanding of what is technique. With [Project Director], it was impossible. He had no technical knowledge." [R4 – P1] [Misfit] **[27]** "As soon as you became more familiar with the software, the way of approaching things changed, now we speak the same language and we have interlocutors who understand what they are doing." [R4 – P2] [Fit]
Alignment between **IS culture** and **project culture**	**[28]** "It changed our way of working. Before, we were free to do what we wanted to do in our internal software. Now, we are limited in our customization capacity. Because the software has its own logic, we cannot do everything we want; the vendor has to approve our customization requests." [R11 – P2] [Misfit] **[29]** "ROROL's project team is trying to do what they did in ROROL's current in-house software because you think it's great; therefore, you think we have to reproduce it, but at the same time, you also have to adapt to our software [speaking about the ERP software] because we're not going to reproduce your in-house software!" [R4 – P1] [Misfit]

	Alignment Between IS Organization and Business Organization
Alignment between **IS strategy** and **organizational strategy**	**[30]** "Our current information systems do no longer allow us to support our growth. We need to set up an integrated information system that allows us to reach our business goals; that is, streamline our operations and provide useful information to our clients, but above all, produce reliable data so that we can quickly detect excesses to adjust our action plans and more broadly, our business strategy." [R6 – P1] [Misfit] **[31]** "One of the most problematic things is that the data that is entered into information systems is sometimes unusable. Without a reliable database, it is very complicated to steer the company, it is very complicated to make informed strategic choices." [R1 – P1] [Misfit] **[32]** "By implementing the new system, we achieved to increase our internal efficiency by removing most of Excel files, manual operations and redundancies. Also, we have standardized the very majority of our process and procedures in Europe and North Africa which will allow us to better monitor our performance and act more quickly in case of gaps." [R6 – P3] [Fit]
Alignment between **IS structure/ process** and **organizational structure/process**	**[33]** "The system is old, changing it has become imperative. For example, slowness is common because the database sometimes becomes too large." [R11 – P2] [Misfit] **[34]** "We face de-optimization every day in our daily activities because we use very outdated IS tools! " [R10 – P1] [Misfit] **[35]** "[Speaking about the former system] There are technological developments that the current system cannot keep up with. For example, I saw an email from a user who asked for the automatic percentage increase on a tariff that is 165 lines and the system cannot do it... " [R11 – P2] [Misfit] **[36]** "[Speaking about the former system] There is a lot of work that we do manually outside of the system because we don't have tools that allow us to speed up, automate and simplify our daily work. We need a system that makes our work easier and above all that reduces the possibility of making mistakes, because when we have to do the same thing four or five times for the same file, there is a high risk of making errors." [R10 – P1] [Misfit] **[37]** "To be frank with you, I have only had good feedback from the operation, they are very happy, they see the benefits brought by the system !" [R9 – P3] [Fit] **[38]** "Overall, the new system is much quicker and better than the old one, it helps us more to do our daily work well. !" [R16 – P3] [Fit] **[39]** "What's great is that we know when the goods have been loaded or delivered, so we no longer have to call the different branches to get the information. On aspects related to quality, the new system allows us to improve." [R14 – P3] [Fit] **[40]** "The system makes it possible to better frame the operational activities because the operators are obliged to follow the sale of the commercial and the system does not allow them to derogate from it which limits the errors. [R15 – P3] [Fit] **[41]** " Compared to the old system, we have much richer data at the invoicing level and it is easier too. On the new system [speaking about the ERP system], we can see all the operations we have to deal with so we can't forget to invoice a client. On the other hand, with the old system, all the work was manual, so we could make mistakes or forget to invoice certain clients." [R17 – P3] [Fit]
Alignment between **IS people** and **organizational people**	**[42]** "Another important point is trust […] When you create something for someone, they have to believe in what you are proposing. If they does not believe in it, it does not fit and it blocks! I felt there was distrust from the general management." [R4 – P1] [Misfit] **[43]** "I had to justify absolutely everything I did. I spent my time justifying the hours billed. I found that it was a very cumbersome and time-consuming way to operate. In fact, I felt it was a lack of confidence; people [speaking about ROROL top management] thought I was trying to bamboozle them." [R8 – P1] [Misfit] **[44]** "It has nothing to do with the former situation. Now, we [speaking about ROROL top management and software vendor A] can talk and understand each other. We managed to create a relationship of trust." [R4 – P2] [Fit]
Alignment between **IS culture** and **organizational culture**	**[45]** "Each contract is confidential, so tomorrow if we make contract details available to different people at the operational level through the ERP, confidentiality is no longer limited to the sales department!" [R12 – P2] [Misfit] **[46]** "With the new software [speaking about the ERP system], we will have all our pricing schedules shared with all company staff and that is not to our advantage. I think that is not right. Why give the prices to the operators? It is not worth sharing the price. It is the job of the salesperson!" [R13 – P2] [Misfit] **[47]** "Why are selling prices communicated to other departments of the company? I think it's really a mistake because we have people who will have access to all the selling prices practiced by the company, these people will not stay in the company and in the long term it can really be a problem." [R18 – P3] [Misfit]

Chapter 9
Cybernetics Principles in the Management of Intelligent Organizations

Stanislas Bigirimana

 https://orcid.org/0000-0002-3735-6102

College of Business, Peace, Leadership, and Governance, Africa University, Zimbabwe

ABSTRACT

Against the background that mechanical principles were applied in management leading to bureaucracy, an application of cybernetics principles in management would imply (1) a behaviouralist approach to organisations, (2) teleology: reintroducing the notion of purpose, (3) managing complexity, (4) systems thinking, (5) managing as building intelligence, (6) managing as integrating knowledge domains. This overcomes the rigidity embedded in bureaucracy where organizations sought stability and equilibrium and operated in a relatively stable environment for a dynamic and integrative approach to organisations which are not closed stable entities but dynamic open systems. Organisations built on cybernetics principles are agile and continuously respond to their environment through information processing and feedback loops. In this context, there is a paradigm shift from top down management processes linked with hierarchy to cross-functional, flexible, adaptable, and open to learning management principles based on knowledge networks. Alternatives to bureaucracy can be suggested in terms of flat, inverted pyramids, matrix, networked and virtual organisational structures which may stipulate a change from Michael Porter's normative approach to strategic management to Mintzberg's descriptive approach. Organisational structures are not cast in stone but respond to changes in the environment, and there is a paradigm shift in corporate culture from organisations as closed stable entities to organisations as open dynamic systems, from competition to trust and collaboration including outsourcing, consortia, joint venture, and conglomerates become better ways of satisfying customer needs. From a corporate culture there is also a change from focusing on power and ownership in decision-making to focusing on knowledge and an increased use of information and communication technologies leading to virtualisation.

DOI: 10.4018/978-1-7998-9687-6.ch009

Copyright © 2024, IGI Global. Copying or distributing in print or electronic forms without written permission of IGI Global is prohibited.

1. INTRODUCTION

Paradigms shifts in management, engineering and science in general are most of the time associated with disruptive technological innovations. A paradigm has been defined by Kuhn (1962) as "universally recognized achievements that for a time provide model problems and solutions to a community of practitioners". A disruptive innovation is an innovation that creates a new market and value network and eventually disrupts an existing market and value network, displacing established market leaders and alliance (Bower & Christensen 1995). Other authors add significant social impact as part of disruptive innovations (Marnix 2006). The link between disruptive technological innovation and unprecedented societal changes is not a new phenomenon. As Wiener (1961) has pointed out:

The thought of every age is reflected in its technique. The civil engineers of ancient days were land surveyors, astronomers and navigators; those of the seventeenth and early eighteenth centuries were clockmakers and grinders of lenses. As in ancient times, the craftsmen made their tools in the image of the heavens. A watch is nothing but a pocket orrery, moving by necessity as do the celestial spheres; and if friction and the dissipation of energy play a role in it, they are effects to be overcome, so that the resulting motion of the hands may be as periodic and regular as possible. The chief technical result of this engineering after the model of Huyghens and Newton was the age of navigation, in which for the first time it was possible to compute longitudes with a respectable precision, and to convert the commerce of the great oceans from a thing of chance and adventure to a regular understood business. It is the engineering of the mercantilists.

Wiener (1961) continues his exemplification of how paradigms have been changing within the area of physics and engineering by noting that:

To the merchant succeeded the manufacturer, and to the chronometer, the steam engine. From the Newcomen engine almost to the present time, the central field of engineering has been the study of prime movers. Heat has been converted into usable energy of rotation and translation, and the physics of Newton has been supplemented by that of Rumford, Carnot, and Joule. Thermodynamics makes its appearance, a science in which time is eminently irreversible; and although the earlier stages of this science seem to represent a region of thought almost without contact with the Newtonian dynamics, the theory of the conservation of energy and the later statistical explanation of the Carnot principle or second law of thermodynamics or principle of the degeneration of energy – that principle that makes the maximum efficiency obtainable by a steam engine depend on the working temperatures of the boiler and the condenser – all these have fused thermodynamics and the Newtonian dynamics into the statistical and the non-statistical aspects of the same science.

As a conclusion Wiener (1961) sets as a contemporary challenge the fact that, "[i]f the seventeenth and the eighteenth centuries are the age of clocks, and the later eighteenth century the age of steam engines, the present age is the age of communication and control". Cybernetics was defined by Wiener (1948) as the science of control and communication in the animal and the machine. Although the concept originated from engineering it was successfully introduced in management by Stafford Beer (Beer, 1959, Beer, 1960, Beer, 1965, Beer, 1966, Beer, 1972, Beer, 1975, Beer, 1979, Beer, 1981) creating the discipline of "management cybernetics" (Rosenhead, 2006). Management cybernetics implies approaching organisations as wholes through "systems thinking" (Espejo, 2006, Jackson 2000,, Jackson, 1991). Systems thinking implies understanding how systems influence one another within a complete entity, or larger system. Therefore, the best way to understand the Viable System Model (VSM) as both a conceptual, diagnosis, design and management tool is to link the VSM with its corollary concepts such as cybernetics and systems thinking.

2. THE NOTION OF CYBERNETICS

The late 1980s and early 1990s a paradigm shift was being pointed by various academic disciplines. For instance, Prigogine and Stengers (1984) pointed out that "interest is shifting from substance to relation, to communication, to time." At the same time, Drucker (1989) postulated a multidimensional change characterized by *The New Realities in Government and Politics, in Economics and Business in Society and World View.* Another voice that begged for a paradigm change was Bernstein (1991)'s calling for a *New Constellation.* However, it is Henry C. Mishkoff who gave the concept of cybernetics its status as a new *weltanschauung* in his book on artificial intelligence. According to Mishkoff (1986):

Norbert Wiener is best known for developing a new approach to understanding the workings of the universe. Since the time of Newton, scientists have concentrated on an energy model, explaining events and processes in terms of the transfer of energy. Wiener suggested a model that has proven to be extremely valuable in understanding computers as well as people – he suggested that the transfer of information rather than energy is the best way to model different kinds of scientific phenomena. Cybernetics was the name Wiener used both to describe his informational approach and to entitle his 1948 book on the subject.

Like any new concept, the concept of cybernetics may be new but the phenomenon it describes is not. Cybernetics did not get immediate acceptance in the scientific community. At the beginning, cybernetics was considered as belonging to the esoteric jargon of highly skilled mathematicians given its origins at the Massachusetts Institute of Technology (Ashby 1956). Syre (1967) warns that the concept of cybernetics came a long way. Before its general acceptance, it had some competing or substituting concepts which instead of overcrowding it revealed its intrinsic link with information science and its richness. In Syre (1967) own words:

The term "cybernetics" has not been universally accepted by mathematicians and engineers who often prefer to speak instead of information theory or of the theory of feedback and control. Use of the term here does not reflect a decision one way or another regarding those issues which incline many specialists from adopting "cybernetics" as a technical term.

The concept of cybernetics like any other encompassing concept refers to such wide and different areas of reality that it is not easy to define. For example, its mechanical counterpart defines reality as "matter in motion" and hence insists on the transmission of energy. We can also describe how mechanical principles apply in machinery, in body functions such as the understanding of speech as the movement of the tongue in the mouth, dying as the impossibility of motion which include the motion of blood in vessels, the motion of air in the lungs, or economics as the motion of goods and services between sellers and buyers (the notion of "financial flow" attests to this). The same wide areas of application are available for the concept of cybernetics. According to Norbert Wiener (1948) the inventor of the concept himself:

Since the end of World War II, I have been working on the many ramifications of the theory of messages. Besides the electrical engineering theory of transmission of messages, there is a larger field which includes not only the study of language but the study of messages as a means of controlling machinery and society, the development of computing machines and other such automata, certain reflections upon psychology and the nervous system, and a tentative theory of scientific method. This larger theory is a probabilistic theory ... Until recently, there was no existing word for this complex of ideas, and in order to embrace the whole field by a single term, I felt constrained to invent one. Hence "Cybernetics", which I derived from the Greek word *kubernetes*, for "steersman," the same Greek word from which we eventually derive our word "governor".

Hence from the subtitle of the book where the founder of cybernetics has systematically exposed this concept, we can define cybernetics as the science of "control and communication, in the machine and the animal" (Wiener 1948). The encompassing character of the concept of cybernetics creates a situation where, as Syre (1967) warns "there is no recognized philosophic theory or school that could properly be termed cybernetics." This is because, "cybernetics stands to the real machine – electronic, mechanical, neural, or economic – much as geometry stands to a real object in our terrestrial space" (Ashby, 1956). In other words, cybernetics

Cybernetics Principles in the Management of Intelligent Organizations

is not a form of description or a separate theory but a framework through which the functioning of both natural and artificial machines can be understood. According to Ashby (1956):

It (cybernetics) treats, not things, but ways of behaving. It does not ask "what is this thing" but "what does it do?" Thus it is very interested in such a statement as "this variable is undergoing simple harmonic oscillation", and is much less concerned with whether the variable is the position of a point on a wheel, or a potential in an electric circuit. It is thus essentially functional and behaviouristic.

This clarification by Ashby confirms Moray (1963)'s definition of cybernetics as the study of the behavior of systems of all kinds. It is the science of "input" and "output". This shift introduces a double dynamism. On the one hand, it requires us to study and understand not the invariant characteristics of systems associated with structure but the variable ones that are associated with behavior. That is why while mechanical models focus on identifying simple immutable laws that can be formulated into simple mathematical relations, cybernetic model focus in how systems respond to changes in their environment either by transforming themselves or by activating feedback processes. That is why Ashby (1956) points out that:

The most fundamental concept in cybernetics is that of "difference", either that two things are recognizably different or that one thing has changed with time ... All the changes that may occur with time are naturally included, for when plants grow and planets age and machines move some change from one state to another is implicit. So our first task will be to develop this concept of "change", not only making it more precise but making it richer, converting it to a form that experience has shown to be necessary if significant developments are to be made.

Change effected at one end of the behaving system is transmitted to other parts of the system or to its environment. In other words, change does not occur merely within the system but the system is both an object and an agent of change. In other words, cybernetics is interested not only in the way both internal and external factors change a given system but also in how this system transmits this change to its environment. This double dynamism points to another aspect of cybernetics, namely, the study of "input" and "output" (Moray 1963) because not only the system is acted upon by its environment but it also acts on its environment. This capacity to be acted on or to receive inputs and the capacity to generate an output create a situation where the system loses its invariant character and is subject to complex processes of change that are triggered by both internal and external factors. Hence, "a system is a set of attributes and the history of the changes of that set of attributes" (Moray, 1963)

3. CYBERNETICS IMPLICATIONS FOR MANAGEMENT

3.1 A Behaviouralist Approach to Organisations

Cybernetics implies a behaviouristic approach to machines and organisms. Rosenblueth, Wiener and Bigelow (1943) defined the behaviouristic approach as "the examination of the output of the object and of the relationship of this output to input" (Rosenblueth et al., 1943). Output is defined as "change produced in the surroundings of the object" (Rosenblueth et al., 1943) while input is "any external event to the object that modifies this object in any manner" (Rosenblueth et al. 1943). This definition of the behavioural approach to systems and organisms follows Moray (1963) definition of cybernetics as the the study of "input" and "output." The behaviouristic approach is contrasted with the functional approach which focuses on the intrinsic organization of the entity studied, its structures and its properties. The relationship between the entity and its surroundings are relatively incidental (Rosenblueth et al. 1943).

A functional approach to business organisations would imply conceiving organisations as stable closed entities while a behavioural approach implies understanding business as dynamic open systems (Bigirimana 2004). Organisations have been traditionally conceived as stable and closed entities aiming at equilibrium (balancing books or avoiding crises). This view exemplifies the way of proceeding of the pyramidal model where the preservation of the structural makeup of organisations made organisations self-serving rather than customer focused. In many instances, the fear of competition or sabotage by ill willed people covered them with secrecy and led to the creation of deep rooted routines borrowed either natural sciences or from other human organisations such as armies. In computer mediated environments, it becomes difficult even impossible to avoid interacting with others. The idea of the corporation (an autonomous body) invites some degree of heteronomy given the fact "interorganisational metabolism" (Lloyd and Boyle 1998) rather than "intraorganisational" metabolism is the norm of the day.

While the bureaucratic model conceives organisations as machines (Morgan, 2006) with laid down principles and processes that makes decisions independent of the bureaucrat, the idea of a corporation (from *corpus* in Latin that means body) implies an organic model with internal dynamics that are as stable as the biological laws of metabolism. From an organisational point of view, while the mechanical model implies a physical metaphor, the cybernetic model implies a biological metaphor. The biological metaphor presents organisations as living organisms hence their capacity to have "life" or viability. Organisations (from Greek *Organon* that means instrument) are not created for their own sake but for fulfilling pre-established goals, hence, the importance of the notion of purpose or teleology in both organizational design and management.

3.2 Teleology: Reintroducing the Notion of Purpose

One of the merits of cybernetics, is the introduction of the notions of purpose and teleology in the description of the behavior of machines and organisations (Rosenblueth et al., 1943). Scientific accounts of the behavior of machines and organisms had discarded this notion mainly because of its link to intentionality, a notion which is considered as inherently subjective but also because of its relation which religion through the definition of God by Aristotle and Thomas Aquinas as "the final cause" or the "immovable mover". In the context of cybernetics, the term purposeful is meant to denote that the act or behavior may be interpreted as directed to the attainment of a goal (Rosenblueth et al., 1943) i.e. a final condition in which the behaving object reaches a definite correlation in time or in space with respect to another object or event (Rosenblueth et al., 1943).

This is because there are actually two types of bahaviour: active behavior and passive behavior. Active behavior is that in which the object is the source of the output energy involved in a given specific reaction (Rosenblueth et al., 1943) while in passive behavior the object is not a sources of energy, all the energy in output can be traced to the immediate input (Rosenblueth et al. 1943). Active behavior may be subdivided in two classes: purposeless (random) and purposeful. That is why Umpleby (1987) have described cybernetics as a "science of goal formulation." This emphasis of goal formulation has been brought into focus by other cybernetics scholars such as Ackoff and Emery (1972), Ackoff (1981), Ackoff, Finnel and Gharajedaghi (1984), Ackoff (1994).

This emphasis on purpose implies that organisations should be geared towards shaping their future rather than preserving current structures and and practices. While the metaphor of the organization as an organism (Morgan 2006) is perceived as a improvement to its mechanical and bureaucratic counterparts (Morgan 2006), the idea of purpose justify the very nature of organisations (from Greek *Organon* that means instrument). Organisations are in their very essence, instruments for fulfilling pre-determined goals. This implies not only putting into place structures and systems i.e. not only putting parts together in a certain pattern of relationships and functions (creating a structure) but also determining the principles, values, procedures, and rules of interaction (creating a culture) (Bigirimana 2004).

3.3 Managing Complexity

Another aspect of organisations which is brought into focus by cybernetics is the idea of complexity. Moray (1963) has noted that "a system is a set of attributes and the history of the changes of that set of attributes." Being a set of attributes and the history of that set of attributes, any system presupposes basically some complexity. This complexity is brought by the fact that on the one hand in order to make a system one must bring many entities or attributes together, and on the other hand, not only these entities but also their various relations are subject to change over time. Hence, adopting cybernetics as a *weltanschauung* implies what Rescher (1998) calls "the complexity of the real." This idea of complexity has been studied in detail by scholars such as Mainzer (2007), Heylighen, Bollen and Riegler (1999), Sandra Mitchell (Mitchell, 2003, Mitchell, 2008, Mitchell, 2009) and Melanie Mitchell (2009).

The complexity of the real becomes more evident with the various patterns of organization and interaction of elements and entities which can be aggregated to form complex beings or which are involved in various relations be they spatio-temporal, exchange of various forms of energy or various possibilities of transformation given both external and internal factors. The degree of complexity can be so high to the extent that the ideas of simplicity, order, and regularity that founded Newton's mechanical model and Descartes' rational model can be called into question. There is increasing literature that claims that reality, at least in some of its aspects, is chaotic. This chaotic aspect has been so well studied to the extent that some scientists have attempted to find its mathematical formulation especially by pushing beyond certain limits the variables of functions which are otherwise simple when their computation are kept in 'normal' limits. It is worth noting the distinction that Toffler (1984) makes when he assesses Progogine and Stengers' ways of thinking. In their view,

Summed and amplified, they hold that while some parts of the universe may operate like machines, these are closed systems, at best form only a small part of the physical universe. Most phenomena of interest to us are, in fact, open systems, exchanging energy or matter [one may add information] with their environment. Surely biological and social systems are open, which means that the attempt to understand them in mechanistic terms is doomed to failure. This suggests, moreover, that most of reality instead of being orderly, stable, and equilibrial, is seething and bubbling with change, disorder, process.

3.4 Systems Thinking

Management cybernetics implies approaching organisations as wholes through "systems thinking" (Espejo, 2006, Jackson, 2000, Jackson, 1991). Systems thinking implies understanding how systems influence one another within a complete entity, or larger system. Systems thinking has been defined as an approach to problem solving that attempts to balance holistic thinking and reductionist thinking. Reductionist thinking implies analysing complex systems by separating their parts. However, Bertalanffy (1968) pointed out that:

Application of the analytical procedure depends on two conditions. The first is that interactions between "parts" be non-existent or weak enough to be neglected for certain research purposes. Only under this condition, can parts be "worked out," actually, logically, mathematically, and then be "put together." The second condition is that the relations describing the behavior of parts be linear; only then is the condition of summativity given, i.e., an equation describing the behavior of the parts; partial processes can be superimposed to obtain the total process, etc., but as by cutting them into their parts.

In other words, we can only analyse systems which are analysable. Systems thinking is a response to Cartesianism i.e. the habit to "break apart problems, to fragment the world" (Drucker 1989). The semi-skilled worker was precious in the industrial society because at that time the industrialist "analyzed tasks and broke them down into individual, unskilled tasks that could be learned quickly" (Drucker 1989). However, this situation is changing radically since the post-industrial society is dominated by the scientists and experts that hold technical and professional positions. Drucker has noted that the "knowledge worker", an expert is replacing the semi-skilled worker of the massive production of the industrial society (Drucker 1989).

Cabrera (2008) has noted that systems thinking itself is the emergent property of complex adaptive system behavior that results from four simple rules of thought. These rules also known as DSRP imply that a system thinker has to display four types of ability namely: (1) making Distinctions i.e. among various objects in a system the system thinker should be able to know which consist of an *identity* and an *other; (2)* Organizing Systems – which consist of *part* and *whole, (3)* recognizing Relationships – which consist of *action* and *reaction* and (4) taking Perspectives – which consist of *point* and *view*. According to Jackson (1986) cybernetics offers an extremely sophisticated account of the nature of organisations. In spite of its strengths, the cybernetic model is not widely known or used in organisation and management theory. One reason might be that perceived weaknesses in the model are seen to outweigh the strengths (Jackson 1986). Jackson (1986) corroborated Clemson (1968)'s view who earlier pointed out that that cybernetics is a new management tool. Espejo (2013) actually is of the view that a cybernetic model would have averted the 2008 financial crisis by weaving financial and economic activities into one organisational system constituted by cohesive and inclusive autonomous systems. The origin of the crisis, according to Espejo (2013) is that financial services as wealth extracting activities [are] detached from the economies they were supposed to serve. Likewise, applying cybernetic principles to the management of institutions of higher education would imply considering universities as complex systems which are in continuous interaction with the communities in which they serve.

3.5 Managing as Integrating Knowledge Domains

A cybernetic model of organization has the advantages of integrating aspects of business which are traditionally considered as separate. Furthermore, a cybernetic model goes beyond academic disciplines and research programmes. For instance, The Organization Orientation Group (OOG) (2011) have showed how a cybernetic model of organisations integrates organization theory ad culture theory through knowledge cybernetics. In their view, every organization is characterised by four domains (culture, strategy, structure, operations) and six processes (cultural guidance, strategy implementation, structural guidance, performance assessment, single- and double-loop learning (OOG, 2011). The cybernetic model that they suggest integrates Schein (1985)'s theory of culture and Hatch and Cunliffe (2006)'s organizational theory. Schein (1985)'s theory of culture comprises 'underlying values' (invisible, unconscious assumptions), 'espoused values'(rules, standard prohibitions) and 'artifacts'(visible behavior). Hatch and Cunliffe (2006)'s organizational theory on the other hand identifies five major fields in organizational theory namely organizational culture and identity, organizational strategy, organizational design and structure, organizational behavior and performance, and strategic response to organizational environment. Taken in isolation, Schein (1985) and Hatch and Cunliffe (2006) models can be represented as shown in Figure 1.

Figure 1.
Source: *OOG (2011: 3)*

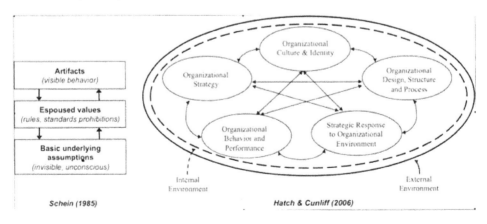

Cybernetics Principles in the Management of Intelligent Organizations

However these models taken in isolation have some limitations. While these model suggests which domains seem to be of utmost importance when analyzing organizations, it does not extend our knowledge about how these domains are related to each other and how they may change over time (OOG, 2011). The same limitation is observed with Schein (1985)'s theory of culture. Schein (1985) still lacks a precise definition of relationships among domains is not provided, which reaches beyond what is commonly defined as 'organizational mechanisms' (Pajunen, 2008). In other words, there is a need to integrate the two theories in order to introduce an element of dynamism which accounts not only for the relationships between various domains but also their possible changes over time. This process of integration was achieved by the OOG (2011) by noticing a relationship of equivalence between knowledge cybernetics, Hatch and Cunliffe (2006)'s organizational theory and Schein (1985)'s theory of culture. Equivalences in these domains has been represented as Table 1.

Following these relationships of equivalence any organization can be defined from the point of view of knowledge cybernetics as having a phenomenal domain, an epistemic domain and an existential domain (OOG 2011). The phenomenal domain of an organization can be understood as a structural coupling between two domains, namely, structures and operations (OOG 2011). Operations make an organization visible as a member of society because they become manifest through action/behavior (OOG 2011). Structures on the other hand, are responsible for the 'internal allocation of tasks, decisions, rules, and procedures for appraisal and reward, selected for the best pursuit of [...] [a] strategy' (Caves, 1980). Changes in the phenomenal domain are triggered by performance feedback of other social systems, i.e. institutions, organizations, interest groups and individuals, which can be subsumed as stakeholders of an organization (Freeman, 1984). According to Yolles (2017), the OOG (2011), (Piaget 1950) the coupling between the distinct domains is cybernetic in nature, with feed-forward and feedback "loops" that are most simply described in terms of operative and figurative intelligence.

The epistemic domain of the organization comprises the strategic orientation of the organization and mechanisms of implementing strategy. A strategic process comprises three stages namely strategy formulation, strategy implementation and strategy evaluation. Strategy itself comprises a vision, a mission, long term goals,

Domains of the Cybernetic Model	Equivalents in Organisational Theory (Hatch & Cunliffe, 2006)	Equivalents in Culture Theory (Schein, 1985)
Existential domain	*Organisational Culture*	*Underlying Values*
Epistemic domain	*Strategy*	*Espoused values*
Phenomenal domain	*Structure, Operations*	*Artifacts*

Source: OOG (2011)

systems and structures and a corporate culture. Menguc and Auh (2005) have noted that strategic orientation formation and strategic orientation implementation are different. Strategic orientation includes "the strategic directions implemented by a firm to create the proper behaviors for the continuous superior performance of the business" (Gatignon and Xuereb 1997: 78). Strategic orientation comprises the organization wide and collective action of firms that is supported by successful communication, interpretation, adoption, and enactment of information (Menguc and Auh 2005). The formation stage includes three activities, namely, the the adoption, interpretation, and communication of information (Menguc and Auh 2005) while enactment, implementation, or execution of such information belongs to the strategic orientation implementation stage (Menguc and Auh 2005). Implementation can be defined as the application of resources to strategy (Day and Wensley 1983) or the "how-to-do-it" aspects (Céspedes 1991). In other words, implementation involves "the organization's competence in executing, controlling, and evaluating its marketing strategy (White et al. 2003).

All in all, the epistemic domain of an organization has both a theoretical and practical dimension. The implementation stage is a key mediator between strategy development styles and firm performance (White et al. 2003). Menguc and Auh (2005) have emphasized the the need of TMT (top management team) diversity and interfunctional coordination in successful strategy orientation formulation while they noted that this diversity may be detrimental to strategy orientation implementation. From a cybernetic point of view, the epistemic domain integrates normative aspects of the value chain (Porter 1998) and emerging properties linked with the multifaceted nature of managerial roles (Mintzberg 1975).

The existential domain is the values and principles which underlying the daily management of the organization. Porter (1998) pointed out that culture is difficult to define. However, he acknowledges different cultures are implied by different generic strategies. Porter (1998) has identified three generic strategies cost leadership, differentiation, and cost focus. For Mintzberg (1973) corporate culture is linked to the strategy making mode and to the context. Mintzberg (1973) distinguished three strategy modes namely the entrepreneurial, the adaptive and the planning mode and five contexts namely the entrepreneurial, the mature, the diversified, the innovation and the professional context (Mintzberg 1983). These contexts invite according to Mintzberg (1983) not only different cultures but also different organizational structures ranging from the simple structure where an entrepreneur has pervasive influence on the environment, the machine bureaucracy, the divisionalised form, adhocracy, or a professional bureaucracy. A comparison of Porter and Mintzberg approaches to strategy can be represented in Table 2.

Table 2.

	PORTER	MINTZERBERG
Approach	Normative	Descriptive
Definition	Plan	• Pattern; • Ploy; • Position; • Perspective • Plan
Process	Top-down Linear (Formulate-Implement-Evaluate)	Vertical and Horizontal Integration Complex and dynamic (Craft through the interaction between the strategic and a context
Context	Mature	Variable (look at the various possible contexts)
Structure	Machine Bureaucracy	Variable (look at different possible configurations)
Culture	Command and Control Employee compliance	Dynamic and Integrative and Interactive (look at the different coordination mechanisms)
Outcomes	Conformity to pre-determined goals	Planning; Entrepreneurial; Adaptive depending on the context, the size of the organisation etc

3.6 Managing as Building Intelligence

Intelligence has been often presented as human prerogative. According to Sternberg (1988) intelligence implies the capability to do two things: (1) to transform or change oneself by adapting, developing and learning, (2) to influence or change the environment if necessary. For Schwaninger (2000) in order to make the concept of an intelligent enterprise operational there is a need to class an enterprise that effectively combines adaptation, learning and development as 'intelligent'. Schwaninger (2000) has defined adaptation as self-transformation in order to meet requirements from outside. Learning signifies an increase in the ability to take effective action (Kim 1993) while creation signifies the growing ability of an organization to meet its own and others' needs (Ackoff 1981). The paternity of the concept of "organizational intelligence" is attributed to Wilensky (1967)'s book on Organizational Intelligence: Knowledge and Policy in Government and Industry. March and Olsen (1975) explored the concept of organizational learning while Quinn (1992) popularized the concept in his book *Intelligent Enterprise.* In addition to Quinn (1992), Thannhuber (2004) and Gupta and Sharma (2004) explored the ins and outs of the concept outside the United States. Contrary to the dominat supportive trend, Palmer (2007) pointed to the limitations of the concept.

Cybernetics Principles in the Management of Intelligent Organizations

Yolles (2005) argued that the concept of intelligence can be applied to organization at least metaphorically. In Yolles (2005)'s terms the notion of organisational intelligence requires a metaphorically defined psychological frame of reference. In trying to formulate this metaphor, there has been a need to explore the collective from a psychological perspective (Yolles, 2005). Applications of the notion of organisational intelligence operate in a variety of areas, and two of these are in organisational learning and managerial cybernetics (Yolles, 2005). Other authors who explored the possible extension of individual cognitive processes to organization include Morgan (2006) who presented organisations as "brains". Presenting organisations as brains implies emphasizing organisations's ability for learning and self-organisation (Morgan 2006) but also organisations that are able to "learn to learn" (Morgan 2006). It is through this ability that Morgan (2006) links the image of the learning organization to cybernetics.

The idea that organization are able to learn was brought to public earlier by Senge (1990) who is perceived as the pioneer of the concept of a "learning organization" but Haeckel and Nolan (1993) have defined organizational intelligence as the institutional ability to deal with complexity, that is, its ability to capture, share, and extract meaning from marketplace signals. This implies that managing intelligent organisations includes integrating knowledge domains but also adequate information management (Choo 1995), knowledge management (Wiig, 2007) and intelligent behavior. This integrative dimension is highlighted by Liebowitz and Wilcox (1997). Haeckel and Nolan (1993) suggest a transfer of the OODA model used by the United States Air Force to management. According to Haeckel and Nolan (1993) the United States Air Force assesses a pilot's ability to learn with the OODA Loop, a model for the mental processes of a fighter pilot. OODA stands for:

- *Observation:* sensing environmental signals;
- *Orientation:* interpreting those signals;
- *Decision:* selecting from a repertoire of available responses;
- *Action:* executing the response selected.

Fighter pilots with faster OODA Loops tend to win dogfights, while those with slower ones get more parachute practice (Haeckel and Nolan, 1993). Haeckel and Nolan (1993) indicate that the loop is iterative: a continuous cycle in which an action leads to the observation of the results of that action that in turn requires a new orientation, decision, and action. This iterative sequence constitutes a *learning loop*. It contains the four functions essential to any adaptive organism: sensing, interpreting, deciding, and acting. By analogy, an enterprise model for a business that incorporates learning is one that systematically creates and links learning loops.

Figure 2.
Source: Haeckel and Nolan (1993)

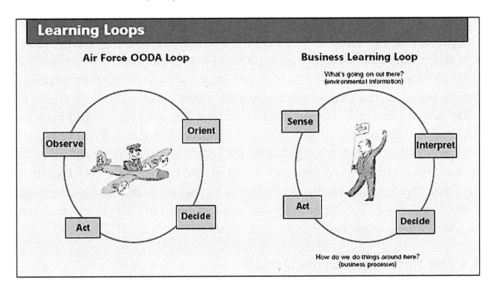

Haeckel and Nolan (1993) have represented the OODA model and its managerial equivalent as Figure 2.

4. CHANGES IN ORGANISATIONAL STRUCTURES

The 1990's saw a wave of organisational changes that included Total Quality Management (TQM), Business Process Reengineering (BPR), Customer Relations Management (CRM) and the Learning Organisation. The whole process started when icons of American wealth such as General Electric, Ford and General motors were finding difficult to face the competition brought by young, swift Japanese competitors with less resources and experience. In a process of self-examination, the American business practices were recounted as follows:

Because of the voracious appetite for cars in America, GM grew rapidly after World War II. Symbolising America's wealth, companies likes GM wrote the marketplace rules while the rest of the world was rebuilding. These rules emphasized finance, size, low cost production, and marketing power. Finance began to dominate GM's corporate decision making during the late 1950s. The Board of Directors' Financial Committee approved all significant strategic decisions. Financial influence proliferated throughout the organisation. This success, coupled with the power that the company had, made GM arrogant. This story however, was repeated in nearly every industry in America. Post-war America was a heady time for business. "From sea to sea" symbolised a relatively closed system for American business. No foreign organisations came close to threatening American business. Business adapted to this system a set of strategies that maintained the equilibrium of marketplaces. Those companies that dominated their industry could easily defend their market share. The nation's antitrust laws kept the largest firms from exploiting their economies of scale and marketing power. The Sloan-type bureaucracy was the appropriate design for this period of time (Vroman & Luchsigner, 1994).

In such a context, it was paradoxical that the Japanese who lacked both the financial and the marketing arm managed to succeed in the American business environment and to push some giants on the wall. Their success was based on "a unique design and effective strategies" (Vroman and Luchsinger 1994). It came to light that "the Sloan bureaucracy was unable to respond to new quality standards in the marketplace. The whole processes and paradigms of changes can therefore be summed up to a process of "debureaucratisation".

4.1 The Networked Organisation

Another problem that the American giants mentioned above faced with bureaucracy was that of coordination. There were many bottlenecks in resource and information circulation not only within departments (from the bottom to the top) but also between departments (from one functional speciality to another). Processes of decision making are often fragmented and levels of the value chain that produce inputs for other levels sometimes provided substandard products, information and services. As a remedy to this state of affair, the networked organisation emerged. As Quinn et al. (1996) have noted, "in the network organization, lateral relations are more important than vertical relations, and hierarchies are either flat or disappear altogether. The network organization appears in different forms such as the infinitely flat organization, the inverted organization, the spider's web organization, the cluster and the starburst. However, in practice the network model appears in many forms. In fact, the fundamental difference between these forms is that they represent different models of deploying intellect, the key to hypercompetitive survival. This implies a change in paradigm, since from the inception of administrative theory, organizational structure has been defined primarily by functional specialization, power relationships, and hierarchy. However, today's managers must focus instead upon how the enterprise develops and deploys intellect (Quinn et al. 1996).

For instance, the models of networked organisations mentioned above deploy the intellect differently. The infinitely flat organization locates the intellect at the center and locates novelty at the nodes. This mode of linkage consists of linking the center to the nodes and its source of leverage is multiplicative. The management problems and challenges that it raises are that there is no career path, the pay depends on individual performance, professional management is isolated, and there is a permanent need to maintain system flexibility. The typical example of an infinitely flat organization is a brokerage firm. The inverted organization locates the intellect and linkage at the nodes and its source of leverage is distributive. The managerial problems and challenges it raises are the loss of formal authority for line managers, the need to simultaneously empower and control the people at nodes. The best illustrations of the inverted organizations are hospitals. The spider's web organization locates the intellect at the nodes and novelty in the project. The linkage occurs from node to node and the source of leverage is exponential.

The managerial problem it raises is the need to foster communication without overloading the system and the management of competition over the nodes. The most common example of a spider's web organization is the internet. The cluster organization, as the name indicates, locates the intellect in the whole cluster and novelty in project. The mode of linkage is from cluster to project and the source of leverage is additive. The problems and challenges it raises are the facts that individuals face pressures from clusters and cross-cluster teams. The whole organization depends on the quality of leadership, breadth of training, and motivation of participants. An example of a cluster organization is the corporate staff. The starburst organization locates the intellects at the center and at the nodes while novelty is located at the nodes. The mode of linkage is from center to nodes and the source of leverage is synthetic. There is a need to balance autonomy and control and to generate significant resources (Quinn et al. 1996).

However, it is worth noticing that: these new forms seldom occur in pure form across the entire entity, integrating all aspects of a major enterprise, and their evolution is not being driven by the emergence of new enterprises. Rather they are forms of organizing, not forms of organization, and they are typically embedded in large organizational structures that are still at least partly bureaucratic. Because these forms are building blocks, with several typically co-existing inside larger organizations, a key challenge for top management in integrating these different forms of organizing into a coherent whole. The organization of the future will not be a hybrid, but will be polymorphic, containing within itself subunits whose fundamental ways of bringing intellect to bear upon problems vastly different from one another (Quinn et al. 1996).

4.2 The Flat Organisation

With the growing awareness the bureaucracy as an organisational design was not only inefficient but also time and resources consumer, many anti-bureaucracy movement emerged. Jack Welch, the CEO of General Electric called bureaucracy a sin (Bower et al. 1995). This was a revolution preceded that has been occurring through human history. While in the pre-industrial society, work was based mainly on physical labour be it of humans or animals, in the industrial society work was massively organized in giant plants around automatic machinery. The new demands of work and life in the modern times introduced new paradigms of work and organisation design such as the division of labour spearheaded by Max Weber. As a paradigm of organisational design, the division of labor fosters a pyramidal organisational model where levels of hierarchy are clearly delineated and where channels of command and control from the top to the bottom of the pyramid are clear and well codified in legal and juridical instruments.

However, with the "debureacratisation" movement, this model of organisational design was brought into disrepute because of many changes in demographics and psychodynamics. For instance, skilled labour emerged with "knowledge workers" who most of the time knows better than their bosses in their area of expertise. These people did not want just to be told what to do but also to have a say not only in their specific areas but also to participate in decision making. This created a predilection for organisational designs that abrogate the hierarchy embedded in the pyramidal model. In this context the concept of the flat organisation emerged and shifts were made from command and control to information-based organization (Quinn et al. 1996). Some authors went as far as turning upside down the pyramid and advocating of an inverted pyramid model of organisation where the wide bottom would be at the top and the narrow pick at the bottom. All these were attempts to reduce inefficiencies due to the fact that in a rigid hierarchy viewpoints are valuable and taken into account in decision making according to the position of the person who express then and not his or her competence or their overall contribution to value creation. Moreover, the flat organisation avoids bottlenecks in resource and information circulation.

4.3 The Learning Organisation

Most of organisational designs assessed so far focused on their own internal workings. For instance, the pyramidal and hierarchical model considered organisations as autonomous (if not isolated) entities and focused on stabilising their internal channels of control and command in a way that these organisations lacked internal flexibility and external adaptability to cope with increasingly complex production systems and versatile markets. Moreover, the customer of the mass production area looked for products quality and service in addition to mere utility and this introduced new pressures especially with the entry of Japanese companies in the American market that brought philosophies such as continuous improvement (Kaizen) and types of loyalty that went beyond the legalistic and contractual understanding of work. The

Cybernetics Principles in the Management of Intelligent Organizations

mechanistic model (a search for universal and immutable laws similar to Newton's laws of motion) that has led to rigid bureaucracies and to stagnation both in management thought and practice and big companies could not anymore face the challenges of increasing competition, customers oriented production methods and services and a new labour that is educated and willing to participate in the running of the business. This mechanistic and rigid system was more and more replaced by a more flexible (even somehow amorphous) model that included in organisational design the notion that businesses are not isolated entities but they are complex and integrative process that are in continuous interaction with their environment. The mechanistic model was replaced by an organic model in attempt to integrate elements of complexity and dynamism and in the academic jargon there was a shift from business systems (internally focused) to business ecosystems (environment minded).

The notion of a business ecosystem has been applied to electronic commerce in a way that some scholars have talked about the Internet ecosystem. As Turban et al. (2004) have noted, the Internet ecosystem is the business of the online economy. The prevailing model of competition in the Internet economy is more like web interrelationships than the hierarchical, command-and-control model of the industrial economy, Unlike the value chain, which rewarded exclusivity, the Internet economy is inclusive and has low barrier entry. Just like an ecosystem in nature, activity in the Internet economy is self-organising. The process of natural selection take place around company profits and value to customers. As the Internet ecosystem evolves both technologically and in population, it will be even easier and likelier for countries/companies/individuals to participate in the Internet economy. (Turban et al. 2004).

Linked to this idea of a self-organising economic ecosystem is the notion of the learning organisation. To survive the turbulence of the electronic marketplace organisation must be flexible and adaptable enough to face the challenges of their own complexities and changes in the environment. The notion of the learning organisation was coined by Peter Senge (1990) and he defines this type of organisation as "an organisation that is continually expanding its capacity to create its future. For such an organisation, it is not enough merely to survive. "Survival learning" or what is more often termed "adaptive learning" is important – indeed is necessary. But for a learning organisation, "adaptive learning" must be joined by "generative learning", learning that enhances our capacity to create (Senge 1990). The learning organisation therefore does not emphasize its own processes and systems but it is alert and ready to make necessary changes to face challenges an to seize opportunities. It is not merely reactive to its context but it is proactive and ready to undergo processes of radical change equated to the Geek word for conversion to Christianity – *metanoia* – that Senge (1990) defines as a "shift of mind". In this context, the capacity to learn becomes a strategic asset at the same level as capital and labour.

205

4.4 The Virtual Organization

There is no agreed definition of what a virtual organisation is. This is due to the fact that virtual in the business ecosystem is a complex notion and many people tend to define the virtual organisation by contrasting it to the traditional brick-and-mortar organisation. Therefore, from the point of view of physical location, people define the virtual organisation as "placeless", located in the Cyberspace. This implies that the virtual organisation is purely an electronic entity made of "bits rather than atoms" (Negroponte 1995). This notion equates the virtual organisation to any online organisations. The different dot.coms that dominated the market in the early 1990's then can be considered as the only virtual organisations. However, a wider view considers the virtual organisation from the point of view of the way resources, people, information and skills are put together in view of creating value for the customer. This leads to defining the virtual organisation from the point of view of business practice and not of essence. The question shifts from "what is a virtual organisation?" to "what does a virtual organisation do?". This second approach brings into focus definitions such as that of Burn et al. (2002) that the virtual organisation is "an entity which comprises a combination of different companies and individuals that have combined to complete projects or business propositions and developments". From this second perspective it seems that the virtual organisation extends the formation of cross-functional teams beyond the traditional boundaries of any single organisation. This aspect underlines another important characteristic of the virtual organisation: inter-organisational systems. For the virtual organisation to operate successfully in the internetworked markets it must be aware that "no organisation is an island". The different aspects will be assessed in details in the next sub-sections.

4.4.1 The Online Organisation

The most known aspect of e-commerce is the fact that it is technology-enabled, technology-mediated, and includes intra- and interorganisational activities to support the exchange (Rayport et al. 2003). This creates the image that the virtual organisation operates solely in computer mediated environments (CME), a phenomenon that may in a near future put an end to brick-and-mortar types of business that the industrial society has created and develop into a cashless society. The role of technology is so important that Barnatt (1995) has coined the concept of "management by wire" Management by wire is possible because the Internet and related technologies allow "near-instantaneous global connectivity" (Barnatt 1995). Therefore, the virtual organisation is not fiction since computer mediated environments creates infrastructures such as computer virtual workplace (CVW), personal virtual workplace (PVW) and computer supported cooperative work

Cybernetics Principles in the Management of Intelligent Organizations

(CSCW). Other infrastructures are computer telephone integration (CTI) and this goes beyond organisational and country boundaries allowing large scale integration (LSI) and very large scale integration (VLSI) communication systems. In this arena, the notion of virtual reality emerges. According to Barnatt (1995), virtual reality is "any structured representation or metaphor of the physical world, encoded in computer software with which human beings may interact". Therefore, "the concept of the virtual organisation is encapsulated in a desire to use information technology to enable relaxation of the traditional physical constraints of organisational formation and adaptation" (Barnatt 1995).

The understanding of the virtual organisation from the point of view of technology brings into focus a wide range of application including simple electronic versions of traditional paper based activity such as record keeping, invoicing, billing, and other innovations such as automated teller machines (ATMs), electronic checks and electronic cash. There are options such as homeworking also called telecommuting since through computer network people can work together without being located at the same place. This creates the possibility of the paperless office since there are ways of carrying all the informational, communicational, distributional and transactional activities through computer networks. A partial solution to the virtual workplace is hot-desks. According to Barnatt (1995), "hot-desk environments abandon the notion of having individual desks for individual employees. Instead, with these re-engineered workplaces, many communal desks or consoles with networked IT facilities are provided. In Digital Equipment Corporations's Stockholm headquarters, such "office of the future" has already been created. With permanent offices and desks scrapped, employees are presented with an open-plan area with terminals that drop down on flexibars. When an employee needs computer access they simply pull down a free terminal, and when they're finished they let it sail back up to the ceiling. Any personal space in the office is confined to the capacity of one's individual drawer in a communal filing cabinet".

Other ways online transactions are transfiguring the workplace is through hotelling and the use of groupeware and virtual teams. As Barnatt (1995), "closely related to hot-desk development, where enough desks will only be provided to accommodate the number of staff likely to be in the office at any one point in time, are *hotelling* arrangements. This system of working, as adopted by consultants Ernst & Young, relies on the notion that many consultants, accountants and so forth spend the majority of their working lives out with clients. They therefore have no need for permanent desks or office back at base. Hotelling employees are instead provided with portable, start-of-the-art computers, and rely on their clients to provide them with a desk from which they stay in touch with base via computer network links and voice-mail. When hotelling employees need to work at base, they simply call on a 'concierge', letting them know when they will be arriving and for how long. A cubicle is then allocated for the duration of the employees's 'visit', on which their nameplate will be displayed by the time they arrive. Like its sister hot-desk, the hotelling concept relies on organisation-wide communications networks and high specification computer hardware through which all work is directed." Telecommuters do not work in isolation although they do not converge at one physical location. Specific software known as groupeware allow them to work into virtual teams. Groupeware as noted earlier is a genre label for the many types of computer software which are designed to enable group rather than individual computer usage (Barnatt 1995). In other instances, some human functions have been replaced by software agents. A software agent is "a 'smart' computer program (or *infomachine*) that will 'serve' its human master in cyberspace. Software agents protect their users from complexity of computer and network operations, and may engage is database searches and transactions based on knowledge of their user's "profile".

Authors such as Barnatt (1995) have defined the virtual organisation from the point of view of technology. In their view, the virtual organisation has three main characteristics:

- A reliance for their functioning and survival on the medium of cyberspace across a wide system of organisational infrastructures.
- No identifiable physical form, and only transient patterns of agent-broker (employee-employer) connectivity.
- Boundaries defined and limited only by the available information technology, rather than bureaucratic rules or cumbersome contractual arrangements.

However, complementary to this view, are views that define the virtual organisation form the point of view of business practice and insist that in addition to being an online organisation the virtual organisation is a collaborative organisation.

4.4.2 The Collaborative Organisation

Gammack and Poon (2013) have ranked the levels of a virtual organisation in the following decreasing order collaboration, conversation, communication and connection. This implies that Internet connectivity is just the first step in an organisation that is moving from brick-and-mortar or virtual organisation. This implies that in addition to technological aspect (going online) there are not only new organisational structures that take place but also a supporting culture that permeates business practices. As Marshall et al. (2001) note, "the virtual organisation may provide the much needed after flexible and synergistic model of this Millenium". Collaboration in virtual organisations have occurred under two main strategies: partnering and outsourcing. In fact, some authors such as Burn (2002) have defined virtual organisations as "partnership networks". This implies that to succeed, virtual organisation either enter into strategic alliances with other organisations or they stick to what they do the best and outsource what they are not best at. As proponents of virtual organisations such as Hedberg (1997) have noted, "Back to basics" and "focusing" have become watch words in efforts to limit a company to activities of vital strategic importance and to areas in which it can be a winner or at least operate efficiently. Accordingly it would be better to subcontract activities not part of this core (outsourcing), or even to discontinue then entirely and buy them from completing suppliers when necessary. For instance, CACC Learning, a distance education college focuses on its core (providing study material, collecting fees, administering exams, and providing qualifications) and sub-contracts some of its activities such as exam invigilating and essay marking or hiring exam halls rather then building them.

In addition to outsourcing many business scholars have noted that companies need to collaborate rather than to compete. This leads to the creation of strategic alliances or establishing "knowledge links". Strategic alliances corroborate Marshall's view of the virtual organisation as an organisational structure based primarily on the notion of collaborating entities. As Marshall (2001) elaborates, "here, firms come together to share competencies, skills, knowledge and other resources for the purpose of producing a particular service or good, or of taking advantage of a particular opportunity." The demands of collaboration create an amorphous type of organisation that keeps changing according to the product or the services the alliance is being formed for. That is why "a key characteristic of the virtual organisation is its adaptability and flexibility in the face of turbulent business environments, a condition sometimes described as "agility" (Goldman et al. 1995 quoted in Marshall 2001).

Virtual organisations appear in various forms according to the type of their presence online and to the type of strategic alliance they are involved in. They range from virtual faces, co-alliances, star alliances, value alliances, market alliances and virtual space. The first model, virtual faces, is the online presence of brick-and-mortar organisations. For instance, the University of Zimbabwe may have a web presence (a virtual face) but that does not dispense this institution from using lecture rooms, libraries and other physical facilities. The second model is made of co-alliance virtual organisations. These are essentially shared partnerships. In this type of virtual organisation, "each partner makes approximately equal contribution to resources, competencies, skills and knowledge to the alliance, then forming consortium (Marshall et al. 2001). The composition and the structure of the consortium may change according to market opportunities and these types of alliance may appear or disappear either by mutual convenience or on a project-by-project basis. Unlike co-alliances that are partnerships between equals, there are other strategic alliances where a big organisation that occupies the centre stage is surrounded by small organisations. This third type of alliance is called star-alliance. According to Marshall et al. (2001), "star-alliance models are co-ordinated networks of interconnected members representing a core surrounded by satellite organisations. The core comprises the leader who is a dominant player in the market. The leader tends to dominate and has the power to direct and dictate the supply of competence, expertise, knowledge and expertise to members." The fourth type, value alliance models, brings together range of interrelated products, services and facilities that are based on an industry value or supply chain" (Marshall et al. 2001) while the fifth type- the market alliance- is made of organisations that come together to coordinate manufacture, marketing, selling, and distribution of a diverse but coherent set of products and services. The market alliance is different from the value-alliance model in the sense that several value chains are likely to be involved (Marshall et al. 2001)

4.4.3 Inter-Organisational Systems

The shift from the brick-and-mortar organisation to the virtual organisation implies a change from the understanding of organisations as static autonomous entities to organisations as dynamic interdependent processes. The flow of resources, people and information in virtual organisations enhances complex and dynamic processes that are captured by computer networks. Whether an organisation is called virtual by the virtue of being online or whether the collaborating aspect is emphasised, or various combinations of the two models it is clear that traditional boundaries be they physical, structural and legal are being regularly modified for the only purpose of creating value for the customer. This implies technically that no organisation is an island and hence cross-functional teams are not enough as long as they are confined to one organisation. The weaknesses of self-centred organisations make then unable to complete since other organisations through outsourcing and strategic alliances can form all stars teams. The introduction of inter-organisational systems becomes not only a prerequisite and a strategic asset but sometimes it is a condition for survival. This subsection will focus on inter-organisational systems and their value-creating role in the context of computer mediated business environments.

Inter-organisational systems (IOS) have been defined by Li (2001) as "the computer and telecommunications infrastructure developed, operated and/or used by two or more firms for the purpose of exchanging information that supports a business operation process." The most known is Zimbabwe is the ZimSwitch function that links all the banks in Zimbabwe in a way that credit card holder can cash at any ATM regardless of which bank she banks with. A similar function exists in the UK's banking sector with LINK network of cash dispensing machines. Another

Cybernetics Principles in the Management of Intelligent Organizations

well known example of an IOS is the online seat reservation and ticket reservation network among major airlines in the USA, and less known such as Demepool in France, an information network created by a group of independent transportation firms for the exchange of jobs and for avoiding the running of empty vehicles on return delivery trips (Li et al. 2001). The role of inter-organisational systems is not limited to the service industries, as the examples above may seem to portray. In the manufacturing industry techniques such as just-in-time have been possible because of inter-organisational systems that have been called integrated core technology. According to Vroman and Luchsinger (1994), integrated core technologies refers to the use of information technology to reshape organisation's relationships with customers and supplier partners and with employee teams. It means redesigning the operations or service delivery to complement the power of these elements. Corollary to integrated technology are improved service quality and a holistic understanding of work and organisation that empowers the front-line employee.

Inter-organisational systems appear in many forms according to their degree of openness to external input. Three models have emerged: (1) the dedicated closed inter-organisational systems, (2) the semi-closed group networks based on value-added network services (VANs) and (3) completely open systems based on mediums such as the Internet. (Li 2001). Inter-organisational systems creates new types of organisations and a new management philosophy by fostering radical changes and introducing new business paradigms. Lloyd and Boyle (1998) have identified the way new technological infrastructures affect both value creation and organisational transformation. For instance, the "net" allows wealth creation and social development leading to internetworked business. Likewise, interenterprise computing allows the recasting of external relationships extending the traditional boundaries of corporations and thus creating "the extended enterprise". From the internal physiognomy of the enterprise, enterprise infrastructure fosters organisational transformation and creates "the integrated enterprise" as opposed to the hierarchical pyramidal model that creates boundaries between management and staff and fragments the enterprise into rigid functional specialities that sometimes lead to bottlenecks in the flow of resources, skills and information. Workgroup computing leads inevitably to business process and job redesign and this creates the high-performance team. From a personal point of view, personal multimedia technology gives the employee access and control over information in such as way that she becomes the effective individual. It is obvious that effective individual freed from the bottlenecks imposed by rigid hierarchies and inflexible functional specialties enter into collaborative relationships that go beyond the physical and legal bounds of their organisation in order to give the customer the best value.

5. CHANGES IN CORPORATE CULTURE

5.1 From Fragmentation to Integration

Traditionally organisations have been defined by their boundaries both physical and legal. However, Barnatt (1995) has noted that computer network facilities have already been noted to "supercharge" organisations, with hierarchical and functional boundaries often short-circuited as interdepartmental problem solving teams spontaneously emerge. In computer networked organisational environments, people with relevant knowledge get drawn into any kind of discussion, with employees forming into "virtual departments". This leads to vertical integration (removal of barriers between management and staff) and horizontal integration (removal of barriers between different functional specialities). This double integration requires from managers some technical know-how that not only help them to make efficient and effective decisions but also that allow them to solve complex problems linked with the sophistication, complexity and elusiveness of computer mediated business environments. These environments require organisations to pull together the best of their resources, skills and people in order to satisfy a more and more demanding customer who has limitless choices since Internet connectivity allows the customer cheap and real-time access to global markets. Moreover, online trade gives the customers the possibility of dictating the features of the products she can buy or the quality of the services that she requires. In this context, only the best can sell and the Biblical metaphor of a kingdom divided applies here. Fragmentation though watertight hierarchical levels and functional speciality is detrimental to the production of quality goods and the provision of quality services.

At the organisational level, this creates a need, not only for new structures but also new principles values and procedures that inevitably involves new skills. Each employee participates in the double process of integration described above though integrating at the personal level of technical and non-technical skills. Technical and non-technical skills at this level are not mutually exclusive; they are different but yet complementary. Companies need either to initiate integrated training programs but the overall school systems need to narrow the gaps between the two. These new training needs lead to what Barnatt (1995) calls convergence. In his own words, "traditionally, research scientists, systems analysts and computer programmers have been isolated from front-line company operations. They have had no contact with customers, and hence have not needed training in customer liaison. However, with many organisations now downsizing away from remote mainframes, and with cybertechnology being used by a greater and greater number of employees, this scenario is changing. Across many institutions, technical employees, and the computer systems and interfaces they create and maintain, are becoming the first point of contact. Take banking as an example. Many customers now never go into a bank at all. They deal with the whole organisation totally via interaction with its hole-in-the-wall machines. Such a trend will explode as home banking, home shopping and other interactive television services become available. Just as companies now spend money training sales reps, marketing personnel and other customer representatives, so in future attention will need to be focused upon the non-technical capabilities of technicians, as their contribution to organizational success emerge from the backroom and into the harsh light of the front-line. All employees will require some degree of customer training. Similarly, future managers will require a high level of technical expertise if they are to reach for the top. A powerful ethos of the New Age is convergence in a myriad of guises. Across industry, demarcations are being decimated on all levels."

5.2 From Stable Closed Entities to Dynamic Open Systems

In addition to integrating technical and non-technical skills at employee level, integrating low and high levels of hierarchies through "debureaucratization", and achieving excellence through cross-functional teams that may go beyond the physical and legal boundaries of one organisation it is important to have a shift of focus. Organisations have been traditionally conceived as stable and closed entities. In many instances, the fear of competition or sabotage by ill willed people covered them with secrecy and led to the creation of deep rooted routines borrowed either natural sciences or from other human organisations such as armies. The idea of the corporation (from *corpus* in Latin that means body) implies an organic model with internal dynamics that are as stable as the biological laws of metabolism. Moreover, to remain healthy, a body needs some degree of autonomy that leads to strict ways of integrating elements from the external environment. There is no wonder that sickness is often conceptualised through the metaphor of attack (by germs, viruses and so forth). From this point of view, purity is equated to health and diversity or integration of external elements is either avoided or submitted to strict screening. From an organisational point of view, this view exemplifies the way of proceeding of the pyramidal model where the preservation of the structural makeup of organisations made self-serving rather than customer focused.

In computer mediated environments, it becomes difficult even impossible to avoid interacting with others. The idea of the corporation (an autonomous body) invites some degree of heteronomy given the fact "interorganisational metabolism" (Lloyd and Boyle 1998) rather than "intraorganisational" metabolism is the norm of the day. This new dynamism questions even the idea of an organisation (from Greek Organon that means body) since organising means putting into place structures and systems i.e. not only putting parts together in a certain pattern of relationships and functions (creating a structure) but also determining the principles, values, procedures, and rules of interaction (creating a culture). However, doing business in the cyberspace seem to creates amorphous organisational patterns where paradoxically the only constant is change and where to survive organisations must respond to the requirements of en ever changing environment. This leads inevitably to an organisational culture characterized by paradoxes and a constant tension that amounts to the "entrepreneurial spirit". In this context, ambiguity and uncertainty seems to take the upper hand over planning and rigor, creativity opposes disciplined analysis while urgency (opportunistic proactive behaviour) overrules the patience and perseverance (that is embedded in building long lasting and bid physical structures such as the massive plants of the industrial revolution). The new context requires organisations to be flexible, adaptive and open to learning if they are to survive. In addition to flexibility, adaptability and openness to learning, organisation that operate in computer mediated environment must be innovative and responsive to external changes instead of abiding to deep rooted orthodoxies and practices that are only applicable in stable environments. Instead of avoiding risks these organisations brave the storm and seem to be interested in current profit rather than in long-term equity. These new ways of doing business make the Internet not only a technological innovation but also the heart of a cultural revolution.

5.3 From Power and Ownership to Knowledge

Unlike the industrial revolution where the transformation of energy was the dominant mode of production, the Internet and e-commerce make information processing the dominant mode of production. This change of focus creates subsequent changes in the attribution of value to different types of stakeholders be they from the point of view of the ownership and valuation of the means of production, or from the point of view of their relative contribution to the value chain. For instance, "across the economies of the world, information itself, rather than oil, land, minerals and industrial plant, has now become the key global resource" (Barnatt 1995). This brings in focus that the owner of information technology and information know-how is slowly replacing the owner of "natural resources" in dictating the rules of the world economy. The traditional economic theory of limiting resources to capital and labour can be questioned from many point of view unless different players accept that information technology, information itself and information know-how are strategic assets, a "digital capital" as Tapscott et al. (2000) point out.

This changes in the valuation of assets shifts the balances of power from owners and to the knowledge worker who, most of times, knows much more than the bosses in his or her specific area of expertise. The "knowledge worker" according to Drucker (1989) is replacing the semi-skilled worker of the massive production era of the industrial society. The semi-skilled worker is in fact the fruit of Cartesianism i.e the habit to "break apart problems, to fragment the world" (Senge 1990). The semi-skilled worker was precious in the industrial society because at that time the industrialist "analyzed tasks and broke them down into individual, unskilled tasks that could be learned quite quickly" (Drucker 1989). In the information society things are different. The professional or the expert more and more replaces the semi-skilled worker and this puts an end to the command-and-control model of organising. This change leads to different patterns of empowerment and sharing of rewards. The distinction between management and staff becomes irrelevant because power is no more at the top of a pyramid but at different nods of complex networks where different members of a team share resources and information. This creates a flat, networked model of organisation that is ruled by equality rather than domination. Daily manifestations of power balance such as routine checks and controls and scheduling are minimized since the knowledge worker has the options of working from home or any other location she pleases and can access central databases twenty four hours a day. This shift in power balance creates also a similar shift in the sharing of rewards since people get rewarded according to their contribution rather than to their position in the organisational structure (in computer mediated environments there may be no structure at all since teams assemble and disassemble following the dictates of the market).

5.4 From Competition to Collaboration

Theories of organisations that followed the industrial revolution were mainly inspired by the command-and-control model that guided armies and emphasized individual achievement and discipline as a way to achievement and greatness. The metaphor of the individual hero emerged and this way of approaching organisation emphasized competition as a core value. This model was later supported by evolutionary theories inspired by Charles Darwin that contended that natural selection and the survival of the fittest were the only ways for species to grow. From the two metaphors introduced previously the marketplace was considered as a battle from where one victory implies one's defeat. From an ethical point of view, theories such as ethical egoism emphasized the fact that in the marketplace every player should follow his or her self-interest and let the "invisible hand" supply and demand regulate the competition. This predilection for competition has been articulated clearly by some business leader such as James Lincoln the CEO of Lincoln Electric. For him:

Competition is the foundation of man's development. It has made the human race what it is. It is the spur that makes progress. Every nation that has eliminated it as the controlling force of its economy has disappeared, or will. We will do the same if we eliminate it by trying to give security, and for the same reason. Competition means that there will be losers as well as winners in the game. Competition will mean the disappearance of the lazy and the incompetent, be they workers, industrialists, or distributors. Competition promotes progress. Competition determines who will be the leader. It is the only known way leadership and progress can be developed if history means anything. It is a hard taskmaster. It is completely necessary for anyone, be he worker, user, distributor, or boss, if he is to grow. If some way could be found to so that competition could be eliminated from life, the result would be disastrous. Any nation and any people disappearing from life becomes too easy. There is no danger from a hard life as all history shows. Danger is from a life that is made soft by lack of competition. (Bower et al. 1995)

However, doing business in the cyberspace portrays a different understanding of the relationships between different players. This crude individualistic understanding of competitions has been replaced by vertical integration (the suppression of hierarchical barriers) and horizontal integration (the formation of cross-functional teams). These patterns of integration lead to sharing resources and information in a way that within the organisation collaboration rather than competition is the order of the day. Barnatt (1995) has noted that interactive information technologies and computer connectivity allow real-time collaboration. These patterns of integration are not limited to isolated organisations. Collaboration between organisations and their customers and suppliers is not common while through outsourcing and strategic alliances competitors can work together in order to give the customer the best value.

This new way of doing business has been called by Burn et al. (2002) "coopetition". For them coopetition is the information and resource sharing strategies that are replacing naked aggression and competition in many business contexts. Collaboration is the way virtual organisations do business. With the global reach that many organisations enjoy the organisation that isolates itself is self-destructive. Burn et al. (2002) have noted the link between collaborating ways of managing and virtual organisations. In their view, "as soon as one mentions managing in a virtual organisation, or of adopting virtual organising as a deliberate strategy, then there is a sense in which one is almost talking about *interorganisational* management, and thus about the *coordinated* and cooperative behaviours and endeavours of acts/ managers who originate in different organisations and who, after a period of time, may again actually be in different organisations."

5.5 From Warfare to Trust

The war metaphor is ingrained into popular beliefs that some electronic commerce scholars have entitled their book *Hyperwars* (Judson and Kelly 1999). This implies

Cybernetics Principles in the Management of Intelligent Organizations

that the marketplace conceived as a battleground is a dangerous place, where one must be very careful in order to brave the fury of the enemy and unveil the enemy's traps. This way of understanding business has created suspicion in the marketplace and one's operations are covered with secrecy. Otherwise, unscrupulous competitors may take advantage of loopholes in one production system either to destroy an organisation or to take an upper hand in the market. In contradistinction to this approach, virtual managing suggests another spirit i.e. trust. To be successful trust must be the order of the day both within and between organisations. Concerning trust within organisations, Jack Welch, the CEO of General Electric has noted that in the processes of "debureaucratization" a new type of loyalty is a must. In his own words, "my concept of loyalty is not "giving time" to some corporate entity and, in turn, being shielded and protected from the outside world. Loyalty is an affinity among people who want to grapple with the outside world and win. Their personal values, dreams, and ambitions cause them to gravitate towards each other and toward a company like GE which gives them resources and opportunities to flourish" (Bower et al. 1995).

Jack Welch calls this new type of loyalty the "psychological contract". Psychological contract, in addition to financial rewards give the employee the feeling that not only do they get from the company their pay check but also that their work goes beyond earning a living and satisfying their vegetative needs. The psychological contract gives job security and a sense of fulfilment and accomplishment. In addition to their financial and other material needs, the psychological contract help the employees to feel that there are not working for "someone else" but that there are "insiders" and that their participation is acknowledged and rewarded. That is why, as a way of implementing the psychological contract Jack Welch testifies: "we try to avoid barriers between management and workers. We're treated equally as much as possible. When I got to work this morning at 7:30, the parking lot was three-quarters full. I parked way out here like anyone would. In don't have a special reserved spot. The same principle holds true in our cafeteria. There is no executive dinning room. We eat with everyone else." (Bower et al. 1995). This way of proceeding fosters trust and other values such as independence, freedom, responsibility and autonomy (Bower et al. 1995). To be effective in real business practice the psychological contract must be supported by the employees' sharing in the financial rewards of the organisations and in their effective participation in decision-making and problem solving. Jack Welch finds that the main limitation of the psychological contract is that it "tends to focus people inward" (Bower et al. 1995). This creates the need for trust not only within organisations but also between organisations. Technically, inter-organisational systems that help the sharing of resources, information and skills exist.

Inter-organisational systems traditionally linked organisations to their customers and suppliers. For instance, in manufacturing the cost of inventory is significantly reduced when the suppliers can access information about the needs of the producers in raw materials. This type of collaboration let at General Electric to "a new plant lay out". As Jack Welch explained, "raw materials entered one side of the plant and finished goods came out the other side. There was no central stock room for materials and or work in process. Instead, everything that entered the plant was transported directly to the work station where it would be used." (Bower et al. 1995). In the same organisation the approach to the customer is different. As Al Patnik, vice-president of sales at GE pointed out: "our approach to the customer is to go and learn what he is doing and show him how to do it better. For many companies our people become their experts in welding. They go in and talk to a foreman. They might say, 'Let me put on a headshield and show you what I am talking about" (Bower et al. 1995). This type of collaboration yield a lot of financial benefits. Electronic commerce however brings collaboration to a higher level the one of putting in place inter-organisational systems that links organisations to their competitors. Obviously, this type of arrangements requires, in addition to technical links and structural convergence, a supporting culture based on trust rather than on suspicion.

Linking organisations to their competitors is paradoxical but it helps both organisations to pull together the best of their resources, personnel, know-how and information to give the best value to the competitor. However, this may amount to the violation of basic business intelligence and to the loss of one intellectual property. In this context, it is difficult to assess whether the competitor really has the real intentions he or she is expressing. The solution to this suspicion is the acceptance by both partners to share the risks involved equally or proportionally to the potential benefits. When the partners know each other agreements in this matter can be worked out. However, the nature of electronic commerce makes some organisations time and space independent and electronic transactions can be impersonal and faceless. It is a fact of human experience that people have difficulties to trust people they have never seen especially when financial transactions are involved. Moreover, people do not like to purchase products and services they do not know. These difficulties can be overcome through product certification and authentication by trusted third party intermediaries or shared security features such as encrypted security messages that can be decoded by the purchaser.

6. CONCLUSION

The unprecedented development and diffusion of computer and related information and communication technologies (ICTs) brought unprecedented changes in the ways people do business, live and play. However, the information age cannot limited to replacing pen and pencils with computers but information and communication

Cybernetics Principles in the Management of Intelligent Organizations

Table 3. The process of debureaucratisation (from mechanics to cybernetics)

Type of Organisation	Bureaucratic	Informated
Structure	Pyramid	Network
Emphasis	Internal Workings to achieve equilibrium	Internal and External environment to adapt to change
Model	Closed Entities	Open System
Layers of Hierarchy	Many	Few or None
Management Method	Command and Control	Interaction
Workforce	Uniform Semi-skilled	Diverse Knowledge workers
Values	Rigidity; Discipline; Compliance Competition Warfare	Flexibility Adaptability Openness to Learning Collaboration Trust
Location	Physical Place	Physical and Virtual
Results Areas	Functional Specialties (Departments)	Cross-Functional Teams
Performance Criteria	Outcomes	Processes
Strategy	Cost cutting; Competition	Adaptation to Change Collaboration (including outsourcing and strategic alliances)
Inspiration	Mechanics	Cybernetics
Decision-Base	Power and Ownership	Knowledge
Organisational Principle	Division of Labour	Integration/Networking

technologies (ICTs) brought changes in business operations, organizational structures and corporate culture. This chapter endeavored to outline not only changes brought in organizational structure and corporate culture but also pointed to a paradigm shift from bureaucracy which is build on mechanical principles to informated organisations which are built on cybernetics. This is not just a shift for paper-based operation and learning or simply the replacement of paper by hardware and software but a change of mindset from bureaucratic to informated organization. This change of mindset implies not only a change in organizational structuers but also a change in corporate culture from organizations based on mechanical principles embedded in bureaucracy to dynamic, agile, and flexible organizations build on dynamic and integrative principles embedded in cybernetics. This implies the changes presented in the table below:

Debureaucratization is supported by a change in corporate culture:

219

(1)   From hierarchies (pyramids) heterachies (networks)
(2)   From organisations as stable closed entities to organisations as dynamic open systems;
(3)   From competition to collaboration;
(4)   From warfare to trust and mutual support;
(5)   From focusing on ownership and power to focus on knoweldge.
(6)   From universality (tendencies to standardize products and procedures) to transversality (creating value through temporal cross-functional teams)
(7)   From making and selling products to sensing and responding to customer needs

REFERENCES

Ackoff, R. L. (1974). *Redesigning the Future –A Systems Approach to Societal Problems.* Wiley.

Ackoff, R. L. (1981). *Creating the corporate future: Plan or be planned for.* Wiley.

Ackoff, R. L. (1994). *The democratic corporation: A radical prescription for recreating corporate America and rediscovering success.* Oxford University Press. doi:10.1093/oso/9780195087277.001.0001

Ackoff, R. L., & Emery, F. E. (1972). *On purposeful systems.* Aldine-Atherton.

Ackoff, Finnel, & Gharajedaghi. (1984). A guide to controlling your corporation's future. New York: Wiley.

Ashby, W. R. (1956). *An Introduction to Cybernetics.* Chapman & Hall. doi:10.5962/bhl.title.5851

Beer, S. (1959). *Cybernetics and Management.* English University Press.

Beer, S. (1960). Towards the cybernetic factory. In *Principles of Self Organization. Symposium of 1960.* Pergamon Press.

Beer, S. (1965). *The world, the flesh and the metal. Nature, 205(4968), 223-231.*

Beer, S. (1966). Decision and Control. Wiley.

Beer, S. (1972). *Brain of the Firm.* Penguin.

Beer, S. (1979) The Heart of Enterprise. Wiley.

Beer, S. (1981) Brain of the Firm (2nd ed.). Wiley.

Beer, S. (1985). *Diagnosing the System for Organisations*. John Wiley & Sons.

Beer, S. (1989). *The Viable System Model: Its Provenance, Development, Methodology and Pathology*. Cwarel Isaf Institute.

Bernstein, R. (1991). *The New Constellation: the Ethical-Political Horizons of Modernity/Postnmodernity*. The MIT Press.

Bower, J. L., Bartlett, C. A., Uyterhoeven, H. E., & Walton, R. E. (1995). *Business Policy: managing strategic processes*. No Title.

Bower, J. L., & Christensen, C. M. (1995, January–February). Disruptive Technologies: Catching the Wave. *Harvard Business Review*, 43–54.

Burn, J., Marshall, P., & Barnett, M. (2007). *E-business strategies for virtual organizations*. Routledge. doi:10.4324/9780080504889

Burn, J., & Robins, G. (2002). A Virtual Organisation Model for E-Government. *AJIS. Australian Journal of Information Systems*, *9*(2), 104–112.

Cabrera, D. (2008). Distinctions, systems, relationships, perspectives: the simple rules of complex conceptual systems: A universal descriptive grammar of cognition. *Proceedings of the 52nd Annual Meeting of the ISSS*, *3*(1).

Caves, R. E. (1980). Industrial organization, corporate strategy, and structure. *Journal of Economic Literature*, *18*, 64–92.

Céspedes, F. V. (1991). *Organizing and Implementing the Marketing Effort*. Addison- Wesley.

Choo, C. W. (1995). *Information Management for the Intelligent Organization*. Information Today/Learned InformatioN.

Chris, W. J., Conant, J. S., & Echambadi, R. (2003). Marketing Strategy Development Styles, Implementation Capability, and Firm Performance: Investigating the Curvilinear Impact of Multiple Strategy-Making Styles. *Marketing Letters*, *14*(2), 111–124. doi:10.1023/A:1025415018239

Clemson, B. (1991). *Cybernetics: A new management tool* (Vol. 4). CRC Press.

Day, G. S., & Wensley, R. (1983). Marketing Theory with a Strategic Orientation. *Journal of Marketing*, *47*(4), 79–89. doi:10.1177/002224298304700409

Drucker, P. (1989). *The New Realities In Government and Politics, in Economics and Business, in Society and World View*. Harper & Row.

Espejo, R. (2006). What is systemic thinking? *System Dynamics Review*, *10*(2-3), 199–212. doi:10.1002dr.4260100208

EspejoR. (2013). Organisational Cybernetics as a Systemic Paradigm: Lessons from the Past - Progress for the Future. https://ssrn.com/abstract=2242459

Freeman, E. (1984). *Strategic Management: A Stakeholder Approach*. Pitman.

Gammack, J., & Poon, S. (2013). Knowledge and teamwork in the virtual organization. In *E-Commerce and V-Business* (pp. 231–249). Routledge.

Gatignon, H., & Xuereb, J. (1997). Strategic Orientation of the Firm and New Product Performance. *JMR, Journal of Marketing Research*, *34*(February), 77–90. doi:10.1177/002224379703400107

Goldman, S. L., Nagel, R. N., & Preiss, K. (1995). Agile competitors and virtual organizations. *Manufacturing Review*, *8*(1), 59–67.

Gupta, J. N. D., & Sharma, S. K. (2004). *Intelligent Enterprises of the 21st Century*. Idea Group Publishing. doi:10.4018/978-1-59140-160-5

Haeckel, S. H., & Nolan, R. A. (1993). Managing by wire. *Harvard Business Review*, *71*(5), 122–132.

Hatch, M. J., & Cunliffe, A. L. (2006). *Organisation Theory*. Oxford University Press.

Heylighen, F., Bollen, J., & Riegler, A. (1999). *The Evolution of Complexity: The Violet Book of "Einstein Meets Magritte*. Kluwer Academic Publishers.

Jackson, M. C. (1986). The Cybernetic Model of the Organisation: An Assessment. In *Cybernetics and Systems'86: Proceedings of the Eighth European Meeting on Cybernetics and Systems Research, organized by the Austrian Society for Cybernetic Studies*. University of Vienna.

Jackson, M. C. (1991). *Systems Methodology for The Management Sciences*. Springer. doi:10.1007/978-1-4899-2632-6

Jackson, M. C. (2000). *Systems Approaches to Management*. BostonL Kluwer Academic Publihsers.

Kim, D. H. (1993) The Link between Individual and Organizational Learning. Sloan Management Review, 37-50.

Kuhn, T. S. (1962). *The Structure of Scientific Revolutions*. The University of Chicago Press.

Li, F., Whalley, J., & Williams, H. (2001). Between physical and electronic spaces: The implications for organisations in the networked economy. *Environment & Planning A*, *33*(4), 699–716. doi:10.1068/a33161

Liebowitz, J., & Wilcox, L. C. (1997). *Knowledge Management and its Integrative Elements*. CRC Press.

Lloyd, P., & Boyle, P. (1998). *Web-Weaving: Intranets, Extranets and Strategic Alliances*. Heinenmann.

Mainzer, K. (2007). *Thinking in Complexity: The Computional Dynamics of Matter, Mind, and Mankind*. Springer.

March, G., & Olson, J. (1975). The Uncertainty of the Past: Organisational Learning Under Ambiguity. *European Journal of Political Research*, *3*(2), 147–171. doi:10.1111/j.1475-6765.1975.tb00521.x

Marnix, A. (2006). Inhibitors of disruptive innovation capability: A conceptual model. *European Journal of Innovation Management*, *9*(2), 215–233. doi:10.1108/14601060610663587

Marshall, A., & Sandberg, J. (2011). Sensemaking in 'real' versus virtual environments: A comparison and challenge. *3rd International Symposium on Process Organization Studies*.

Menguc, B., & Auh, S. (2005, Spring). A Test of Strategic Orientation Formation versus Strategic Orientation Implementation: The Influence of TMT Functional Diversity and Inter-Functional Coordination. *Journal of Marketing Theory and Practice*, *13*(2), 4–19. doi:10.1080/10696679.2005.11658540

Mintzberg, H. (1973). Strategy-Making in Three Modes. *California Management Review*, *16*(2), 44–53.

Mintzberg, H. (1975). *The Manager's Job: Folklore and Fact. Harvard Business Review*.

Mintzberg, H. (1983). *Structure in Fives: Designing Effective Organisations*. Prentice Hall.

Mishkoff, H. C. (1986). *Understanding Artificial Intelligence*. Texas Instruments Incorporated.

Mitchell, M. (2009). *Complexity: A Guided Tour*. Oxford University Press. doi:10.1093/oso/9780195124415.001.0001

Mitchell, S. (2003). *Biological Complexity and Integrative Pluralism*. Cambridge University Press. doi:10.1017/CBO9780511802683

Mitchell, S. (2008). *Komplexitäten: Warum wir erst anfangen, die Welt zu verstehen*. Suhrkamp.

Mitchell, S. (2009). *Unsimple Truths: Science,Complexity and Policy*. University of Chicago Press. doi:10.7208/chicago/9780226532653.001.0001

Moray, N. (1963). *Cybernetics*. Hawthorn Books.

Morgan, G. (2006). *Images of Organisastion*. Sage Publication.

Negroponte, N. (1996). *(1995). Being Digital*. Knopf.

Pajunen, K. (2008). 'The nature of organisational mechanisms'. *Organization Studies*, *29*(11), 1449–1468. doi:10.1177/0170840607096384

Palmer, K. D. (2007). *Exploring Intelligent Entreprise System Limitations*. INCOSE Planning.

Piaget, J. (1950). *The Psychology of Intelligence*. Harcourt and Brace.

Porter, M. E. (1998). *The Competitive Advantage: Creating and Sustaining Superior Performance*. Free Press. doi:10.1007/978-1-349-14865-3

Prigogine, I., & Stengers, I. (1984). *Order out of Chaos: Man's New Dialogue with Nature*. Bentam Books.

Quinn, J. B. (1992). *Intelligent Enterprise: A knowledge and service based paradigm*. The Free Press.

Quinn, J. B., Anderson, P., & Finkelstein, S. (2009). Managing professional intellect: making the most of the best. In *The strategic Management of Intellectual capital* (pp. 87–98). Routledge.

Rayport, J. F., & Jaworski, B. J. (2003). *Introduction to e-commerce*. McGraw-Hill, Inc.

Rescher, N. (1998). *Complexity: A philosophical overview*. Transaction Publishers.

Rosenblueth, A., Wiener, N., & Bigelow, J. (1943, January). Behaviour, Purpose and Teleology. *Philosophy of Science*, *10*(1), 18–24. doi:10.1086/286788

Rosenhead, J. (2006). IFORS' Operational Research Hall of Fame Stafford Beer. *International Transactions in Operational Research*, *13*(6), 577–578. doi:10.1111/j.1475-3995.2006.00565.x

Schein, E. H. (1985) *Organisational Culture and Leadership*. Jossey-Bass.

Schwaninger, M. (2000). Managing Complexity—The Path Toward Intelligent Organizations. *Systemic Practice and Action Research*, *13*(2), 207–241. doi:10.1023/A:1009546721353

Senge, P. (1990). *The fifth discipline*. The Art & Practice of Learning Organization.

Senge, P. (1990). *The Fifth Discipline: The Art and the Practice of the Learning Organization*. Random House.

Sternberg, R. J. (1988). Mental self-government: A theory of intellectual styles and their development. *Human Development*, *31*(4), 197–224. doi:10.1159/000275810

Syre, K. D. (2007). *Exploring Intelligent Entreprise System Limitations*. INCOSE Planning.

Syre, K. M. (1967). Philosophy and Cybernetics. In F. J. Crosson & K. M. Syre (Eds.), *Philosophy and Cybernetics*. Simon and Schuster.

Tapscott, D., Ticoll, D., & Lowy, A. (2000). Digital capital: Harnessing the power of business webs. *Ubiquity*, *2000*(May), 3. doi:10.1145/341836.336231

Toffler, A. (1984). *Science and Change. In Order out of Chaos: Man's New Dialogue with Nature*. Bentam Books.

Turban, E., King, D., Lee, J., & Viehland, D. (2004). *Electronic Commerce: a managerial perspective 2004*. Pearson Education.

Umpleby, S. (2006). *Fundamentals and history of cybernetics: Development of the theory of complex adaptive systems*. Retrieved March 10, 2015, from: http://info-sciiis.org/IIIS_Videos/website/IIISV06.asp

von Bertalanffy, L. (1968) *General System Theory: Foundations, Development, Applications*. George.

Vroman, H. W., & Luchsinger, V. P. (1994). *Managing organization quality*. Academic Press.

Wiener, N. (1948). *Cybernetics: Or Control and Communication in the Animal and the Machine*. Academic Press.

Wiener, N. (1961). *Cybernetics or Control and Communication in The Animal and The Machine* (2nd ed.). The MIT Press.

Wiig, K. M. (2007). *The Intelligent Enterprise and Knowledge Management1*. Knowledge Research Institute, Inc.

Wilensky, H. (1967). *Organizational Intelligence: Knowledge and Policy in Government and Industry.* Basic Books.

Yolles, M. (2017). Corporate joint alliances, their children and cultural figurative intelligence. *European Journal of Cross-Cultural Competence and Management,* *4*(3-4), 201–217. doi:10.1504/EJCCM.2017.084520

Chapter 10
Customer Churn Prediction for Financial Institutions Using Deep Learning Artificial Neural Networks in Zimbabwe

Panashe Chiurunge
Chinhoyi University of Technology, Zimbabwe

Agripah Kandiero
https://orcid.org/0000-0001-8201-864X
Instituto Superior Mutasa, Mozambique & Africa University, Zimbabwe

Sabelo Chizwina
https://orcid.org/0000-0001-9842-4060
North-West University, South Africa

ABSTRACT

The research was conducted to develop a customer churn predictive modelling using deep neural networks for financial institutions in Zimbabwe using a local leading financial institution. This was based on a need to perform a customer churn analysis and develop a very high accurate and reliable customer churn predictive model. In this era, every customer counts, hence once acquired a business should do everything in its power to keep that customer because the cost of acquiring a new customer is far greater than the cost of keeping an existing one. Therefore the need to ascertain customers who have churned and also be at a position to anticipate those who are churning or are about to churn then take corrective measures to keep such customers on board. The study followed one of the data science research methodologies called CRoss industry standard process for data mining (CRISP-DM) which involves understanding the business, understanding the data, data preparation, modelling, validating the model then deployment of the model.

DOI: 10.4018/978-1-7998-9687-6.ch010

Copyright © 2024, IGI Global. Copying or distributing in print or electronic forms without written permission of IGI Global is prohibited.

1. INTRODUCTION

This section entails the problem statement and the aims of this study. Hence, the section covers the background of the study, problem statement, research objectives and questions

1.1 Background of the Study

According to Ahmed et al (2017), customer churn prediction models done through machine learning techniques gained massive popularity in just a few decades ago. Similarly, so as the trend in the financial industry where predictions have been done to predict dissatisfied customers who were likely to go for other service providers primarily using traditional machine learning techniques such as Support Vector Machine (SMV) and Decision Trees (DTs). Globally, Farquad, Vadlamani, Ravi, Bapi and Raju (2014) states that the Germany N26 Bank and American Express from America successfully implemented customer churn prediction. The American Express now relies on sophisticated predictive modelling that forecasts and prevents customer churn. This was achieved through the analysis of past customer transactions hence identification of customer accounts that are likely going to close and take preventive action to mitigate the problem. Amuda and Adeyemo (2019), argues that the cost of retaining existing customers is lower than the cost of acquiring new customers when they did a customer churn prediction using multi-layer perceptron for financial institutions in Nigeria. In the African continent, International Financial Corporation (IFC) World Bank (2018) states that Greenfield Microfinance in Sub-Sahara Africa is a business model to advanced financial inclusion which successfully implemented churn predictions. The following was its customer churn rate in the year of implementation.

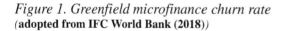

Figure 1. Greenfield microfinance churn rate
(**adopted from IFC World Bank (2018)**)

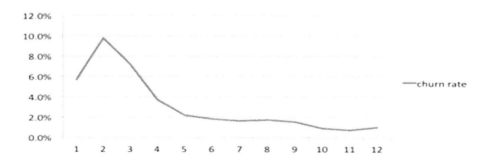

This led to a 43 percent of adults in this continent to have access of formal financial services in comparison with a 23 percent as per the year 2011. It also states that its subsidiaries in South Africa managed to incorporate customer churn prediction which led to a successful avoidance of customer attrition. In Zimbambe, customer churn prediction has been done for mobile network operators by Kusotera, Chimire and Mapuwei (2018) in their study titled An Analysis of Customer Churn for Mobile Network Operators in Zimbabwe. Upon observation no bank has engaged in customer attrition predictions yet. This study aims at developing a customer churn prediction model using a case of one of the leading financial institutions in Zimbabwe.

1.2 Statement of the Problem

According to Amuda and Adeyemo (2019) tones and tones of data is being generated as a result of technological advancement hence data has become oil of the twenty first century however oil is just useless unless it is refined into fuel. Several techniques and methods were introduced for hidden meaningful and salient information to be extracted from this data. The techniques include traditional machine learning and deep learning artificial neural networks. Customer churn is a critical challenge for corporates as this entails loss of customers to competitors. An in advance prediction of customer churning behaviour is therefore crucial for high valuable insight extraction in order to retain and maximise a corporate's customer base. In Zimbabwe, many if not all financial institutions have not yet implemented customer churn prediction hence failure to realise the benefits of customer retention at the expense of acquiring new customers. Therefore the purpose of this study is to develop a deep learning customer churn prediction model using customer past transactional data.

1.3 Objectives of the Study

1.3.1 Aim

Develop a very high accurate customer churn predictive model for financial institutions using deep learning artificial neural networks.

1.3.2 Objectives

1. To determine which features contribute towards customer attrition.
2. To assess the relationship between features that contribute towards customer attrition and customer churn.
3. To conduct customer churn analysis on the current data of the organisation.
4. To assess the effectiveness of deep neural networks in customer churn prediction.

1.4 Research Questions

1. What are the features that contribute to customer attrition?
2. What is the relationship between features that contribute towards customer attrition and customer churn?
3. What is the current situation on customer churn within the organisation?
4. Will deep learning neural networks help develop a desired customer churn predictive model for the organisation?

2. LITERATURE REVIEW

This section discusses the relevant literature, the study's goals, and the relevant ideas to the study. It examines, analyses, and critiques applicable empirical and theoretical research on customer churn analysis and prediction.

2.1 Empirical Evidence

2.1.1 Features Pertaining to Customer Churn Data

Features, in this context, refers to independent variables that causes customer churn. Features are extracted from data sources used to store customer transaction history such as transaction relational databases. According to Amuda and Adeyemo (2019) in their study they used data extracted from a database of one of the leading financial institutions in Nigeria. The data had 42 attributes but they determined only 19 for their study some of them are:

- Gender – Male or Female
- Transactional status – Active or Inactive
- Marital status – Divorced, Married, Single
- Occupation – Customer job description
- Religion – Christian, Islam, Other Religion
- Current account for individuals
- Current Account for
- xclusive_subscript - High Net worth Individuals with monthly income above N1m
- Hida – High interest deposit account
- Mobapp_Lifestyle_Count - The total number of times the customer paid for travel tickets or movie tickets or other event ticket.
- Tenure

230

Kaya, Dong, Suhara, Balcisoy and Bozkaya (2018), on the other hand, used the following features in their study titled "Behavioural Attributes and Financial Churn Prediction":

- Gender
- Marital status
- Educational status
- Job type
- Tenure
- Income
- Age
- Transaction Status

Both Kaya et al (2018), and Amuda and Adeyemo (2019) agrees that Recency, Frequency and Monetary value are other essential features that helps in determining customer churn.

2.1.2 Relationships Between Features and Customer Churn

Cai, Luo, Wang and Yang (2019) argues that high dimensional data analysis is becoming a challenge for engineers and researchers in the field of Data Mining and Machine Learning. This therefore means that there is need for feature selection since not all features are relevant in the development of a model. Subramanya and Somani (2017) argues that features which have a relationship with the predicted variable are relevant in model building hence they ensure a better accuracy. Those with no relationship with the predicted variable should be dropped out as they reduce the accuracy of a model.

2.1.3 Customer Churn Analysis

According to Celik and Osmanoglu (2019) customer churn analysis and customer churn prediction are two different subjects. Customer churn analysis helps ascertain the current status on how many customers have left the organisation and how many are left. Therefore it helps understand customers churn rate as well as the distribution of the customer base in terms of those who have churn and those who have not churned whereas customer churn prediction is forecasting the probability that the customer will churn or not using before the customer churns. Customer churn prediction is done using customer historical transaction data. Amuda and Adeyemo (2019) in their study entitled, 'Customers Churn Prediction in Financial Institution Using Artificial Neural Network' concluded a 33% churn rate and 67%

of customers not churned by the time they conducted their study. On the other hand Kaya et al (2018) concluded a 28% customer churn rate and 72% of those who did not churn in their similar study.

2.1.4 Customer Churn Prediction Related Work

Amuda and Adeyemo (2019) researched customer churn prediction for one of the leading financial institutions in Nigeria using a multi-layer perceptron neural networks. The data contained 50 000 customers and 42 features. Their predictive model had a 97.53% accuracy.

Amin et al (2019) in their research title "Customer churn prediction in the telecommunication sector using a rough set approach" did customer churn prediction models using tradition machine learning logistic regression and naïve bayes model and achieved model accuracies of 87.8% and 92.6% respectively. Ahmad, Jafar and Aljoumaa (2019) did a customer churn prediction model in similar industry using an experiment of four traditional machine learning algorithms which are Random Forest, Decision Tree, Gradient Boost Machine Tree(GBM) and Extreme Gradient Boost (XGBOOST). The XGBOOST achieved the best accuracy of 89%.

Deep learning neural networks have better accuracy compared to traditional machine learning. According the above information, neural networks achieved 97.53% compared to a highest of 92.6% from traditional neural networks.

2.2 Theory

2.2.1 Artificial Intelligence (AI), Machine Learning, and Deep Learning

According to Bini (2018) Artificial Intelligence expressed in terms of academic discipline, was established in 1956. The motive then, as well as now, was to facilitate computers to carry out tasks that can be seen as uniquely human: those that need intelligence. AI, then, simply refers to an outcome of a computer whereby that computer exhibits intelligence that is artificial through carrying out a task mimicking human intelligence. Jeong (2020) argues that the term AI itself does not say much about how those tasks are carried out hence many different techniques include expert systems or rule-based, one category of such techniques embarked on widely being used in the 1980s is machine learning.

Bini (2018) argues that it is not just about mimicking human behaviour (AI) but mimicking how humans learn hence Machine Learning and Deep Learning. Also states that Machine Learning is a subset of AI whereas Deep Learning is a subset of Machine Learning. Cook (2016) defines Machine Learning as a process of providing data (as input) to a computer, then train allowing it to learn trends and patterns with that data (through building a model or an algorithm) so that the computer produces desired output that will provide actionable insights as well as data driven decision making. For example, feeding an algorithm vast amounts of financial transactions data, telling it which ones are not fraudulent, and allow it to work out on what indicates fraud so that it can be able to predict fraud in future.

According to Bini (2018) also argues that Deep Learning is the only part of Machine Learning that makes use artificial neural networks designed to mimic human brains. Deep artificial neural networks are a set of algorithms achieving new levels of great accuracy for quite several significant problems, such as recommender systems, sound recognition and image recognition. According to www.blogs.nvidia. com Deep learning has managed to break down tasks in ways that makes all kinds of machine assists seem possible, even likely, which is the reason why self-driving cars, better preventive healthcare, as well as better movie recommendations, are all here today or on the horizon.

Jeong (2020) also agrees on the relationships between AI, Machine Learning and Deep Learning as shown on fig. 2:

2.2.2 Why Deep Learning Is Superior to Machine Learning

With few data, shallow networks (Machine Learning Algorythms) are still effective. A deep network has at least two hidden layers and its performance continues to increase as the amount of data increases as shown on the diagram above. Older learning algorithms are the machine learning algorithms and examples of them are Random Forest, Decision Tree, Gradient Boost Machine Tree and XGBOOST.

2.2.3 Customer Churn

Tripling, vanden Broucke, Antonio, Baesens and Snoeck (2018) argues that customer churn which is also known as customer attrition, is when a customer ceases any form of a relationship with the business. Tripling et al (2018) also states that total cost of churn is an aggregate of both marketing costs involved with replacing customers churned with new ones and lost revenue. It is therefore a goal for every business to reduce customer churn.

Borah, Prakhya and Sharma (2020) agrees with Tripling et al (2018) that customer churn or attrition, is a measurement of how much business a company has lost, the loss which can be assessed as a percentage of total customer base and as revenue lost.

- Percent of total customer base – also called customer churn which measures how many customers a company has lost within a specified period.

Figure 2. AI, machine learning, and deep learning
(adopted from Jeong (2020), page 6)

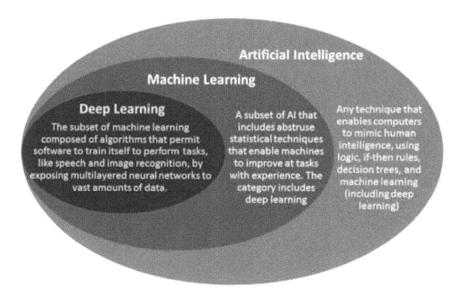

Figure 3. Effectiveness of deep learning over machine learning
(adapted from Bini (2018))

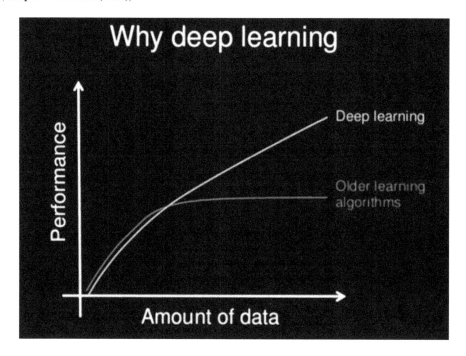

- Revenue lost – also called revenue churn which measures the amount of money a company has lost within a specified period.

Shirazi and Mohammadi (2019) also agrees with the above authors that customer churn or customer attrition means the loss of subscribers or customers for any given reason at any point in time. Companies measure and track churn as a percentage of lost customers against total customer base over a given period.

2.2.4 Importance of Customer Churn Analysis and Prediction

Tripling et al (2018) argues that the ability to anticipate that a given customer is at high risk to churn, whilst having considerable time to do something about it, entails excellent potential source of revenue for a company. Avoiding such a customer from churning results in retaining revenue supposed to have been lost by losing that customer.

- Coussement, Lessmann and Verstraeten (2017) states that it is reasonably very costly to acquire new customers and lose existing customers however cheap to retain existing customers as the act ensures repeated purchase. Therefore by predicting which customers are likely to churn gives a company the room to take corrective measures in retaining such customers before they churn.
- Shirazi and Mohammadi (2019) alluded that with the rise in competition within the markets there is high risk of losing customers to competitors hence customer churn analysis and prediction is of great importance as it helps in avoiding customers to fall for competitors.
- The process also helps businesses to focus through offering incentives on repeated purchases by the soon to churn customers.
- Borah, Prakhya and Sharma (2020) also argues that the intension to stop consuming a company's product(s) is a decision done by customers over time. Hence the company has to understand and determine which customers intend to stop purchasing to convince them to stay and keep purchasing. This is achievable through customer attrition analysis and prediction.
- According to www.superoffice.com the cost of acquiring new customers is 5 times greater than the cost retaining existing customers as well as that the most significant retail revenue driver is customer retention as shown on the fig below:

Figure 4. Most significant retail revenue drivers
(**adopted from** *https://www.superoffice.com/blog/reduce-customer-churn/*)

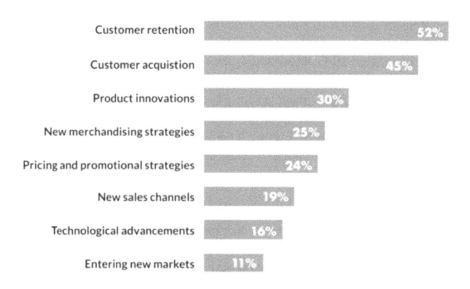

2.2.5 Ways to Reduce Customer Churn

Hassouna, Tarhini, Elyas and AbouTrab (2016) argues that it is only after customer churn analysis and predictive modelling for an organisation to be able to apply ways to reduce customer churn. The following are ways to reduce customer churn:

- *Analysis of why customers churn* – Hassouna et al (2016) stresses that it is the task of a business to find out the reason(s) why customers are leaving. Almost 68% of customers leave for competitors because they feel a company is not giving adequate care (Hassouna et al, 2016). It is not adequate to send customers exist surveys but rather make actual phone calls asking why they are leaving as this proves how an organisation is concerned about the its customers.
- *Engaging with customers* - Shirazi and Mohammadi (2019) on the other hand argues that a business must be involved with customers daily. It is a company's job remind its customers why it is essential for them to keep consuming its products or acquiring its services daily. Tripling et al (2018) even suggests that a company should engage with its customers through

various communication platforms such as social media, emails, websites and blogs.

- *Keeping loyal customers* – Bhattacharyya and Dash (2020) stresses that it of paramount importance for a company to provide its loyal customers with reason of why they should stick to its brand. This is because loyal customers does not only do repeated purchases but rather give family, friends and relatives recommendations to do the same.

- *Provision of exceptional customer services* - Tripling et al (2018) recommends that a business should exceptionally provide customers with services that will avoid them to go for competitors. This is definitely because the key to loyalty is customer service and provision of it exceptionally results in very few chances of churn. Hence being better than competitors is crucial and can be achieved by not just offering a service or product but rather adding more and more value to the service or product.

- *Educating the customers* - Hassouna et al (2016) emphasises that a company must do whatever it takes to inform customers about its services and products; and suggests that this might be done through product demos, free trainings, video tutorials as well as webinars so that customers feel informed and comfortable.

2.2.6 Recency, Frequency, and Monetary Value (RFM)

According to Khodabandehlou and Rahman (2017) RFM analysis is a method that can be used for determining which of your current customers are most likely to churn or stay. The following basic theory underpins RFM analysis:

- *Recency* - Mena, Caigny, Coussement, De Bock and Lessmann (2019) argues that recency is an essential factor in determining which consumers are most likely to churn or stay. Customers who have made a recent purchase are more likely to make another purchase (stay) than those who have made a purchase way well in the past (are most likely to churn, if they have not yet churned).

- *Frequency* – On the other hand Jha, Parekh, Mouhoub and Makkar (2020) states that frequency is another significant factor. Customers who have made a larger number of purchases in the past are more likely to stay than those who have made a smaller number of purchases.

- *Monetary value* - Khodabandehlou and Rahman (2017) also states that the total amount a customer brings into a business, also known as monetary value, is another significant feature. Customers who have spent more in the past (in total for all purchases) are more likely stay than customers who have brought less into the bustiness.

2.3 Information and Computer Technology (ICT) Theories

Korpelainen (2011) argues that there is quite several theories that are used for ICT systems adoption and implementation. Amongst others these include; Technology Acceptancy Theory (TAM), Theory of Reasoned Action (TRA), Diffusion of Innovations (DOI), Theory of Planned Behaviour (TPB) and Information Systems Success Model. The following theories were reviewed with the mind that Data Science and Artificial Intelligence technologies are new dogs on the market especially in the nation of Zimbabwe.

2.3.1 Technology Acceptancy Theory

The Technology Acceptance Model was the most cited theory (TAM). Davis (1985) proposed a theoretical model which is aimed at predicting as well as explaining ICT use behaviour hence what induces potential adopters to support or reject the use of technology. Koufaris (2002) argues that the Theory of Reasoned Action is the theoretical foundation of TAM (TRA) where perceived utility and perceived ease of use are fundamental determinants of system use in TAM, and attitudes toward system use, that is, the user's willingness to use the system. Perceived utility refers to how much a person believes that using a particular system will improve his or her job performance, whereas perceived ease of use refers to how much a person believes that using a particular system will be painless. Hassouna et al (2016) mentions that across the globe, deep neural networks through python programming language libraries are perceived efficient and the predictions outcome are ease to interpret as well as the models are ease to use.

2.3.2 Theory of Reasoned Action

Fishbein (1979) states that according to the theory of rational action (TRA), attitude and subjective norms are critical for persuasion. TRA was created by Fishbein and Ajzen in 1975 to describe the connections between people's values, perceptions, norms, intentions, and behaviours. According to the theory, a person's conduct is dictated by their behavioural purpose to execute it, which is determined by the person's behaviours and subjective norms toward the behaviour. The subjective standard is described as "a person's belief that the majority of important people in his life believe he should or should not conduct the action in question" (Fishbein, 1979). Sarver (1983) states that Ajzen and Fishbein in 1980 did a book which focused on the prediction and interpretation of human actions to aid in the solution of practical problems and policy decisions. The authors claim that TRA can research

2.3.3 Diffusion of Innovations

According to Sahin (2006) the diffusion of inventions theory describes how new technological and other advancements spread across societies and cultures, from their introduction to widespread acceptance. The diffusion of inventions theory attempts to understand how and why new ideas and methods are implemented over time, with timelines theoretically spanning decades. Dearing and Cox (2018) argues that AI, machine learning and deep learning technologies are being implemented and spreading according DOI.

According to Thurber and Fahey (2009) DOI is a broad theory of how new ideas spread and accepted in a society, attempting to understand how communication networks and opinion leaders influence adoption. Sahin (2006) states that Rogers in 1983 introduced the first method model, a five-stage model of organisational innovation implementation and adoption:

i. *Innovators* - Some individuals want to be among the first to try a new product. They are daring and curious about new concepts. These people are also the first to create new ideas and are willing to take risks. To cater to this demographic, very little, if anything, needs to be done.

ii. *Early Adopters* - They are those individuals who serve influential people. They enjoy taking on leadership positions and are open to new experiences. These people are well aware of the need for improvement and are also open to new ideas. How-to guides and information sheets on implementation are examples of strategies to cater to this demographic. They do not need facts to change their minds.

iii. *Early Majority* – They are those individuals that are seldom leaders, but they are the first to embrace new ideas. However, before they can implement an idea, they usually need to see proof that it works. Success stories and proof of the innovation's efficacy are two strategies for appealing to this demographic. Upon observation, several organisations within Zimbabwe are in this stage when data science and Artificial Intelligence technologies come.

iv. *Late Majority* - These individuals are wary of change and will only accept a new technology after being tried by many people. Knowledge about how many other people have tried the innovation and successfully followed it is one strategy for appealing to this demographic.

v. *Laggards* - Tradition binds these individuals, and they are staunch conservatives. They are the most resistant to change and the most difficult to persuade.

Statistics, anxiety appeals, and pressure from other adopter groups are all used to cater to this demographic.

2.3.4 Theory of Planned Behaviour

Accord to Ajzen (2011) TPB is a theoretical model proposed by Ajzen in 1991 that focuses on cognitive self-regulation. It is very similar to the TRA model, except that it includes a new construct, namely perceived behavioural regulation. The interpretation of control over the output of a given action is referred to as perceived behavioural control. Objective factors determine individual decisions and actions in TRA, and individual motives dictate conduct. Individuals' plans and reasons to perform a particular act are referred to as intentions. Individual perceptions and the degree to which individuals view a particular act as advantageous or favourable are often reflected in intentions. According to the theory, human behaviour is influenced by personal attitudes and social influences and a sense of power. Sniehotta, Presseau and Araújo-Soares (2014) argues that TPB was derived on the basis that the TRA makes the statement that actions are under an individual's volitional influence. This assumption, however, is more likely to be impractical in some instances, as volitional regulation of behaviours can vary depending on the situation.

2.3.5 Information Systems Success Model

DeLone and McLean (2002) reviewed previous research and introduced a taxonomy of factors that influence information system performance. The authors looked at

Figure 5. Information systems success model
(**adopted from DeLone and McLean, 2002**)

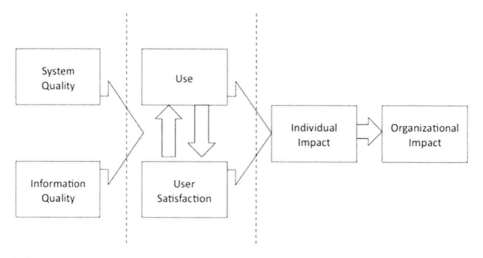

the literature on IT performance and divided it into system quality, knowledge quality, usage, user satisfaction, personal impact, and organisational impact. These six interconnected and interdependent categories provide a holistic view of IS performance.

3. METHODOLOGY

This section covers the data science research methodology employed. It contains the research design, population, and sampling and sampling procedures, tools, and libraries that were used to develop the desired customer churn desired model.

3.1 CRISP-DM Design Methodology

According to d'Aquin, Troullinou, O'Connor, Cullen, Faller and Holden (2018, December) data science research design involves a plan of the processes that needs

Figure 6. Experiment design flowchart
(**Adopted from** *www.datascience-pm.com*)

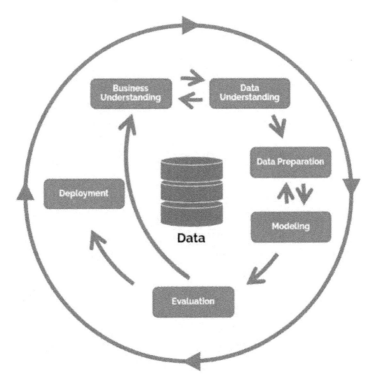

to be followed to carry out a large data sets experimental analytical research. The plan involves the steps also called procedures towards attaining objectives about an innovative idea(s) whilst ensuring the accuracy and integrity of the findings ethically. Schäfer, Zeiselmair, Becker and Otten (2018) defines that CRoss Industry Standard Process for Data Mining (CRISP-DM) as a process model that consists of six phases which naturally details a Data Science Life Cycle and these phases are; Business understanding, Data understanding, Data preparation, Modelling, Evaluation and Deployment.

3.1.1 Business Understanding

This involves determining the business need and what needs to be done to achieve that business need. In this study, the bank needed to anticipate whether a customer is churning or not using past transactional data to take corrective measures in avoiding its customers from churning. It also needed to understand the current churn status to deploy the proper techniques in retaining such customers. The bank also needed to ascertain features that causes customer churn and the extent to which they cause customer churn (relationships between those features and customer churn) hence knowing what features to monitor and consider when performing customer churn predictive modelling.

3.1.2 Data Understanding

This involves gathering data that the business has, then ascertain what data is needed to accomplish the business need and the cleanness. After understanding the data, one will establish the kind of preparation that needs to be done on that data. The data was collected from a customer transaction relational data base using structured query language queries. Transactional data pertaining 135,207 customers was collected and it contained 1,896,901 records. The data had the following columns:

- TRN_DT – The date that the transaction occurred.
- TXN_ACC – The customer's bank account
- ACCOUNT_CLASS - The customer's account class
- CHG_AMT_1 – The charge amount which is revenue that the bank gets from charging its customers per transaction.
- PRODUCT_CODE – services offered by the bank to its customers
- BRANCH_CODE – the location of the customer.
- DORMANT – whether the account is active or dormant. 1 represents yes the account is dormant, and 0 represents no the account is not dormant (is active).

Customer Churn Prediction for Financial Institutions Using DL ANN

Table 1. Missing values

Feature	Number of missing values
TRN_DT	0
TXN_ACC	0
ACCOUNT_CLASS	0
CHG_AMT_1	11,397
PRODUCT_CODE	0
BRANCH_CODE	0
DORMANT	0

In charge amount feature there were 11,397 missing values. Since there are 2,311,784 records within the dataset

3.1.3 Data Preparation

Usually, data comes with missing values and different characters, hence removing or filling in those values. Data cleaning is therefore a crucial stage in model development as it helps in making the data complete.

3.1.3.1 Dealing With Missing Values

The researcher opted to drop all records without the charge amount. After dropping the charge amount, the number of missing values became zeros.

3.1.3.2 Anonymising the Dataset

It is an essential step to do in ensuring ethics. It is the company's right to remain anonymous in this study. The data categorical features were transformed to numerical values using Label Encoding (replacing (encoding) column elements with a numbers starting from zero so that these numbers will mean the categories within a particular column). Below is a sample of the anonymised dataset:

The customers' accounts were used to create the CUSTOMER_ID feature since an account is unique per customer.

3.1.3.3 Created RFM Features

According to literature review of this study Recency, Frequency and Monetary features are also crucial in customer churn prediction. Below is a sample of these features after they were created from the anonymised dataset where LTDate is the Last Transacted Date by a customer:

Customer Churn Prediction for Financial Institutions Using DL ANN

Table 2. After dropping missing values

Feature	Number of missing values
TRN_DT	0
TXN_ACC	0
ACCOUNT_CLASS	0
CHG_AMT_1	0
PRODUCT_CODE	0
BRANCH_CODE	0
DORMANT	0

Table 3. Anonymized dataset

	TRN_DT	ACCOUNT_CLASS	CHG_AMT_1	PRODUCT_CODE	BRANCH_CODE	DORMANT	CUSTOMER_ID
0	2021-03-05	0	0.00	27	15	0	397129
1	2021-03-05	0	13.04	27	15	0	397129
3	2021-03-06	0	0.00	15	106	0	441026
4	2021-03-08	0	140.00	19	106	0	441026
5	2021-03-04	0	0.00	1	11	0	342883

Table 4. RFM features

	CUSTOMER_ID	LTDate	Recency	Frequency	Monetary
0	100000	2021-03-07	17	5	230.20
1	100013	2021-03-24	0	24	88.60
2	100018	2021-03-24	0	20	2611.28
3	100023	2021-03-20	4	25	0.00
4	100025	2021-03-16	8	26	163.73

Customer Churn Prediction for Financial Institutions Using DL ANN

3.1.3.4 Merging RFM Features to the Primary Dataset

The data was merged to develop a complete set of features to enhance customer churn prediction model building.

Table 5. Merged dataset

CUSTOMER_ID	Recency	Frequency	Monetary	ACCOUNT_CLASS	CHG_AMT_1	PRODUCT_CODE	BRANCH_CODE	DORMANT
100000	17	5	230.2	9	0.0	3	29	0
100000	17	5	230.2	9	2.8	12	29	0
100000	17	5	230.2	9	3.4	12	29	0
100000	17	5	230.2	9	120.0	27	29	0
100000	17	5	230.2	9	104.0	27	29	0

3.1.3.5 EDA

Exploratory Data Analysis is a process whereby the developer familiarises with the data to understand its properties, distribution, relevance, and relationships amongst features. This is where relevant features are demined which are those that strongly causes the predicted variable.

3.1.3.6 Data Information

The data has 1,896,901 records. All the columns' data types are numeric. Machine learning and deep learning models only accept numeric values as input hence converting all features to numeric values is a crucial stage in model building.s

Figure 7. Data information

```
<class 'pandas.core.frame.DataFrame'>
Int64Index: 1896901 entries, 0 to 474225
Data columns (total 8 columns):
 #   Column         Dtype
---  ------         -----
 0   Recency        int64
 1   Frequency      int64
 2   Monetary       float64
 3   ACCOUNT_CLASS  int64
 4   CHG_AMT_1      float64
 5   PRODUCT_CODE   int64
 6   BRANCH_CODE    int64
 7   DORMANT        int64
dtypes: float64(2), int64(6)
memory usage: 130.2 MB
```

Figure 8. Distribution and data ranges

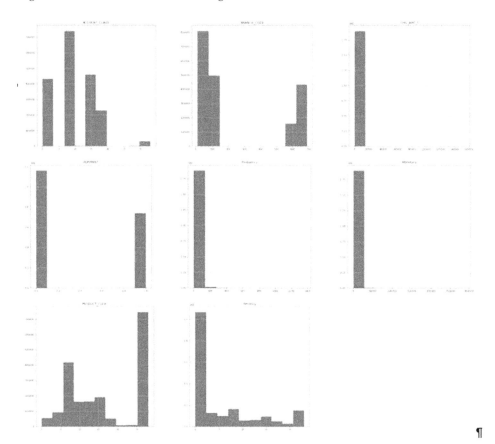

3.1.3.7 Distribution and Data Ranges

The histograms show the distribution and data ranges. Figure 7 shows that the data is not normally distributed hence the need to normalise the data in the feature engineering section. Feature ranges are varying much from one another. For example, ACCOUNT_CLASS RANGES from 0 to 30 whilst CHG_AMT_1 ranges from 0 to 160,000.00; hence normalisation is needed. Normalising data helps in bring all data ranges within the same range. This helps a deep neural network model to focus hence higher accuracy in terms of its predictive capabilities.

3.1.3.8 Feature Selection and Engineering

This involves enriching the data and selecting relevant features. Enriching data includes feature scaling in order to bring data values into values within the same range so as to reduce noise for the model training process. In enriching the data,

Figure 9. Normalised and scaled data sample

```python
X = zwl_data[columns].values
Y = zwl_data[['DORMANT']].values


power = PowerTransformer()


X = power.fit_transform(X)


X

array([[ 0.7880679 ,  0.17019098,  0.57079844, ..., -0.85670457,
        -2.25032929,  1.29084696],
       [ 0.7880679 ,  0.17019098,  0.57079844, ..., -0.85670457,
        -1.19059319,  1.29084696],
       [ 0.7880679 ,  0.17019098,  0.57079844, ..., -0.85670457,
         1.12736448,  1.29084696],
       ...,
       [ 0.21946256, -1.27115454, -1.22119216, ..., -0.85670457,
        -0.08047839,  0.23065785],
       [ 1.19185358, -0.95834974, -1.22119216, ..., -0.85670457,
        -0.08047839,  0.14416132],
       [ 1.48589438, -1.27115454, -1.22119216, ..., -0.85670457,
        -0.91771761, -1.27653932]])
```

the power transformer a Sci-kit Learn pre-processing library which normalises and scales data at once whilst maintaining data meaning and integrity. Sample of transformed data:

3.1.4 Modelling

This is the phase at which a particular type of model to use is determined. Based on empirical evidence and related literature, deep learning neural networks proved to be effective given that the bank had vast amounts of past customer transactional data (big data, millions of records) deep neural networks were considered appropriate in this study. Hence a deep neural network model was built. Deep neural networks have become a standard for data science as they can be used for various types of models ranging from binary classification, multi-classification, regression, natural language processing, time series predictive modelling and computer vision.

3.1.4.1 Deep Neural Network One

The model has three hidden layers and was built without any special techniques such as model early stopping or checkpointing. When training a deep neural network model, model checkpointing helps in saving the best model that is in each iteration of training if the model improves then the model is saved and if it does not improve then the model is not saved. Model early stopping ensures that the model stops training when it gradually starts to decrease its performance in training.

Figure 10. Model one

```
model = Sequential()
model.add(Dense(50,input_dim=X_train.shape[1],activation='relu'))
model.add(Dense(50,activation='relu'))
model.add(Dense(50,activation='relu'))
model.add(Dense(1,activation='sigmoid'))

model.summary()

Model: "sequential"
```

Layer (type)	Output Shape	Param #
dense (Dense)	(None, 50)	400
dense_1 (Dense)	(None, 50)	2550
dense_2 (Dense)	(None, 50)	2550
dense_3 (Dense)	(None, 1)	51

```
Total params: 5,551
Trainable params: 5,551
Non-trainable params: 0
```

compile the model

```
model.compile(loss="binary_crossentropy",
              optimizer = "adam",
              metrics = ["accuracy"])
```

Training the model

```
history = model.fit(X_train,
                    y_train,
                    epochs=50,
                    batch_size = 10,
                    validation_split=0.2,
                    verbose = 1)
```

3.1.4.2 Deep Neural Network Two

The model has three hidden layers and was built with any special techniques such as model early stopping or check pointing.

Customer Churn Prediction for Financial Institutions Using DL ANN

Figure 11. Model two

Create the model

```
model1 = Sequential()
model1.add(Dense(50,input_dim=X_train.shape[1],activation='relu'))
model1.add(Dense(50,activation='relu'))
model1.add(Dense(50,activation='relu'))
model1.add(Dense(1,activation='sigmoid'))
```

compile the model

```
model1.compile(loss="binary_crossentropy",optimizer = "adam",metrics = ["accuracy"])

from tensorflow.keras.callbacks import EarlyStopping, ModelCheckpoint

early = EarlyStopping('val_accuracy',patience=10,verbose=1)
mcp = ModelCheckpoint('churn_prediction1.h5',save_best_only=True,monitor='val_accuracy',verbose=1)
```

Training the model

```
history = model1.fit(X_train,Y_train,epochs=100,batch_size = 12,
                validation_split=0.2,callbacks=[early, mcp],verbose = 1)
```

3.1.4.3 Training and Testing the Model

The built models were trained and tested using the training and testing data. Data was split into 80% training set and 20% testing set so as to ensure that the model is exposed to more data in training hence more capability of exhibiting knowledge obtained through training on unseen data (testing set as well as in natural world production environment). The 80% training data was further split into 80% of 80% training set and 20% of 80% validation.

3.1.5 Model Evaluation

3.1.5.1 Testing Performance of the Model on Unseen Data

Each of the models is then exposed on the testing data (unseen data) to see if the model accuracy is worth bringing the model into the real world. Test accuracy determines the significance of a model in natural world production environment.

3.1.5.2 Model Results and Conclusion

Model training history, classification report and classification report will be used for model performance and results. This will be done through section four of this study.

3.1.6 Model Deployment

The best model is then deployed into the real world if its performance is satisfactory. The bank will do the deployment on their deployment platforms.

3.2 Tools and Libraries

3.2.1 Anaconda

An open source software distribution of Python and R programming languages used for scientific computing for example data science. It is an intuitive interface which provides actionable insights usable to drive better quality decisions. Machine learning and deep learning are best done in this software. This tool will be used for the achievement of all the objectives as it provides all the tools needed for building the entire model

3.2.2 Jupyter Notebook

A free open source web application used for data simulation, statistical modelling, data visualisation, data cleaning and transformation, descriptive analytics, diagnostic analytics, predictive analytics and prescriptive analytics. The entire model will be built in jupyter notebook.

3.2.3 Pandas

It is a stylish package in python programming language that provides flexible, expensive and powerful data structures which makes data analysis and manipulation very easy. This will provide data for analysis that will help achieve objective one and two.

3.2.4 Numpy

A crucial package in Python Programming language used for financial computing and also contains a compelling multi-dimensional array objects plus very useful linear algebra. Numpy will help achieve objective two and three by transforming data to numerical values as deep learning models understand numerical values only.

3.2.5 Matplotlib and Seaborn

Python Programming language unique libraries used for any kind of two-dimensional array plots (Matplotlib and Seaborn) and multi-dimensional array plots (Seaborn). High dimensionality data can be visualised easily to make it easily understandable. Helps in achieving objectives one and two through visualisations.

3.2.6 Sci-Kit Learn

A free traditional machine learning library in python programming language. It is used for regression, classification and clustering algorithms such as linear and logistic regression, support vector machines, XGBOOST, K-means just to mention a few. It will be used for data pre-processing as well as data splitting into training and testing sets.

3.2.7 TensorFlow

An open source Python Programming language library used for deep learning applications such as artificial neural networks and uses Keras as a backend.

3.2.8 Keras

It is an artificial neural network framework for python which provides a very convenient environment to define and train almost all kinds of deep learning models. Helps achieve objective three.

4. PRESENTATION ANALYSIS OF DATA AND RESULTS

The section provides presentation, analysis and interpretation of the research findings on features that causes customer churn, relationships of such features with customer churn, current status of customer churn within the bank as well as customer churn prediction modelling significance using deep neural networks.

4.1 Features That Cause Customer Churn

A correlation matrix shows whether a relationship exists between two of each and every feature within a given dataset. The presented correlation matrix is showing the relationships between the labelled features. It was used to determine features that have a relationship with the customer churn (DORMANT) feature. Recency,

Figure 12. Feature correlation matrix

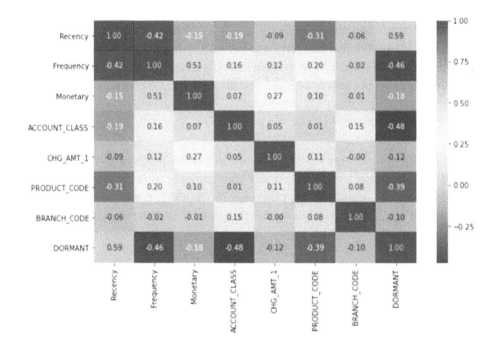

frequency, monetary, account class, charge amount, product type and location of the account that is the customer (BRANCH_CODE) they both determine dormancy. There is no feature without a relationship customer churn. A correlation coefficient of zero denotes no relationship.

4.2 Relationships Between Features and Customer Churn

The above figure shows correlation coefficients between features that causes customer churn and customer churn itself. These coefficients were extracted from the correlation matrix. The relationship between customer churn and recency is positive with a correlation coefficient of 0.59 and this means that when increases (the number of days since last purchase) that customer is more likely to or have churned. Customer churn and frequency have a weak negative relationship of 0.46 detailing that when the number of times a customer consumes the bank's service(s) or product(s) increases a customer is more likely not going to churn. Monetary value from customers and customer churn have poor negative relationship of 0.18 which means if a customer is bring more and more monetary value to the business, there is a chance that the customer will stay. Customer churn and account class have a week negative relationship of 0.48 hence the more classes a customer falls into the lesser

Customer Churn Prediction for Financial Institutions Using DL ANN

Figure 13. Relationships between features and customer churn

```
corr_coefs

{'Recency & Churn': 0.59,
 'Frequency & Churn': -0.46,
 'Monetary & Churn': -0.18,
 'ACCOUNT_CLASS & Churn': -0.48,
 'CHG_AMT_1 & Churn': -0.12,
 'PRODUCT_CODE & Churn': -0.39,
 'BRANCH_CODE & Churn': -0.1}
```

the chances that the customer will churn. The charge amount and customer churn have a poor negative relationship of 0.12 and the relationship is negative because the more the charges a customer gets the more the transactions a customer is doing therefore there is chance that customer will stay. Customer churn and product type have a weak negative relationship of 0.39 meaning that lesser the products a customer consumes the more likely that customer will churn. Churn and location has have an impoverished negative relationship of 0.1 which means that only few chances that where a customer is located will determine whether that customer will churn or not.

4.3 Customer Churn Analysis for the Organisation

The figure shows churn class distribution in term of the number of transactions by customers within each class. There are 738,082 instances pertaining dormant accounts and this means that the bank lost a potential of 738,082 transactions of a similar upcoming period to the period under study.

The pie chart shows the percentage distribution of dormant accounts in relation to active accounts. There a 38.9% dormancy within the bank and this means that 38.9% of its potential revenue is lying within customers that the bank can retain instead of acquiring new customers.

4.4 Customer Churn Prediction

4.4.1 Deep Neural Network One Results

The first deep learning neural network was developed without any special techniques that help in increasing model accuracy such as model check pointing and early stopping.

Figure 14. Customer churn distribution

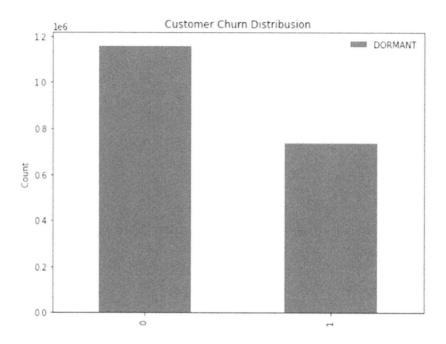

Figure 15. Customer churn analysis pie chart

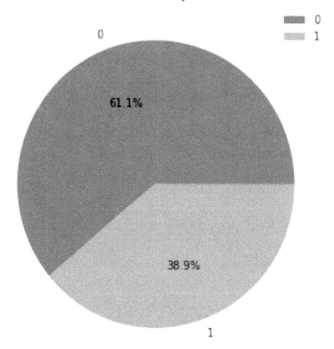

Customer Churn Prediction for Financial Institutions Using DL ANN

4.4.1.1 Model Training History

The model loss and validation loss are converging towards loss equal to zero. The lesser the loss the more the accuracy as shown on the following figure. Epochs are number of iterations a model take whilst training and learning the trends and patterns within the data. Validation is used to monitor if a model is overfitting hence if they both follow the same trend then the model's performance on training is good.

Figure 16. Model one loss training history

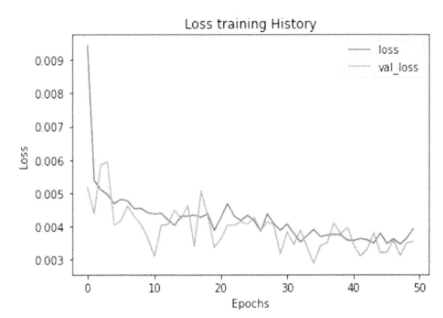

The model accuracy and validation accuracy are diverging towards accuracy equal to 100%. The figure shows an exemplary model training performance as both training and validation accuracy are not diverging from one another but rather both towards very high accuracy.

4.4.1.2 Model Accuracy

The first model's accuracy on test data (unseen data) is as follows:

The model accuracy on unseen data, natural world production environment is 99.95% to two significant figures. This means that for every 200 customers only one customer is misclassified.

Figure 17. Model one accuracy training history

Figure 18. Model one accuracy

```
print("The model accuracy is:",model.evaluate(X_test,Y_test,verbose=0)[1]*100,'%')
The model accuracy is: 99.95255470275879 %
```

Figure 19. Model one classification report

```
print(classification_report(Y_test,y_pred))
              precision    recall  f1-score   support

           0       1.00      1.00      1.00    231578
           1       1.00      1.00      1.00    147803

    accuracy                           1.00    379381
   macro avg       1.00      1.00      1.00    379381
weighted avg       1.00      1.00      1.00    379381
```

4.4.1.3 Classification Report

A classification report shows how precise, sensitive (recall) a model is as well significance of the model. The classification report is showing a 100% precision, recall and f1-score for both classes 0 (active) and 1 (dormant). This is because a classification report is to 2 decimal places. The number of active accounts (0) records is 231,578 and dormancy related records is 147,803. This proves significance of the model as it managed to classify the classes correctly given that there is an imbalance in classes.

4.4.1.4 Confusion Matrix

A confusion matrix shows actual test labels and the model's predicted outcome. On the y-axis is the actual classes and the x-axis is the predicted classes. The model predicted all records pertaining class 1 to be class 1, and 0 records of class 1 were predicted as class 0 (no misclassification). The model also classified 231,398 records belonging to class 0 as class 0 and misclassified 180 records belonging to class 0 as class 1. The model has a misclassification rate of (180/ (231,438+180))

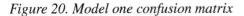

Figure 20. Model one confusion matrix

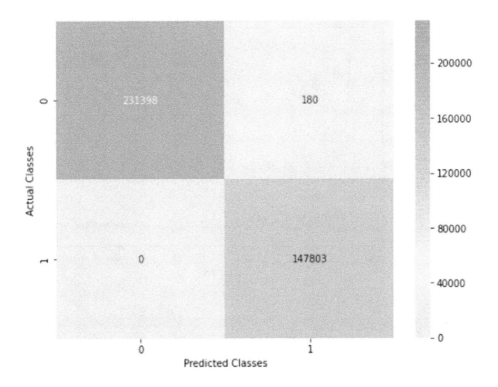

x 100 which is equal to 0.08% to 2 decimal places on class 0 and a 0% on class 1. All records pertaining dormancy were correctly classified hence the model has a 100% accuracy on predicting customers who are churning.

4.4.2 Deep Neural Network Two Results

The second deep learning neural network was developed two special techniques that help in increasing model accuracy which are model check pointing and early stopping.

4.4.2.1 Model Training History

The model loss and validation loss are converging towards loss equal to zero. Figure 21 is showing a better (less zig zag) trend for both training loss and validation loss hence model two is better than model one.

The model training and validation accuracy are diverging towards accuracy equal to 100%. Figure 22 is showing a better (less zig zag) trend for both training accuracy and validation accuracy hence model two as well is better than model one.

Figure 21. Model two loss training history

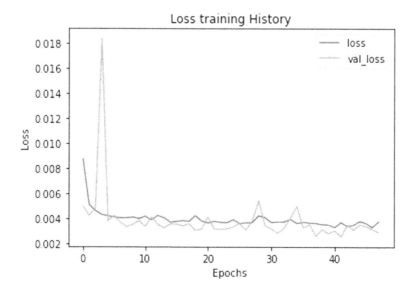

Figure 22. Model two accuracy training history

4.4.2.2 Model Accuracy

The model accuracy on unseen data, natural world production environment is 99.96% to two significant figures. This means that for about every 220 customers only one customer is misclassified.

Figure 23 Model two accuracy

```
m1 = tf.keras.models.load_model('churn_prediction1.h5')
```
```
print("The model accuracy is:",m1.evaluate(X_test,Y_test,verbose=0)[1]*100,'%')
```
```
The model accuracy is: 99.96204376220703 %
```

4.4.3.3 Classification Report

A classification report for model 2 also shows how precise, sensitive (recall) a model is as well significance of the mode and the report is showing a 100% precision, recall and f1-score for both classes 0 (active) and 1 (dormant). The number of active accounts (0) records is 231,578 and dormancy related records is 147,803. This proves significance of the model as it managed to classify the classes correctly given that there is an imbalance in classes.

Figure 24. Model two classification report

```
print(classification_report(Y_test,y_pred))
              precision    recall  f1-score   support

           0       1.00      1.00      1.00    231578
           1       1.00      1.00      1.00    147803

    accuracy                           1.00    379381
   macro avg       1.00      1.00      1.00    379381
weighted avg       1.00      1.00      1.00    379381
```

4.4.4.4 Confusion Matrix

A confusion matrix shows actual test labels and the model's predicted outcome. On the y-axis is the actual classes and the x-axis is the predicted classes. The model

Figure 25. Model one confusion matrix

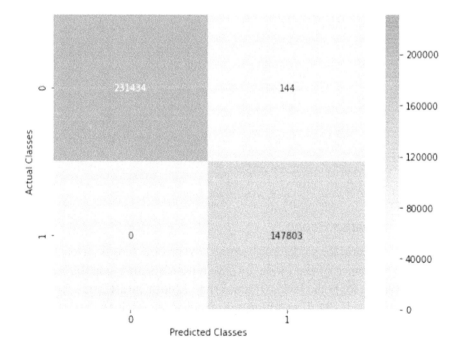

predicted all records pertaining class 1 to be class 1, and 0 records of class 1 were predicted as class 0 (no misclassification). The model also classified 231,434 records belonging to class 0 as class 0 and misclassified 144 records belonging to class 0 as class 1. The model has a misclassification rate of (144/(231,434+144)) x 100 which is equal to 0.06% to 2 decimal places on class 0 and a 0% on class 1. All records pertaining dormancy were correctly classified hence the model has a 100% accuracy on predicting customers who are churning. This model is very significant compared to the first model which misclassified 180 records compared to 144.

5. CONCLUSION AND RECOMMENDATIONS

This section summarises the results that were discovered in the previous section in order to address the research questions related to the study's objectives. The results were then used to draw conclusions and make specific recommendations to the financial institutions as well as the one under study.

5.1 Summary of Findings

5.1.1 Features That Cause Customer Churn

The features that causes customer churn in a financial institutions are Recency, frequency, monetary, account class, charge amount, product type and location of the account that is the customer.

5.1.2 Relationships Between Features and Customer Churn

Only Recency have a positive relationships with customer churn whereas the rest of the features that were concluded to be causing customer churn in this study have a negative relationship with customer churn.

5.1.3 Customer Churn Analysis for the Organisation

There more active customers within the bank as compared to those who have churned and there is currently a 38.9% churn rate within the bank.

5.1.2 Customer Churn Prediction

Both neural networks have an outstanding performance on unseen data with the first neural network having accuracy of 99.95% and the second one a 99.96%.

5.2 Conclusion

All the features that contribute towards customer churn are essential as input to the model. Quality features leads to quality models hence elimination of features that have no relationship with the predicted variable is very important. The targeted variable (customer churn) had significant representation of each class as this problem is a binary classification one. This therefore led to quality deep neural networks models with the second model being the ultimate best model. In relation to literature of this study and the results of this study proved well that deep neural networks are very effective on vast amounts of data as in customer churn predictive modelling.

5.3 Recommendations

- Financial institutions willing to begin their journey in customer churn predictive modelling should consider features used in this study as their first step and add other features as per their business set up such as tenure in their modelling.
- The bank should consider retaining the 38.9% customers who have churned (have gone dormant) as the cost of this is considered less than the cost acquiring new customers in order to maintain the same customer base.
- Predictive modelling on vast amounts of data using deep learning neural networks requires intensive computational resources, therefore the bank should consider running the best model on their massive computational capabilities infrastructure since the model have great potential of moving to an accuracy of 100%.

REFERENCES

Ahmad, A. K., Jafar, A., & Aljoumaa, K. (2019). Customer churn prediction in telecom using Machine learning in big data platform. *Journal of Big Data*, *6*(1), 28. doi:10.118640537-019-0191-6

Ahmed, M., Afzal, H., Majeed, A., & Khan, B. (2017). A Survey of Evolution in Predictive Models and Impacting Factors in Customer Churn. *Advances in Data Science and Adaptive Analysis.*, *1750007*(3), 1750007. doi:10.1142/S2424922X17500073

Ajzen, I. (2011). *The theory of planned behaviour: Reactions and reflections.*

Alvi, M. (2016). *A manual for selecting sampling techniques in research.*

Amin, A., Anwar, S., Adnan, A., Nawaz, M., Alawfi, K., Hussain, A., & Huang, K. (2017). Customer churn prediction in the telecommunication sector using a rough set approach. *Neurocomputing*, *237*, 242–254. doi:10.1016/j.neucom.2016.12.009

Amuda, K. A., & Adeyemo, A. B. (2019). Customers Churn Prediction in Financial Institution Using Artificial Neural Network. *arXiv preprint arXiv:1912.11346*.

Bhattacharyya, J., & Dash, M. K. (2020). Investigation of customer churn insights and intelligence from social media: A netnographic research. *Online Information Review*, *45*(1), 174–206. doi:10.1108/OIR-02-2020-0048

Bini, S. A. (2018). Artificial intelligence, machine learning, deep learning, and cognitive computing: What do these terms mean and how will they impact health care? *The Journal of Arthroplasty*, *33*(8), 2358–2361. doi:10.1016/j.arth.2018.02.067 PMID:29656964

Borah, S. B., Prakhya, S., & Sharma, A. (2020). Leveraging service recovery strategies to reduce customer churn in an emerging market. *Journal of the Academy of Marketing Science*, *48*(5), 848–868. doi:10.100711747-019-00634-0

Cai, J., Luo, J., Wang, S., & Yang, S. (2018). Feature selection in machine learning: A new Perspective. *Neurocomputing*, *300*, 70–79. doi:10.1016/j.neucom.2017.11.077

Celik, O., & Osmanoglu, U. O. (2019). Comparing to techniques used in customer churn analysis. *Journal of Multidisciplinary Developments*, *4*(1), 30–38.

Cook, D. (2016). *Practical machine learning with H2O: robust, scalable techniques for deep learning and AI*. O'Reilly Media, Inc.

Coussement, K., Lessmann, S., & Verstraeten, G. (2017). A comparative analysis of data preparation algorithms for customer churn prediction: A case study in the telecommunication industry. *Decision Support Systems*, *95*, 27–36. doi:10.1016/j.dss.2016.11.007

d'Aquin, M., Troullinou, P., O'Connor, N. E., Cullen, A., Faller, G., & Holden, L. (2018, December). Towards an" ethics by design" methodology for AI research projects. In *Proceedings of the 2018 AAAI/ACM Conference on AI, Ethics, and Society* (pp. 54-59). ACM. 10.1145/3278721.3278765

Daniel, J. (2012). *Sampling Essentials: Practical Guidelines for Making Sampling Choices*. Copyright by SAGE Publications, Inc. doi:10.4135/9781452272047

Davis, F. D. (1985). *A technology acceptance model for empirically testing new end-user information systems: Theory and results* [Doctoral dissertation, Massachusetts Institute of Technology].

Dearing, J. W., & Cox, J. G. (2018). Diffusion of innovations theory, principles, and practice. *Health Affairs*, *37*(2), 183–190. doi:10.1377/hlthaff.2017.1104 PMID:29401011

DeLone, W. H., & McLean, E. R. (2002, January). Information systems success revisited. In *Proceedings of the 35th Annual Hawaii International Conference on System Sciences* (pp. 2966-2976). IEEE. 10.1109/HICSS.2002.994345

Etikan, I., & Bala, K. (2017). Sampling and sampling methods. *Biometrics & Biostatistics International Journal*, *5*(6), 00149. doi:10.15406/bbij.2017.05.00149

Farquad, H., Ravi, V., & Raju, S. B. (2014). Churn Prediction using Comprehensible Support Vector Machine: An Analytical CRM Application. *Applied Soft Computing*, *19*, 31–40. Advance online publication. doi:10.1016/j.asoc.2014.01.031

Fishbein, M. (1979). *A theory of reasoned action: some applications and implications.*

Gorny, A., & Napierała, J. (2016). Comparing the effectiveness of respondent-driven sampling and quota sampling in migration research. *International Journal of Social Research Methodology*, *19*(6), 645–661. doi:10.1080/13645579.2015.1077614

Hassouna, M., Tarhini, A., Elyas, T., & AbouTrab, M. S. (2016). Customer churn in mobile markets a comparison of techniques. *arXiv preprint arXiv:1607.07792.*

International Financial Corporation World Bank Group (2018). *Digital Access: The Future of Financial Inclusion in Africa.* World Bank.

Jeong, G. H. (2020). Artificial intelligence, machine learning, and deep learning in women's health nursing. *Korean Journal of Women Health Nursing*, *26*(1), 5–9. doi:10.4069/kjwhn.2020.03.11 PMID:36311852

Jha, N., Parekh, D., Mouhoub, M., & Makkar, V. (2020, May). Customer Segmentation and Churn Prediction in Online Retail. In *Canadian Conference on Artificial Intelligence* (pp. 328-334). Springer, Cham. 10.1007/978-3-030-47358-7_33

Kaya, E., Dong, X., Suhara, Y., Balcisoy, S., Bozkaya, B., & Pentland, A. S. (2018). Behavioral Attributes and Financial churn prediction. *EPJ Data Science*, *7*(1), 41. doi:10.1140/epjds13688-018-0165-5

Khodabandehlou, S., & Rahman, M. Z. (2017). Comparison of supervised machine learning techniques for customer churn prediction based on analysis of customer behavior. *Journal of Systems and Information Technology*, *19*(1/2), 65–93. doi:10.1108/JSIT-10-2016-0061

Korpelainen, E. (2011). Theories of ICT system implementation and adoption. *Critical Review.*

Koufaris, M. (2002). Applying the technology acceptance model and flow theory to online consumer behavior. *Information Systems Research, 13*(2), 205–223. doi:10.1287/isre.13.2.205.83

Kusotera, B., Chimire, F., & Mapuwei, T. W. (2018). *An Analysis Of Customer Churn For Mobile Network Operators In Zimbabwe.*

Mena, C. G., De Caigny, A., Coussement, K., De Bock, K. W., & Lessmann, S. (2019). Churn prediction with sequential data and deep neural networks. A comparative analysis. *arXiv preprint arXiv:1909.11114.*

Sahin, I. (2006). Detailed review of Rogers' diffusion of innovations theory and educational technology-related studies based on Rogers' theory. *Turkish Online Journal of Educational Technology-TOJET, 5*(2), 14–23.

Sarver, V. T. (1983). Ajzen and Fishbein's" theory of reasoned action": A critical assessment.

Schäfer, F., Zeiselmair, C., Becker, J., & Otten, H. (2018, November). Synthesizing CRISP-DM and quality management: A data mining approach for production processes. In *2018 IEEE International Conference on Technology Management, Operations and Decisions (ICTMOD)* (pp. 190-195). IEEE. 10.1109/ITMC.2018.8691266

Shirazi, F., & Mohammadi, M. (2019). A big data analytics model for customer churn prediction in the retiree segment. *International Journal of Information Management, 48*, 238–253. doi:10.1016/j.ijinfomgt.2018.10.005

Sniehotta, F. F., Presseau, J., & Araújo-Soares, V. (2014). Time to retire the theory of planned behaviour. *Health Psychology Review, 8*(1), 1–7. doi:10.1080/1743719 9.2013.869710 PMID:25053004

Stripling, E., vanden Broucke, S., Antonio, K., Baesens, B., & Snoeck, M. (2018). Profit maximising logistic model for customer churn prediction using genetic algorithms. *Swarm and Evolutionary Computation, 40*, 116–130. doi:10.1016/j. swevo.2017.10.010

Subramanya, K. B., & Somani, A. (2017, January). Enhanced feature mining and classifier Models to predict customer churn for an E-retailer. In *2017 7th International Conference on Cloud Computing, Data Science & Engineering-Confluence* (pp. 531-536). IEEE. 10.1109/CONFLUENCE.2017.7943208

Thurber, M. D., & Fahey, J. W. (2009). Adoption of Moringa oleifera to combat under-nutrition viewed through the lens of the "Diffusion of Innovations" theory. *Ecology of Food and Nutrition, 48*(3), 212–225. doi:10.1080/03670240902794598 PMID:20161339

Compilation of References

Abdelwahab, H. T., & Abdel-Aty, M. A. (2001). Development of Artificial Neural Network Models to Predict Driver Injury Severity in Traffic Accidents at Signalized Intersections *Transportation Research Record: Journal of the Transportation Research Board*, *1746*(1), 6–13. doi:10.3141/1746-02

Abdulhafedh, A. (2016). Crash frequency analysis *Journal of Transportation Technologies*, *6*(4), 169–180. doi:10.4236/jtts.2016.64017

Abdulhafedh, A. (2017). Road crash prediction models: Different statistical modeling approaches. *Journal of Transportation Technologies*, *7*(2), 190–205. doi:10.4236/jtts.2017.72014

Aboelmaged, M. G. (2010). Predicting e-procurement adoption in a developing country: An empirical integration of technology acceptance model and theory of planned. *Industrial Management & Data Systems*, *110*(3), 392–41. doi:10.1108/02635571011030042

Ackoff, Finnel, & Gharajedaghi. (1984). A guide to controlling your corporation's future. New York: Wiley.

Ackoff, R. L. (1974). *Redesigning the Future –A Systems Approach to Societal Problems*. Wiley.

Ackoff, R. L. (1981). *Creating the corporate future: Plan or be planned for*. Wiley.

Ackoff, R. L. (1994). *The democratic corporation: A radical prescription for recreating corporate America and rediscovering success*. Oxford University Press. doi:10.1093/oso/9780195087277.001.0001

Ackoff, R. L., & Emery, F. E. (1972). *On purposeful systems*. Aldine-Atherton.

Adetoyi, O. E., & Raji, O. A. (2020). Electronic health record design for inclusion in sub- Saharan Africa medical record informatics. *Scientific African*, *7*, e00304. doi:10.1016/j.sciaf.2020.e00304

Agrawal, T. K., Kumar, V., Pal, R., Wang, L., & Chen, Y. (2021). Blockchain-based framework for supply chain traceability: A case example of textile and clothing industry. *Computers & Industrial Engineering*, *154*, 107130. doi:10.1016/j.cie.2021.107130

Ahmad, A. K., Jafar, A., & Aljoumaa, K. (2019). Customer churn prediction in telecom using Machine learning in big data platform. *Journal of Big Data*, *6*(1), 28. doi:10.118640537-019-0191-6

Compilation of References

Ahmadi, H., Nilashi, M., & Ibrahim, O. (2015). Organizational decision to adopt hospital information system: An empirical investigation in the case of Malaysian public hospitals. *International Journal of Medical Informatics*, *84*(3), 166–188. doi:10.1016/j.ijmedinf.2014.12.004 PMID:25612792

Ahmadi, H., Nilashi, M., Shahmoradi, L., & Ibrahim, O. (2017). Hospital Information System adoption: Expert perspectives on an adoption framework for Malaysian public hospitals. *Computers in Human Behavior*, *67*, 161–189. doi:10.1016/j.chb.2016.10.023

Ahmad, W., Kim, W. G., Choi, H., & Haq, J. U. (2021). Modelling behavioural intention to use travel reservation apps: A cross-cultural examination between US and China. *Journal of Retailing and Consumer Services*, *63*, 102689. doi:10.1016/j.jretconser.2021.102689

Ahmed, M., Afzal, H., Majeed, A., & Khan, B. (2017). A Survey of Evolution in Predictive Models and Impacting Factors in Customer Churn. *Advances in Data Science and Adaptive Analysis.*, *1750007*(3), 1750007. doi:10.1142/S2424922X17500073

Ajzen, I. (2011). *The theory of planned behaviour: Reactions and reflections.*

Ajzen, I. (1991). The theory of planned behavior. *Organizational Behavior and Human Decision Processes*, *50*(2), 179–211. doi:10.1016/0749-5978(91)90020-T

Albalate, D., & Xavier, F. (2021). On the relationship between congestion and road safety in cities. *Transport Policy*, *105*, 145–152. doi:10.1016/j.tranpol.2021.03.011

Albirini, A. (2006). Teachers' attitudes toward information and communication technologies: The case of Syrian EFL teachers. *Computers & Education*, *47*(4), 373–398. doi:10.1016/j.compedu.2004.10.013

Al-Gahtani, S. S., Hubona, G. S., & Wang, J. (2007). Information technology (IT) in Saudi-Arabia: Culture and the acceptance and use of IT. *Information & Management*, *44*(8), 681–691. doi:10.1016/j.im.2007.09.002

Al-Ghamdi, A. (2002). Using Logistic Regression to Estimate the Influence of Accident Factors on Accident Severity. *Accident; Analysis and Prevention*, *34*(6), 729–741. doi:10.1016/S0001-4575(01)00073-2 PMID:12371778

Alharahsheh, H. H., & Pius, A. (2020). A review of key paradigms: Positivism vs Interpretivism. *Global Academic Journal of Humanities and Social Science*, *2*(3), 39–43.

Ali, O., Shrestha, A., Osmanaj, V., & Muhammed, S. (2020). Cloud computing technology adoption: An evaluation of key factors in local governments. *Information Technology & People*, *34*(2), 666–703. doi:10.1108/ITP-03-2019-0119

Almogren, A. S., & Aljammaz, N. A. (2022). The integrated social cognitive theory with the TAM model: The impact of M-learning in King Saud University art education. *Educational Psychology*, *13*, 1050532. doi:10.3389/fpsyg.2022.1050532 PMID:36506961

Alrahbi, D. A., Khan, M., Gupta, S., Modgil, S., & Chiappetta Jabbour, C. J. (2020). Challenges for developing healthcare knowledge in the digital age. *Journal of Knowledge Management.*

Alsaleh, D. A., Elliott, M. T., Fu, F. Q., & Thakur, R. (2019). Cross-cultural differences in the adoption of social media. *Journal of Research in Interactive Marketing*, *13*(1), 119–140. doi:10.1108/JRIM-10-2017-0092

Alsalman, D., Alumran, A., Alrayes, S., Althumairi, A., Almubarak, S., Agrawal, S., & Alanzi, T. (2021). Implementation status of health information systems in hospitals in the eastern province of Saudi Arabia. *Informatics in Medicine Unlocked, 22*, 100499.

Alsudiri, T., Al-Karaghouli, W., & Eldabi, T. (2013). Alignment of large project management process to business strategy: A review and conceptual framework. *Journal of Enterprise Information Management*, *26*(5), 596–615. doi:10.1108/JEIM-07-2013-0050

Altbach, P. A., & Knight, J. (2007). The Internationalisation of Higher Education: Motivations and Realities. *Journal of Studies in International Education*, *11*(3-4), 290–305. doi:10.1177/1028315307303542

Alvarado, G. S. M. (1988). *Organizational pathology. 26th International Conference of the Institute of Management Sciences*, Copenhagen, Denmark.

Alvi, M. (2016). *A manual for selecting sampling techniques in research*.

Ames, G. M., Duke, M. R., Moore, R. S., & Cunradi, C. B. (2009). The impact of occupational culture on the drinking behavior of young adults in the US navy. *Journal of Mixed Methods Research*, *3*(2), 129–150. doi:10.1177/1558689808328534

Amin, A., Anwar, S., Adnan, A., Nawaz, M., Alawfi, K., Hussain, A., & Huang, K. (2017). Customer churn prediction in the telecommunication sector using a rough set approach. *Neurocomputing*, *237*, 242–254. doi:10.1016/j.neucom.2016.12.009

Aminbeidokhti, A. A., Talebi, A., & Nemati, M. A. (2014). Studying the Effect of Cybernetic Pattern on Quality Assurance by Reviewing The Role of Learning Organisation Mediator Variable in General Universities of Tehran. *Kuwait Chapter of Arabian Journal of Business and Management Review*, *3*(10), 12–22. doi:10.12816/0018387

Amuda, K. A., & Adeyemo, A. B. (2019). Customers Churn Prediction in Financial Institution Using Artificial Neural Network. *arXiv preprint arXiv:1912.11346*.

Anand, A., & Fosso Wamba, S. (2013). The business value of RFID-enabled healthcare transformation projects. *Business Process Management Journal*, *19*(1), 111–145. doi:10.1108/14637151311294895

Antwi, K. S., & Hamza, K. (2015). Qualitative and Quantitative Research Paradigms in Business Research: A Philosophical Reflection. *European Journal of Business and Management*, *7*(3), 217–225.

Arpaci, I., & Baloglu, M. (2016). The impact of cultural collectivism on knowledge sharing among information technology majoring undergraduates. *Computers in Human Behavior*, *56*, 65–71. doi:10.1016/j.chb.2015.11.031

Compilation of References

Ashby, W. R. (1956). *An Introduction to Cybernetics*. Chapman & Hall. doi:10.5962/bhl.title.5851

Atasoy, H., Greenwood, B. N., & McCullough, J. S. (2019). The Digitization of Patient Care: A Review of the Effects of Electronic Health Records on Health Care Quality and Utilization. *Annual Review of Public Health, 40*(1), 487–500. doi:10.1146/annurev-publhealth-040218-044206 PMID:30566385

Aurini, D. J., Health, M., & Howells, S. (2016). *The How to of Qualitative Research*. SAGE.

Aversano, L., Grasso, C., & Tortorella, M. (2016). Managing the alignment between business processes and software systems. *Information and Software Technology, 72*, 171–188. doi:10.1016/j.infsof.2015.12.009

Awa, H. O., Ukoha, O., & Igwe, S. R. (2017). Revisiting technology-organization-environment (T-O-E) theory for enriched applicability. *The Bottom Line (New York, N.Y.), 30*(01), 2–22. doi:10.1108/BL-12-2016-0044

Ayaad, O., Alloubani, A., ALhajaa, E. A., Farhan, M., Abuseif, S., Al Hroub, A., & Akhu-Zaheya, L. (2019). The role of electronic medical records in improving the quality of health care services: Comparative study. *International Journal of Medical Informatics, 127*(April), 63–67. doi:10.1016/j.ijmedinf.2019.04.014 PMID:31128833

Babbie, C. (2017). *The basics of Social Research* (7th ed.). Cengage.

Baccarini, D. (1999). The logical framework method for defining project success. *Project Management Journal, 30*(4), 25–32. doi:10.1177/875697289903000405

Badan Pengkajian dan Penerapan Teknologi. (2020). *Strategi Nasional Kecerdasan Artifisial Indonesia*.

Bai, C., Quayson, M., & Sarkis, J. (2022). Analysis of Blockchain's enablers for improving sustainable supply chain transparency in Africa cocoa industry. *Journal of Cleaner Production, 358*, 131896. doi:10.1016/j.jclepro.2022.131896

Bailey, C. A. (2007). *A guide to Qualitative Field Research* (2nd ed.). Pine Forge Press. doi:10.4135/9781412983204

Bain & Company. (2020). *Asia-Pacific Front Line of Healthcare Report 2020*. Bain & Company.

Baloc, R. A., Sha, N., & Panhwar, K. N. (2014). The relationship of slack resources with subjective wellbeing at work: Empirical study of sugar mills from Pakistan. *International Strategic Management Review, 2*(2), 89–97. doi:10.1016/j.ism.2014.10.002

Bandura, A. (1999). Social cognitive theory of personality. Handbook of personality, 2, 154-96.

Bandyopadhyay, K., & Fraccastoro, K. A. (2007). The Effect of Culture on User Acceptance of Information Technology. *Communications of the Association for Information Systems, 19*(23). doi:10.17705/1CAIS.01923

Barney, J., Wright, M., & Ketchen, D. J. Jr. (2001). The resource-based view of the firm: Ten years after 1991. *Journal of Management, 27*(6), 625–641. doi:10.1177/014920630102700601

Barut, M., Faisst, W., & Kanet, J. J. (2002). Measuring supply chain coupling: An information system perspective. *European Journal of Purchasing & Supply Management, 8*(3), 161–171. doi:10.1016/S0969-7012(02)00006-0

Beer, S. (1960). Towards the cybernetic factory. In *Principles of Self Organization. Symposium of 1960*. Pergamon Press.

Beer, S. (1966). Decision and Control. Wiley.

Beer, S. (1979) The Heart of Enterprise. Wiley.

Beer, S. (1981) Brain of the Firm (2nd ed.). Wiley.

Beer, S. (1959). *Cybernetics and Management*. English University Press.

Beer, S. (1965). *The world, the flesh and the metal. Nature, 205(4968), 223-231.*

Beer, S. (1972). *Brain of the Firm*. Penguin.

Beer, S. (1985). *Diagnosing the System for Organisations*. John Wiley & Sons.

Beer, S. (1989). *The Viable System Model: Its Provenance, Development, Methodology and Pathology*. Cwarel Isaf Institute.

Beins, B. C. (2009). *Research Methods. A tool for life* (2nd ed.). Pearson Education.

Belhadi, A., Kamble, S., Fosso Wamba, S., & Queiroz, M. M. (2022). Building supply-chain resilience: An artificial intelligence-based technique and decision-making framework. *International Journal of Production Research, 60*(14), 4487–4507. doi:10.1080/00207543.2021.1950935

Benbasat, I., Goldstein, D. K., & Mead, M. (1987). The case research strategy in studies of information systems. *Management Information Systems Quarterly, 11*(3), 369–386. doi:10.2307/248684

Berg, B. L. (2009). *Qualitative Research Methods for the Social Sciences* (7th ed.). Pearson.

Bernstein, R. (1991). *The New Constellation: the Ethical-Political Horizons of Modernity/Postnmodernity*. The MIT Press.

Besbes, A., Legohérel, P., Kucukusta, D. M., & Law, R. (2016). A Cross-Cultural Validation of the Tourism Web Acceptance Model (T-WAM) in different cultural contexts. *Journal of International Consumer Marketing, 28*(3), 211–226. doi:10.1080/08961530.2016.1152524

Bharadwaj, S., Bharadwaj, A., & Bendoly, E. (2007). The performance effects of complementarities between information systems, marketing, manufacturing, and supply chain processes. *Information Systems Research, 18*(4), 437–453. doi:10.1287/isre.1070.0148

Compilation of References

Bhattacharyya, J., & Dash, M. K. (2020). Investigation of customer churn insights and intelligence from social media: A netnographic research. *Online Information Review*, *45*(1), 174–206. doi:10.1108/OIR-02-2020-0048

Bhuyan, S. S., Zhu, H., Chandak, A., Kim, J., & Stimpson, J. P. (2014). Do service innovations influence the adoption of electronic health records in long-term care organizations? Results from the US National Survey of residential care facilities. *International Journal of Medical Informatics*, *83*(12), 975–982. doi:10.1016/j.ijmedinf.2014.09.007 PMID:25453201

Bini, S. A. (2018). Artificial intelligence, machine learning, deep learning, and cognitive computing: What do these terms mean and how will they impact health care? *The Journal of Arthroplasty*, *33*(8), 2358–2361. doi:10.1016/j.arth.2018.02.067 PMID:29656964

Binkmann, S. C., & Kvle, S. (2005). Interviews learning the Craft of Qualitative Research Interviewing, 3rd edition. London. Thousand Oaks. CA.

Blagoeva, K. T., & Mijoska, M. (2017). Applying TAM to study online shopping adoption among youth in the Republic of Macedonia. *Management International Conference*, Venice, Italy.

Blomquist, T., & Packendorff, J. (1998). Learning from renewal projects: Content, context and embeddedness. In R. A. Lundin & C. Midler (Eds.), *Projects as arenas for renewal and learning processes* (pp. 37–46). Springer. doi:10.1007/978-1-4615-5691-6_4

Blumberg, F. Boris, Cooper, R.D & Schindler, P.S (2011). Business Research Methods (4th Edition). London: McGraw-Hill Higher Education.

Boneva, B., Kraut, R., & Frohlich, D. (2001). Using e-mail for personal relationships: The difference gender makes. *The American Behavioral Scientist*, *45*(3), 530–549. doi:10.1177/00027640121957204

Borah, S. B., Prakhya, S., & Sharma, A. (2020). Leveraging service recovery strategies to reduce customer churn in an emerging market. *Journal of the Academy of Marketing Science*, *48*(5), 848–868. doi:10.100711747-019-00634-0

Botha, N., & Atkins, K. (2005). *An assessment of five different theoretical frameworks to study the uptake of innovations.* Paper presented at the 2005 NZARES Conference, Tahuma Conference Centre, New Zealand.

Bower, J. L., Bartlett, C. A., Uyterhoeven, H. E., & Walton, R. E. (1995). *Business Policy: managing strategic processes*. No Title.

Bower, J. L., & Christensen, C. M. (1995, January–February). Disruptive Technologies: Catching the Wave. *Harvard Business Review*, 43–54.

Box, S., & Platts, K. (2005). Business process management: Establishing and maintaining project alignment. *Business Process Management Journal*, *11*(4), 370–387. doi:10.1108/14637150510609408

Bozeman, D. P., Kacmar, K. M. (1997) A Cybernetic Model of Impression Management Processes in Organizations, *Organisational Behaviour and Human Decision-Processes, 69*(1), 9-30.

Braun, V., Clarke, V., & Gray, D. (2017). *Collecting Qualitative Data. A practical Guide to Textual, Media and Virtual Techniques.* Cambridge University Press. doi:10.1017/9781107295094

Broadbent, J., & Unerman, J. (2011). Developing the relevance of the accounting academy. *Meditari Accountancy Research, 19*(1/2), 7–21. doi:10.1108/10222521111178600

Bryman, A. (2004). *Social Research Methods* (3rd ed.). Oxford University Press.

Bryman, A., & Bell, E. (2014). *Research methodology, Business and Management Context.* Oxford University Press.

Bunge, M. (1977). Treatise on basic philosophy: Vol. 3. *Ontology I: The furniture of the world.* D. Reidel Publishing Company.

Bunge, M. (1979). Treatise on basic philosophy: Vol. 4. *Ontology II: A world of systems.* D. Reidel Publishing Company.

Burgess, N., & Wake, N. (2012). The applicability of the Viable Systems Model as a diagnostic for small to medium sized enterprises. *International Journal of Productivity and Performance Management, 62*(1), 29–46. doi:10.1108/17410401311285282

Burn, J., Marshall, P., & Barnett, M. (2007). *E-business strategies for virtual organizations.* Routledge. doi:10.4324/9780080504889

Burn, J., & Robins, G. (2002). A Virtual Organisation Model for E-Government. *AJIS. Australian Journal of Information Systems, 9*(2), 104–112.

Burton-Jones, A., McLean, E. R., & Monod, E. (2015). Theoretical perspectives in IS research: From variance and process to conceptual latitude and conceptual fit. *European Journal of Information Systems, 24*(6), 664–679. doi:10.1057/ejis.2014.31

Cabrera, D. (2008). Distinctions, systems, relationships, perspectives: the simple rules of complex conceptual systems: A universal descriptive grammar of cognition. *Proceedings of the 52nd Annual Meeting of the ISSS, 3*(1).

Cai, J., Luo, J., Wang, S., & Yang, S. (2018). Feature selection in machine learning: A new Perspective. *Neurocomputing, 300*, 70–79. doi:10.1016/j.neucom.2017.11.077

Case, O. D. (2012). Looking for information: A survey of Research on Information Seeking, Needs, and Behaviour. Third Edition. Library and Information Science. Emerald.

Caves, R. E. (1980). Industrial organization, corporate strategy, and structure. *Journal of Economic Literature, 18*, 64–92.

Celik, O., & Osmanoglu, U. O. (2019). Comparing to techniques used in customer churn analysis. *Journal of Multidisciplinary Developments, 4*(1), 30–38.

Compilation of References

Céspedes, F. V. (1991). *Organizing and Implementing the Marketing Effort*. Addison- Wesley.

Chang, L. (2005). Analysis of Freeway Accident Frequencies: Negative Binomial Regression Versus Artificial Neural Network. *Safety Science, 43*(8), 541–557. doi:10.1016/j.ssci.2005.04.004

Chen, W. H., & Jovanis, P. P. (2000). Method for Identifying Factors Contributing to Driver-Injury Severity in Traffic Crashes. *Transportation Research Record: Journal of the Transportation Research Board, 1717*(1), 1–9. doi:10.3141/1717-01

Chikaraishi, M., Garg, P., Varghese, V., Yoshizoe, K., Urata, J., Shiomi, Y., & Watanabe, R. (2022). On the possibility of short-term traffic prediction during disaster with machine learning approaches: An exploratory analysis. *Transport Policy, 98*, 91–104. doi:10.1016/j.tranpol.2020.05.023

Choo, C. W. (1995). *Information Management for the Intelligent Organization*. Information Today/Learned InformatioN.

Chopdar, P. K., Korfiatis, N., Sivakumar, V.J. & Lytras, M. D. (2018). Mobile shopping app adoption and perceived risks: A cross-country perspective utilizing the Unified Theory of Acceptance and Use of Technology. *Computers in Human Behavior, 86(2018), 109e128.*

Chou, C. C., Hwang, N. C. R., Li, C. W., Wang, T., & Wang, Y. Y. (2023). Implementing a multichain framework using hyperledger for supply chain transparency in a dynamic partnership: A feasibility study. *Computers & Industrial Engineering, 175*, 108906. doi:10.1016/j.cie.2022.108906

Chouinard, M., D'Amours, S., & Ait-Kadi, D. (2005). Integration of reverse logistics activities within a supply chain information system. *Computers in Industry, 56*(1), 105–124. doi:10.1016/j.compind.2004.07.005

Chris, W. J., Conant, J. S., & Echambadi, R. (2003). Marketing Strategy Development Styles, Implementation Capability, and Firm Performance: Investigating the Curvilinear Impact of Multiple Strategy-Making Styles. *Marketing Letters, 14*(2), 111–124. doi:10.1023/A:1025415018239

Clarke, F., Dean, G., & Edwards, J. R. (2013) *An historical perspective from the work of Chambers from: The Routledge Companion to Accounting Communication*. Routledge. https://www.routledgehandbooks.com/doi/10.4324/9780203593493.ch3

Clarke, R., Davison, M. R., & Jia, W. (2020). Researcher perspective in the IS discipline: An empirical study of articles in the basket of 8 journals. Researcher perspective in the IS discipline. *Information Technology & People, 33*(6), 1515–1541. doi:10.1108/ITP-04-2019-0189

Clemson, B. (1991). *Cybernetics: A new management tool* (Vol. 4). CRC Press.

Clipper, B. (2020). The Influence of the COVID-19 Pandemic on Technology: Adoption in Health Care. *Nurse Leader, 18*(5), 500–503. doi:10.1016/j.mnl.2020.06.008 PMID:32837346

Closs, D. J., Goldsby, T. J., & Clinton, S. R. (1997). Information technology influences on world class logistics capability. *International Journal of Physical Distribution & Logistics Management, 27*(1), 4–17. doi:10.1108/09600039710162259

Coffey, R. M., Buck, J. A., Kassed, C. A., Dilonardo, J., Forhan, C., Marder, W. D., & Vandivort-Warren, R. (2008). Transforming mental health and substance abuse data systems in the United States. *Psychiatric Services (Washington, D.C.)*, *59*(11), 1257–1263. doi:10.1176/ps.2008.59.11.1257 PMID:18971401

Cohen, W. M., & Levinthal, D. A. (1990). Absorptive capacity: A new perspective on learning and innovation. *Administrative Science Quarterly*, *35*(1), 128–152. doi:10.2307/2393553

Cook, D. (2016). *Practical machine learning with H2O: robust, scalable techniques for deep learning and AI*. O'Reilly Media, Inc.

Cooke-Davies, T. (2002). The "real" success factors on projects. *International Journal of Project Management*, *20*(3), 185–190. doi:10.1016/S0263-7863(01)00067-9

Cook, K., Cochran, G., Gali, H., Hatch, T., Awdishu, L., & Lander, L. (2021). Pharmacy students' readiness to use the electronic health record: A tale of two institutions. *Currents in Pharmacy Teaching & Learning*, *13*(4), 327–332. doi:10.1016/j.cptl.2020.11.005 PMID:33715792

Corley, K. G., & Gioia, D. A. (2011). Building theory about theory building: What constitutes a theoretical contribution? *Academy of Management Review*, *36*(1), 12–32. doi:10.5465/amr.2009.0486

Coussement, K., Lessmann, S., & Verstraeten, G. (2017). A comparative analysis of data preparation algorithms for customer churn prediction: A case study in the telecommunication industry. *Decision Support Systems*, *95*, 27–36. doi:10.1016/j.dss.2016.11.007

Creswell, J. W. (2014). Research Design: Qualitative, Quantitative, Mixed Methods approaches. International Students Edition 4th Edition. New Jersey: Pearson.

Creswell, J. W., & Creswell, J. D. (2018). Research Design: Qualitative, Quantitative, and Mixed Methods Approaches. SAGE Publishing (Five Edit). California: SAGE Publisher.

Creswell, J. W. (2005). *Educational Research. Planning, Conducting and Evaluating Quantitative and Qualitative Research* (2nd ed.). Pearson.

Cruz-Jesus, F., Pinheiro, A., & Oliveira, T. (2019). Understanding CRM adoption stages: Empirical analysis building on the TOE framework. *Computers in Industry*, *109*, 1–13. doi:10.1016/j.compind.2019.03.007

Curtis, B., & Curtis, C. (2011). Social Research: A practical introduction. London: SAGE: London. doi:10.4135/9781526435415

d'Aquin, M., Troullinou, P., O'Connor, N. E., Cullen, A., Faller, G., & Holden, L. (2018, December). Towards an" ethics by design" methodology for AI research projects. In *Proceedings of the 2018 AAAI/ACM Conference on AI, Ethics, and Society* (pp. 54-59). ACM. 10.1145/3278721.3278765

Dai, H., & Palvia, P. C. (2009). Mobile commerce adoption in China and the United States: A cross-cultural study. *The Data Base for Advances in Information Systems*, *40*(4), 43–61. doi:10.1145/1644953.1644958

Compilation of References

Dana, R., & Shaun, P. (2005). Some of the philosophical Issues underpinning research in information systems – from Positivism to Critical Realism. *SACTJT, 35*, 50–79.

Daniel, J. (2012). *Sampling Essentials: Practical Guidelines for Making Sampling Choices.* Copyright by SAGE Publications, Inc. doi:10.4135/9781452272047

Davis, F. D. (1985). *A technology acceptance model for empirically testing new end-user information systems: Theory and results* [Doctoral dissertation, Massachusetts Institute of Technology].

Davis, F. D. (1987). *User acceptance of information systems: the technology acceptance model.* TAM.

Davis, F. D. (1989). Perceived usefulness, perceived ease of use, and user acceptance of information technology. *Management Information Systems Quarterly, 13*(3), 319–340. doi:10.2307/249008

Day, G. S., & Wensley, R. (1983). Marketing Theory with a Strategic Orientation. *Journal of Marketing, 47*(4), 79–89. doi:10.1177/002224298304700409

De Vos, A. S., Strydom, H., Fouche, C. B., & Delport, C. S. L. (2017). *Research at Grassroots. For the Social Sciences and Huan service professions eth edition.* Van Schaik.

De Wit, A. (1988). Measurement of project success. *International Journal of Project Management, 6*(3), 164–170. doi:10.1016/0263-7863(88)90043-9

Dearing, J. W., & Cox, J. G. (2018). Diffusion of innovations theory, principles, and practice. *Health Affairs, 37*(2), 183–190. doi:10.1377/hlthaff.2017.1104 PMID:29401011

Deci, E. L., & Ryan, R. M. (2012). Self-determination theory. Handbook of theories of social psychology, 1(20), 416-436.

Defour- Howard. S (2015). Research Methods. A handbook for Beginners. Denver: Outskirts Press.

deGuinea, A. O., & Webster, J. (2015). The missing links: Cultural, software, task and personal influences on computer self-efficacy. *International Journal of Human Resource Management, 26*(7), 905–931. doi:10.1080/09585192.2012.655758

Delen, D. R., Sharda, R., & Bessonov, M. (2006). Sharda., Bessonov, M.: Identifying significant predictors of injury severity in traffic accidents using a series of artificial neural networks. *Accident; Analysis and Prevention, 38*(3), 434–444. doi:10.1016/j.aap.2005.06.024 PMID:16337137

DeLone, W. H., & McLean, E. R. (2002, January). Information systems success revisited. In *Proceedings of the 35th Annual Hawaii International Conference on System Sciences* (pp. 2966-2976). IEEE. 10.1109/HICSS.2002.994345

DeLone, W. H., & McLean, E. R. (2003). The DeLone and McLean model of information systems success: A ten-year update. *Journal of Management Information Systems, 19*(4), 9–30. doi:10.1080/07421222.2003.11045748

Denzin, K. N., & Linoln, Y. S. (2013). *Collecting and Interpreting Qualitative Materials.* SAGE.

Dhagarra, D., Goswami, M., & Kumar, G. (2020). Impact of Trust and Privacy Concerns on Technology Acceptance in Healthcare: An Indian Perspective. *International Journal of Medical Informatics*, *141*, 141. doi:10.1016/j.ijmedinf.2020.104164 PMID:32593847

DiMaggio, P. J. (1995). Comments on" What theory is not. *Administrative Science Quarterly*, *40*(3), 391–397. doi:10.2307/2393790

Dinev, T., Goo, J., Hu, Q. & Nam, K. (2009). User behaviour towards protective information technologies: the role of national cultural differences. *Info Systems J, 19*(2009), 391-412. . doi:. doi:10.1111/j.1365-2575.2007.00289.x

Dolgui, A., & Ivanov, D. (2022). 5G in digital supply chain and operations management: Fostering flexibility, end-to-end connectivity and real-time visibility through internet-of-everything. *International Journal of Production Research*, *60*(2), 442–451. doi:10.1080/00207543.2021.2002969

Dougherty, M. (1995). A review of Neural Network applied to Transport. *Transportation Research Part C, Emerging Technologies*, *3*(4), 247–260. doi:10.1016/0968-090X(95)00009-8

Drucker, P. (1989). *The New Realities In Government and Politics, in Economics and Business, in Society and World View*. Harper & Row.

Ebrahim, S., & Hossain, Q. S. (2018). An Artificial Neural Network Model for Road Accident Prediction: A Case Study of Khulna Metropolitan City. *Proceedings of the 4th International Conference on Civil Engineering for Sustainable Development (ICCESD 2018)*.

Eisenhardt, K. M. (1989). Building theories from case study research. *Academy of Management Review*, *14*(4), 532–550. doi:10.2307/258557

Eisenhardt, K. M., & Martin, J. A. (2000). Dynamic capabilities: What are they? *Strategic Management Journal*, *21*(10-11), 1105–1121. doi:10.1002/1097-0266(200010/11)21:10/11<1105::AID-SMJ133>3.0.CO;2-E

Elliott, T. E., Holmes, J. H., Davidson, A. J., La Chance, P.-A., Nelson, A. F., & Steiner, J. F. (2013). Data Warehouse Governance Programs in Healthcare Settings: A Literature Review and a Call to Action. *EGMs (Generating Evidence & Methods to Improve Patient Outcomes)*, *1*(1), 15.

El-Telbany, O., & Elragal, A. (2014). Business-information systems strategies: A focus on misalignment. *Procedia Technology*, *16*, 250–262. doi:10.1016/j.protcy.2014.10.090

Engwall, M. (2003). No project is an island: Linking projects to history and context. *Research Policy*, *32*(5), 789–808. doi:10.1016/S0048-7333(02)00088-4

Espejo, R. (1993) Giving Requisite Variety to Strategy and Information Systems in Stowell et al. (1993). Systems Science, New York, Plenum Press.

Espejo, R. (2006). What is systemic thinking? *System Dynamics Review*, *10*(2-3), 199–212. doi:10.1002dr.4260100208

276

Compilation of References

EspejoR. (2013). Organisational Cybernetics as a Systemic Paradigm: Lessons from the Past - Progress for the Future. https://ssrn.com/abstract=2242459

Etikan, I., & Bala, K. (2017). Sampling and sampling methods. *Biometrics & Biostatistics International Journal, 5*(6), 00149. doi:10.15406/bbij.2017.05.00149

Falsafinejad, M., & Hashembeik, N. (2013, September). A Cybernetic Modelling Framework in Higher Education Administration (Case study: Isfahan Medical Sciences UniversityIsfahan Medical Sciences University). *International Journal of Scientific and Research Publications, 3*(9), 1–4.

Faqih, K. M. S., & Jarada, M. R. M. (2015). Assessing the moderating effect of gender differences and individualism-collectivism at individual-level on the adoption of mobile commerce technology: TAM3 perspective. *Journal of Retailing and Consumer Services, 22*, 37–52. doi:10.1016/j.jretconser.2014.09.006

Farquad, H., Ravi, V., & Raju, S. B. (2014). Churn Prediction using Comprehensible Support Vector Machine: An Analytical CRM Application. *Applied Soft Computing, 19*, 31–40. Advance online publication. doi:10.1016/j.asoc.2014.01.031

Fishbein, M. (1979). *A theory of reasoned action: some applications and implications.*

Flick, U. (2015). *Designing Qualitative Research.* SAGE.

Fox, W., & Bayat, M. S. (2012). *A guide to Managing Research.* Juta.

Freeman, E. (1984). *Strategic Management: A Stakeholder Approach.* Pitman.

Freeman, R. E. (2001). A stakeholder theory of the modern corporation. *Perspectives in Business Ethics Sie, 3*(144), 38–48.

Freese, L. (1984). Cumulative problem solving in family sociology. *Journal of Family Issues, 5*(4), 447–469. doi:10.1177/019251384005004002

Frisina, P. G., Munene, E. N., Finnie, J., Oakley, J. E., & Ganesan, G. (2020). Analysis of end- user satisfaction with electronic health records in college/university healthcare. *Journal of American College Health, 0*(0), 1–7. PMID:32529959

Fusilier, M., & Durlabhji, S. (2005). An exploration of student internet use in India the technology acceptance model and the theory of planned behaviour. *Campus-Wide Information Systems, 22*(4), 233–246. doi:10.1108/10650740510617539

Gammack, J., & Poon, S. (2013). Knowledge and teamwork in the virtual organization. In *E-Commerce and V-Business* (pp. 231–249). Routledge.

Gangwar, H., Date, H., & Ramaswamy, R. (2015). Understanding determinants of cloud computing adoption using an integrated TAM-TOE model. *Journal of Enterprise Information Management, 28*(1), 107–130. doi:10.1108/JEIM-08-2013-0065

Gartner. (2021). *Gartner forecasts worldwide IT spending to exceed $4 trillion in 2022*. Gartner Consulting. https://www.gartner.com/en/newsroom/press-releases/2021-10-20-gartner-forecasts-worldwide-it-spending-to-exceed-4-trillion-in-2022

Gatignon, H., & Xuereb, J. (1997). Strategic Orientation of the Firm and New Product Performance. *JMR, Journal of Marketing Research*, *34*(February), 77–90. doi:10.1177/002224379703400107

Gault, R. H. (1907). A history of the questionnaire method of research in psychology. *Research in Psychology.*, *14*(3), 366–383. doi:10.1080/08919402.1907.10532551

Gebauer, M. M., McElvany, N., Köller, O., & Schöber, C. (2021). · Köller, O. & Schöber, C. (2021). Cross-cultural differences in academic self-efficacy and its sources across socialization contexts. *Social Psychology of Education*, *24*(6), 1407–1432. doi:10.100711218-021-09658-3

Gilchrist, A., Burton-Jones, A., & Green, P. (2018). The process of social alignment and misalignment within a complex IT project. *International Journal of Project Management*, *36*(6), 845–860. doi:10.1016/j.ijproman.2018.04.004

Gillani, F., Chatha, K. A., Sadiq Jajja, M. S., & Farooq, S. (2020). Implementation of digital manufacturing technologies: Antecedents and consequences. *International Journal of Production Economics*, *229*, 107748. doi:10.1016/j.ijpe.2020.107748

Göğüş, A., Nistor, N., & Lerche, T. (2012). Educational technology acceptance across cultures: A validation of the Unified Theory of Acceptance And Use of Technology in the context of Turkish national culture. *The Turkish Online Journal of Educational Technology*, *11*(4).

Goldman, G. A. (2016). Multiparadigmatic, Cooperative Opportunities for the Study of Business Management. *Management Dynamics*, *25*(3), 2–15.

Goldman, S. L., Nagel, R. N., & Preiss, K. (1995). Agile competitors and virtual organizations. *Manufacturing Review*, *8*(1), 59–67.

Goodhue, D. L., & Thompson, R. L. (1995). Task-technology fit and individual performance. *Management Information Systems Quarterly*, *19*(2), 213–236. doi:10.2307/249689

Gorman, G. E., & Clayton, P. (2005). *Qualitative Research for the Information Professional: A Practical Handbook* (2nd ed.). Facet.

Gorny, A., & Napierała, J. (2016). Comparing the effectiveness of respondent-driven sampling and quota sampling in migration research. *International Journal of Social Research Methodology*, *19*(6), 645–661. doi:10.1080/13645579.2015.1077614

Grabher, G. (2002). Cool projects, boring institutions: Temporary collaboration in social context. *Regional Studies*, *36*(3), 205–214. doi:10.1080/00343400220122025

Grbich, C. (2013). *Qualitative Data Analysis: An introduction*. Sage. doi:10.4135/9781529799606

Gregor, S. (2006). The nature of theory in information systems. *Management Information Systems Quarterly*, *30*(3), 611. doi:10.2307/25148742

278

Compilation of References

Griffith, A. F., & Gibson, G. E. Jr. (2001). Alignment during preproject planning. *Journal of Management Engineering, 17*(2), 69–76. doi:10.1061/(ASCE)0742-597X(2001)17:2(69)

Griffith, T. L., Sawyer, J. E., & Neale, M. A. (2003). Virtualness and knowledge in teams: Managing the love triangle of organizations, individuals, and information technology. *Management Information Systems Quarterly, 27*(2), 265–287. doi:10.2307/30036531

Grover, P., Kar, A. K., & Dwivedi, Y. K. (2022). Understanding artificial intelligence adoption in operations management: Insights from the review of academic literature and social media discussions. *Annals of Operations Research, 308*(1-2), 177–213. doi:10.100710479-020-03683-9

Grover, V., & Lyytinen, K. (2023). The pursuit of innovative theory in the digital age. *Journal of Information Technology, 38*(1), 45–59. doi:10.1177/02683962221077112

Grover, V., Lyytinen, K., Srinivasan, A., & Tan, B. C. (2008). Contributing to rigorous and forward-thinking explanatory theory. *Journal of the Association for Information Systems, 9*(2), 40–47. doi:10.17705/1jais.00151

Guillemette, M. G., & Paré, G. (2012). Toward a new theory of the contribution of the IT function in organizations. *Management Information Systems Quarterly, 36*(2), 529–551. doi:10.2307/41703466

Gunasekaran, A., & Ngai, E. W. (2004). Information systems in supply chain integration and management. *European Journal of Operational Research, 159*(2), 269–295. doi:10.1016/j.ejor.2003.08.016

Gupta, J. N. D., & Sharma, S. K. (2004). *Intelligent Enterprises of the 21st Century*. Idea Group Publishing. doi:10.4018/978-1-59140-160-5

Gupta, M., & Galloway, K. (2003). Activity-based costing/management and its implications for operations management. *Technovation, 23*(2), 131–138. doi:10.1016/S0166-4972(01)00093-1

Hader, M., Tchoffa, D., El Mhamedi, A., Ghodous, P., Dolgui, A., & Abouabdellah, A. (2022). Applying integrated Blockchain and Big Data technologies to improve supply chain traceability and information sharing in the textile sector. *Journal of Industrial Information Integration, 28*, 100345. doi:10.1016/j.jii.2022.100345

Haeckel, S. H., & Nolan, R. A. (1993). Managing by wire. *Harvard Business Review, 71*(5), 122–132.

Hancock, D. R., & Algozzine, B. (2011). *Doing Case Study Research: A practical guide for beginning researchers* (2nd ed.). Teachers College Press.

Handy, C. B. (2020). *Gods of management: The four cultures of leadership*. Profile Books.

Haneem, F., Kama, N., Taskin, N., Pauleen, D., & Abu Bakar, N. A. (2019). Determinants of master data management adoption by local government organizations: An empirical study. *International Journal of Information Management, 45*(October 2018), 25–43.

Hartzel, K. S., Marley, K. A., & Spangler, W. E. (2016). Online Social Network Adoption: A Cross-Cultural Study. *Journal of Computer Information Systems*, *56*(2), 87–96. doi:10.1080/0 8874417.2016.1117367

Hartz-Karp, J., & Marinova, D. (2017). *Methods for Sustainability Research*. Edward Elgar. doi:10.4337/9781786432735

Hassan, L. M., Shiu, E., & Parry, S. (2016). Addressing the cross-country applicability of the theory of planned behaviour (TPB): A structured review of multi-country TPB studies. *Journal of Consumer Behaviour*, *15*(1), 72–86. doi:10.1002/cb.1536

Hassan, N. R., & Lowry, P. B. (2015, December). Seeking middle-range theories in information systems research. In *International Conference on Information Systems (ICIS 2015), Fort Worth, TX, December*.

Hassan, N. R., Lowry, P. B., & Mathiassen, L. (2022). Useful products in information systems theorizing: A discursive formation perspective. [JAIS]. *Journal of the Association for Information Systems*, *23*(2), 418–446. doi:10.17705/1jais.00730

Hassan, N. R., Mathiassen, L., & Lowry, P. B. (2019). The process of information systems theorizing as a discursive practice. *Journal of Information Technology*, *34*(3), 198–220. doi:10.1177/0268396219832004

Hassouna, M., Tarhini, A., Elyas, T., & AbouTrab, M. S. (2016). Customer churn in mobile markets a comparison of techniques. *arXiv preprint arXiv:1607.07792*.

Hatch, M. J., & Cunliffe, A. L. (2006). *Organisation Theory*. Oxford University Press.

Hawash, B., Mokhtar, U. A., Yusof, Z. M., & Mukred, M. (2020). The adoption of electronic records management system (ERMS) in the Yemeni oil and gas sector: Influencing factors. *Records Management Journal*, *30*(1), 1–22. doi:10.1108/RMJ-03-2019-0010

Helo, P., & Szekely, B. (2005). Logistics information systems: An analysis of software solutions for supply chain coordination. *Industrial Management & Data Systems*, *105*(1), 5–18. doi:10.1108/02635570510575153

Henderson, C., & Venkatraman, N. (1993). Strategic alignment: Leveraging information technology for transforming organizations. *IBM Systems Journal*, *32*(1), 4–16. doi:10.1147j.382.0472

Herath, T. C., Herath, H. S. B., & D'Arcy, J. (2020). Organizational Adoption of Information Security Solutions. *The Data Base for Advances in Information Systems*, *51*(2), 12–35. doi:10.1145/3400043.3400046

Heylighen, F. (1992). Principles of Systems and Cybernetics: an evolutionary perspective. In Trappl, R. (1992) (ed.) Cybernetics and Systems. Singapore: World Science.

Heylighen, F., Bollen, J., & Riegler, A. (1999). *The Evolution of Complexity: The Violet Book of "Einstein Meets Magritte*. Kluwer Academic Publishers.

Compilation of References

Hilder, T. (1995). *The Viable System Model Cavendish Software Ltd.*

Hirschheim, R. (2019). Against theory: With apologies to Feyerabend. *Journal of the Association for Information Systems*, *20*(9), 8.

Hofstede, G. (2001). *Culture's Consequences: Comparing values, behaviors, institutions, and organizations across nations.* Sage.

Hofstede, G. (2011). Dimensionalizing cultures: The Hofstede model in context. *Online Readings in Psychology and Culture*, *2*(1), 8. doi:10.9707/2307-0919.1014

Holland, C. P. (1995). Cooperative supply chain management: The impact of interorganizational information systems. *The Journal of Strategic Information Systems*, *4*(2), 117–133. doi:10.1016/0963-8687(95)80020-Q

Holland, C. R., & Light, B. (1999). A critical success factors model for ERP implementation. *IEEE Software*, *16*(3), 30–36. doi:10.1109/52.765784

Hong, K.-K., & Kim, Y.-G. (2002). The critical success factors for ERP implementation: An organizational fit perspective. *Information & Management*, *40*(1), 25–40. doi:10.1016/S0378-7206(01)00134-3

Hospital Insights Asia. (2019). *How this hospital is overcoming the IT skills shortage.*

Hossain, A., Quaresma, R., & Rahman, H. (2019). Investigating factors influencing the physicians' adoption of electronic health record (EHR) in healthcare system of Bangladesh: An empirical study. *International Journal of Information Management, 44*(September 2018), 76–87.

Huang, W., D'Ambra, J., & Bhalla, V. (2002). An empirical investigation of the adoption of eGovernment in Australian citizens: Some unexpected research findings. *Journal of Computer Information Systems*, *43*(1), 15–22.

Hue, T. T. (2019). The determinants of innovation in Vietnamese manufacturing firms: An empirical analysis using a technology–organization–environment framework. *Eurasian Business Review*, *9*(3), 247–267. doi:10.100740821-019-00125-w

Hughes, L., Dwivedi, Y. K., Misra, S. K., Rana, N. P., Raghavan, V., & Akella, V. (2019). Blockchain research, practice and policy: Applications, benefits, limitations, emerging research themes and research agenda. *International Journal of Information Management*, *49*(February), 114–129. doi:10.1016/j.ijinfomgt.2019.02.005

Humphreys, P. K., Lai, M. K., & Sculli, D. (2001). An inter-organisational information system for supply chain management. *International Journal of Production Economics*, *70*(3), 245–255. doi:10.1016/S0925-5273(00)00070-0

Hussain, S. & Bashir-Dar, I. (2020). Comments on "The nature of theory in information systems". *Future Business Journal. 6*(1).

Hustad, E., Haddara, M., & Kalvenes, B. (2016). ERP and organizational misfits: An ERP customization journey. *Procedia Computer Science*, *100*, 429–439. doi:10.1016/j.procs.2016.09.179

International Financial Corporation World Bank Group (2018). *Digital Access*: *The Future of Financial Inclusion in Africa.* World Bank.

Iqbal, U., Ho, C.-H., Li, Y.-C., Nguyen, P.-A., Jian, W.-S., & Wen, H.-C. (2013). The relationship between usage intention and adoption of electronic health records at primary care clinics. *Computer Methods and Programs in Biomedicine*, *112*(3), 731–737. doi:10.1016/j.cmpb.2013.09.001 PMID:24091088

Iriarte, C., & Bayona, S. (2020). IT projects success factors: A literature review. *International Journal of Information Systems and Project Management*, *8*(2), 49–78. doi:10.12821/ijispm080203

Isaac, O., Abdullah, Z., Aldholay, A. H. & Ameen, A. A. (2019). Antecedents and outcomes of Internet usage within organisations in Yemen: An extension of the Unified Theory of Acceptance and Use of Technology (UTAUT) model. *Asia Pacific Management Review, 24.*

Iyamu, T. (2021). *Applying theories for information systems research.* Routledge. doi:10.4324/9781003184119

Jackson, M. C. (1986). The Cybernetic Model of the Organisation: An Assessment. In *Cybernetics and Systems'86: Proceedings of the Eighth European Meeting on Cybernetics and Systems Research, organized by the Austrian Society for Cybernetic Studies.* University of Vienna.

Jackson, M. C. (1991). *Systems Methodology for The Management Sciences.* Springer. doi:10.1007/978-1-4899-2632-6

Jackson, M. C. (2000). *Systems Approaches to Management.* BostonL Kluwer Academic Publihsers.

Jadil, Y., Rana, N. P. & Dwivedi, Y. K. (2023). A meta-analysis of the UTAUT model in the mobile banking literature: The moderating role of sample size and culture. *Journal of Business Research, 132*, 354–372.

Jan, J., Alshare, K. A., & Lane, P. L. (2022). Hofstede's cultural dimensions in technology acceptance models: A meta-analysis. *Universal Access in the Information Society.* doi:10.100710209-022-00930-7

Janssen, M., Brous, P., Estevez, E., Barbosa, L. S., & Janowski, T. (2020). Data governance: Organizing data for trustworthy Artificial Intelligence. *Government Information Quarterly*, *37*(3), 101493. doi:10.1016/j.giq.2020.101493

Janz, N. K., Zimmerman, M. A., Wren, P. A., Israel, B. A., Freudenberg, N., & Carter, R. J. (1996). Evaluation of 37 AIDS prevention projects: Successful approaches and barriers to program effectiveness. *Health Education & Behavior*, *23*(1), 80–97. PMID:8822403

Jayaram, J., Vickery, S. K., & Droge, C. (2000). The effects of information system infrastructure and process improvements on supply-chain time performance. *International Journal of Physical Distribution & Logistics Management*, *30*(3/4), 314–330. doi:10.1108/09600030010326082

Compilation of References

Jenkin, T. A., & Chan, Y. E. (2010). IS project alignment – A process perspective. *Journal of Information Technology*, *25*(1), 35–55. doi:10.1057/jit.2009.10

Jeong, G. H. (2020). Artificial intelligence, machine learning, and deep learning in women's health nursing. *Korean Journal of Women Health Nursing*, *26*(1), 5–9. doi:10.4069/kjwhn.2020.03.11 PMID:36311852

Jha, N., Parekh, D., Mouhoub, M., & Makkar, V. (2020, May). Customer Segmentation and Churn Prediction in Online Retail. In *Canadian Conference on Artificial Intelligence* (pp. 328-334). Springer, Cham. 10.1007/978-3-030-47358-7_33

Jianxun, C., Arkorful, V. E., & Shuliang, Z. (2021). Electronic health records adoption: Do institutional pressures and organizational culture matter? *Technology in Society*, *65*(96), 101531. doi:10.1016/j.techsoc.2021.101531

Johnson, J. (2020). *CHAOS 2020: Beyond infinity*. The Standish Group. https://www.standishgroup.com/news/49

Johnson, R. D., & Diman, K. (2017). An Investigation of the Factors Driving the Adoption of Cloud-Based Human Resource Information Systems by Small- and Medium-Sized Businesses. In *Electronic HRM in the Smart Era* (pp. 1–31). Emerald Publishing Limited. doi:10.1108/978-1-78714-315-920161001

Joseph, R. (2021). Determining the singularity and transdisciplinarity properties of the theory evaluation scale: A literature review. *Journal of Evidence-Based Social Work*, *18*(6), 650–662.

Jugdev, K., & Müller, R. (2005). A retrospective look at our evolving understanding of project success. *Project Management Journal*, *36*(4), 19–31. doi:10.1177/875697280503600403

Kahneman, D., & Tversky, A. (2013). Prospect theory: An analysis of decision under risk. In Handbook of the fundamentals of financial decision making: Part I (pp. 99-127).

Kankam, K. P. (2019). The use of Paradigms in information research. *Library & Information Science Research*, *41*(2), 85–92. doi:10.1016/j.lisr.2019.04.003

Kapadia, M., Sarkar, S., Roy, B. C., & Sinha, R. C. (2022). Critical Appraisal of Parameters for Successful Implementation of BRTS in India. *Periodica Polytechnica Transportation Engineering*, *50*(2), 165–183. doi:10.3311/PPtr.16508

Kapungu, R. S. (2008). *The Pursuit of Higher Education in Zimbabwe: A Futile Effort?* Center for International Private Enterprise Economic Reform Feature Service.

Karjaluoto, H., Shaikha, A. A., Saarijarvib, H., & Saraniemi, S. (2019). How perceived value drives the use of mobile *financial services apps. International Journal of Information Management*, *47*, 252–261. doi:10.1016/j.ijinfomgt.2018.08.014

Kaya, E., Dong, X., Suhara, Y., Balcisoy, S., Bozkaya, B., & Pentland, A. S. (2018). Behavioral Attributes and Financial churn prediction. *EPJ Data Science*, *7*(1), 41. doi:10.1140/epjds13688-018-0165-5

Kay, R., Alder, J., Brown, D., & Houghton, P. (2013). Management Cybernetics: A New Institutional Framework for Coastal Management. *Coastal Management*, *31*(3), 213–227. doi:10.1080/08920750390198513

Kerlinger, F. N., Lee, H. B., & Bhanthumnavin, D. (2000). Foundations of behavioral research: The most sustainable popular textbook by Kerlinger & Lee (2000). *Journal of Social Development*, *13*, 131–144.

Khodabandehlou, S., & Rahman, M. Z. (2017). Comparison of supervised machine learning techniques for customer churn prediction based on analysis of customer behavior. *Journal of Systems and Information Technology*, *19*(1/2), 65–93. doi:10.1108/JSIT-10-2016-0061

Kim, D. H. (1993) The Link between Individual and Organizational Learning. Sloan Management Review, 37-50.

Kim, D., Cavusgil, S. T., & Calantone, R. J. (2006). Information system innovations and supply chain management: Channel relationships and _rm performance. *Journal of the Academy of Marketing Science*, *34*(1), 40–54. doi:10.1177/0092070305281619

Kim, S. W., & Narasimhan, R. (2002). Information system utilisation in supply chain integration efforts. *International Journal of Production Research*, *40*(18), 4585–4609. doi:10.1080/0020754021000022203

King, N., Horrocks, C., & Broks, J. (2017). *Interviews in Qualitative Research* (2nd ed.). SAGE.

Klimkeit, D. (2013). Organizational context and collaboration on international projects: The case of a professional service firm. *International Journal of Project Management*, *31*(3), 366–377. doi:10.1016/j.ijproman.2012.08.001

Koo, C., & Chung, N. (2014). Examining the eco-technological knowledge of Smart Green IT adoption behaviour: A self-determination perspective. *Technological Forecasting and Social Change*, *88*, 140–155. doi:10.1016/j.techfore.2014.06.025

Korpelainen, E. (2011). Theories of ICT system implementation and adoption. *Critical Review*.

Koufaris, M. (2002). Applying the technology acceptance model and flow theory to online consumer behavior. *Information Systems Research*, *13*(2), 205–223. doi:10.1287/isre.13.2.205.83

Krumbholz, M., & Maiden, N. A. M. (2000). How culture might impact on the implementation of enterprise resource planning packages. In B. Wangler & L. Bergman (Eds.), *Advanced Information Systems Engineering* (pp. 279–293). Springer. doi:10.1007/3-540-45140-4_19

Kuada, J. (2012). Research Methodology: A project Guide for University Students. Aalborg University, Denmark: Samfundslitteratur.

Kuhn, T. S. (1962). *The Structure of Scientific Revolutions*. The University of Chicago Press.

Kurasha, P. (2015, July). The Future of Higher Education in Zimbabwe: A Constantly Moving Target. *Zimbabwe Journal of Educational Research*, *27*(2), 204–220.

Compilation of References

Kusotera, B., Chimire, F., & Mapuwei, T.W. (2018). *An Analysis Of Customer Churn For Mobile Network Operators In Zimbabwe.*

Kwarteng, M. A., Ntsiful, A., Diego, L. F. P., & Novak, P. (2022). Extending UTAUT with competitive pressure for SMEs digitalization adoption in two European nations: A multi-group analysis. *Aslib Journal of Information Management.* doi:10.1108/AJIM-11-2022-0482

Ladley, J. (2020). *Data Governance.* Elsevier.

Largan, C., & Morris, T. (2019). *Qualitative Secondary Research. A step-by-step guide.* SAGE.

Latino, M. E., Menegoli, M., Lazoi, M., & Corallo, A. (2022). Voluntary traceability in food supply chain: A framework leading its implementation in Agriculture 4.0. *Technological Forecasting and Social Change, 178*, 121564. doi:10.1016/j.techfore.2022.121564

Lau, H. C., & Lee, W. B. (2000). On a responsive supply chain information system. *International Journal of Physical Distribution & Logistics Management, 30*(7/8), 598–610. doi:10.1108/09600030010346242

Leedy, D. P., & Ormrod, E. J. (2015). *Practical Research Planning and Design* (11th ed.). Pearson.

Lee, J., Yoon, T., Kwon, S., & Lee, J. (2019). Model evaluation for forecasting traffic accident severity in rainy seasons using machine learning algorithms: Seoul city study. *Applied Sciences (Basel, Switzerland), 10*(1), 129. doi:10.3390/app10010129

Lee, S., Trimi, S., & Kim, K. (2013). The impact of cultural differences on technology adoption. *Journal of World Business, 48*(1), 20–29. doi:10.1016/j.jwb.2012.06.003

Leidner, D. E., & Kayworth, T. (2006). Review: A review of culture in information systems research: Toward a theory of information technology culture conflict. *Management Information Systems Quarterly, 30*(2), 357–399. doi:10.2307/25148735

Levitt, B., & March, J. G. (1988). Organizational learning. *Annual Review of Sociology, 14*(1), 319–338. doi:10.1146/annurev.so.14.080188.001535

Lidow, D. (1999). Duck alignment theory: Going beyond classic project management to maximize project success. *Project Management Journal, 30*(4), 8–14. doi:10.1177/875697289903000403

Liebowitz, J., & Wilcox, L. C. (1997). *Knowledge Management and its Integrative Elements.* CRC Press.

Li, F., Whalley, J., & Williams, H. (2001). Between physical and electronic spaces: The implications for organisations in the networked economy. *Environment & Planning A, 33*(4), 699–716. doi:10.1068/a33161

Lim, J., Sharma, S., Colyer, T., & Lee, S. (2018). *The Future of the Indonesian Healthcare Ecosystem, 21.*

Lim, S., Saldanha, J. J. V., Mallachi, S., & Melville, N. P. (2014). Theories used in information system research: Insights from complex network analysis. [A publication of the Association for Information Systems.]. *Journal of Information Technology Theory and Application*, *14*(2), 5–46.

Lin, F., Fofanah, S. S & Liang, D. (2011). Assessing citizen adoption of e-government initiatives in the Gambia. *Validation of the tech,* 271-279.

Lin, C. A., & Kim, T. (2016). Predicting user response to sponsored advertising on social media via the technology acceptance model. *Computers in Human Behavior*, *64*, 710–718. doi:10.1016/j. chb.2016.07.027

Lin, H. (2014). An investigation of the effects of cultural differences on physicians' perceptions of information technology acceptance as they relate to knowledge management systems. *Computers in Human Behavior*, *38*, 368–380. doi:10.1016/j.chb.2014.05.001

Lin, H.-F. (2014). Understanding the determinants of electronic supply chain management system adoption: Using the technology–organization–environment framework. *Technological Forecasting and Social Change*, *86*, 80–92. doi:10.1016/j.techfore.2013.09.001

Lloyd, P., & Boyle, P. (1998). *Web-Weaving: Intranets, Extranets and Strategic Alliances.* Heinenmann.

Loseke, R. D. (2017). Methodological Thinking Second Edition. Basic Principles of Social Research Design. London: SAGE

Lowry, G. (2004). Translation and Validation of the Technology Acceptance Model and instrument for use in the Arab World. *ACIS 2004 Proceedings. 105.* https://aisel.aisnet.org/acis2004/105

Lucas, S. R. (2014). Beyond the Existence Proof: Ontological Conditions, Epistemological Implications, and In-Depth Interview Research. *Quality & Quantity*, *48*(1), 387–408. doi:10.100711135-012-9775-3

Lui, K. J., McGee, D., Rhodes, P., & Pollock, D. (1988). An Application of a Conditional Logistic Regression to a Study the Effects of Safety Belts, Principal Impact Points, and Car Weights on Drivers' Fatalities. *Journal of Safety Research*, *19*(4), 197–203. doi:10.1016/0022-4375(88)90024-2

Lundin, R. A., & Söderholm, A. (1995). A theory of the temporary organization. *Scandinavian Journal of Management*, *11*(4), 437–455. doi:10.1016/0956-5221(95)00036-U

Lu, Y., Panetto, H., Ni, Y., & Gu, X. (2013). Ontology alignment for networked enterprise information system interoperability in supply chain environment. *International Journal of Computer Integrated Manufacturing*, *26*(1-2), 140–151. doi:10.1080/0951192X.2012.681917

Lyaruu, T. (2021). *Integrating Records Management into the extractive industries transparency initiative in Tanzania.* [Thesis, University of South Africa]. Pretoria.

Mabika, B. (2019). *The Use of Mobile Phones in Disseminating Agricultural Information to Farmers in Mashonaland West Province of Zimbabwe*. [Thesis, University of South Africa]. Pretoria.

Compilation of References

Mack, N., Woodsong, C., MacQueen, K. M., Guest, G., & Namey, E. (2005). *Qualitative research methods: A data collector's field guide*. Family Health International.

Magwa, W. (2015, July). Enhancing Africa's Renewal through Internationalisation of Higher Education: A Review of Management Strategies and Issues. *Zimbabwe Journal of Educational Research, 27*(2), 255–272.

Mainzer, K. (2007). *Thinking in Complexity: The Computional Dynamics of Matter, Mind, and Mankind*. Springer.

Malik, F. (2016). *Strategies for Managing Complex Systems: A Contribution to Management Cybernetics for Complex Systems, Frankfurt-am-Main*. Campus Verlag.

Manning, S. (2008). Embedding projects in multiple contexts – A structuration perspective. *International Journal of Project Management, 26*(1), 30–37. doi:10.1016/j.ijproman.2007.08.012

Marchewka, J. T. (2012). *Information technology project management: Providing measurable organizational value* (4th ed.). Wiley.

March, G., & Olson, J. (1975). The Uncertainty of the Past: Organisational Learning Under Ambiguity. *European Journal of Political Research, 3*(2), 147–171. doi:10.1111/j.1475-6765.1975.tb00521.x

Markus, M. L., & Robey, D. (1988). Information technology and organizational change: Causal structure in theory and research. *Management Science, 34*(5), 583–598. doi:10.1287/mnsc.34.5.583

Markus, M. L., & Rowe, F. (2018). Is IT changing the world? Conceptions of causality for information systems theorizing. *Management Information Systems Quarterly, 42*(4), 1255–1280.

Marnix, A. (2006). Inhibitors of disruptive innovation capability: A conceptual model. *European Journal of Innovation Management, 9*(2), 215–233. doi:10.1108/14601060610663587

Marshall, A., & Sandberg, J. (2011). Sensemaking in 'real' versus virtual environments: A comparison and challenge. *3rd International Symposium on Process Organization Studies*.

Mathai, N., McGill, T., & Toohey, D. (2020). Factors Influencing Consumer Adoption of Electronic Health Records. *Journal of Computer Information Systems, 00*(00), 1–11.

Mathieson, K. (1991). Predicting User Intentions: Comparing the Technology Acceptance Model with the Theory of Planned Behaviour. *Information Systems Research, 2*(3), 173–191. doi:10.1287/isre.2.3.173

Matlala, E. (2019). Long-term preservation of digital records at the University of Kwazulu-Natal archives. *Journal of the South African Society of Archivists, 52*, 95–109.

Matua, G. A. (2015). Choosing phenomenology as a guiding philosophy for nursing research. *Nurse Researcher, 22*(4), 30–34. doi:10.7748/nr.22.4.30.e1325 PMID:25783150

Mawonde, A. (2015). Government to Wean Off Universities. *The Herald*.

Maxwell, J. A. (2013). *Qualitative Research Design. An Interactive Approach* (3rd ed.). SAGE.

McChesney, K., & Aldridge, J. (2019). Weaving an Interpretivist stance throughout mixed methods research. *International Journal of Research & Method in Education*, *42*(3), 225–238. doi:10.1080/1743727X.2019.1590811

McCormick, J., Alavi, S. B., & Hanham, J. (2015). *The importance of context when applying social cognitive theory in organisations. Faculty of Social Sciences, Papers (Archive).* The University of Wollongong.

Mehmet, K. M., Aghayan, I., & Noii, N. (2011). Prediction for traffic accident severity: Comparing the artificial neural network, genetic algorithm, combined genetic algorithm and pattern search methods. *Transport*, *26*(4), 353–366.

Mena, C. G., De Caigny, A., Coussement, K., De Bock, K. W., & Lessmann, S. (2019). Churn prediction with sequential data and deep neural networks. A comparative analysis. *arXiv preprint arXiv:1909.11114*.

Menguc, B., & Auh, S. (2005, Spring). A Test of Strategic Orientation Formation versus Strategic Orientation Implementation: The Influence of TMT Functional Diversity and Inter-Functional Coordination. *Journal of Marketing Theory and Practice*, *13*(2), 4–19. doi:10.1080/10696679 .2005.11658540

Merhi, M., Hone, K., & Tarhi, A. (2019). A cross-cultural study of the intention to use mobile banking between Lebanese and British consumers: Extending UTAUT2 with security, privacy and trust. *Technology in Society*, *59*, 101151. doi:10.1016/j.techsoc.2019.101151

Metallo, C., Agrifoglio, R., Lepore, L., & Landriani, L. (2022). Explaining users' technology acceptance through national cultural values in the hospital context. *BMC Health Services Research*, *2022*(22), 84. doi:10.118612913-022-07488-3 PMID:35039014

Meyer, J. W., & Rowan, B. (1977). Institutionalized organizations: Formal structure as myth and ceremony. *American Journal of Sociology*, *83*(2), 340–363. doi:10.1086/226550

Mhukahuru, C. (2015) Universities brace for 50% government cuts to salaries. *University World News*, 367. https://www.universityworldnews.com/article.php?story=20150513172957289

Mikalef, P., Boura, M., Lekakos, G., & Krogstie, J. (2019). Big data analytics and firm performance: Findings from a mixed-method approach. *Journal of Business Research, 98*(July 2018), 261–276.

Miles, M. B., Huberman, A. M., & Saldana, J. (2014). Qualitative Data Analysis. Los Angels: SAGE.

Miles, M. B., & Huberman, A. M. (1994). Qualitative data analysis: An expanded sourcebook. *Sage (Atlanta, Ga.).*

Miles, M. B., Huberman, A. M., & Saldaña, J. (2020). Qualitative data analysis: A methods sourcebook. *Sage (Atlanta, Ga.).*

Compilation of References

Miller, D. (1981). Toward a new contingency approach: The search for organizational gestalts. *Journal of Management Studies*, *18*(1), 1–26. doi:10.1111/j.1467-6486.1981.tb00088.x

Minton, E. A., Spielmann, N., Kahle, L. R., & Kim, C. (2018). The subjective norms of sustainable consumption: A cross-cultural Exploration. *Journal of Business Research*, *82*, 400–408. doi:10.1016/j.jbusres.2016.12.031

Mintzberg, H. (1973). Strategy-Making in Three Modes. *California Management Review*, *16*(2), 44–53.

Mintzberg, H. (1975). *The Manager's Job: Folklore and Fact. Harvard Business Review*.

Mintzberg, H. (1983). *Structure in Fives: Designing Effective Organisations*. Prentice Hall.

Mishkoff, H. C. (1986). *Understanding Artificial Intelligence*. Texas Instruments Incorporated.

Mishra, S. (2014). Adoption of M-commerce in India: Applying Theory of Planned Behaviour Model. *Journal of Internet Banking and Commerce*, *19*(1).

Mitchell, M. (2009). *Complexity: A Guided Tour*. Oxford University Press. doi:10.1093/oso/9780195124415.001.0001

Mitchell, S. (2003). *Biological Complexity and Integrative Pluralism*. Cambridge University Press. doi:10.1017/CBO9780511802683

Mitchell, S. (2008). *Komplexitäten: Warum wir erst anfangen, die Welt zu verstehen*. Suhrkamp.

Mitchell, S. (2009). *Unsimple Truths: Science,Complexity and Policy*. University of Chicago Press. doi:10.7208/chicago/9780226532653.001.0001

Mohammed, Z. A., & Tejay, G. P. (2017). Examining privacy concerns and e-commerce adoption in developing countries: The impact of culture in shaping individuals' perceptions toward technology. *Computers & Security*, *67*, 254–265. doi:10.1016/j.cose.2017.03.001

Moray, N. (1963). *Cybernetics*. Hawthorn Books.

Morgan, G. (2006). *Images of Organisastion*. Sage Publication.

Morquin, D., Ologeanu-Taddei, R., Paré, G., & Wagner, G. (2023). A method for resolving organisation-enterprise system misfits: An action research study in a pluralistic organisation. *Information Systems Journal*, *33*(5), 995–1028. doi:10.1111/isj.12433

Morris, P. W., & Geraldi, J. (2011). Managing the institutional context for projects. *Project Management Journal*, *42*(6), 20–32. doi:10.1002/pmj.20271

Mosweu, O. (2016). Critical Success factors in electronic document and records management systems implementation at the Ministry of Trade and Industry in Botswana. *ESARBICA Journal*, *35*(1), 1–13. doi:10.4314/esarjo.v38i1.1

Muhammad, S. J., Mat, I. S. A., & Miah, J. S. (2021). Constituent of an Information governance framework for a successful implementation in Nigerian Universities. *Education and Information Technologies*, *26*(5), 6447–6460. doi:10.100710639-021-10528-w

Muk, A., & Chung, C. (2015). Applying the technology acceptance model in a two-country study of SMS advertising. *Journal of Business Research*, *68*(1), 1–6. doi:10.1016/j.jbusres.2014.06.001

Muller, B., & Urbach, N. (2017). Understanding the Why, What and How of theories in IS research. *Communications of the Association for Information Systems*, *41*, 349–388. doi:10.17705/1CAIS.04117

Müller, R., & Jugdev, K. (2012). Critical success factors in projects: Pinto, Slevin, and Prescott–the elucidation of project success. *International Journal of Managing Projects in Business*, *5*(4), 757–775. doi:10.1108/17538371211269040

Mussone, L., Ferrari, A., & Oneta, M. (1999). An analysis of urban collisions using an artificial intelligence model. *Accident; Analysis and Prevention*, *31*(6), 705–718. doi:10.1016/S0001-4575(99)00031-7 PMID:10487346

Nah, F. F. H., Lau, J. L. S., & Delgado, S. (2006). Critical success factors for enterprise resource planning implementation and upgrade. *Journal of Computer Information Systems*, *46*(5), 99–113. doi:10.1080/08874417.2006.11645928

Nah, F. F. H., Lau, J. L. S., & Kuang, J. (2001). Critical factors for successful implementation of enterprise systems. *Business Process Management Journal*, *7*(3), 285–296. doi:10.1108/14637150110392782

Narasimhan, R., & Kim, S. W. (2001). Information system utilisation strategy for supply chain integration. *Journal of Business Logistics*, *22*(2), 51–75. doi:10.1002/j.2158-1592.2001.tb00003.x

Neaverth, M. P. (2015). Project management and governance in the Project Management Office (PMO): Analysis of the variables associated with project success. *ProQuest Dissertations and Theses*, (March), 153.

Negroponte, N. (1996). *(1995). Being Digital*. Knopf.

Ngulube, P. (2016). *Postgraduate workshop on methodology at UNISA. (unpublished College of Graduate Studies.* UNISA: Pretoria Padilla-Diaz, M (2015). Phenomenology in Educational Qualitative Research: Philosophy as science or philosophical science? *International Journal of Educational Excellence*, *1*(2), 101–110.

Niederman, F., & March, S. (2019a). The "theoretical lens" concept: We all know what it means, but do we all know the same thing? *Communications of the Association for Information Systems*, *44*(1), 1–33. doi:10.17705/1CAIS.04401

Niederman, F., & March, S. T. (2019b). Broadening the conceptualization of theory in the information systems discipline: A meta-theory approach. *The Data Base for Advances in Information Systems*, *50*(2), 18–44. doi:10.1145/3330472.3330476

Compilation of References

Nilsson Vestola, E., Eriksson, P. E., Larsson, J., & Karrbom Gustavsson, T. (2021). Temporary and permanent aspects of project organizing–operation and maintenance of road infrastructure. *International Journal of Managing Projects in Business*, *14*(7), 1444–1462. doi:10.1108/IJMPB-09-2020-0279

Nilsson, A. (2015). IT project alignment in practice. In S. Gao & L. Rusu (Eds.), *Modern techniques for successful IT project management* (pp. 21–47). Business Science Reference. doi:10.4018/978-1-4666-7473-8.ch002

O'Halloran, K. L., Tan, S., Pham, D. S., Bateman, J., & Vande Moere, A. (2018). A digital mixed methods research design: Integrating multimodal analysis with data mining and information visualization for big data analytics. *Journal of Mixed Methods Research*, *12*(1), 11–30. doi:10.1177/1558689816651015

O'Leary, T., & Williams, T. (2012). Managing the social trajectory: A practice perspective on project management. *IEEE Transactions on Engineering Management*, *60*(3), 566–580. doi:10.1109/TEM.2012.2228206

Oliveira, T., Thomas, M., & Espadanal, M. (2014). Assessing the determinants of cloud computing adoption: An analysis of the manufacturing and services sectors. *Information & Management*, *51*(5), 497–510. doi:10.1016/j.im.2014.03.006

Oni, A. A., Oni, S., Mbarika, V., & Ayo, C. K. (2017). An empirical study of user acceptance of online political participation: Integrating Civic Voluntarism Model and Theory of Reasoned Action. *Government Information Quarterly*, *34*(2), 317–328. doi:10.1016/j.giq.2017.02.003

Oshlyyansky, L., Cairns, P., & Thimbleby, H. (2007). Validating the unified theory of acceptance and use of technology (UTAUT) tools cross-culturally. *Conference: Proceedings of the 21st British HCI Group Annual Conference on HCI 2007: HCI...but not as we know it - Volume 2, BCS HCI 2007*. University of Lancaster, United Kingdom.

Oyedepo, O. J., & Makinde, O. (2010). Accident Prediction Models for Akure – Ondo Carriageway, Ondo State Southwest Nigeria; Using Multiple Linear Regressions. *African Research Review*, *4*(2), 30–49. doi:10.4314/afrrev.v4i2.58286

Özer, Ö., Özkan, O., & Budak, F. (2020). The Relationship between the Nurses' Perception of Electronic Health Records and Patient Privacy. *Hospital Topics*, *98*(4), 155–162. doi:10.1080/00185868.2020.1799729 PMID:32757888

Packendorff, J. (1995). Inquiring into the temporary organization: New directions for project management research. *Scandinavian Journal of Management*, *11*(4), 319–333. doi:10.1016/0956-5221(95)00018-Q

Pajunen, K. (2008). 'The nature of organisational mechanisms'. *Organization Studies*, *29*(11), 1449–1468. doi:10.1177/0170840607096384

Palas, M. J. U., & Bunduchi, R. (2021). Exploring interpretations of blockchain's value in healthcare: A multi-stakeholder approach. *Information Technology & People*, *34*(2), 453–495. doi:10.1108/ITP-01-2019-0008

Palmer, K. D. (2007). *Exploring Intelligent Entreprise System Limitations*. INCOSE Planning.

Park, H. S. (2000). Relationships among attitudes and subjective norms: Testing the theory of reasoned action across cultures. *Communication Studies*, *51*(2), 162–175. doi:10.1080/10510970009388516

Park, N., Roman, R., Lee, S., & Chung, J. E. (2009). User acceptance of a digital library system in developing countries: An application of the Technology acceptance model. *International Journal of Information Management*, *29*(3), 196–209. doi:10.1016/j.ijinfomgt.2008.07.001

Patanakul, P., & Shenhar, A. J. (2012). What project strategy really is: The fundamental building block in strategic project management. *Project Management Journal*, *43*(1), 4–20. doi:10.1002/pmj.20282

Pattern, L. M., & Newhat, M. (2018). *Understanding Research Methods. AN overview of the Essentials* (10th ed.). Routledge.

Peña-García, N., Gil-Saura, I., Rodríguez-Orejuela, A., & Siqueira-Juni, J. R. (2020). Purchase intention and purchase behaviour online: A cross-cultural approach. *Heliyon*, *6*(6), e04284. doi:10.1016/j.heliyon.2020.e04284 PMID:32613132

Perez-Alvarez, C. (2006). Uncertainty avoidance, IT perceptions, use and adoption: Distributed teams in two cultures. *Journal of Academic and Business Ethics*.

Perkmen, S., Toy, S., & Caracuel, A. (2023). Extended Social Cognitive Model Explains Pre-Service Teachers' Technology Integration Intentions with Cross-Cultural Validity. *Computers in the Schools*, *40*(2), 173–193. doi:10.1080/07380569.2022.2157690

Pfeffer, J. (2005). Developing resource dependence theory: how theory is affected by its environment. In K. G. Smith & M. A. Hitt (Eds.), *Great Minds in Management: The Process of Theory Development*. Oxford University Press. doi:10.1093/oso/9780199276813.003.0021

Phiri, M. J. (2016*). Managing university records and documents in the world of governance, audit and documents in the world of governance, audit and risk: case studies from South Africa and Malawi*. [Thesis, University of Glasgow, Glasgow].

Piaget, J. (1950). *The Psychology of Intelligence*. Harcourt and Brace.

Pickard, A. J. (2013). *Research Methods in information* (2nd ed.). Facet Publishing.

Pinto, J. K. (2019). *Project management: Achieving competitive advantage* (5th ed.). Pearson.

Popper, K. (2005). *The logic of scientific discovery*. Routledge. doi:10.4324/9780203994627

Porter, M. E. (1997). Competitive strategy. *Measuring Business Excellence*, *1*(2), 12–17. doi:10.1108/eb025476

Porter, M. E. (1998). *The Competitive Advantage: Creating and Sustaining Superior Performance.* Free Press. doi:10.1007/978-1-349-14865-3

Post, C., Sarala, R., Gatrell, C., & Prescott, J. E. (2020). Advancing theory with review articles. *Journal of Management Studies*, *57*(2), 351–376. doi:10.1111/joms.12549

Pradhan, B., & Sameen, M. I. (2020). Review of traffic accident predictions with neural networks. In *Advances in Science, Technology, and Innovation book series (ASTI)* (pp. 97–109). Springer. doi:10.1007/978-3-030-10374-3_8

Preece, G., Shaw, D., & Hayashi, H. (2015). Application of the Viable System Model to analyse communications structures: A case study of disaster response in Japan. *European Journal of Operational Research*, *243*(1), 312–322. doi:10.1016/j.ejor.2014.11.026

Premkumar, G., Ramamurthy, K., & Nilakanta, S. (1994). Implementation of electronic data interchange: An innovation diffusion perspective. *Journal of Management Information Systems*, *11*(2), 157–186. doi:10.1080/07421222.1994.11518044

Prigogine, I., & Stengers, I. (1984). *Order out of Chaos: Man's New Dialogue with Nature.* Bentam Books.

Puche, J., Ponte, B., Costas, J., Pino,R., de la Fuente, D. (2016) Systemic approach to supply chain management through the viable system model and the theory of constraints. *Production Planning & Control, 27*(5), 421-430.

Punch, F. K., & Qancea, A. (2009). *Introduction to Research Methods in Education* (2nd ed.). SAGE.

Quinn, J. B. (1992). *Intelligent Enterprise: A knowledge and service based paradigm.* The Free Press.

Quinn, J. B., Anderson, P., & Finkelstein, S. (2009). Managing professional intellect: making the most of the best. In *The strategic Management of Intellectual capital* (pp. 87–98). Routledge.

Qu, K., & Liu, Z. (2022). Green innovations, supply chain integration and green information system: A model of moderation. *Journal of Cleaner Production*, *339*, 130557. doi:10.1016/j.jclepro.2022.130557

Rahmadiliyani, N. R., Putri, P., & Gunarti, R. (2019). Implementasi Electronic Health Record (EHR) Pada Poli Rawat Jalan Di Rumah Sakit Umum Daerah Ratu Zalecha Martapura. *Jurnal Kesehatan Indonesia*, *9*(3), 135. doi:10.33657/jurkessia.v9i3.186

Ramayah, T., Rouibah, K., Gopi, M., & Rangel, G. J. (2009). A decomposed theory of reasoned action to explain the intention to use Internet stock trading among Malaysian investors. *Computers in Human Behavior*, *25*(6), 1222–1230. doi:10.1016/j.chb.2009.06.007

Ramírez-Correa, P. (2016, May). Most popular theories in information systems research. In *Anais Do XII Simpósio Brasileiro de Sistemas de Informação* (pp. 582–584). SBC. doi:10.5753bsi.2016.6017

Ram, J., & Corkindale, D. (2014). How "critical" are the critical success factors (CSFs)? Examining the role of CSFs for ERP. *Business Process Management Journal, 20*(1), 151–174. doi:10.1108/BPMJ-11-2012-0127

Rasmi, M., Alazzam, M. B., Alsmadi, M. K., Almarashdeh, I. A., Alkhasawneh, R. A., & Alsmadi, S. (2020). Healthcare professionals' acceptance Electronic Health Records system: Critical literature review (Jordan case study). *International Journal of Healthcare Management, 13*(sup1, S1), 48–60. doi:10.1080/20479700.2017.1420609

Rayport, J. F., & Jaworski, B. J. (2003). *Introduction to e-commerce*. McGraw-Hill, Inc.

Ren, X., Yan, Z., Wang, Z., & He, J. (2019). Inter-project knowledge transfer in project-based organizations: An organizational context perspective. *Management Decision, 58*(5), 844–863. doi:10.1108/MD-11-2018-1211

Rescher, N. (1998). *Complexity: A philosophical overview*. Transaction Publishers.

Richards, R. J., Prybutok, V. R., & Ryan, S. D. (2012). Electronic medical records: Tools for competitive advantage. *International Journal of Quality and Service Sciences, 4*(2), 120–136. doi:10.1108/17566691211232873

Rios, J. P. (2012). *Design and Diagnosis for Sustainable Organisations: The Viable System Model*. Springer-Verlag. doi:10.1007/978-3-642-22318-1

Rivard, S. (2021). Theory building is neither an art nor a science. It is a craft. *Journal of Information Technology, 36*(3), 316–328. doi:10.1177/0268396220911938

Rogers, E. M., Singhal, A., & Quinlan, M. M. (2014). Diffusion of innovations. In *An integrated approach to communication theory and research* (pp. 432–448). Routledge.

Rosenblueth, A., Wiener, N., & Bigelow, J. (1943, January). Behaviour, Purpose and Teleology. *Philosophy of Science, 10*(1), 18–24. doi:10.1086/286788

Rosenhead, J. (2006). IFORS' Operational Research Hall of Fame Stafford Beer. *International Transactions in Operational Research, 13*(6), 577–578. doi:10.1111/j.1475-3995.2006.00565.x

Rourke, A. J., & Coleman, K. S. (2011). Pedagogy Leading Technology in higher education: New Technologies, New Pedagogies. Champaign, Il: Common Ground Publishing.

Rubbio, I., Bruccoleri, M., Pietrosi, A., & Ragonese, B. (2019). Digital health technology enhances resilient behaviour: Evidence from the ward. *International Journal of Operations & Production Management, 40*(1), 34–67. doi:10.1108/IJOPM-02-2018-0057

Rule, P., & John, V. (2011). *Your Guide to Case Study Research*. Van Schaik.

Saccomanno, F. F., Nassar, S. A., & Shortreed, J. H. (1996). Reliability of Statistical Road Accident Injury Severity Models. *Transportation Research Record: Journal of the Transportation Research Board, 1542*(1), 14–23. doi:10.1177/0361198196154200103

Compilation of References

Sahin, I. (2006). Detailed review of Rogers' diffusion of innovations theory and educational technology-related studies based on Rogers' theory. *Turkish Online Journal of Educational Technology-TOJET*, *5*(2), 14–23.

Salkind, N. (2018). *Exploring Research* (9th ed.). Pearson.

Sandberg, J., & Alvesson, M. (2021). Meanings of theory: Clarifying theory through typification. *Journal of Management Studies*, *58*(2), 487–516. doi:10.1111/joms.12587

Sarkar, A., Sahoo, G., & Sahoo, U. C. (2016). Feature Selection in Accident Data: An Analysis of its Application in Classification Algorithms. *International Journal of Data Analysis Techniques and Strategies*, *8*(2), 108–121. doi:10.1504/IJDATS.2016.077484

Sarkar, A., Sahoo, U. C., & Sahoo, G. (2012). Accident prediction models for urban roads. *International Journal of Vehicle Safety*, *6*(2), 149–161. doi:10.1504/IJVS.2012.049020

Sarkar, A., & Sarkar, S. (2020). Comparative Assessment Between Statistical and Soft Computing Methods for Accident Severity Classification. *Journal of Institution of Engineers India Series A*, *101*(1), 27–40. doi:10.100740030-019-00422-7

Sarver, V. T. (1983). Ajzen and Fishbein's" theory of reasoned action": A critical assessment.

Saunders, M., Lewis, P., & Thornhill, A. (2009). *Research methods for business students* (4th ed.). Person Education Limited.

Schäfer, F., Zeiselmair, C., Becker, J., & Otten, H. (2018, November). Synthesizing CRISP-DM and quality management: A data mining approach for production processes. In *2018 IEEE International Conference on Technology Management, Operations and Decisions (ICTMOD)* (pp. 190-195). IEEE. 10.1109/ITMC.2018.8691266

Schein, E. H. (1985) *Organisational Culture and Leadership*. Jossey-Bass.

Schwalbe, K. (2019). *Information technology project management* (9th ed.). Cengage.

Schwaninger, M. (2000). Managing Complexity—The Path Toward Intelligent Organizations. *Systemic Practice and Action Research*, *13*(2), 207–241. doi:10.1023/A:1009546721353

Schwaninger, M. (2006). Design for Viable Organisations: The Diagnostic Power of the Viable System Model, Kybernetes. *The International Journal of Systems and Cybernetics*, *35*(7/8), 955–971. doi:10.1108/03684920610675012

Seiler, D. (2020). *How COVID-19 has pushed companies over the technology tipping point—and transformed business forever*. Strategy & Corporate Finance. https://www.mckinsey.com/business-functions/strategy-and-corporate-finance/our-insights/how-covid-19-has-pushed-companies-over-the-technology-tipping-point-and-transformed-business-forever

Senge, P. (1990). *The fifth discipline*. The Art & Practice of Learning Organization.

Senge, P. (1990). *The Fifth Discipline: The Art and the Practice of the Learning Organization*. Random House.

Shah, R., Goldstein, S. M., & Ward, P. T. (2002). Aligning supply chain management characteristics and interorganizational information system types: An exploratory study. *IEEE Transactions on Engineering Management*, *49*(3), 282–292. doi:10.1109/TEM.2002.803382

Shahzad, K., Jianqiu, Z., Zubedi, A., Xin, W., Wang, L., & Hashim, M. (2020). DANP-based method for determining the adoption of hospital information system. *International Journal of Computer Applications in Technology*, *62*(1), 57. doi:10.1504/IJCAT.2020.103900

Shaik, M. E., & Hossain, Q. S. (2019). Accident prediction by using Poisson regression for unsignalised junction in Khulna Metropolitan City, Bangladesh. In *Proceedings of International Conference on Planning, Architecture and Civil Engineering*. Rajshahi University of Engineering & Technology.

Shane, S. A. (2003). *A general theory of entrepreneurship: The individual-opportunity nexus*. Edward Elgar Publishing. doi:10.4337/9781781007990

Shanks, G. (2002). Guidelines for conducting positivist case study research in information systems. *AJIS. Australasian Journal of Information Systems*, *10*(Special Issue), 76–85. doi:10.3127/ajis. v10i1.448

Sharma, S. K., Al-Badi, A. H., Govindaluri, S. M., & Al-Kharusi, M. H. (2016). Predicting motivators of cloud computing adoption: A developing country perspective. *Computers in Human Behavior*, *62*, 61–69. doi:10.1016/j.chb.2016.03.073

Shenhar, A. J. (1999). Strategic project management: The new framework. *PICMET '99: Portland International Conference on Management of Engineering and Technology (Vol-1)*. 10.1109/PICMET.1999.808262

Shenhar, A. J., Levy, O., & Dvir, D. (1997). Mapping the dimensions of project success. *Project Management Journal*, *28*(2), 5–13.

Shirazi, F., & Mohammadi, M. (2019). A big data analytics model for customer churn prediction in the retiree segment. *International Journal of Information Management*, *48*, 238–253. doi:10.1016/j. ijinfomgt.2018.10.005

Shizha, E., & Kariwo, M. (2011). *"The Development of Higher Education in Zimbabwe" in Shizha, E. &Kariwo, M. (2011) Education and Development in Zimbabwe: A Social, Political and Economic Analysis*. Springer.

Shtub, A., & Karni, R. (1999). *Enterprise resource planning (ERP): the dynamics of operations management*. Kluwer Academic Publishers.

Sia, S. K., & Soh, C. (2007). An assessment of package–organisation misalignment: Institutional and ontological structures. *European Journal of Information Systems*, *16*(5), 568–583. doi:10.1057/palgrave.ejis.3000700

Siggelkow, N. (2007). Persuasion with case studies. *Academy of Management Journal*, *50*(1), 20–24. doi:10.5465/amj.2007.24160882

Compilation of References

Simeonova, B., Bogolyubov, P., Blagov, E., & Kharabsheh, R. (2014). Cross-cultural validation of UTAUT: The case of University VLEs in Jordan, Russia and the UK. *Electronic Journal of Knowledge Management, 12*(1), 25–34.

Simon, H. A. (1950). Administrative behaviour.

Simons, S. M. J., Cillessen, F. H. J. M., & Hazelzet, J. A. (2016). Determinants of a successful problem list to support the implementation of the problem-oriented medical record according to recent literature. *BMC Medical Informatics and Decision Making, 16*(1), 1–9. doi:10.118612911-016-0341-0 PMID:27485127

Singhal, S., Kayyali, B., Levin, R., & Greenberg, Z. (2020). *The next wave of healthcare innovation: The evolution of ecosystems How healthcare stakeholders can win within evolving healthcare ecosystems.*

Singh, N., Fassott, G., Chao, M. C. H., & Hoffmann, J. A. (2004). Understanding international website usage A cross-national study of German, Brazilian, and Taiwanese online consumers. *International Marketing Review, 23*(1), 83–97. doi:10.1108/02651330610646304

Sivathanu, B. (2018). Adoption of internet of things (IoT) based wearables for healthcare of older adults – a behavioural reasoning theory (BRT) approach. *Journal of Enabling Technologies, 12*(4), 169–185. doi:10.1108/JET-12-2017-0048

Skulmoski, G. J., & Hartman, F. T. (1999). Project alignment: The key to successful cost engineering. *AACE International Transactions*, PM41.

Smallwood, R. F. (2020). *Information Governance*. John Wiley & Sons.,Inc.

Sniehotta, F. F., Presseau, J., & Araújo-Soares, V. (2014). Time to retire the theory of planned behaviour. *Health Psychology Review, 8*(1), 1–7. doi:10.1080/17437199.2013.869710 PMID:25053004

Soh, C., Kien, S. S., & Tay-Yap, J. (2000). Enterprise resource planning: Cultural fits and misfits: Is ERP a universal solution? *Communications of the ACM, 43*(4), 47–51. doi:10.1145/332051.332070

Srivannaboon, S., & Milosevic, D. Z. (2006). A two-way influence between business strategy and project management. *International Journal of Project Management, 24*(6), 493–505. doi:10.1016/j.ijproman.2006.03.006

Stablein, T., Loud, K. J., DiCapua, C., & Anthony, D. L. (2018). The Catch to Confidentiality: The Use of Electronic Health Records in Adolescent Health Care. *The Journal of Adolescent Health, 62*(5), 577–582. doi:10.1016/j.jadohealth.2017.11.296 PMID:29422435

Steinhaeusser, T., Elezi, F., Tommelein, I. D., & Lindemann, U. (2015). Management Cybernetics as a Theoretical Basis for Lean Construction Thinking. *Lean Construction Journal*, 01-14

Sternberg, R. J. (1988). Mental self-government: A theory of intellectual styles and their development. *Human Development, 31*(4), 197–224. doi:10.1159/000275810

Straub, D., Karen, L., & Hill, C. E. (2001). Transfer of information technology to the Arab world: A test of cultural influence modelling. *Journal of Global Information Management*, *9*(4), 6–28. doi:10.4018/jgim.2001100101

Straub, D., Keil, M., & Brenner, W. (1997). Testing the technology acceptance model across cultures: A three-country study. *Information & Management*, *33*(1), 1–11. doi:10.1016/S0378-7206(97)00026-8

Stripling, E., vanden Broucke, S., Antonio, K., Baesens, B., & Snoeck, M. (2018). Profit maximising logistic model for customer churn prediction using genetic algorithms. *Swarm and Evolutionary Computation*, *40*, 116–130. doi:10.1016/j.swevo.2017.10.010

Strong, D. M., & Volkoff, O. (2010). Understanding organization—Enterprise system fit: A path to theorizing the information technology artifact. *Management Information Systems Quarterly*, *34*(4), 731–756. doi:10.2307/25750703

Struwig, F. W., & Stead, G. b (2016). Research: Planning, Designing Second Edition. Cape Town: Pearson Education South Africa (PTY).

Subramani, M. (2004). How do suppliers benefit from information technology use in supply chain relationships? *Management Information Systems Quarterly*, *28*(1), 45–73. doi:10.2307/25148624

Subramanya, K. B., & Somani, A. (2017, January). Enhanced feature mining and classifier Models to predict customer churn for an E-retailer. In *2017 7th International Conference on Cloud Computing, Data Science & Engineering-Confluence* (pp. 531-536). IEEE. 10.1109/CONFLUENCE.2017.7943208

Sunny, J., Undralla, N., & Pillai, V. M. (2020). Supply chain transparency through blockchain-based traceability: An overview with demonstration. *Computers & Industrial Engineering*, *150*, 106895. doi:10.1016/j.cie.2020.106895

Suprapto, Y. L., Wibowo, A., & Harsono, H. (2018). Intra-firm causal ambiguity on cross-functional project team's performance: Does openness and an integrative capability matter? *International Journal of Managing Projects in Business*, *11*(4), 901–912. doi:10.1108/IJMPB-09-2017-0109

Sutton, R. I., & Staw, B. M. (1995). What theory is not. *Administrative Science Quarterly*, *40*(3), 371–384. doi:10.2307/2393788

Svejvig, P., & Andersen, P. (2015). Rethinking project management: A structured literature review with a critical look at the brave new world. *International Journal of Project Management*, *33*(2), 278–290. doi:10.1016/j.ijproman.2014.06.004

Sydow, J., & Windeler, A. (2020). Temporary organizing and permanent contexts. *Current Sociology*, *68*(4), 510–531. doi:10.1177/0011392120907629

Syre, K. D. (2007). *Exploring Intelligent Entreprise System Limitations*. INCOSE Planning.

Syre, K. M. (1967). Philosophy and Cybernetics. In F. J. Crosson & K. M. Syre (Eds.), *Philosophy and Cybernetics*. Simon and Schuster.

Compilation of References

Tachinardi, U., Gutierrez, M. A., Moura, L., & Melo, C. P. (1993). Integrating Hospital Information Systems. The challenges and advantages of (re-)starting now. *Proceedings / the ... Annual Symposium on Computer Application [Sic] in Medical Care. Symposium on Computer Applications in Medical Care*, (pp. 84–87). NIH.

Taherdoost, H. (2018). A review of technology acceptance and adoption models and theories. *Procedia Manufacturing*, *22*, 960–967. doi:10.1016/j.promfg.2018.03.137

Takieddine, S., & Sun, J. (2015). Internet banking diffusion: A country-level analysis. *Electronic Commerce Research and Applications*, *14*(5), 361–371. doi:10.1016/j.elerap.2015.06.001

Tan, M. L., Prasanna, R., Stock, K., Doyle, E. E. H., Leonard, G., & Johnston, D. (2020). Usability factors influencing the continuance intention of disaster apps: A mixed-methods study. *International Journal of Disaster Risk Reduction*, *50*(April), 101874. doi:10.1016/j.ijdrr.2020.101874

Tao, D., Shao, F., Wang, H., Yan, M., & Qu, X. (2019). Integrating usability and social cognitive theories with the technology acceptance model to understand young users' acceptance of a health information portal. *Health Informatics Journal*, *26*(2), 1347–1362. doi:10.1177/1460458219879337 PMID:31603378

Tapscott, D., Ticoll, D., & Lowy, A. (2000). Digital capital: Harnessing the power of business webs. *Ubiquity*, *2000*(May), 3. doi:10.1145/341836.336231

Tarhini, A., Hassouna, M., Abbasi, M. S., & Orozco, J. (2015). Towards the Acceptance of RSS to Support Learning: An empirical study to validate the Technology Acceptance Model in Lebanon. *Electronic Journal of e-Learning*, *13*(1), 30–41.

Teo, T. M., Luan, W. S., & Sing, C. C. (2008). A cross-cultural examination of the intention to use technology between Singaporean and Malaysian pre-service teachers on application of the technology acceptance model (TAM). *Journal of Educational Technology & Society*, *11*(4), 265–280.

Tepic, M., Kemp, R., Omta, O., & Fortuin, F. (2013). Complexities in innovation management in companies from the European industry: A path model of innovation project performance determinants. *European Journal of Innovation Management*, *16*(4), 517–550. doi:10.1108/EJIM-05-2012-0053

Themistocleous, M., Irani, Z., & Love, P. E. (2004). Evaluating the integration of supply chain information systems: A case study. *European Journal of Operational Research*, *159*(2), 393–405. doi:10.1016/j.ejor.2003.08.023

Thomas, G., & Fernández, W. (2008). Success in IT projects: A matter of definition? *International Journal of Project Management*, *26*(7), 733–742. doi:10.1016/j.ijproman.2008.06.003

Thompson, R. L., Higgins, C. A., & Howel, J. M. (1991). Personal Computing: Towards a Conceptual Model of Utilization. *Management Information Systems Quarterly*, *15*(1), 125–143. doi:10.2307/249443

Thurber, M. D., & Fahey, J. W. (2009). Adoption of Moringa oleifera to combat under-nutrition viewed through the lens of the "Diffusion of Innovations" theory. *Ecology of Food and Nutrition*, *48*(3), 212–225. doi:10.1080/03670240902794598 PMID:20161339

Toffler, A. (1984). *Science and Change. In Order out of Chaos: Man's New Dialogue with Nature*. Bentam Books.

Tornatzky, L. G., & Fleischer, M. (1990). *Processes of Technological Innovation*. Lexington Books.

Tracy, S. J. (2013). *Qualitative Research Methods. Collecting Evidence. Crafting analysis, Communicating impact*. Wiley Blackwell.

Truex, D., Holmstrom, J., & Keil, M. (2006). Theory in information systems research: A reflexive analysis of the adaptation of theory in information systems research. *Journal of the Association for Information Systems*, *7*(12), 797–821. doi:10.17705/1jais.00109

Turban, E., King, D., Lee, J., & Viehland, D. (2004). *Electronic Commerce: a managerial perspective 2004*. Pearson Education.

Umpleby, S. (2006). *Fundamentals and history of cybernetics: Development of the theory of complex adaptive systems*. Retrieved March 10, 2015, from: http://info-sciiis.org/IIIS_Videos/website/IIISV06.asp

Umpleby, S. (2006). *Fundamentals and history of cybernetics: Development of the theory of complex adaptive systems*. SCIIIS. http://info-sciiis.org/IIIS_Videos/website/IIISV06.asp

Vaishnavi, V., Suresh, M., & Dutta, P. (2019). Modelling the readiness factors for agility in healthcare organization: An TISM approach. *Benchmarking*, *26*(7), 2372–2400. doi:10.1108/BIJ-06-2018-0172

van der Hoorn, B., & Whitty, S. J. (2017). The praxis of 'alignment seeking' in project work. *International Journal of Project Management*, *35*(6), 978–993. doi:10.1016/j.ijproman.2017.04.011

Van Vliet, V. (2011). *Management cybernetics*. ToolsHero. https://www.toolshero.com/change-management/management-cybernetics

Varghese, N. V. (2008) Globalisation of higher education and cross border student mobility. *UNESCO IIEP Research Paper*. Springer.

Veltri, N. F., & Elgarah, W. (2009). The Role of national cultural differences in user adoption of social networking. *Proceedings of the Southern Association for Information Systems Conference*, Charleston, SC.

Venkatesh, V., Morris, M. G., Davis, G. B., & Davis, F. D. (2003). User acceptance of information technology: Toward a unified view. *Management Information Systems Quarterly*, *27*(3), 425–478. doi:10.2307/30036540

Compilation of References

Villachica, S. W., Stone, D. L., & Endicott, J. (2004). Project alignment ensuring successful development and implementation from day one. *Performance Improvement*, *43*(10), 9–15. doi:10.1002/pfi.4140431005

Vogt, A. & Barred, J. G. (n.d.). *Accident Models for Two-Lane Rural Road: Segment and Intersection.* Federal Highway Administration, McLean, Virginia. FHWA-RD-98-133.

von Bertalanffy, L. (1968) *General System Theory: Foundations, Development, Applications.* George.

Vroman, H. W., & Luchsinger, V. P. (1994). *Managing organization quality.* Academic Press.

Wahyuni, D. (2012). The Research Design Maze: Understanding Paradigms, Cases. *Methods and Methodologies.*, *10*(2), 69–81.

Wang, Y., & Hajli, N. (2017a). Exploring the path to big data analytics success in healthcare. *Journal of Business Research*, *70*, 287–299. doi:10.1016/j.jbusres.2016.08.002

Weber, R. (2012). Evaluating and developing theories in the information systems discipline. *Journal of the Association for Information Systems*, *13*(1), 2. doi:10.17705/1jais.00284

Weick, K. E. (1995). *Sensemaking in organizations* (Vol. 3). Sage.

Wei, K., Teo, H., Chan, C., & Tan, C. (2011). Conceptualising and testing the social cognitive model of the digital divide. *Information Systems Research*, *22*(1), 170–187. doi:10.1287/isre.1090.0273

Weitzman, P. F., & Levkoff, S. E. (2000). Combining Qualitative and Quantitative Methods in Health Research with Minority Elders: Lessons from a Study of Dementia Caregiving. *Field Methods*, *12*(3), 195–208. doi:10.1177/1525822X0001200302

Whang, S. (2000). Information sharing in a supply chain. *International Journal of Technology Management*, *20*(3/4), 373–387. doi:10.1504/IJTM.2000.002867

Whetten, D. A. (1989). What constitutes a theoretical contribution? *Academy of Management Review*, *14*(4), 490–495. doi:10.2307/258554

White, A. E. D. M., Daniel, E. M., & Mohdzain, M. (2005). The role of emergent information technologies and systems in enabling supply chain agility. *International Journal of Information Management*, *25*(5), 396–410. doi:10.1016/j.ijinfomgt.2005.06.009

Wiegers, K., & Beatty, J. (2013). *Software requirements* (3rd ed.). Pearson.

Wiener, N. (1948) Cybernetics: Or Control and Communication in the Animal and the Machine. Mass. MIT Press.

Wiener, N. (1948). *Cybernetics: Or Control and Communication in the Animal and the Machine.* Academic Press.

Wiener, N. (1961). *Cybernetics or Control and Communication in The Animal and The Machine* (2nd ed.). The MIT Press.

Wiig, K. M. (2007). *The Intelligent Enterprise and Knowledge Management1.* Knowledge Research Institute, Inc.

Wilensky, H. (1967). *Organizational Intelligence: Knowledge and Policy in Government and Industry.* Basic Books.

Williamson, O. E. (1998). Transaction cost economics: How it works; where it is headed. *De Economist, 146*(1), 23–58. doi:10.1023/A:1003263908567

Winter, M., Smith, C., Morris, P., & Cicmil, S. (2006). Directions for future research in project management: The main findings of a UK government-funded research network. *International Journal of Project Management, 24*(8), 638–649. doi:10.1016/j.ijproman.2006.08.009

World Health Organization. (2018). *Global status report on road safety.* WHO.

Wu, J., & Wang, S. (2005). What drives mobile commerce? An empirical evaluation of the revised technology acceptance model. *Information & Management, 42*(5), 719–729. doi:10.1016/j.im.2004.07.001

Wu, M. (2020). Organizational Acceptance of Social Media Marketing: A Cross-Cultural Perspective. *Journal of Intercultural Communication Research, 49*(4), 313–329. doi:10.1080/17475759.2020.1771752

Yazdani, M., Zarate, P., Coulibaly, A., & Zavadskas, E. K. (2017). A group decision making support system in logistics and supply chain management. *Expert Systems with Applications, 88,* 376–392. doi:10.1016/j.eswa.2017.07.014

Yin, R. K. (2018). *Case Study Research Design and Methods* (5th ed.). Sage.

Yolles, M. (2017). Corporate joint alliances, their children and cultural figurative intelligence. *European Journal of Cross-Cultural Competence and Management, 4*(3-4), 201–217. doi:10.1504/EJCCM.2017.084520

Yu, C. C. (2006). An artificial neural network-based expert system for the appraisal of two-car crash accidents. *Accident; Analysis and Prevention, 38*(4), 777–785. doi:10.1016/j.aap.2006.02.006 PMID:16556433

Yusuf, Y., Gunasekaran, A., & Abthorpe, M. S. (2004). Enterprise information systems project implementation: A case study of ERP in Rolls-Royce. *International Journal of Production Economics, 87*(3), 251–266. doi:10.1016/j.ijpe.2003.10.004

Yu, Z., Yan, H., & Edwin Cheng, T. C. (2001). Benefits of information sharing with supply chain partnerships. *Industrial Management & Data Systems, 101*(3), 114–121. doi:10.1108/02635570110386625

Zhang, M., & Gable, G. G. (2017). A systematic framework for multilevel theorizing in information systems research. *Information Systems Research, 28*(2), 203–224. doi:10.1287/isre.2017.0690

Compilation of References

Zheng, Z., Yang, Y., Liu, J., Dai, H. N., & Zhang, Y. (2019). Deep and embedded learning approach for traffic flow prediction in urban informatics. *IEEE Transactions on Intelligent Transportation Systems*, *20*(10), 3927–3939. doi:10.1109/TITS.2019.2909904

Zhou, H., & Benton, W. C. Jr. (2007). Supply chain practice and information sharing. *Journal of Operations Management*, *25*(6), 1348–1365. doi:10.1016/j.jom.2007.01.009

About the Contributors

Agripah Kandiero has a BSc. Computer Science (UZ), BSc Honours Information Systems (UNISA), MBA (UZ), MSc Computer Science (WU), MPhil ICTs in Education (UCT), and University of Witwatersrand PhD candidate in ICTs in Education. Currently working for Africa University as Computer Science lecturer after opting for career change from mainstream corporate world to academia in 2011. Positions held in the corporate world include Regional ICT Manager for Southern Africa (ExxonMobil), Mozambique Country Manager (Workgroup Africa), Director of Administration (University of St. Thomas), Chief Information Officer (University of St. Thomas). Member of the Zimbabwe National Nanotechnology Coordinating Commission (NNCC) and Board Member of Africa Learning Development Network (ALDN). A career professional turned academic practitioner with a passion for positive social change.

Stanislas Bigirimana a citizen of Burundi is a Senior Lecturer at the College of Business, Peace, Leadership and Governance at Africa University. He is a holder of Doctor of Philosophy (PhD) from the Ruprecht-Karls-University, Heidelberg (Germany). He is a multi-disciplinary academic who also holds the Masters in Intellectual Property from Africa University; Master's in Business Intelligence from the Chinhoyi University of Technology, a Master of Business Administration and a Master of Arts in Philosophy from the Azaliah University, Albuquerque, New Mexico (USA) and the University of Zimbabwe respectively. Dr. Bigirimanas' expertise are in Business Intelligence, Management Information Systems, Intellectual Property, Innovation, Entrepreneurship, International Marketing, Organisational Behaviour, Public Sector Management, Cybernetics, and Dynamic and Integrative Epistemology. He has published over 40 journal articles, 3 book chapters and 1 monograph. He has supervised 2 doctoral theses, 60 master's theses and 40 undergraduate dissertations. He has also made presentations at over 50 academic conferences in Africa, Europe and the Americas. Dr Bigirimana's current research interests are in the areas of Integrating Non-Conventional Intellectual Property Assets in Agricultural and Social Policy for Sustainable Development, The valuation and Exploitation of Intangible

About the Contributors

Assets, Intellectual Property Rights Protection in New Plant Varieties and Traditional Knowledge Systems, Intellectual Property Protection in Cyberspace, Applications of the viable system model (VSM), Transitioning Institutions of Higher Education towards Education 5.0. He is a member of the Editorial boards of the International Journal of E-business Research and the Zimbabwe Journal of Economics, Business and Management. He has reviewed for prestigious publishing houses such as Emerald Insight, Sage, Springer and IGI Global. He is the Chairperson of the Board of Trustees of the Information and Communication Technologies Association of Zimbabwe (ICTAZ) and member of the advisor board of the Catholic Commission Justice and Peace (CCJP). Dr. Bigirimana is a co-founder and co-owner of Code Empire, a software development company based in Harare. Code Empire was recipient of the 2019 Research Council of Zimbabwe's Presidential Award for outstanding research and commercialisation of research results and he won the Second Prize at an Essay Competition organised by the Hannover Philosophical Research Institute (Germany) in 2009. He has collaborated with prestigious research and academic bodies such as the American Society for Cybernetics (ASC), the International Systems Sciences Society (ISSS), the Royal Academy for Engineering (RAE), the European Innovation Alliance (EIA), the South African Academy of the Sciences, the Association of African Studies, the Refugee Law Project at Makerere University, Uganda, the Association of Africa Universities and the Council for the Development of Social Sciences in Africa (CODESRIA). Dr. Bigirimana is happily married to Madame Assumpta and they are blessed with three boys.

Sabelo Chizwina holds a PhD in Information Science is currently a Director responsible for Information and Learning Services at North-West University in South Africa. He holds a Bachelor of Information Science Honors Degree (University of Pretoria), a Masters in Information Science (University of Pretoria), Masters in Education with specialization in ICT (University of Cape Town) and a PhD in Information Science (University of South Africa). He has published extensively in academic journals and has several book chapters. He is a researcher with interests in fields such as the use of Artificial Intelligence in teaching and learning, the use of social media, information systems research and embedded librarianship.

***

Eddy Bajolle is a PhD candidate in Management Sciences at Aix-Marseille University, CERGAM Research Department. He holds Master's degree in Economics and Management from Aix-Marseille University (France) and a B.A. in Information System Management from Munster Technological University (Ireland). For over a decade, he has served as a project manager in logistics service providers, playing

305

About the Contributors

a pivotal role in shaping and implementing information systems, with a specific focus on ERP systems. His doctoral research is centered on investigating the intricacies of IS project alignment within a prominent transportation company based in Maghreb and Europe.

Kelvin Joseph Bwalya is a full professor in the School of Consumer Intelligence and Information Systems. He is NRF rated at C1, vice chairperson of the UJ Senate Academic Freedom Committee, Fellow of the International Engineering and Technology Institute (Hong Kong), and member of the Board of Directors for the Institute of Data Science and Artificial Intelligence (Singapore). Prof Bwalya is a visiting professor at three different universities: Rajamangla University of Technology, Sri Lanka; Alagappa University, India; and the Information and Communications University, Zambia. He has supervised 6 PhDs to completion and significant Masters students. He is currently supervising 3 PhD students intending to submit their thesis at the end of this year. Kelvin has a PhD in Information Management (University of Johannesburg), a Master's in Computer Science (Korea Advanced Institute of Science and Technology - KAIST), and a Bachelor's in Electrical Electronics Engineering (Moscow PE Technical University). He has worked as a Senior Windows Programming Researcher at Samsung Electronics (Taejŏn, South Korea) specializing in Digital Image Processing and MPEG 7/21 Digital Media Adaption. He has also worked at the University of Botswana as a senior scholar and at Zambia Research and Development Centre as Executive Director – Research and Development. Prof Bwalya has delivered numerous keynote speeches at reputable international conferences. He has a Google Scholar H-Index of 19 (1708 citations) and a Scopus H index of 10 with a field-weighted citation index of 1.06 (6% more than the world average). Prof Bwalya has a substantial international network. He is currently serving as vice Dean with significant impact.

Nathalie Fabbe-Costes is a Full Professor of Management Sciences at the Faculty of Economics and Management, and a member of the CERGAM research center at Aix-Marseille University, France. Her numerous national and international publications are at the interface of logistics, strategy and information systems. She is heavily involved in supervising doctoral projects and industry-academia collaborative research projects. She has worked on supply chain integration, plug-and-play/unplug mechanisms, sustainable supply chains, traceability systems and performance management systems. She is currently developing research on the digitalisation of strategic inter-organisational processes, the management of the 'sustainable' transformation of companies and of their value chains, and the inter-organisational dynamics of innovation in these contexts.

About the Contributors

Cécile Godé is a full professor at Aix-Marseille University, CERGAM Research Department. Her expertise covers coordination and decision making in extreme contexts, with the support of information technologies in various organizational settings (including military and homeland security organizations). Her work has been published in academic journals such as Organization Studies, Group & Organization Management, Scandinavian Journal of Management, European Management Journal, The International Journal of Technology and Human Interaction and Systèmes d'Information et Management (The French Journal of MIS). She also authored five books, two of which were award-winning. She finally conducted and participated to research funded by public and private organizations, including the French ministries of Defense and Interior.

Ganyanhewe Masanga holds a PhD in Industrial Management, an MSc in Engineering Production and Management and a BSc in Mechanical Engineering. He is a consultant and trainer in Strategic Management and Training and Development. Dr Masanga is a senior lecturer at Chinhoyi University of Technology, Graduate Business School and teaches the following courses: Strategic Management, Strategic Entrepreneurship, Scenario Planning, Modelling and Forecasting, Training and Development. He has a wide experience in management, serving as Managing Director of Zimbabwean companies for 22 years, including 12 years as Group Managing Director for the Zimbabwe Iron and Steel Company(ZISCO). For the 22 years he spent in industry, Dr Masanga held various board level appointments including ZISCO's subsidiaries in South Africa, Botswana, Namibia, Zambia and Mozambique. He has a wide experience of setting up cross-border and joint-venture companies within the SADC region. He made a number of company acquisitions and joint ventures for ZISCO. Dr Masanga supervised the rehabilitation of ZISCO and built its distribution network, from zero in South Africa, Botswana, Namibia, Mozambique and Zambia. He was instrumental in creating the ZISCO Management Development Centre, where regional steel industry managers from the COMESA region were trained.

Elisha Mupaikwa is a lecturer in the Department of Library and Information Science at the National University of Science and Technology, Zimbabwe. His lecturing career began in 1999 when he was employed as a lecturer in the Information Technology department at the Bulawayo Polytechnic College. In 2012, he joined the Department of Library and Information Science as a lecturer (the post he holds). In this department, he has actively participated in curriculum development, recommending courses that are in line with the technological developments globally. This has been both at undergraduate and postgraduate levels. His major areas of research have been in the disciplines of information systems and development communication. A holder of a Higher National Diploma in Computer Studies, Bachelor of Science degree in Computer Studies, Diploma in Technical and Vocational Education, Master of Science in Library and Information Science, and Ph.D. in Library and Information Science.

Nkholedzeni Sidney Netshakhuma is currently the Postdoctoral Research Fellowship with the University of Cape Town, Centre for African Studies effective from January 2023. His research interest includes Records Management, Archives management and Heritage management, and Political and liberation movements archives. He has published more than 60 articles and book chapters. He currently served as a Deputy Chairperson of the South Africa Higher Education Records and Archives Management Forum. He reviewed more than 60 research articles and book chapters. He obtained Ph.D. Information Science, Masters of Information Science, Post Diploma in Archival Studies, BTECH (Archival Studies at the University of South Africa (UNISA), BPHIL (Information Science at the University of Stellenbosch), BA (History and Political Studies at the University of Venda.

Yulita Hanum Iskandar is a Senior Lecturer in Graduate School of Business, Universiti Sains Malaysia. She currently teaches 'Management Information Systems' and 'Technology Management' for postgraduates and specializes in research related to technological and innovation.

Mampilo Phahlane is a senior lecturer at the university of South Africa for more than a decade in the school of computing. Her research interest include but not limited to ICT in education, government and healthcare in developing countries. She is currently supervising post graduate students and that takes up a lot of her time, her plans include being an NRF rated scholar.

Ahmad Said is a Faculty member - International Business Management Program, Management Department, Bina Nusantara University, Jakarta, Indonesia and a Ph.D. Student in Universiti Sains Malaysia at Graduated School of Business.

Amrita Sarkar is a graduate engineer in information technology with a postgraduate degree in remote sensing and has completed her Ph.D. in computer science and engineering from BIT, Mesra She has two years of experience at BIT, Mesra as an SRF. After completing her Ph.D., she has almost six years of teaching experience. She is presently an Assistant Professor at the Department of Computer Science, Birla Institute of Technology, Mesra, Off Campus Lalpur, Ranchi. She has several research publications in reputed journals. She is also the author of a book related to

About the Contributors

her field of research. Her areas of interest include Artificial Intelligence, Machine Learning, Soft Computing, Data Mining, and Algorithms.

Satyaki Sarkar, Professor, Department of Architecture and Planning is in the field of academics and research for the last two decades. He has published numerous research papers, and books and has been involved with numerous research projects throughout his career.

Index

A

Adaptive Neuro-fuzzy inference system 50, 53, 72-73
Alignment 35, 101, 111, 155-163, 167-172, 174-184
Alignment Between the Business Organization and the Project Organization 168, 172, 184
Alignment Between the IS Organization and Project Organization 184
Alignment Between the IS Organization and the Business Organization 168, 184
Archives and records management 29-37, 40
Artificial Neural Networks 52, 74, 227, 229, 233, 251

C

Case study 29-30, 34-35, 38, 40, 42-45, 47-49, 74, 91, 105, 107-108, 112, 132-133, 155, 157, 163, 176-177, 179, 183, 263
Comprehensive framework 155, 157, 161, 163, 172, 176-177
Constructivism 34, 49
Cross-cultural Technology Acceptance 28

D

Decision-Making 8, 83, 86, 94-96, 99, 107-110, 169, 187, 217
Deep Learning 227, 229-230, 232-234, 239, 245, 247, 250-251, 253, 258, 262-264

E

Electronic Healthcare Record 77
Enterprise resource planning 99, 112, 155, 180-181, 183
Environment 8, 13, 20, 28, 35, 39, 41, 43, 77, 80, 82-86, 89-90, 106-107, 111, 115, 117, 119, 125, 130-131, 142-144, 153, 159-161, 165, 177, 187, 191, 194, 196, 198-199, 202, 205, 213-214, 223, 249, 251, 255, 259
Epistemology 49

F

Frameworks 22, 94-96, 106, 109, 146, 155, 163

H

Higher Education 13, 17, 45, 113-115, 119-120, 128-134, 196
Hofstede 1-3, 8-9, 11, 14-17, 20, 23-24, 28, 144, 152
Hofstede cultural Dimensions 28

I

Individualism 10, 12, 14-17, 20, 28
Information Systems 1-3, 5, 12, 14-17, 20-25, 27-28, 46, 48, 83, 87, 89-90, 92, 94-96, 98-105, 107-112, 114, 118, 132, 135-136, 138, 142-143, 150-155, 158, 170-171, 178-183, 221, 238-240, 263-265

Index

Information Systems discipline 135-136, 153-154
Information Systems Theory 28
Interpretivism 30-34, 37-38, 42, 44-45, 49
IS Project Alignment 155-156, 171, 175, 180, 184
IS Project Contextual Alignments 184
IS Project Non-Supportive Organizational Context 184
IS project organizational context 184
IS Project Supportive Organizational Context 184

L

Literature Review 33, 89, 91, 94, 104, 115, 152, 158, 180, 183, 230, 243
Logistics service provider 155, 157, 164, 176

M

Management Cybernetics 113, 115, 117-119, 133-134, 189, 194
Masculinity-Feminity 28

O

Organization 31, 35, 37-40, 42-43, 75, 79-86, 89-90, 92, 107, 115-119, 121-122, 124-128, 135, 142-144, 155-157, 159-164, 167-174, 176-178, 180, 182-184, 192-194, 196-200, 202-204, 206, 219-225

P

Positivism 29, 31, 34, 44-46, 49
Power-distance 8, 28

Q

Qualitative methodology 49

R

Road accident prediction 74

S

Supply Chain 90, 94-103, 105-112, 134, 210
Supply Chain Partnership 96, 102, 109

T

Technology 1-5, 8-28, 46, 50, 73, 75, 77-84, 86-91, 94-96, 99-100, 105-108, 110, 112, 114, 119, 127, 129, 134-135, 137, 144-145, 148, 150-154, 157, 178-184, 190, 206-208, 211, 214, 227, 238-239, 263-265
Technology Acceptance Model 3, 14, 21-22, 24-28, 137, 144, 151, 238, 263, 265
Technology Across Cultures 28
Theorizing 135-136, 140-142, 145-146, 148-149, 152-154, 183
Theory 2-3, 9, 12, 14-16, 18-28, 30, 32, 49, 85, 87, 92, 102, 134, 136-154, 157, 160, 176, 180, 188, 190-191, 195-197, 202, 214, 221-223, 225, 232, 237-240, 262-265
Transparency 42, 47, 94-96, 100, 105-107, 109-110, 112, 127, 131, 172

V

Viable System model (VSM) 113-115, 118-119, 130-131, 189

Recommended Reference Books

IGI Global's reference books are available in three unique pricing formats:
Print Only, E-Book Only, or Print + E-Book.
Order direct through IGI Global's Online Bookstore at www.igi-global.com or through your preferred provider.

Autoethnographic Perspectives on Multilingual Life Stories

ISBN: 9781668437384
EISBN: 9781668437407
© 2022; 343 pp.
List Price: US$ 215

Innovative Technologies for Enhancing Knowledge Access in Academic Libraries

ISBN: 9781668433645
EISBN: 9781668433669
© 2022; 317 pp.
List Price: US$ 215

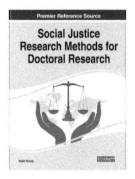

Social Justice Research Methods for Doctoral Research

ISBN: 9781799884798
EISBN: 9781799884804
© 2022; 397 pp.
List Price: US$ 215

Opportunities and Challenges for Computational Social Science Methods

ISBN: 9781799885535
EISBN: 9781799885559
© 2022; 277 pp.
List Price: US$ 215

Global Perspectives on Sustainable Library Practices

ISBN: 9781668459645
EISBN: 9781668459652
© 2023; 376 pp.
List Price: US$ 240

Research Anthology on Innovative Research Methodologies and Utilization Across Multiple Disciplines

ISBN: 9781668438817
EISBN: 9781668438824
© 2022; 663 pp.
List Price: US$ 415

Do you want to stay current on the latest research trends, product announcements, news, and special offers?
Join IGI Global's mailing list to receive customized recommendations, exclusive discounts, and more.
Sign up at: **www.igi-global.com/newsletters.**

Publisher of Timely, Peer-Reviewed Inclusive Research Since 1988

www.igi-global.com | Sign up at www.igi-global.com/newsletters | facebook.com/igiglobal | twitter.com/igiglobal

Ensure Quality Research is Introduced to the Academic Community

Become an Evaluator for IGI Global Authored Book Projects

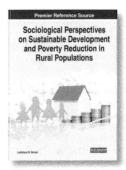

The overall success of an authored book project is dependent on quality and timely manuscript evaluations.

Applications and Inquiries may be sent to:
development@igi-global.com

Applicants must have a doctorate (or equivalent degree) as well as publishing, research, and reviewing experience. Authored Book Evaluators are appointed for one-year terms and are expected to complete at least three evaluations per term. Upon successful completion of this term, evaluators can be considered for an additional term.

If you have a colleague that may be interested in this opportunity, we encourage you to share this information with them.

Easily Identify, Acquire, and Utilize Published Peer-Reviewed Findings in Support of Your Current Research

IGI Global OnDemand

Purchase Individual IGI Global OnDemand Book Chapters and Journal Articles

For More Information:
www.igi-global.com/e-resources/ondemand/

Browse through 150,000+ Articles and Chapters!

Find specific research related to your current studies and projects that have been contributed by international researchers from prestigious institutions, including:

- Accurate and Advanced Search
- Affordably Acquire Research
- Instantly Access Your Content
- Benefit from the InfoSci Platform Features

It really provides **an excellent entry into the research literature of the field.** *It presents a manageable number of* **highly relevant sources** *on topics of interest to a wide range of researchers. The sources are* **scholarly, but also accessible** *to 'practitioners'.*

- Ms. Lisa Stimatz, MLS, University of North Carolina at Chapel Hill, USA

Interested in Additional Savings?

Subscribe to
IGI Global OnDemand *Plus*

Learn More

Acquire content from over 128,000+ research-focused book chapters and 33,000+ scholarly journal articles for as low as US$ 5 per article/chapter (original retail price for an article/chapter: US$ 37.50).

7,300+ E-BOOKS.
ADVANCED RESEARCH.
INCLUSIVE & AFFORDABLE.

IGI Global e-Book Collection

- **Flexible Purchasing Options** (Perpetual, Subscription, EBA, etc.)
- Multi-Year Agreements with **No Price Increases** Guaranteed
- **No Additional Charge** for Multi-User Licensing
- No Maintenance, Hosting, or Archiving Fees
- Continually Enhanced & Innovated **Accessibility Compliance Features** (WCAG)

Handbook of Research on Digital Transformation, Industry Use Cases, and the Impact of Disruptive Technologies
ISBN: 9781799877127
EISBN: 9781799877141

Handbook of Research on New Investigations in Artificial Life, AI, and Machine Learning
ISBN: 9781799886860
EISBN: 9781799886877

Handbook of Research on Future of Work and Education
ISBN: 9781799882756
EISBN: 9781799882770

Research Anthology on Physical and Intellectual Disabilities in an Inclusive Society (4 Vols.)
ISBN: 9781668435427
EISBN: 9781668435434

Innovative Economic, Social, and Environmental Practices for Progressing Future Sustainability
ISBN: 9781799895909
EISBN: 9781799895923

Applied Guide for Event Study Research in Supply Chain Management
ISBN: 9781799889694
EISBN: 9781799889717

Mental Health and Wellness in Healthcare Workers
ISBN: 9781799888130
EISBN: 9781799888147

Clean Technologies and Sustainable Development in Civil Engineering
ISBN: 9781799898108
EISBN: 9781799898122

Request More Information, or Recommend the IGI Global e-Book Collection to Your Institution's Librarian

For More Information or to Request a Free Trial, Contact IGI Global's e-Collections Team: eresources@igi-global.com | 1-866-342-6657 ext. 100 | 717-533-8845 ext. 100

Printed in the USA
CPSIA information can be obtained
at www.ICGtesting.com
LVHW081538150324
774517LV00042B/1841